Praise for *Practical Natural Language Processing*

Practical NLP focuses squarely on an overlooked demographic: the practitioners and business leaders in industry! While many great books focus on ML's algorithmic fundamentals, this book exposes the anatomy of real-world systems: from e-commerce applications to virtual assistants. Painting a realistic picture of modern production systems, the book teaches not only deep learning, but also the heuristics and patchwork pipelines that define the (actual) state of the art for deployed NLP systems. The authors zoom out, teaching problem formulation, and aren't afraid to zoom in on the grimy details, including handling messy data and sustaining live systems. This book will prove invaluable to industry professionals keen to build and deploy NLP in the wild.

—*Zachary Lipton, Assistant Professor, Carnegie Mellon University, Scientist at Amazon AI, Author of* Dive into Deep Learning

This book does a great job bridging the gap between natural language processing (NLP) research and practical applications. From healthcare to e-commerce and finance, it covers many of the most sought-after domains where NLP is being put to use and walks through core tasks in a clear and understandable manner. Overall, the book is a great manual on how to get the most out of current NLP in your industry.

—*Sebastian Ruder, Research Scientist, Google DeepMind*

There are two kinds of computer science books on the market: academic textbooks that give you a deep understanding of a domain but can be difficult to access for a non-academic, and "cookbooks" that outline solutions to very specific problems without providing the technical foundations that would allow the reader to generalize the recipes. This book offers the best of both worlds: it is thorough yet accessible. It provides the reader with a solid foundation in natural-language processing. . . . If you would like to go from zero to one in NLP, this book is for you!

—*Marc Najork, Research Engineering Director, Google AI, ACM & IEEE Fellow*

There are text books or research papers or books on programming tips, but not a book that tells us how to build an end-to-end NLP system from scratch. I am happy to see this book on practical NLP, which fills this much needed gap. The authors have meticulously, thoughtfully and lucidly covered each and every aspect of NLP that one has to be aware of while building large scale practical systems; at the same time, this book has also managed to cover a large number of examples and varied application areas and verticals. This book is a must for all aspiring NLP engineers, entrepreneurs who want to build companies around language technologies, and also academic researchers who would like to see their inventions reach the real users.

—*Monojit, Principal Researcher, Microsoft Research India,*
Adjunct Faculty at IIIT Hyderabad, Ashoka University, IIT Kharagpur

This book bridges the gap between theory and practice by explaining the underlying concepts while keeping in mind varied real-world deployments across different business verticals. There is much hard-fought practical advice from the trenches whether it is about tweaking parameters of open source libraries, setting up data pipelines for building models, or optimizing for fast inference. A must-read for engineers building NLP applications.

—*Vinayak Hegde, CTO-in-Residence, Microsoft For Startups*

This book shows how to put NLP to practice. It bridges the gap between NLP theory and practical engineering. The authors achieved a rare feat by simplifying the esoteric art of design and architecture of production quality machine learning systems.

I wish I had access to this book early on in my professional career and evaded the mistakes I made along the way. . . . I am deeply convinced that this book is an essential read for anybody aiming to develop involved in developing a robust, high-performing NLP system.

—*Siddharth Sharma, ML Engineer, Facebook*

I feel this is not only an essential book for NLP practitioners, it is also a valuable reference for the research community to understand the problem spaces in real-world applications. I very much appreciate this book and wish this could be a long-term project with up-to-date NLP application trending!

—*Mengting Wan, Data Scientist (ML&NLP) at Airbnb,*
Microsoft Research Fellow

Practical Natural Language Processing

A Comprehensive Guide to Building Real-World NLP Systems

Sowmya Vajjala, Bodhisattwa Majumder,
Anuj Gupta, and Harshit Surana

Beijing · Boston · Farnham · Sebastopol · Tokyo

Practical Natural Language Processing

by Sowmya Vajjala, Bodhisattwa Majumder, Anuj Gupta, and Harshit Surana

Published by O'Reilly Media, Inc., 1005 Gravenstein Highway North, Sebastopol, CA 95472.

O'Reilly books may be purchased for educational, business, or sales promotional use. Online editions are also available for most titles (*http://oreilly.com*). For more information, contact our corporate/institutional sales department: 800-998-9938 or *corporate@oreilly.com*.

Acquisitions Editor: Jonathan Hassell
Developmental Editor: Melissa Potter
Production Editor: Beth Kelly
Copyeditor: Holly Forsyth
Proofreader: Charles Roumeliotis

Indexer: nSight Inc.
Interior Designer: David Futato
Cover Designer: Karen Montgomery
Illustrator: Rebecca Demarest

June 2020:   First Edition

Revision History for the First Edition
2020-06-17:   First Release

See *http://oreilly.com/catalog/errata.csp?isbn=9781492054054* for release details.

978-1-492-05405-4

[LSI]

This book is dedicated to our respective advisors: Detmar Meurers, Julian McAuley, Kannan Srinathan, and Luis von Ahn.

Table of Contents

Part I.   Foundations

Part II. Essentials

Part III. Applied

Part IV.   Bringing It All Together

Foreword

The field of natural language processing (NLP) has undergone a dramatic shift in recent years, both in terms of methodology and in terms of the applications supported. Methodological advances have ranged from new ways of representing documents to new techniques for language synthesis. With these have come new applications ranging from open-ended conversational systems to techniques that use natural language for model interpretability. Finally, these advances have seen NLP gain a foothold in related areas, such as computer vision and recommender systems, some of which my lab is working on with support from Amazon, Samsung, and the National Science Foundation.

As NLP is expanding into these exciting new areas, so too has the audience of practitioners wanting to make use of NLP techniques. In the Data Science course (CSE 258) that I take at the University of California–San Diego, which is often the most attended in the computer science department, I see that more and more students are doing their projects on NLP-based topics. NLP is rapidly becoming a necessary skill required by engineers, product managers, scientists, students, and enthusiasts wishing to build applications on top of natural language data. On one hand, new tools and libraries for NLP and machine learning have made natural language modeling more accessible than ever. But on the other hand, resources for learning NLP must target this ever-growing and diverse audience. This is especially true for organizations that have recently adopted NLP or for students working with natural language data for the first time.

It has been my pleasure over the last few years to collaborate with Bodhisattwa Majumder on exciting new applications in NLP and dialog, so I was thrilled to hear about his efforts (along with Sowmya Vajjala, Anuj Gupta, and Harshit Surana) to write a book on NLP. They have a wide experience in scaling NLP including at early-stage startups, the MIT Media Lab, Microsoft Research, and Google AI.

I am excited by the end-to-end approach taken in their book, which will make it useful for a range of scenarios and will help readers to work with the labyrinth of possible options while building NLP applications. I am especially thrilled about the emphasis on modern NLP applications such as chatbots, as well as the focus on interdisciplinary topics such as ecommerce and retail. These topics will be especially useful for industry leaders and researchers, and are critical subjects that have been given only limited coverage in existing textbooks. This book is ideal both as a first resource to discover the field of natural language processing and a guide for seasoned practitioners looking to discover the latest developments in this exciting area.

— Julian McAuley
Professor of Computer Science and Engineering
University of California, San Diego

Preface

Natural language processing (NLP) is a field at the intersection of computer science, artificial intelligence, and linguistics. It concerns building systems that can process and understand human language. Since its inception in the 1950s and until very recently, NLP has primarily been the domain of academia and research labs, requiring long formal education and training. The past decade's breakthroughs have resulted in NLP being increasingly used in a range of diverse domains such as retail, healthcare, finance, law, marketing, human resources, and many more. There are a range of driving forces for these developments:

- Widely available and easy-to-use NLP tools, techniques, and APIs are now all-pervading in the industry. There has never been a better time to build quick NLP solutions.

- Development of more interpretable and generalized approaches has improved the baseline performance for even complex NLP tasks, such as open-domain conversational tasks and question answering, which were not practically feasible before.

- More and more organizations, including Google, Microsoft, and Amazon, are investing heavily in more interactive consumer products, where language is used as the primary medium of communication.

- Increased availability of useful open source datasets, along with standard benchmarks on them, has acted as a catalyst in this revolution, as opposed to being impeded by proprietary datasets only available to limited organizations and individuals.

- The viability of NLP has moved beyond English or other major languages. Datasets and language-specific models are being created for the less-frequently digitized languages too. A fruitful product that came out this effort was a near-perfect automatic machine translation tool available to all individuals with a smartphone.

With this rapidly expanding usage, a growing proportion of the workforce that builds these NLP systems is grappling with limited experience and theoretical knowledge about the topic. This book addresses this need from an applied perspective. Our book aims to guide the readers to build, iterate, and scale NLP systems in a business setting, and to tailor them for various industry verticals.

Why We Wrote This Book

There are many popular books on NLP available. While some of these serve as textbooks, focusing on theoretical aspects, some others aim to introduce NLP concepts through a lot of code examples. There are a few others that focus on specific NLP or machine learning libraries and provide "how-to" guides on solving different NLP problems using the libraries. So, why do we need another book on NLP?

We have been building and scaling NLP solutions for over a decade at leading universities and technology companies. While mentoring colleagues and other engineers, we noticed a gap between NLP practice in the industry and the NLP skill sets of new engineers and those who are just starting with NLP in particular. We started understanding these gaps even better during NLP workshops we were conducting for industry professionals, where we noticed that business and engineering leaders also have these gaps.

Most online courses and books tackle NLP problems using toy use cases and popular (often large, clean, and well-defined) datasets. While this imparts the general methods of NLP, we believe it does not provide enough of a foundation to tackle new problems and develop specific solutions in the real world. Commonly encountered problems while building real-world applications, such as data collection, working with noisy data and signals, incremental development of solutions, and issues involved in deploying the solutions as a part of a larger application, are not dealt with by existing resources, to the best of our knowledge. We also saw that best practices to develop NLP systems were missing in most scenarios. We felt a book was needed to bridge this gap, and that is how this book was born!

The Philosophy

We want to provide a holistic and practical perspective that enables the reader to successfully build real-world NLP solutions embedded in larger product setups. Thus, most chapters are accompanied by code walkthroughs in the associated Git repository. The book is also supplemented with extensive references for readers who want to delve deeper. Throughout the book, we start with a simple solution and incrementally build more complex solutions by taking a minimum viable product (MVP) approach, as commonly found in industry practice. We also give tips based on our experience and learnings. Where possible, each chapter is accompanied by a discussion on the state-of-the-art in that topic. Most chapters conclude with a case study of real-world use cases.

Consider the task of building a chatbot or text classification system at your organization. In the beginning there may be little or no data to work with. At this point, a basic solution using rule-based systems or traditional machine learning will be apt. As you accumulate more data, more sophisticated NLP techniques (which are often data intensive) can be used, including deep learning. At each step of this journey there are dozens of alternative approaches one can take. This book will help you navigate this maze of options.

Scope

This book provides a comprehensive view on building real-world NLP applications. We will cover the complete lifecycle of a typical NLP project—from data collection to deploying and monitoring the model. Some of these steps are applicable to any ML pipeline, while some are very specific to NLP. We also introduce task-specific case studies and domain-specific guides to build an NLP system from scratch. We specifically cover a gamut of tasks ranging from text classification to question answering to information extraction and dialog systems. Similarly, we provide recipes to apply these tasks in domains ranging from e-commerce to healthcare, social media, and finance. Owing to the depth and breadth of the topics and scenarios we cover, we will not go step by step explaining the code and all the concepts. For details of the implementation, we have provided detailed source code notebooks. The code snippets in this book cover the core logic and often skip introductory steps like setting up a library or importing a package as they are covered in the associated notebooks. To cover the wide range of concepts we have given more than 450 extensive references to delve deeper into these topics. This book will be a day-to-day cookbook giving you a pragmatic view while building any NLP system, as well as be a stepping stone to broaden the application of NLP into your domain.

Who Should Read This Book

This book is for anyone involved in building NLP applications for real-world use cases. This includes software developers and testers, machine learning engineers, data engineers, MLOps engineers, NLP engineers, data scientists, product managers, people managers, VPs, CXOs, and startup founders. This also includes those involved in data creation and annotation processes—in short anyone and everyone who is involved in any way in building NLP systems in industry. While not all chapters are useful for people with all roles, we tried to give lucid explanations using less technical jargon and more intuitive understanding wherever possible. We believe there is something in every chapter for all potential readers interested in getting a holistic perspective about building NLP applications.

Some chapters or sections can be understood without much coding experience and code bits can be skipped as needed. For example, the first two sections in Chapter 1 and Chapter 9, or the sections "The Data Science Process" and "Making AI succeed in your organization" in Chapter 11 can be understood without any coding experience by all groups of readers. As you progress through the book, you will find more such sections in all chapters. However, to extract maximum benefit from this book, its notebooks, and references, we expect the reader to have the following background:

- Intermediate proficiency in Python programming. For example, understanding Python features such as list comprehension, writing functions and classes, and using existing libraries.

- Familiarity with various aspects of the software development life cycle (SDLC) such as design, development, testing, DevOps, etc.

- Basics of machine learning, including familiarity with commonly used machine learning algorithms such as logistic regression and decision trees and the ability to use them in Python with existing libraries such as scikit-learn.

- Basic knowledge of NLP is useful but not mandatory. Having an idea of tasks such as text classification and named entity recognition is also helpful.

What You Will Learn

Our primary audience is comprised of engineers and scientists involved in building real-world NLP systems for different verticals. Some of the common job titles are: Software Engineer, NLP Engineer, ML Engineer, and Data Scientist. The book may also be helpful for product managers and engineering leaders. However, it may not be as helpful for those pursuing cutting-edge research in NLP because we do not cover in-depth theoretical and technical details related to NLP concepts. With this book, you will:

- Understand the wide spectrum of problem statements, tasks, and solution approaches within NLP.

- Gain experience in implementing and evaluating different NLP applications and applying machine learning and deep learning methods for this process.

- Fine-tune an NLP solution based on the business problem and industry vertical.

- Evaluate various algorithms and approaches for the given task, dataset, and stage of the NLP product.

- Plan the lifecycle of the NLP product and produce software solutions following best practices around release, deployment, and DevOps for NLP systems.

- Understand best practices, opportunities, and the roadmap for NLP from a business and product leader's perspective.

You will also learn to adapt your solutions for different industry verticals like healthcare, finance, and retail. Moreover, you will learn about specific caveats you will encounter in each.

Structure of the Book

The book is divided into four sections. Figure P-1 illustrates the chapter organization. Isolated chapters that are not directly connected to other chapters are easiest to skip while moving forward.

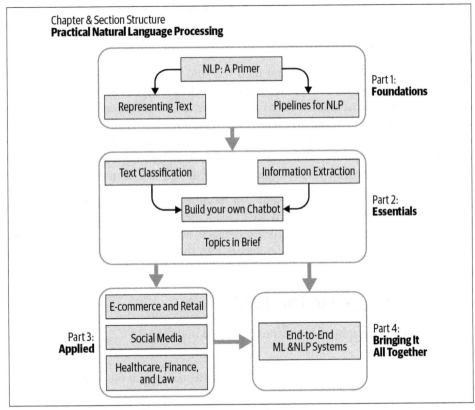

Figure P-1. How the book's sections are structured

Part I, *Foundations* acts as a bedrock for the rest of the book, by giving an overview of NLP (Chapter 1), discussing typical data processing and modeling pipelines used in building NLP systems (Chapter 2), and introducing different ways of representing textual data in NLP (Chapter 3).

Part II, *Essentials*, focuses on the most common NLP applications, with an emphasis on real-world use cases. Where possible, we show multiple solutions to the problem at hand to demonstrate how to choose among different options. Some applications include text classification (Chapter 4), information extraction (Chapter 5), and the building of chat bots (Chapter 6). We also introduce other applications, such as search, topic modeling, text summarization, and machine translation, along with a discussion about practical use cases (Chapter 7).

Part III, *Applied* (Chapters 8–10) specifically focuses on three industry verticals where NLP is heavily used, with a detailed discussion on those domains' specific problems and how NLP is useful in addressing them.

Finally, Part IV (Chapter 11) brings all the learning together by dealing with the issues involved in end-to-end deployment of NLP systems in practice.

How to Read This Book

How one reads the book depends on their role and objective. For a data scientist or an engineer delving into NLP, we recommend reading Chapters 1–6 and then focusing on the particular domain or subproblem of interest. For someone in a leadership role, we recommend focusing on Chapters 1, 2, and 11. They might want to give extra focus to case studies for Chapters 3–7, which provide more ideas on the process of building NLP applications from scratch. A product leader might want to delve deep into the references provided for relevant chapters, as well as Chapter 11.

NLP applications for various domains can be different from the general problems covered in Chapters 3–7. That is why we have focused more on certain domains such as e-commerce, social media, healthcare, finance, and law. If your interest or work takes you to these areas, you can dig deeper into those chapters and corresponding references.

Conventions Used in This Book

The following typographical conventions are used in this book:

Italic
    Indicates new terms, URLs, email addresses, filenames, and file extensions.

`Constant width`
    Used for program listings, as well as within paragraphs to refer to program elements such as variable or function names, databases, data types, environment variables, statements, and keywords.

`Constant width bold`
    Shows commands or other text that should be typed literally by the user.

Constant width italic

Shows text that should be replaced with user-supplied values or by values determined by context.

This element signifies a tip or suggestion.

This element signifies a general note.

This element indicates a warning or caution.

Using Code Examples

Supplemental material (code examples, exercises, etc.) is available for download at *https://oreil.ly/PracticalNLP*.

If you have a technical question or a problem using the code examples, please send email to *bookquestions@oreilly.com*.

This book is here to help you get your job done. In general, if example code is offered with this book, you may use it in your programs and documentation. You do not need to contact us for permission unless you're reproducing a significant portion of the code. For example, writing a program that uses several chunks of code from this book does not require permission. Selling or distributing examples from O'Reilly books does require permission. Answering a question by citing this book and quoting example code does not require permission. Incorporating a significant amount of example code from this book into your product's documentation does require permission.

We appreciate, but generally do not require, attribution. An attribution usually includes the title, author, publisher, and ISBN. For example: "*Practical Natural Language Processing* by Sowmya Vajjala, Bodhisattwa Majumder, Anuj Gupta, and Harshit Surana (O'Reilly). Copyright 2020 Anuj Gupta, Bodhisattwa Prasad Majumder, Sowmya Vajjala, and Harshit Surana, 978-1-492-05405-4."

If you feel your use of code examples falls outside fair use or the permission given above, feel free to contact us at *permissions@oreilly.com*.

O'Reilly Online Learning

 For more than 40 years, *O'Reilly Media* has provided technology and business training, knowledge, and insight to help companies succeed.

Our unique network of experts and innovators share their knowledge and expertise through books, articles, and our online learning platform. O'Reilly's online learning platform gives you on-demand access to live training courses, in-depth learning paths, interactive coding environments, and a vast collection of text and video from O'Reilly and 200+ other publishers. For more information, visit *http://oreilly.com*.

How to Contact Us

Please address comments and questions concerning this book to the publisher:

O'Reilly Media, Inc.
1005 Gravenstein Highway North
Sebastopol, CA 95472
800-998-9938 (in the United States or Canada)
707-829-0515 (international or local)
707-829-0104 (fax)

We have a web page for this book, where we list errata, examples, and any additional information. You can access this page at *https://oreil.ly/PNLP*.

Email *bookquestions@oreilly.com* to comment or ask technical questions about this book.

For news and information about our books and courses, visit *http://oreilly.com*.

Find us on Facebook: *http://facebook.com/oreilly*

Follow us on Twitter: *http://twitter.com/oreillymedia*

Watch us on YouTube: *http://youtube.com/oreillymedia*

Further Information

In the GitHub repo (*https://oreil.ly/PracticalNLP*) you will find notebooks explaining various concepts covered in the book. The notebooks have been organized by chapter. We also provide additional notebooks, not necessarily covered in the book.

Book website: *http://www.practicalnlp.ai*

The world of NLP is always evolving. To stay updated on how concept mentioned in the book fit into the broader context one, two, and five years from now, follow our blog (*http://www.practicalnlp.ai/blog*). We keep it updated with relevant writeups and articles, and tag every post with the book's corresponding chapter title.

Contact the authors:

Email: *authors@practicalnlp.ai*
Linkedin: *https://linkedin.com/company/practical-nlp*
Twitter: *https://twitter.com/PracticalNLProc*
Facebook: *https://oreil.ly/facebookPNLP*

Acknowledgments

A book like this is a compendium of knowledge; hence, it cannot exist in isolation. While writing this book, we drew a lot of inspiration and information from several books, research papers, software projects and numerous other resources on the internet. We thank the NLP and Machine Learning community for all their efforts. We have merely stood on the shoulders on these giants. We also thank various people who attended some of the authors' talks and workshops and participated in discussions that lead to the idea of writing this book and shaping its premise. This book is the result of a long collaborative effort and several people supported us in different ways in our endeavor.

We thank the O'Reilly reviewers Will Scott, Darren Cook, Ramya Balasubramaniam, Priyanka Raghavan, and Siddharth Narayanan for their meticulous, invaluable, and detailed comments which helped us improve earlier drafts. Detailed feedback from Siddharth Sharma, Sumod Mohan, Vinayak Hegde, Aasish Pappu, Taranjeet Singh, Kartikay Bagla, and Varun Purushotham were instrumental in improving the quality of the content.

We are also very thankful to Rui Shu, Shreyans Dhankhar, Jitin Kapila, Kumarjit Pathak, Ernest Kirubakaran Selvaraj, Robin Singh, Ayush Datta, Vishal Gupta, and Nachiketh for helping us prepare the early versions of code notebooks. We would especially like to thank Varun Purushotham, who spent several weeks reading and rereading our drafts and preparing and cross-checking the code notebooks. This book would not be the same without his contribution.

We would like to thank the O'Reilly Media team, without whom this would not have been possible: Jonathan Hassell, for giving us this opportunity; Melissa Potter, for regularly following up with us throughout this journey and patiently answering all our questions! Beth Kelly and Holly Forsyth, for all the help and support in shaping it into a book from the chapter drafts.

Finally, the following are personal thank you notes by each author:

Sowmya: My first and biggest thank you goes to my daughter, Sahasra Malathi, whose birth and first year of life coincided with the writing of this book. It is not easy to write a book, and not easy at all to write it with a newborn. And yet, here we are. Thank you, Sahasra! My mom, Geethamani, and my husband, Sriram, supported my writing by taking up baby care and household duties at different phases of writing. My friends, Purnima and Visala, were always available to listen to my excited updates as well as rants about the book. My boss, Cyril Goutte, encouraged me and checked on my writing progress throughout. Discussions with my former colleagues, Chris Cardinal and Eric Le Fort, taught me a lot about developing NLP solutions for industry problems, without which I perhaps would never have thought of being a part of this kind of book. I thank all of them for their support.

Bodhisattwa: I would like to take this opportunity to thank my parents, their unquestionable sacrifice, and the constant encouragement that made me the person I am today. Their efforts have instilled in me the love and dedication to learning in my life. I am eternally grateful to my advisors, Prof. Animesh Mukherjee and Pawan Goyal, who introduced me to this world of NLP; and Prof. Julian McAuley, who is nothing less than fundamental to my technical, academic, and personal development in my PhD career. The courses taken by my other professors—Taylor Berg-Kirkpatrick, Lawrence Saul, David Kriegman, Debasis Sengupta, Sudeshna Sarkar, and Sourav Sen Gupta—have significantly shaped my learning on the subject. In the early days of the book, my colleagues from Walmart Labs—especially Subhasish Misra, Arunita Das, Smaranya Dey, Sumanth Prabhu, and Rajesh Bhat—gave me the motivation for this crazy idea. To my mentors at Google AI, Microsoft Research, Amazon Alexa, and my labmates from the UCSD NLP Group, thank you for being supportive and helpful in this entire journey. Also, my friends Sanchaita Hazra, Sujoy Paul, and Digbalay Bose, who stood by me through thick and thin in this mammoth project, deserve a special mention. At last, none of this would have been possible without my coauthors, who believed in this project and stayed together till the last bit of it!

Anuj: First and foremost, I would like to express my sincere gratitude to my wife, Anu, and my son, Nirvaan. Without their unwavering support, I would not have been able to devote the last three years to this endeavor. Thank you so much! I would also like to thank my parents and family for their encouragement. A big shout out goes to Saurabh Arora, for introducing me to the world of NLP. Many thanks to my friends, the late Vivek Jain and Mayur Hemani; they have always encouraged me to keep going, especially in hard times. I would also like to thank all of the amazing people involved in machine learning communities in Bangalore; especially: Sumod Mohan, Vijay Gabale, Nishant Sinha, Ashwin Kumar, Mukundhan Srinivasan, Zainab Bawa, and Naresh Jain for all the wonderful and thought-provoking discussions. I would like to thank my colleagues—former and present—at CSTAR, Airwoot, FreshWorks, Huawei Research, Intuit, and Vahan, Inc., for everything they taught me. To my professors, Kannan Srinathan, P.R.K Rao, and B. Yegnanarayana, whose teachings have had a profound impact on me.

Harshit: I want to thank my parents, who have supported and encouraged me to pursue every crazy idea I have had. I cannot thank my dear friends Preeti Shrimal and Dev Chandan enough. They have been with me throughout the book's entire journey. To my cofounders, Abhimanyu Vyas and Aviral Mathur, thank you for adjusting our startup endeavor to help me complete the book. I want to thank all my former colleagues at Quipio and Notify.io who helped crystalize my thinking, especially Zubin Wadia, Amit Kumar, and Naveen Koorakula. None of this would have been possible without my professors and everything they taught me—thank you, Prof. Luis von Ahn, Anil Kumar Singh, Alan W Black, William Cohen, Lori Levin, and Carlos Guestrin. I also want to acknowledge Kaustuv DeBiswas, Siddharth Narayanan, Siddharth Sharma, Alok Parlikar, Nathan Schneider, Aasish Pappu, Manish Jawa, Sumit Pandey, and Mohit Ranka, who have supported me at various junctures of this journey.

## PART I

Foundations

## CHAPTER 1

NLP: A Primer

> *A language is not just words. It's a culture, a tradition,*
> *a unification of a community,*
> *a whole history that creates what a community is.*
> *It's all embodied in a language.*
> —*Noam Chomsky*

Imagine a hypothetical person, John Doe. He's the CTO of a fast-growing technology startup. On a busy day, John wakes up and has this conversation with his digital assistant:

John: "How is the weather today?"

Digital assistant: "It is 37 degrees centigrade outside with no rain today."

John: "What does my schedule look like?"

Digital assistant: "You have a strategy meeting at 4 p.m. and an all-hands at 5:30 p.m. Based on today's traffic situation, it is recommended you leave for the office by 8:15 a.m."

While he's getting dressed, John probes the assistant on his fashion choices:

John: "What should I wear today?"

Digital assistant: "White seems like a good choice."

You might have used smart assistants such as Amazon Alexa, Google Home, or Apple Siri to do similar things. We talk to these assistants not in a programming language, but in our natural language—the language we all communicate in. This natural language has been the primary medium of communication between humans since time immemorial. But computers can only process data in binary, i.e., 0s and 1s. While we can represent language data in binary, how do we make machines understand the language? This is where natural language processing (NLP) comes in. It is an area of computer science that deals with methods to analyze, model, and understand human language. Every intelligent application involving human language has some NLP behind it. In this book, we'll explain what NLP is as well as how to use NLP to build and scale intelligent applications. Due to the open-ended nature of NLP problems, there are dozens of alternative approaches one can take to solve a given problem. This book will help you navigate this maze of options and suggests how to choose the best option based on your problem.

This chapter aims to give a quick primer of what NLP is before we start delving deeper into how to implement NLP-based solutions for different application scenarios. We'll start with an overview of numerous applications of NLP in real-world scenarios, then cover the various tasks that form the basis of building different NLP applications. This will be followed by an understanding of language from an NLP perspective and of why NLP is difficult. After that, we'll give an overview of heuristics, machine learning, and deep learning, then introduce a few commonly used algorithms in NLP. This will be followed by a walkthrough of an NLP application. Finally, we'll conclude the chapter with an overview of the rest of the topics in the book. Figure 1-1 shows a preview of the organization of the chapters in terms of various NLP tasks and applications.

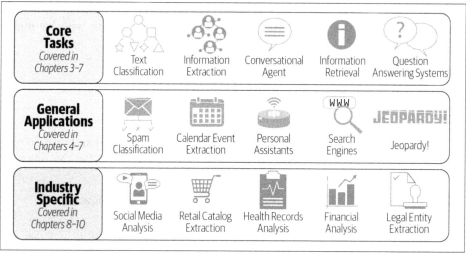

Figure 1-1. NLP tasks and applications

Let's start by taking a look at some popular applications you use in everyday life that have some form of NLP as a major component.

NLP in the Real World

NLP is an important component in a wide range of software applications that we use in our daily lives. In this section, we'll introduce some key applications and also take a look at some common tasks that you'll see across different NLP applications. This section reinforces the applications we showed you in Figure 1-1, which you'll see in more detail throughout the book.

Core applications:

- Email platforms, such as Gmail, Outlook, etc., use NLP extensively to provide a range of product features, such as spam classification, priority inbox, calendar event extraction, auto-complete, etc. We'll discuss some of these in detail in Chapters 4 and 5.

- Voice-based assistants, such as Apple Siri, Google Assistant, Microsoft Cortana, and Amazon Alexa rely on a range of NLP techniques to interact with the user, understand user commands, and respond accordingly. We'll cover key aspects of such systems in Chapter 6, where we discuss chatbots.

- Modern search engines, such as Google and Bing, which are the cornerstone of today's internet, use NLP heavily for various subtasks, such as query understanding, query expansion, question answering, information retrieval, and ranking and grouping of the results, to name a few. We'll discuss some of these subtasks in Chapter 7.

- Machine translation services, such as Google Translate, Bing Microsoft Translator, and Amazon Translate are increasingly used in today's world to solve a wide range of scenarios and business use cases. These services are direct applications of NLP. We'll touch on machine translation in Chapter 7.

Other applications:

- Organizations across verticals analyze their social media feeds to build a better and deeper understanding of the voice of their customers. We'll cover this in Chapter 8.

- NLP is widely used to solve diverse sets of use cases on e-commerce platforms like Amazon. These vary from extracting relevant information from product descriptions to understanding user reviews. Chapter 9 covers these in detail.

- Advances in NLP are being applied to solve use cases in domains such as healthcare, finance, and law. Chapter 10 addresses these.

- Companies such as Arria [1] are working to use NLP techniques to automatically generate reports for various domains, from weather forecasting to financial services.

- NLP forms the backbone of spelling- and grammar-correction tools, such as Grammarly and spell check in Microsoft Word and Google Docs.

- *Jeopardy!* is a popular quiz show on TV. In the show, contestants are presented with clues in the form of answers, and the contestants must phrase their responses in the form of questions. IBM built the Watson AI to compete with the show's top players. Watson won the first prize with a million dollars, more than the world champions. Watson AI was built using NLP techniques and is one of the examples of NLP bots winning a world competition.

- NLP is used in a range of learning and assessment tools and technologies, such as automated scoring in exams like the Graduate Record Examination (GRE), plagiarism detection (e.g., Turnitin), intelligent tutoring systems, and language learning apps like Duolingo.

- NLP is used to build large knowledge bases, such as the Google Knowledge Graph, which are useful in a range of applications like search and question answering.

This list is by no means exhaustive. NLP is increasingly being used across several other applications, and newer applications of NLP are coming up as we speak. Our main focus is to introduce you to the ideas behind building these applications. We do so by discussing different kinds of NLP problems and how to solve them. To get a perspective on what you are about to learn in this book, and to appreciate the nuances that go into building these NLP applications, let's take a look at some key NLP tasks that form the bedrock of many NLP applications and industry use cases.

NLP Tasks

There is a collection of fundamental tasks that appear frequently across various NLP projects. Owing to their repetitive and fundamental nature, these tasks have been studied extensively. Having a good grip on them will make you ready to build various NLP applications across verticals. (We also saw some of these tasks earlier in Figure 1-1.) Let's briefly introduce them:

Language modeling
> This is the task of predicting what the next word in a sentence will be based on the history of previous words. The goal of this task is to learn the probability of a sequence of words appearing in a given language. Language modeling is useful for building solutions for a wide variety of problems, such as speech recognition, optical character recognition, handwriting recognition, machine translation, and spelling correction.

Text classification

This is the task of bucketing the text into a known set of categories based on its content. Text classification is by far the most popular task in NLP and is used in a variety of tools, from email spam identification to sentiment analysis.

Information extraction

As the name indicates, this is the task of extracting relevant information from text, such as calendar events from emails or the names of people mentioned in a social media post.

Information retrieval

This is the task of finding documents relevant to a user query from a large collection. Applications like Google Search are well-known use cases of information retrieval.

Conversational agent

This is the task of building dialogue systems that can converse in human languages. Alexa, Siri, etc., are some common applications of this task.

Text summarization

This task aims to create short summaries of longer documents while retaining the core content and preserving the overall meaning of the text.

Question answering

This is the task of building a system that can automatically answer questions posed in natural language.

Machine translation

This is the task of converting a piece of text from one language to another. Tools like Google Translate are common applications of this task.

Topic modeling

This is the task of uncovering the topical structure of a large collection of documents. Topic modeling is a common text-mining tool and is used in a wide range of domains, from literature to bioinformatics.

Figure 1-2 shows a depiction of these tasks based on their relative difficulty in terms of developing comprehensive solutions.

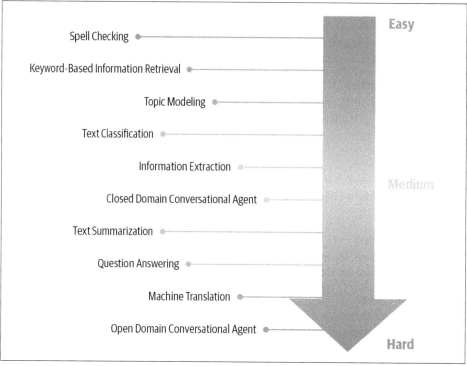

Figure 1-2. NLP tasks organized according to their relative difficulty

In the rest of the chapters in this book, we'll see these tasks' challenges and learn how to develop solutions that work for certain use cases (even the hard tasks shown in the figure). To get there, it is useful to have an understanding of the nature of human language and the challenges in automating language processing. The next two sections provide a basic overview.

What Is Language?

Language is a structured system of communication that involves complex combinations of its constituent components, such as characters, words, sentences, etc. Linguistics is the systematic study of language. In order to study NLP, it is important to understand some concepts from linguistics about how language is structured. In this section, we'll introduce them and cover how they relate to some of the NLP tasks we listed earlier.

We can think of human language as composed of four major building blocks: phonemes, morphemes and lexemes, syntax, and context. NLP applications need knowledge of different levels of these building blocks, starting from the basic sounds of language (phonemes) to texts with some meaningful expressions (context).

Figure 1-3 shows these building blocks of language, what they encompass, and a few NLP applications we introduced earlier that require this knowledge. Some of the terms listed here that were not introduced earlier in this chapter (e.g., parsing, word embeddings, etc.) will be introduced later in these first three chapters.

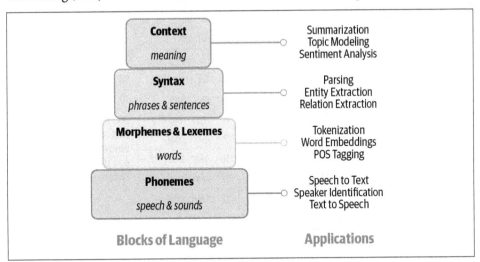

Figure 1-3. Building blocks of language and their applications

Building Blocks of Language

Let's first introduce what these blocks of language are to give context for the challenges involved in NLP.

Phonemes

Phonemes are the smallest units of sound in a language. They may not have any meaning by themselves but can induce meanings when uttered in combination with other phonemes. For example, standard English has 44 phonemes, which are either single letters or a combination of letters [2]. Figure 1-4 shows these phonemes along with sample words. Phonemes are particularly important in applications involving speech understanding, such as speech recognition, speech-to-text transcription, and text-to-speech conversion.

Consonant phonemes, with sample words		Vowel phonemes, with sample words	
1. /b/ – bat	13. /s/ – sun	1. /a/ – ant	13. /oi/ – coin
2. /k/ – cat	14. /t/ – tap	2. /e/ – egg	14. /ar/ – farm
3. /d/ – dog	15. /v/ – van	3. /i/ – in	15. /or/ – for
4. /f/ – fan	16. /w/ – wig	4. /o/ – on	16. /ur/ – hurt
5. /g/ – go	17. /y/ – yes	5. /u/ – up	17. /air/ – fair
6. /h/ – hen	18. /z/ – zip	6. /ai/ – rain	18. /ear/ – dear
7. /j/ – jet	19. /sh/ – shop	7. /ee/ – feet	19. /ure/[4] – sure
8. /l/ – leg	20. /ch/ – chip	8. /igh/ – night	20. /ə/ – corner (the 'schwa' – an unstressed vowel sound which is close to /u/)
9. /m/ – map	21. /th/ – thin	9. /oa/ – boat	
10. /n/ – net	22. /**th**/ – then	10. /**oo**/ – boot	
11. /p/ – pen	23. /ng/ – ring	11. /oo/ – look	
12. /r/ – rat	24. /zh/[3] – vision	12. /ow/ – cow	

Figure 1-4. Phonemes and examples

Morphemes and lexemes

A morpheme is the smallest unit of language that has a meaning. It is formed by a combination of phonemes. Not all morphemes are words, but all prefixes and suffixes are morphemes. For example, in the word "multimedia," "multi-" is not a word but a prefix that changes the meaning when put together with "media." "Multi-" is a morpheme. Figure 1-5 illustrates some words and their morphemes. For words like "cats" and "unbreakable," their morphemes are just constituents of the full word, whereas for words like "tumbling" and "unreliability," there is some variation when breaking the words down into their morphemes.

Figure 1-5. Morpheme examples

Lexemes are the structural variations of morphemes related to one another by meaning. For example, "run" and "running" belong to the same lexeme form. Morphological analysis, which analyzes the structure of words by studying its morphemes and lexemes, is a foundational block for many NLP tasks, such as tokenization, stemming, learning word embeddings, and part-of-speech tagging, which we'll introduce in the next chapter.

Syntax

Syntax is a set of rules to construct grammatically correct sentences out of words and phrases in a language. Syntactic structure in linguistics is represented in many different ways. A common approach to representing sentences is a parse tree. Figure 1-6 shows an example parse tree for two English sentences.

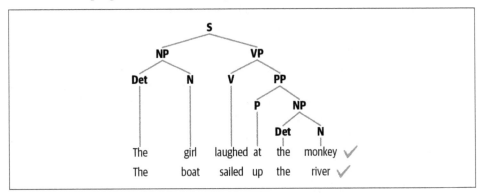

Figure 1-6. Syntactic structure of two syntactically similar sentences

This has a hierarchical structure of language, with words at the lowest level, followed by part-of-speech tags, followed by phrases, and ending with a sentence at the highest level. In Figure 1-6, both sentences have a similar structure and hence a similar syntactic parse tree. In this representation, N stands for noun, V for verb, and P for preposition. Noun phrase is denoted by NP and verb phrase by VP. The two noun phrases are "The girl" and "The boat," while the two verb phrases are "laughed at the monkey" and "sailed up the river." The syntactic structure is guided by a set of grammar rules for the language (e.g., the sentence comprises an NP and a VP), and this in turn guides some of the fundamental tasks of language processing, such as parsing. Parsing is the NLP task of constructing such trees automatically. Entity extraction and relation extraction are some of the NLP tasks that build on this knowledge of parsing, which we'll discuss in more detail in Chapter 5. Note that the parse structure described above is specific to English. The syntax of one language can be very different from that of another language, and the language-processing approaches needed for that language will change accordingly.

Context

Context is how various parts in a language come together to convey a particular meaning. Context includes long-term references, world knowledge, and common sense along with the literal meaning of words and phrases. The meaning of a sentence can change based on the context, as words and phrases can sometimes have multiple meanings. Generally, context is composed from semantics and pragmatics. Semantics is the direct meaning of the words and sentences without external context. Pragmatics adds world knowledge and external context of the conversation to enable us to infer implied meaning. Complex NLP tasks such as sarcasm detection, summarization, and topic modeling are some of tasks that use context heavily.

Linguistics is the study of language and hence is a vast area in itself, and we only introduced some basic ideas to illustrate the role of linguistic knowledge in NLP. Different tasks in NLP require varying degrees of knowledge about these building blocks of language. An interested reader can refer to the books written by Emily Bender [3, 4] on the linguistic fundamentals for NLP for further study. Now that we have some idea of what the building blocks of language are, let's see why language can be hard for computers to understand and what makes NLP challenging.

Why Is NLP Challenging?

What makes NLP a challenging problem domain? The ambiguity and creativity of human language are just two of the characteristics that make NLP a demanding area to work in. This section explores each characteristic in more detail, starting with ambiguity of language.

Ambiguity

Ambiguity means uncertainty of meaning. Most human languages are inherently ambiguous. Consider the following sentence: "I made her duck." This sentence has multiple meanings. The first one is: I cooked a duck for her. The second meaning is: I made her bend down to avoid an object. (There are other possible meanings, too; we'll leave them for the reader to think of.) Here, the ambiguity comes from the use of the word "made." Which of the two meanings applies depends on the context in which the sentence appears. If the sentence appears in a story about a mother and a child, then the first meaning will probably apply. But if the sentence appears in a book about sports, then the second meaning will likely apply. The example we saw is a direct sentence.

When it comes to figurative language—i.e., idioms—the ambiguity only increases. For example, "He is as good as John Doe." Try to answer, "How good is he?" The answer depends on how good John Doe is. Figure 1-7 shows some examples illustrating ambiguity in language.

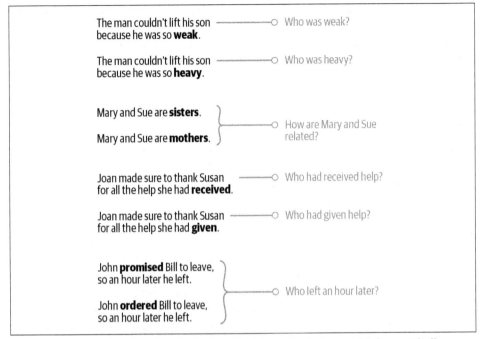

The man couldn't lift his son ———○ Who was weak?
because he was so **weak**.

The man couldn't lift his son ———○ Who was heavy?
because he was so **heavy**.

Mary and Sue are **sisters**.
                              ———○ How are Mary and Sue
Mary and Sue are **mothers**.   related?

Joan made sure to thank Susan ———○ Who had received help?
for all the help she had **received**.

Joan made sure to thank Susan ———○ Who had given help?
for all the help she had **given**.

John **promised** Bill to leave,
so an hour later he left.
                              ———○ Who left an hour later?
John **ordered** Bill to leave,
so an hour later he left.

Figure 1-7. Examples of ambiguity in language from the Winograd Schema Challenge

The examples come from the Winograd Schema Challenge [5], named after Professor Terry Winograd of Stanford University. This schema has pairs of sentences that differ by only a few words, but the meaning of the sentences is often flipped because of this minor change. These examples are easily disambiguated by a human but are not solvable using most NLP techniques. Consider the pairs of sentences in the figure and the questions associated with them. With some thought, how the answer changes should be apparent based on a single word variation. As another experiment, consider taking an off-the-shelf NLP system like Google Translate and try various examples to see how such ambiguities affect (or don't affect) the output of the system.

Common knowledge

A key aspect of any human language is "common knowledge." It is the set of all facts that most humans are aware of. In any conversation, it is assumed that these facts are known, hence they're not explicitly mentioned, but they do have a bearing on the meaning of the sentence. For example, consider two sentences: "man bit dog" and "dog bit man." We all know that the first sentence is unlikely to happen, while the second one is very possible. Why do we say so? Because we all "know" that it is very unlikely that a human will bite a dog. Further, dogs are known to bite humans. This knowledge is required for us to say that the first sentence is unlikely to happen while the second one is possible. Note that this common knowledge was not mentioned in either sentence. Humans use common knowledge all the time to understand and process any language. In the above example, the two sentences are syntactically very similar, but a computer would find it very difficult to differentiate between the two, as it lacks the common knowledge humans have. One of the key challenges in NLP is how to encode all the things that are common knowledge to humans in a computational model.

Creativity

Language is not just rule driven; there is also a creative aspect to it. Various styles, dialects, genres, and variations are used in any language. Poems are a great example of creativity in language. Making machines understand creativity is a hard problem not just in NLP, but in AI in general.

Diversity across languages

For most languages in the world, there is no direct mapping between the vocabularies of any two languages. This makes porting an NLP solution from one language to another hard. A solution that works for one language might not work at all for another language. This means that one either builds a solution that is language agnostic or that one needs to build separate solutions for each language. While the first one is conceptually very hard, the other is laborious and time intensive.

All these issues make NLP a challenging—yet rewarding—domain to work in. Before looking into how some of these challenges are tackled in NLP, we should know the common approaches to solving NLP problems. Let's start with an overview of how machine learning and deep learning are connected to NLP before delving deeper into different approaches to NLP.

Machine Learning, Deep Learning, and NLP: An Overview

Loosely speaking, artificial intelligence (AI) is a branch of computer science that aims to build systems that can perform tasks that require human intelligence. This is sometimes also called "machine intelligence." The foundations of AI were laid in the 1950s at a workshop organized at Dartmouth College [6]. Initial AI was largely built out of logic-, heuristics-, and rule-based systems. Machine learning (ML) is a branch of AI that deals with the development of algorithms that can learn to perform tasks automatically based on a large number of examples, without requiring handcrafted rules. Deep learning (DL) refers to the branch of machine learning that is based on artificial neural network architectures. ML, DL, and NLP are all subfields within AI, and the relationship between them is depicted in Figure 1-8.

While there is some overlap between NLP, ML, and DL, they are also quite different areas of study, as the figure illustrates. Like other early work in AI, early NLP applications were also based on rules and heuristics. In the past few decades, though, NLP

---

application development has been heavily influenced by methods from ML. More recently, DL has also been frequently used to build NLP applications. Considering this, let's do a short overview of ML and DL in this section.

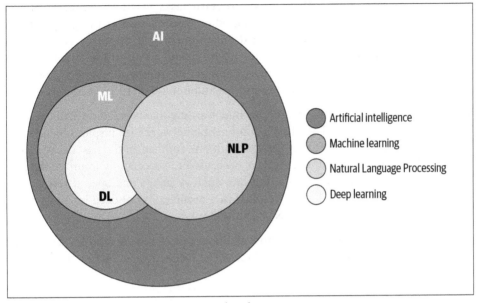

Figure 1-8. How NLP, ML, and DL are related

The goal of ML is to "learn" to perform tasks based on examples (called "training data") without explicit instruction. This is typically done by creating a numeric representation (called "features") of the training data and using this representation to learn the patterns in those examples. Machine learning algorithms can be grouped into three primary paradigms: supervised learning, unsupervised learning, and reinforcement learning. In supervised learning, the goal is to learn the mapping function from input to output given a large number of examples in the form of input-output pairs. The input-output pairs are known as *training data*, and the outputs are specifically known as *labels* or *ground truth*. An example of a supervised learning problem related to language is learning to classify email messages as spam or non-spam given thousands of examples in both categories. This is a common scenario in NLP, and we'll see examples of supervised learning throughout the book, especially in Chapter 4.

Unsupervised learning refers to a set of machine learning methods that aim to find hidden patterns in given input data without any reference output. That is, in contrast to supervised learning, unsupervised learning works with large collections of unlabeled data. In NLP, an example of such a task is to identify latent topics in a large collection of textual data without any knowledge of these topics. This is known as *topic modeling*, and we'll discuss it in Chapter 7.

Common in real-world NLP projects is a case of semi-supervised learning, where we have a small labeled dataset and a large unlabeled dataset. Semi-supervised techniques involve using both datasets to learn the task at hand. Last but not least, reinforcement learning deals with methods to learn tasks via trial and error and is characterized by the absence of either labeled or unlabeled data in large quantities. The learning is done in a self-contained environment and improves via feedback (reward or punishment) facilitated by the environment. This form of learning is not common in applied NLP (yet). It is more common in applications such as machine-playing games like go or chess, in the design of autonomous vehicles, and in robotics.

Deep learning refers to the branch of machine learning that is based on artificial neural network architectures. The ideas behind neural networks are inspired by neurons in the human brain and how they interact with one another. In the past decade, deep learning–based neural architectures have been used to successfully improve the performance of various intelligent applications, such as image and speech recognition and machine translation. This has resulted in a proliferation of deep learning–based solutions in industry, including in NLP applications.

Throughout this book, we'll discuss how all these approaches are used for developing various NLP applications. Let's now discuss the different approaches to solve any given NLP problem.

Approaches to NLP

The different approaches used to solve NLP problems commonly fall into three categories: heuristics, machine learning, and deep learning. This section is simply an introduction to each approach—don't worry if you can't quite grasp the concepts yet, as they'll be discussed in detail throughout the rest of the book. Let's jump in by discussing heuristics-based NLP.

Heuristics-Based NLP

Similar to other early AI systems, early attempts at designing NLP systems were based on building rules for the task at hand. This required that the developers had some expertise in the domain to formulate rules that could be incorporated into a program. Such systems also required resources like dictionaries and thesauruses, typically compiled and digitized over a period of time. An example of designing rules to solve an NLP problem using such resources is lexicon-based sentiment analysis. It uses counts of positive and negative words in the text to deduce the sentiment of the text. We'll cover this briefly in Chapter 4.

Besides dictionaries and thesauruses, more elaborate knowledge bases have been built to aid NLP in general and rule-based NLP in particular. One example is Wordnet [7], which is a database of words and the semantic relationships between them. Some examples of such relationships are synonyms, hyponyms, and meronyms. Synonyms refer to words with similar meanings. Hyponyms capture is-type-of relationships. For example, baseball, sumo wrestling, and tennis are all hyponyms of sports. Meronyms capture is-part-of relationships. For example, hands and legs are meronyms of the body. All this information becomes useful when building rule-based systems around language. Figure 1-9 shows an example depiction of such relationships between words using Wordnet.

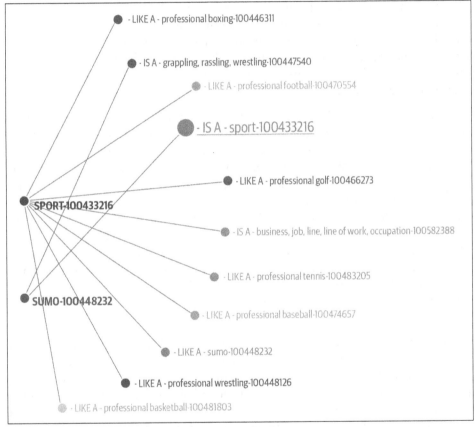

Figure 1-9. Wordnet graph for the word "sport" [8]

More recently, common sense world knowledge has also been incorporated into knowledge bases like Open Mind Common Sense [9], which also aids such rule-based systems. While what we've seen so far are largely lexical resources based on word-level information, rule-based systems go beyond words and can incorporate other forms of information, too. Some of them are introduced below.

Regular expressions (regex) are a great tool for text analysis and building rule-based systems. A regex is a set of characters or a pattern that is used to match and find substrings in text. For example, a regex like '^([a-zA-Z0-9_\-\.]+)@([a-zA-Z0-9_\-\.]+)\.([a-zA-Z]{2,5})$' is used to find all email IDs in a piece of text. Regexes are a great way to incorporate domain knowledge in your NLP system. For example, given a customer complaint that comes via chat or email, we want to build a system to automatically identify the product the complaint is about. There is a range of product codes that map to certain brand names. We can use regexes to match these easily.

Regexes are a very popular paradigm for building rule-based systems. NLP software like StanfordCoreNLP includes TokensRegex [10], which is a framework for defining regular expressions. It is used to identify patterns in text and use matched text to create rules. Regexes are used for deterministic matches—meaning it's either a match or it's not. Probabilistic regexes is a sub-branch that addresses this limitation by including a probability of a match. Interested readers can look at software libraries such as pregex [11]. Last accessed June 15, 2020.

Context-free grammar (CFG) is a type of formal grammar that is used to model natural languages. CFG was invented by Professor Noam Chomsky, a renowned linguist and scientist. CFGs can be used to capture more complex and hierarchical information that a regex might not. The Earley parser [12] allows parsing of all kinds of CFGs. To model more complex rules, grammar languages like JAPE (Java Annotation Patterns Engine) can be used [13]. JAPE has features from both regexes as well as CFGs and can be used for rule-based NLP systems like GATE (General Architecture for Text Engineering) [14]. GATE is used for building text extraction for closed and well-defined domains where accuracy and completeness of coverage is more important. As an example, JAPE and GATE were used to extract information on pacemaker implantation procedures from clinical reports [15]. Figure 1-10 shows the GATE interface along with several types of information highlighted in the text as an example of a rule-based system.

Rules and heuristics play a role across the entire life cycle of NLP projects even now. At one end, they're a great way to build first versions of NLP systems. Put simply, rules and heuristics help you quickly build the first version of the model and get a better understanding of the problem at hand. We'll discuss this point in depth in Chapters 4 and 11. Rules and heuristics can also be useful as features for machine learning–based NLP systems. At the other end of the spectrum of the project life cycle, rules and heuristics are used to plug the gaps in the system. Any NLP system built using statistical, machine learning, or deep learning techniques will make mistakes. Some mistakes can be too expensive—for example, a healthcare system that looks into all the medical records of a patient and wrongly decides to not advise a critical test. This mistake could even cost a life. Rules and heuristics are a great way to plug such gaps in production systems. Now let's turn our attention to machine learning techniques used for NLP.

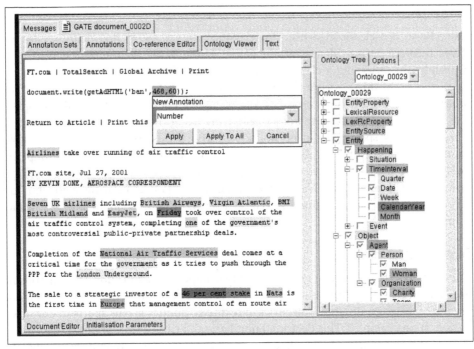

Figure 1-10. GATE tool

Machine Learning for NLP

Machine learning techniques are applied to textual data just as they're used on other forms of data, such as images, speech, and structured data. Supervised machine learning techniques such as classification and regression methods are heavily used for various NLP tasks. As an example, an NLP classification task would be to classify news articles into a set of news topics like sports or politics. On the other hand, regression techniques, which give a numeric prediction, can be used to estimate the price of a stock based on processing the social media discussion about that stock. Similarly, unsupervised clustering algorithms can be used to club together text documents.

Any machine learning approach for NLP, supervised or unsupervised, can be described as consisting of three common steps: extracting features from text, using the feature representation to learn a model, and evaluating and improving the model. We'll learn more about feature representations for text specifically in Chapter 3 and evaluation in Chapter 2. We'll now briefly outline some of the commonly used supervised ML methods in NLP for the second step (using the feature representation to learn a model). Having a basic idea of these methods will help you understand the concepts discussed in later chapters.

Naive Bayes

Naive Bayes is a classic algorithm for classification tasks [16] that mainly relies on Bayes' theorem (as is evident from the name). Using Bayes' theorem, it calculates the probability of observing a class label given the set of features for the input data. A characteristic of this algorithm is that it assumes each feature is independent of all other features. For the news classification example mentioned earlier in this chapter, one way to represent the text numerically is by using the count of domain-specific words, such as sport-specific or politics-specific words, present in the text. We assume that these word counts are not correlated to one another. If the assumption holds, we can use Naive Bayes to classify news articles. While this is a strong assumption to make in many cases, Naive Bayes is commonly used as a starting algorithm for text classification. This is primarily because it is simple to understand and very fast to train and run.

Support vector machine

The support vector machine (SVM) is another popular classification [17] algorithm. The goal in any classification approach is to learn a decision boundary that acts as a separation between different categories of text (e.g., politics versus sports in our news classification example). This decision boundary can be linear or nonlinear (e.g., a circle). An SVM can learn both a linear and nonlinear decision boundary to separate data points belonging to different classes. A linear decision boundary learns to represent the data in a way that the class differences become apparent. For two-dimensional feature representations, an illustrative example is given in Figure 1-11, where the black and white points belong to different classes (e.g., sports and politics news groups). An SVM learns an optimal decision boundary so that the distance between points across classes is at its maximum. The biggest strength of SVMs are their robustness to variation and noise in the data. A major weakness is the time taken to train and the inability to scale when there are large amounts of training data.

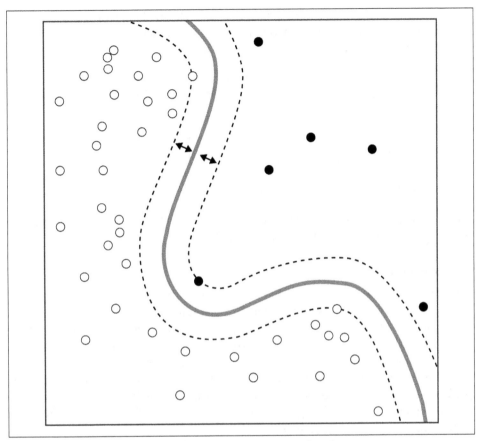

Figure 1-11. A two-dimensional feature representation of an SVM

Hidden Markov Model

The hidden Markov model (HMM) is a statistical model [18] that assumes there is an underlying, unobservable process with hidden states that generates the data—i.e., we can only observe the data once it is generated. An HMM then tries to model the hidden states from this data. For example, consider the NLP task of part-of-speech (POS) tagging, which deals with assigning part-of-speech tags to sentences. HMMs are used for POS tagging of text data. Here, we assume that the text is generated according to an underlying grammar, which is hidden underneath the text. The hidden states are parts of speech that inherently define the structure of the sentence following the language grammar, but we only observe the words that are governed by these latent states. Along with this, HMMs also make the Markov assumption, which means that each hidden state is dependent on the previous state(s). Human language is sequential in nature, and the current word in a sentence depends on what occurred before it. Hence, HMMs with these two assumptions are a powerful tool for modeling textual data. In Figure 1-12, we can see an example of an HMM that learns parts of speech from a given sentence. Parts of speech like JJ (adjective) and NN (noun) are hidden states, while the sentence "natural language processing (nlp)..." is directly observed.

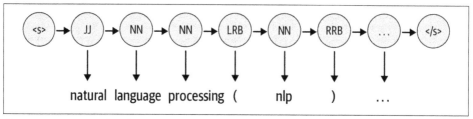

Figure 1-12. A graphical representation of a hidden Markov model

For a detailed discussion on HMMs for NLP, refer to Chapter 8 in the book *Speech and Language Processing* by Professor Jurafsky [19].

Conditional random fields

The conditional random field (CRF) is another algorithm that is used for sequential data. Conceptually, a CRF essentially performs a classification task on each element in the sequence [20]. Imagine the same example of POS tagging, where a CRF can tag word by word by classifying them to one of the parts of speech from the pool of all POS tags. Since it takes the sequential input and the context of tags into consideration, it becomes more expressive than the usual classification methods and generally performs better. CRFs outperform HMMs for tasks such as POS tagging, which rely on the sequential nature of language. We discuss CRFs and their variants along with applications in Chapters 5, 6, and 9.

These are some of the popular ML algorithms that are used heavily across NLP tasks. Having some understanding of these ML methods helps to understand various solutions discussed in the book. Apart from that, it is also important to understand when to use which algorithm, which we'll discuss in the upcoming chapters. To learn more about other steps and further theoretical details of the machine learning process, we recommend the textbook *Pattern Recognition and Machine Learning* by Christopher Bishop [21]. For a more applied machine learning perspective, Aurélien Géron's book [22] is a great resource to start with. Let's now take a look at deep learning approaches to NLP.

Deep Learning for NLP

We briefly touched on a couple of popular machine learning methods that are used heavily in various NLP tasks. In the last few years, we have seen a huge surge in using neural networks to deal with complex, unstructured data. Language is inherently complex and unstructured. Therefore, we need models with better representation and learning capability to understand and solve language tasks. Here are a few popular deep neural network architectures that have become the status quo in NLP.

Recurrent neural networks

As we mentioned earlier, language is inherently sequential. A sentence in any language flows from one direction to another (e.g., English reads from left to right). Thus, a model that can progressively read an input text from one end to another can be very useful for language understanding. Recurrent neural networks (RNNs) are specially designed to keep such sequential processing and learning in mind. RNNs have neural units that are capable of remembering what they have processed so far. This memory is temporal, and the information is stored and updated with every time step as the RNN reads the next word in the input. Figure 1-13 shows an unrolled RNN and how it keeps track of the input at different time steps.

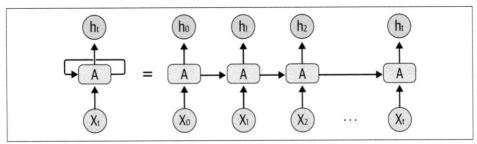

Figure 1-13. An unrolled recurrent neural network [23]

RNNs are powerful and work very well for solving a variety of NLP tasks, such as text classification, named entity recognition, machine translation, etc. One can also use RNNs to generate text where the goal is to read the preceding text and predict the next word or the next character. Refer to "The Unreasonable Effectiveness of Recurrent Neural Networks" [24] for a detailed discussion on the versatility of RNNs and the range of applications within and outside NLP for which they are useful.

Long short-term memory

Despite their capability and versatility, RNNs suffer from the problem of forgetful memory—they cannot remember longer contexts and therefore do not perform well when the input text is long, which is typically the case with text inputs. Long short-term memory networks (LSTMs), a type of RNN, were invented to mitigate this shortcoming of the RNNs. LSTMs circumvent this problem by letting go of the irrelevant context and only remembering the part of the context that is needed to solve the task at hand. This relieves the load of remembering very long context in one vector representation. LSTMs have replaced RNNs in most applications because of this workaround. Gated recurrent units (GRUs) are another variant of RNNs that are used mostly in language generation. (The article written by Christopher Olah [23] covers the family of RNN models in great detail.) Figure 1-14 illustrates the architecture of a single LSTM cell. We'll discuss specific uses of LSTMs in various NLP applications in Chapters 4, 5, 6, and 9.

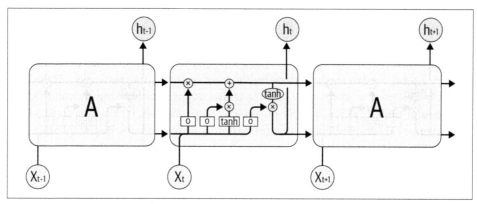

Figure 1-14. Architecture of an LSTM cell [23]

Convolutional neural networks

Convolutional neural networks (CNNs) are very popular and used heavily in computer vision tasks like image classification, video recognition, etc. CNNs have also seen success in NLP, especially in text-classification tasks. One can replace each word in a sentence with its corresponding word vector, and all vectors are of the same size (*d*) (refer to "Word Embeddings" in Chapter 3). Thus, they can be stacked one over another to form a matrix or 2D array of dimension $n \times d$, where n is the number of words in the sentence and d is the size of the word vectors. This matrix can now be treated similar to an image and can be modeled by a CNN. The main advantage CNNs have is their ability to look at a group of words together using a context window. For example, we are doing sentiment classification, and we get a sentence like, "I like this movie very much!" In order to make sense of this sentence, it is better to look at words and different sets of contiguous words. CNNs can do exactly this by definition of their architecture. We'll touch on this in more detail in later chapters. Figure 1-15 shows a CNN in action on a piece of text to extract useful phrases to ultimately arrive at a binary number indicating the sentiment of the sentence from a given piece of text.

As shown in the figure, CNN uses a collection of convolution and pooling layers to achieve this condensed representation of the text, which is then fed as input to a fully connected layer to learn some NLP tasks like text classification. More details on the usage CNNs for NLP can be found in [25] and [26]. We also cover them in Chapter 4.

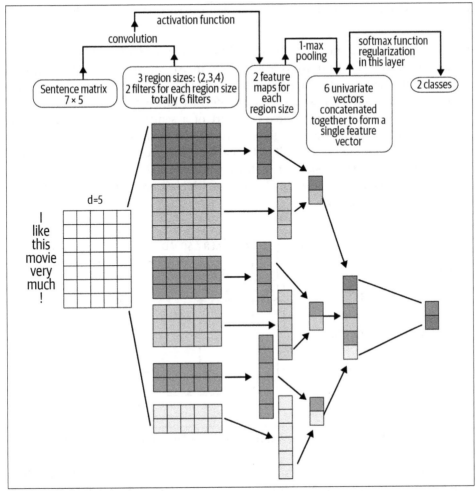

Figure 1-15. CNN model in action [27]

Transformers

Transformers [28] are the latest entry in the league of deep learning models for NLP. Transformer models have achieved state of the art in almost all major NLP tasks in the past two years. They model the textual context but not in a sequential manner. Given a word in the input, it prefers to look at all the words around it (known as *self-attention*) and represent each word with respect to its context. For example, the word "bank" can have different meanings depending on the context in which it appears. If the context talks about finance, then "bank" probably denotes a financial institution. On the other hand, if the context mentions a river, then it probably indicates a bank of the river. Transformers can model such context and hence have been used heavily in NLP tasks due to this higher representation capacity as compared to other deep networks.

Recently, large transformers have been used for *transfer learning* with smaller downstream tasks. Transfer learning is a technique in AI where the knowledge gained while solving one problem is applied to a different but related problem. With transformers, the idea is to train a very large transformer mode in an unsupervised manner (known as *pre-training*) to predict a part of a sentence given the rest of the content so that it can encode the high-level nuances of the language in it. These models are trained on more than 40 GB of textual data, scraped from the whole internet. An example of a large transformer is BERT (Bidirectional Encoder Representations from Transformers) [29], shown in Figure 1-16, which is pre-trained on massive data and open sourced by Google.

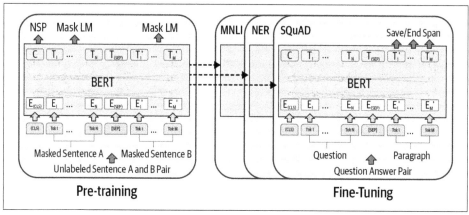

Figure 1-16. BERT architecture: pre-trained model and fine-tuned, task-specific models

The pre-trained model is shown on the left side of Figure 1-16. This model is then fine-tuned on downstream NLP tasks, such as text classification, entity extraction, question answering, etc., as shown on the right of Figure 1-16. Due to the sheer amount of pre-trained knowledge, BERT works efficiently in transferring the knowledge for downstream tasks and achieves state of the art for many of these tasks. Throughout the book, we have covered various examples of using BERT for various tasks. Figure 1-17 illustrates the workings of a self-attention mechanism, which is a key component of a transformer. Interested readers can look at [30] for more details on self-attention mechanisms and transformer architecture. We cover BERT and its applications in Chapters 4, 6, and 10.

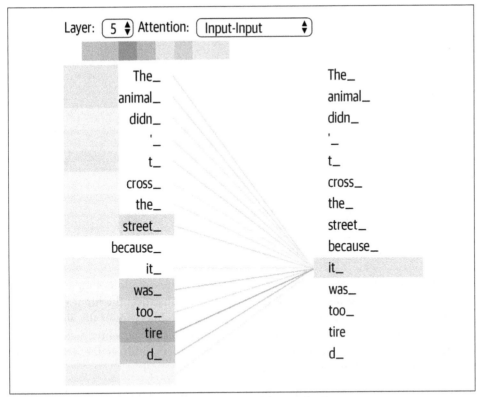

Figure 1-17. Self-attention mechanism in a transformer [30]

Autoencoders

An autoencoder is a different kind of network that is used mainly for learning compressed vector representation of the input. For example, if we want to represent a text by a vector, what is a good way to do it? We can learn a mapping function from input text to the vector. To make this mapping function useful, we "reconstruct" the input back from the vector representation. This is a form of unsupervised learning since you don't need human-annotated labels for it. After the training, we collect the vector representation, which serves as an encoding of the input text as a dense vector. Autoencoders are typically used to create feature representations needed for any downstream tasks. Figure 1-18 depicts the architecture of an autoencoder.

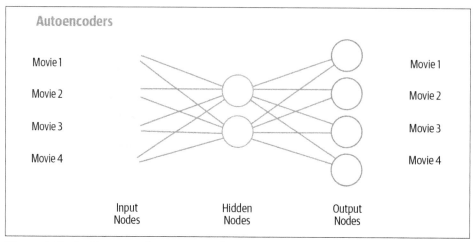

Figure 1-18. Architecture of an autoencoder

In this scheme, the hidden layer gives a compressed representation of input data, capturing the essence, and the output layer (decoder) reconstructs the input representation from the compressed representation. While the architecture of the autoencoder shown in Figure 1-18 cannot handle specific properties of sequential data like text, variations of autoencoders, such as LSTM autoencoders, address these well. More information about autoencoders can be found in [31].

We briefly introduced some of the popular DL architectures for NLP here. For a more detailed study of deep learning architectures in general, refer to [31], and specifically for NLP, refer to [25]. We hope this introduction gives you enough background to understand the use of DL in the rest of this book.

Going by all the recent achievements of DL models, one might think that DL should be the go-to way to build NLP systems. However, that is far from the truth for most industry use cases. Let's look at why this is the case.

Why Deep Learning Is Not Yet the Silver Bullet for NLP

Over the last few years, DL has made amazing advances in NLP. For example, in text classification, LSTM- and CNN-based models have surpassed the performance of standard machine learning techniques such as Naive Bayes and SVM for many classification tasks. Similarly, LSTMs have performed better in sequence-labeling tasks like entity extraction as compared to CRF models. Recently, powerful transformer models have become state of the art in most of these NLP tasks, ranging from classification to sequence labeling. A huge trend right now is to leverage large (in terms of number of parameters) transformer models, train them on huge datasets for generic NLP tasks like language models, then adapt them to smaller downstream tasks. This approach (known as *transfer learning*) has also been successful in other domains, such as computer vision and speech.

Despite such tremendous success, DL is still not the silver bullet for all NLP tasks when it comes to industrial applications. Some of the key reasons for this are as follows:

Overfitting on small datasets
DL models tend to have more parameters than traditional ML models, which means they possess more expressivity. This also comes with a curse. Occam's razor [32] suggests that a simpler solution is always preferable given that all other conditions are equal. Many times, in the development phase, sufficient training data is not available to train a complex network. In such cases, a simpler model should be preferred over a DL model. DL models overfit on small datasets and subsequently lead to poor generalization capability, which in turn leads to poor performance in production.

Few-shot learning and synthetic data generation
In disciplines like computer vision, DL has made significant strides in few-shot learning (i.e., learning from very few training examples) [33] and in models that can generate superior-quality images [34]. Both of these advances have made training DL-based vision models on small amounts of data feasible. Therefore, DL has achieved much wider adoption for solving problems in industrial settings. We have not yet seen similar DL techniques be successfully developed for NLP.

Domain adaptation
If we utilize a large DL model that is trained on datasets originating from some common domains (e.g., news articles) and apply the trained model to a newer domain that is different from the common domains (e.g., social media posts), it may yield poor performance. This loss in generalization performance indicates that DL models are not always useful. For example, models trained on internet texts and product reviews will not work well when applied to domains such as law, social media, or healthcare, where both the syntactic and semantic structure of the language is specific to the domain. We need specialized models to encode the domain knowledge, which could be as simple as domain-specific, rule-based models.

Interpretable models
Apart from efficient domain adaptation, controllability and interpretability is hard for DL models because, most of the time, they work like a black box. Businesses often demand more interpretable results that can be explained to the customer or end user. In those cases, traditional techniques might be more useful. For example, a Naive Bayes model for sentiment classification may explain the effect of strong positive and negative words on the final prediction of sentiment.

As of today, obtaining such insights from an LSTM-based classification model is difficult. This is in contrast to computer vision, where DL models are not black boxes. There are plenty of techniques [35] in computer vision that are used to gain insight into why a model is making a particular prediction. Such approaches for NLP are not as common.

Common sense and world knowledge

Even though we have achieved good performance on benchmark NLP tasks using ML and DL models, language remains a bigger enigma to scientists. Beyond syntax and semantics, language encompasses knowledge of the world around us. Language for communication relies on logical reasoning and common sense regarding events from the world. For example, "I like pizza" implies "I feel happy when I eat pizza." A more complex reasoning example would be, "If John walks out of the bedroom and goes to the garden, then John is not in the bedroom anymore, and his current location is the garden." This might seem trivial to us humans, but it requires multistep reasoning for a machine to identify events and understand their consequences. Since this world knowledge and common sense are inherent in language, understanding them is crucial for any DL model to perform well on various language tasks. Current DL models may perform well on standard benchmarks but are still not capable of common sense understanding and logical reasoning. There are some efforts to collect common sense events and logical rules (such as if-them reasoning), but they are not well integrated yet with ML or DL models.

Cost

Building DL-based solutions for NLP tasks can be pretty expensive. The cost, in terms of both money and time, stems from multiple sources. DL models are known to be data guzzlers. Collecting a large dataset and getting it labeled can be very expensive. Owing to the size of DL models, training them to achieve desired performance can not only increase your development cycles but also result in a heavy bill for the specialized hardware (GPUs). Further, deploying and maintaining DL models can be expensive in terms of both hardware requirements and effort. Last but not least, because they're bulky, these models may cause latency issues during inference time and may not be useful in cases where low latency is a must. To this list, one can also add technical debt arising from building and maintaining a heavy model. Loosely speaking, technical debt is the cost of rework that arises from prioritizing speedy delivery over good design and implementation choices.

On-device deployment

For many use cases, the NLP solution needs to be deployed on an embedded device rather than in the cloud—for example, a machine-translation system that helps tourists speak the translated text even without the internet. In such cases, owing to limitations of the device, the solution must work with limited memory and power. Most DL solutions do not fit such constraints. There are some efforts in this direction [36, 37, 38] where one can deploy DL models on edge devices, but we're still quite far from generic solutions.

In most industry projects, one or more of the points mentioned above plays out. This leads to longer project cycles and higher costs (hardware, manpower), and yet the performance is either comparable or sometimes even lower than ML models. This results in a poor return on investment and often causes the NLP project to fail.

Based on this discussion, it may be apparent that DL is not always the go-to solution for all industrial NLP applications. So, this book starts with fundamental aspects of various NLP tasks and how we can solve them using techniques ranging from rule-based systems to DL models. We emphasize the data requirements and model-building pipeline, not just the technical details of individual models. Given the rapid advances in this area, we anticipate that newer DL models will come in the future to advance the state of the art but that the fundamentals of NLP tasks will not change substantially. This is why we'll discuss the basics of NLP and build on them to develop models of increasing complexity wherever possible, rather than directly jumping to the cutting edge.

Echoing Professor Zachary Lipton from Carnegie Mellon University and Professor Jacob Steinhardt from UC Berkeley [39], we also want to provide a word of caution about consuming a lot of scientific articles, research papers, and blogs on ML and NLP without context and proper training. Following a large volume of cutting-edge work may cause confusion and not-so-precise understanding. Many recent DL models are not interpretable enough to indicate the sources of empirical gains. Lipton and Steinhardt also recognize the possible conflation of technical terms and misuse of language in ML-related scientific articles, which often fail to provide any clear path to solving the problem at hand. Therefore, in this book, we carefully describe various technical concepts in the application of ML in NLP tasks via examples, code, and tips throughout the chapters.

So far, we've covered some foundational concepts related to language, NLP, ML, and DL. Before we wrap up Chapter 1, let's look at a case study to help get a better understanding of the various components of an NLP application.

An NLP Walkthrough: Conversational Agents

Voice-based conversational agents like Amazon Alexa and Apple Siri are some of the most ubiquitous applications of NLP, and they're the ones most people are already familiar with. Figure 1-19 shows the typical interaction model of a conversational agent.

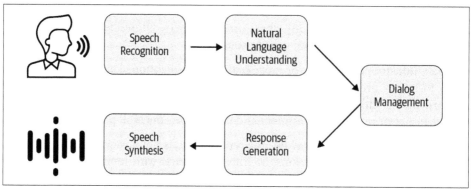

Figure 1-19. Flow of conversation agents

Here, we'll walk through all the major NLP components used in this flow:

1. *Speech recognition and synthesis*: These are the main components of any voice-based conversational agent. Speech recognition involves converting speech signals to their phonemes, which are then transcribed as words. Speech synthesis achieves the reverse process by transforming textual results into spoken language to the user. Both of these techniques have advanced considerably in the last decade, and we recommend using cloud APIs for most standard cases.

2. *Natural language understanding*: This is the next component in the conversational agent pipeline, where the user response received (transcribed as text) is analyzed using a natural language understanding system. This can be broken into many small NLP subtasks, such as:

   - *Sentiment analysis*: Here, we analyze the sentiment of the user response. This will be covered in Chapter 4.

   - *Named entity recognition*: Here, we identify all the important entities the user mentioned in their response. This will be covered in Chapter 5.

   - *Coreference resolution*: Here, we find out the references of the extracted entities from the conversation history. For example, a user may say "*Avengers Endgame* was awesome" and later refer back to the movie, saying "The movie's special effects were great." In this case, we would want to link that "movie" is referring to *Avengers Endgame*. This is covered briefly in Chapter 5.

3. *Dialog management*: Once we've extracted the useful information from the user's response, we may want to understand the user's intent—i.e., if they're asking a factual question like "What is the weather today?" or giving a command like "Play Mozart songs." We can use a text-classification system to classify the user response as one of the pre-defined intents. This helps the conversational agent know what's being asked. Intent classification will be covered in Chapters 4 and 6. During this process, the system may ask a few clarifying questions to elicit fur-

ther information from the user. Once we've figured out the user's intent, we want to figure out which suitable action the conversational agent should take to fulfill the user's request. This is done based on the information and intent extracted from the user's response. Examples of suitable actions could be generating an answer from the internet, playing music, dimming lights, or asking a clarifying question. We'll cover this in Chapter 6.

4. *Response generation*: Finally, the conversational agent generates a suitable action to perform based on a semantic interpretation of the user's intent and additional inputs from the dialogue with the user. As mentioned earlier, the agent can retrieve information from the knowledge base and generate responses using a pre-defined template. For example, it might respond by saying, "Now playing Symphony No. 25" or "The lights have been dimmed." In certain scenarios, it can also generate a completely new response.

We hope this brief case study provided an overview of how different NLP components we'll be discussing throughout this book will come together to build one application: a conversational agent. We'll see more details about these components as we progress through the book, and we'll discuss conversational agents specifically in Chapter 6.

Wrapping Up

From the broader contours of what a language is to a concrete case study of a real-world NLP application, we've covered a range of NLP topics in this chapter. We also discussed how NLP is applied in the real world, some of its challenges and different tasks, and the role of ML and DL in NLP. This chapter was meant to give you a baseline of knowledge that we'll build on throughout the book. The next two chapters (Chapters 2 and 3) will introduce you to some of the foundational steps necessary for building NLP applications. Chapters 4–7 focus on core NLP tasks along with industrial use cases that can be solved with them. In Chapters 8–10, we discuss how NLP is used across different industry verticals such as e-commerce, healthcare, finance, etc. Chapter 11 brings everything together and discusses what it takes to build end-to-end NLP applications in terms of design, development, testing, and deployment. With this broad overview in place, let's start delving deeper into the world of NLP.

References

[1] Arria.com. "NLG for Your Industry" (*https://oreil.ly/R8hSI*). Last accessed June 15, 2020.

[2] UCL. Phonetic symbols for English (*https://oreil.ly/5jnsl*). Last accessed June 15, 2020.

[3] Bender, Emily M. "Linguistic Fundamentals for Natural Language Processing: 100 Essentials From Morphology and Syntax." *Synthesis Lectures on Human Language Technologies* 6.3 (2013): 1–184.

[4] Bender, Emily M. and Alex Lascarides. "Linguistic Fundamentals for Natural Language Processing II: 100 Essentials from Semantics and Pragmatics." *Synthesis Lectures on Human Language Technologies* 12.3 (2019): 1–268.

[5] Levesque, Hector, Ernest Davis, and Leora Morgenstern. "The Winograd Schema Challenge." *The Thirteenth International Conference on the Principles of Knowledge Representation and Reasoning* (2012).

[6] Wikipedia. "Dartmouth workshop" (*https://oreil.ly/6NZGh*). Last modified March 30, 2020.

[7] Miller, George A. "WordNet: A Lexical Database for English." *Communications of the ACM* 38.11 (1995): 39–41.

[8] Visual Thesaurus of English Collocations. "Visual Wordnet with D3.js" (*https://oreil.ly/EY1HB*). Last accessed June 15, 2020.

[9] Singh, Push, Thomas Lin, Erik T. Mueller, Grace Lim, Travell Perkins, and Wan Li Zhu. "Open Mind Common Sense: Knowledge Acquisition from the General Public," Meersman R. and Tari Z. (eds), *On the Move to Meaningful Internet Systems 2002: CoopIS, DOA, and ODBASE. OTM 2002. Lecture Notes in Computer Science*, vol. 2519. Berlin, Heidelberg: Springer.

[10] The Stanford Natural Language Processing Group. Stanford TokensRegex (*https://oreil.ly/M3KnK*), (software). Last accessed June 15, 2020.

[11] Hewitt, Luke. Probabilistic regular expressions (*https://oreil.ly/BqhJX*), (GitHub repo).

[12] Earley, Jay. "An Efficient Context-Free Parsing Algorithm." *Communications of the ACM* 13.2 (1970): 94–102.

[13] "Java Annotation Patterns Engine: Regular Expressions over Annotations" (*https://oreil.ly/dmdOs*). *Developing Language Processing Components with GATE Version 9 (a User Guide)*, Chapter 8. Last accessed June 15, 2020.

[14] General Architecture for Text Engineering (GATE) (*https://gate.ac.uk*). Last accessed June 15, 2020.

[15] Rosier, Arnaud, Anita Burgun, and Philippe Mabo. "Using Regular Expressions to Extract Information on Pacemaker Implantation Procedures from Clinical Reports." *AMIA Annual Symposium Proceedings* v.2008 (2008): 81–85.

[16] Zhang, Haiyi and Di Li. "Naïve Bayes Text Classifier." *2007 IEEE International Conference on Granular Computing* (GRC 2007): 708.

[17] Joachims, Thorsten. *Learning to Classify Text Using Support Vector Machines*, Vol. 668. New York: Springer Science & Business Media, 2002. ISBN: 978-1-4615-0907-3

[18] Baum, Leonard E. and Ted Petrie. "Statistical Inference for Probabilistic Functions of Finite State Markov Chains." *The Annals of Mathematical Statistics* 37.6 (1966): 1554–1563.

[19] Jurafsky, Dan and James H. Martin. *Speech and Language Processing*, Third Edition (Draft) (*https://oreil.ly/sZfWl*), 2018.

[20] Settles, Burr. "Biomedical Named Entity Recognition Using Conditional Random Fields and Rich Feature Sets." *Proceedings of the International Joint Workshop on Natural Language Processing in Biomedicine and its Applications (NLPBA/BioNLP)* (2004): 107–110.

[21] Bishop, Christopher M. *Pattern Recognition and Machine Learning*. New York: Springer, 2006. ISBN: 978-0-3873-1073-2

[22] Géron, Aurélien. *Hands-On Machine Learning with Scikit-Learn, Keras, and TensorFlow: Concepts, Tools, and Techniques to Build Intelligent Systems*. Boston: O'Reilly, 2019. ISBN: 978-1-492-03264-9

[23] Olah, Christopher. "Understanding LSTM Networks" (*https://oreil.ly/X6dwG*). August 27, 2015.

[24] Karpathy, Andrej. "The Unreasonable Effectiveness of Recurrent Neural Networks" (*https://oreil.ly/qTAxV*). May 21, 2015.

[25] Goldberg, Yoav. "Neural Network Methods for Natural Language Processing." *Synthesis Lectures on Human Language Technologies* 10.1 (2017): 1–309.

[26] Britz, Denny. "Understanding Convolutional Neural Networks for NLP" (*https://oreil.ly/vJppc*). November 7, 2015.

[27] Le, Hoa T., Christophe Cerisara, and Alexandre Denis. "Do Convolutional Networks need to be Deep for Text Classification?" *Workshops at the Thirty-Second AAAI Conference on Artificial Intelligence*, 2018.

[28] Vaswani, Ashish, Noam Shazeer, Niki Parmar, Jakob Uszkoreit, Llion Jones, Aidan N. Gomez, Łukasz Kaiser, and Illia Polosukhin. "Attention Is All You Need." *Advances in Neural Information Processing Systems*, 2017: 5998–6008.

[29] Devlin, Jacob, Ming-Wei Chang, Kenton Lee, and Kristina Toutanova. "BERT: Pre-training of Deep Bidirectional Transformers for Language Understanding" (*https://oreil.ly/xdtmX*). October 11, 2018.

[30] Alammar, Jay. "The Illustrated Transformer" (*https://oreil.ly/Fl9n3*). June 27, 2018.

[31] Goodfellow, Ian, Yoshua Bengio, and Aaron Courville. *Deep Learning*. Cambridge: MIT Press, 2016. ISBN: 978-0-262-03561-3

[32] Varma, Nakul. COMS 4771: Introduction to Machine Learning (*https://oreil.ly/yRJZP*), Lecture 6, Slide 7. Last accessed June 15, 2020.

[33] Wang, Yaqing, Quanming Yao, James Kwok, and Lionel M. Ni. "Generalizing from a Few Examples: A Survey on Few-Shot Learning" (*https://oreil.ly/LyMxm*), (2019).

[34] Wang, Zhengwei, Qi She, and Tomas E. Ward. "Generative Adversarial Networks in Computer Vision: A Survey and Taxonomy" (*https://oreil.ly/OFvz7*), (2019).

[35] Olah, Chris, Arvind Satyanarayan, Ian Johnson, Shan Carter, Ludwig Schubert, Katherine Ye, and Alexander Mordvintsev. "The Building Blocks of Interpretability." *Distill* 3.3 (March 2018): e10.

[36] Nan, Kaiming, Sicong Liu, Junzhao Du, and Hui Liu. "Deep Model Compression for Mobile Platforms: A Survey." *Tsinghua Science and Technology* 24.6 (2019): 677–693.

[37] TensorFlow. "Get started with TensorFlow Lite" (*https://oreil.ly/Jxsuc*). Last modified March 21, 2020.

[38] Ganesh, Prakhar, Yao Chen, Xin Lou, Mohammad Ali Khan, Yin Yang, Deming Chen, Marianne Winslett, Hassan Sajjad, and Preslav Nakov. "Compressing Large-Scale Transformer-Based Models: A Case Study on BERT" (*https://oreil.ly/VSQvc*), (2020).

[39] Lipton, Zachary C. and Jacob Steinhardt. "Troubling Trends in Machine Learning Scholarship" (*https://oreil.ly/lpay1*), (2018).

## CHAPTER 2

NLP Pipeline

*The whole is more than the sum of its parts. It is more correct to say that the whole is
something else than the sum of its parts, because summing up is a meaningless procedure,
whereas the whole-part relationship is meaningful.*
—*Kurt Koffka*

In the previous chapter, we saw examples of some common NLP applications that we
might encounter in everyday life. If we were asked to build such an application, think
about how we would approach doing so at our organization. We would normally
walk through the requirements and break the problem down into several subproblems, then try to develop a step-by-step procedure to solve them. Since language
processing is involved, we would also list all the forms of text processing needed at
each step. This step-by-step processing of text is known as a *pipeline*. It is the series of
steps involved in building any NLP model. These steps are common in every NLP
project, so it makes sense to study them in this chapter. Understanding some common procedures in any NLP pipeline will enable us to get started on any NLP problem encountered in the workplace. Laying out and developing a text-processing
pipeline is seen as a starting point for any NLP application development process. In
this chapter, we will learn about the various steps involved and how they play important roles in solving the NLP problem and we'll see a few guidelines about when and
how to use which step. In later chapters, we'll discuss specific pipelines for various
NLP tasks (e.g., Chapters 4–7).

Figure 2-1 shows the main components of a generic pipeline for modern-day, data-
driven NLP system development. The key stages in the pipeline are as follows:

1. Data acquisition
2. Text cleaning
3. Pre-processing

4. Feature engineering

5. Modeling

6. Evaluation

7. Deployment

8. Monitoring and model updating

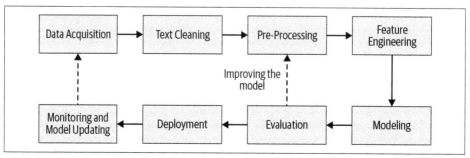

Figure 2-1. Generic NLP pipeline

The first step in the process of developing any NLP system is to collect data relevant to the given task. Even if we're building a rule-based system, we still need some data to design and test our rules. The data we get is seldom clean, and this is where text cleaning comes into play. After cleaning, text data often has a lot of variations and needs to be converted into a canonical form. This is done in the pre-processing step. This is followed by feature engineering, where we carve out indicators that are most suitable for the task at hand. These indicators are converted into a format that is understandable by modeling algorithms. Then comes the modeling and evaluation phase, where we build one or more models and compare and contrast them using a relevant evaluation metric(s). Once the best model among the ones evaluated is chosen, we move toward deploying this model in production. Finally, we regularly monitor the performance of the model and, if need be, update it to keep up its performance.

Note that, in the real world, the process may not always be linear as it's shown in the pipeline in Figure 2-1; it often involves going back and forth between individual steps (e.g., between feature extraction and modeling, modeling and evaluation, and so on). Also, there are loops in between, most commonly going from evaluation to pre-processing, feature engineering, modeling, and back to evaluation. There is also an overall loop that goes from monitoring to data acquisition, but this loop happens at the project level.

Note that exact step-by-step procedures may depend on the specific task at hand. For example, a text-classification system may require a different feature extraction step compared to a text-summarization system. We will focus on application-specific pipeline stages in subsequent chapters in the book. Also, depending on the phase of the project, different steps can take different amounts of time. In the initial phases, most of the time is used in modeling and evaluation, whereas once the system matures, feature engineering can take far more time.

For the rest of this chapter, we'll look at the individual stages of the pipeline in detail along with examples. We'll describe some of the most common procedures at each stage and discuss some use cases to illustrate them. Let's start with the first step: data acquisition.

Data Acquisition

Data is the heart of any ML system. In most industrial projects, it is often the data that becomes the bottleneck. In this section, we'll discuss various strategies for gathering relevant data for an NLP project.

Let's say we're asked to develop an NLP system to identify whether an incoming customer query (for example, using a chat interface) is a sales inquiry or a customer care inquiry. Depending on the type of query, it should be automatically routed to the right team. How can one go about building such a system? Well, the answer depends on the type and amount of data we have to work with.

In an ideal setting, we'll have the required datasets with thousands—maybe even millions—of data points. In such cases, we don't have to worry about data acquisition. For example, in the scenario we just described, we have historic queries fro m previous years, which sales and support teams responded to. Further, the teams tagged these queries as sales, support, or other. So, not only do we have the data, but we also have the labels. However, in many AI projects, one is not so lucky. Let's look at what we can do in a less-than-ideal scenario.

If we have little or no data, we can start by looking at patterns in the data that indicate if the incoming message is a sales or support query. We can then use regular expressions and other heuristics to match these patterns to separate sales queries from support queries. We evaluate this solution by collecting a set of queries from both categories and calculating what percentage of the messages were correctly identified by our system. Say we get OK-ish numbers. We would like to improve the system performance.

Now we can start thinking about using NLP techniques. For this, we need labeled data, a collection of queries where each one is labeled with sales or support. How can we get such data?

Use a public dataset

We could see if there are any public datasets available that we can leverage. Take a look at the compilation by Nicolas Iderhoff [1] or search Google's specialized search engine for datasets [2]. If you find a suitable dataset that's similar to the task at hand, great! Build a model and evaluate. If not, then what?

Scrape data

We could find a source of relevant data on the internet—for example, a consumer or discussion forum where people have posted queries (sales or support). Scrape the data from there and get it labeled by human annotators.

For many industrial settings, gathering data from external sources does not suffice because the data doesn't contain nuances like product names or product-specific user behavior and thus might be very different from the data seen in production environments. This is when we'll have to start looking for data inside the organization.

Product intervention

In most industrial settings, AI models seldom exist by themselves. They're developed mostly to serve users via a feature or product. In all such cases, the AI team should work with the product team to collect more and richer data by developing better instrumentation in the product. In the tech world, this is called *product intervention*.

Product intervention is often the best way to collect data for building intelligent applications in industrial settings. Tech giants like Google, Facebook, Microsoft, Netflix, etc., have known this for a long time and have tried to collect as much data as possible from as many users as possible.

Data augmentation

While instrumenting products is a great way to collect data, it takes time. Even if you instrument the product today, it can take anywhere between three to six months to collect a decent-sized, comprehensive dataset. So, can we do something in the meantime?

NLP has a bunch of techniques through which we can take a small dataset and use some tricks to create more data. These tricks are also called *data augmentation,* and they try to exploit language properties to create text that is syntactically similar to source text data. They may appear as hacks, but they work very well in practice. Let's look at some of them:

Synonym replacement

Randomly choose "k" words in a sentence that are not stop words. Replace these words with their synonyms. For synonyms, we can use Synsets in Wordnet [3, 4].

Back translation

Say we have a sentence, S1, in English. We use a machine-translation library like Google Translate to translate it into some other language—say, German. Let the corresponding sentence in German be S2. Now, we'll use the machine-translation library again to translate back to English. Let the output sentence be S3.

We'll find that S1 and S3 are very similar in meaning but are slight variations of each other. Now we can add S3 to our dataset. This trick works beautifully for text classification. Figure 2-2 [5] shows an example of back translation in action.

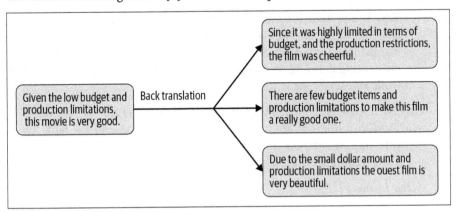

Figure 2-2. Back translation

TF-IDF–based word replacement

Back translation can lose certain words that are crucial to the sentence. In [5], the authors use TF-IDF (*https://oreil.ly/jeUJ8*), a concept we'll introduce in Chapter 3, to handle this.

Bigram flipping

Divide the sentence into bigrams. Take one bigram at random and flip it. For example: "I am going to the supermarket." Here, we take the bigram "going to" and replace it with the flipped one: "to going."

Replacing entities

Replace entities like person name, location, organization, etc., with other entities in the same category. That is, replace person name with another person name, city with another city, etc. For example, in "I live in California," replace "California" with "London."

Adding noise to data

In many NLP applications, the incoming data contains spelling mistakes. This is primarily due to characteristics of the platform where the data is being generated (for example, Twitter). In such cases, we can add a bit of noise to data to train robust models. For example, randomly choose a word in a sentence and replace it with another word that's closer in spelling to the first word. Another source of noise is the "fat finger" problem [6] on mobile keyboards. Simulate a QWERTY keyboard error by replacing a few characters with their neighboring characters on the QWERTY keyboard.

Advanced techniques

There are other advanced techniques and systems that can augment text data. Some of the notable ones are:

Snorkel [7, 8, 52]

This is a system for building training data automatically, without manual labeling. Using Snorkel, a large training dataset can be "created"—without manual labeling—using heuristics and creating synthetic data by transforming existing data and creating new data samples. This approach was shown to work well at Google in the recent past [9].

Easy Data Augmentation (EDA) [10, 11] and NLPAug [12]

These two libraries are used to create synthetic samples for NLP. They provide implementation of various data augmentation techniques, including some techniques that we discussed previously.

Active learning [13]

This is a specialized paradigm of ML where the learning algorithm can interactively query a data point and get its label. It is used in scenarios where there is an abundance of unlabeled data but manually labeling is expensive. In such cases, the question becomes: for which data points should we ask for labels to maximize learning while keeping the labeling cost low?

In order for most of the techniques we discussed in this section to work well, one key requirement is a clean dataset to start with, even if it's not very big. In our experience, data augmentation techniques can work really well. Further, in day-to-day ML practice, datasets come from heterogeneous sources. A combination of public datasets, labeled datasets, and augmented datasets are used for building early-stage production models, as we often may not have large datasets for our custom scenarios to start with. Once we have the data we want for a given task, we proceed to the next step: text cleaning.

Text Extraction and Cleanup

Text extraction and cleanup refers to the process of extracting raw text from the input data by removing all the other non-textual information, such as markup, metadata, etc., and converting the text to the required encoding format. Typically, this depends on the format of available data in the organization (e.g., static data from PDF, HTML or text, some form of continuous data stream, etc.), as shown in Figure 2-3.

Text extraction is a standard data-wrangling step, and we don't usually employ any NLP-specific techniques during this process. However, in our experience, it is an important step that has implications for all other aspects of the NLP pipeline. Further, it can also be the most time-consuming part of a project. While the design of text-extraction tools is beyond the scope of this book, we'll look at a few examples to illustrate different issues involved in this step in this section. We'll also touch on some of the important aspects of text extraction from various sources as well as cleanup to make them consumable in downstream pipelines.

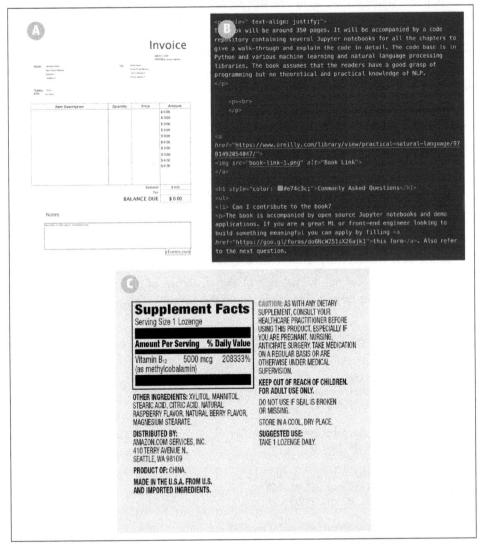

Figure 2-3. (a) PDF invoice, [14] (b) HTML texts, and (c) text embedded in an image [15]

HTML Parsing and Cleanup

Say we're working on a project where we're building a forum search engine for pro-gramming questions. We've identified Stack Overflow as a source and decided to extract question and best-answer pairs from the website. How can we go through the text-extraction step in this case? If we observe the HTML markup of a typical Stack Overflow question page, we notice that questions and answers have special tags asso-ciated with them. We can utilize this information while extracting text from the HTML page. While it may seem like writing our own HTML parser is the way to go, for most cases we encounter, it's more feasible to utilize existing libraries such as Beautiful Soup [16] and Scrapy [17], which provide a range of utilities to parse web pages. The following code snippet shows how to use Beautiful Soup to address the problem described here, extracting a question and its best-answer pair from a Stack Overflow web page:

```
from bs4 import BeautifulSoup
from urllib.request import urlopen
myurl = "https://stackoverflow.com/questions/415511/ \
   how-to-get-the-current-time-in-python"
html = urlopen(myurl).read()
soupified = BeautifulSoup(html, "html.parser")
question = soupified.find("div", {"class": "question"})
questiontext = question.find("div", {"class": "post-text"})
print("Question: \n", questiontext.get_text().strip())
answer = soupified.find("div", {"class": "answer"})
answertext = answer.find("div", {"class": "post-text"})
print("Best answer: \n", answertext.get_text().strip())
```

Here, we're relying on our knowledge of the structure of an HTML document to extract what we want from it. This code shows the output as follows:

```
Question:
What is the module/method used to get the current time?
Best answer:
 Use:
>>> import datetime
>>> datetime.datetime.now()
datetime.datetime(2009, 1, 6, 15, 8, 24, 78915)

>>> print(datetime.datetime.now())
2009-01-06 15:08:24.789150

And just the time:
>>> datetime.datetime.now().time()
datetime.time(15, 8, 24, 78915)

>>> print(datetime.datetime.now().time())
15:08:24.789150

See the documentation for more information.
```

```
To save typing, you can import the datetime object from the datetime module:
>>> from datetime import datetime
```

```
Then remove the leading datetime. from all of the above.
```

In this example, we had a specific need: extracting a question and its answer. In some scenarios—for example, extracting postal addresses from web pages—we would get all the text (instead of only parts of it) from the web page first, before doing anything else. Typically, all HTML libraries have some function that can strip off all HTML tags and return only the content between the tags. But this often results in noisy output, and you may end up seeing a lot of JavaScript in the extracted content as well. In such cases, we should look to extract content between only those tags that typically contain text in web pages.

Unicode Normalization

As we develop code for cleaning up HTML tags, we may also encounter various Unicode characters, including symbols, emojis, and other graphic characters. A handful of Unicode characters are shown in Figure 2-4.

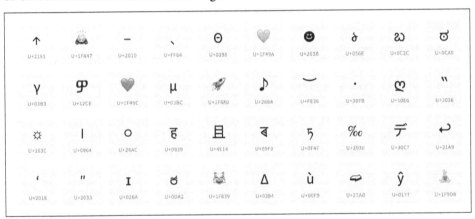

Figure 2-4. Unicode characters [18]

To parse such non-textual symbols and special characters, we use Unicode normalization. This means that the text we see should be converted into some form of binary representation to store in a computer. This process is known as *text encoding*. Ignoring encoding issues can result in processing errors further in the pipeline.

There are several encoding schemes, and the default encoding can be different for different operating systems. Sometimes (more commonly than you think), especially when dealing with text in multiple languages, social media data, etc., we may have to convert between these encoding schemes during the text-extraction process. Refer to [19] for an introduction to how language is represented on computers and what difference an encoding scheme makes. Here is an example of Unicode handling:

```
text = 'I love 🍕!  Shall we book a 🚕 to gizza?'
Text = text.encode("utf-8")
print(Text)
```

which outputs:

```
b'I love Pizza \xf0\x9f\x8d\x95!  Shall we book a cab \xf0\x9f\x9a\x95
  to get pizza?'
```

This processed text is machine readable and can be used in downstream pipelines. We address issues regarding handling Unicode characters with this same example in more detail in Chapter 8.

Spelling Correction

In the world of fast typing and fat-finger typing [6], incoming text data often has spelling errors. This can be prevalent in search engines, text-based chatbots deployed on mobile devices, social media, and many other sources. While we remove HTML tags and handle Unicode characters, this remains a unique problem that may hurt the linguistic understanding of the data, and shorthand text messages in social micro-blogs often hinder language processing and context understanding. Two such examples follow:

> **Shorthand typing:** Hllo world! I am back!
> **Fat finger problem [20]:** I pronise that I will not bresk the silence again!

While shorthand typing is prevalent in chat interfaces, fat-finger problems are common in search engines and are mostly unintentional. Despite our understanding of the problem, we don't have a robust method to fix this, but we still can make good attempts to mitigate the issue. Microsoft released a REST API [21] that can be used in Python for potential spell checking:

```
import requests
import json

api_key = "<ENTER-KEY-HERE>"
example_text = "Hollo, wrld" # the text to be spell-checked

data = {'text': example_text}
params = {
    'mkt':'en-us',
    'mode':'proof'
    }
headers = {
    'Content-Type': 'application/x-www-form-urlencoded',
    'Ocp-Apim-Subscription-Key': api_key,
    }
response = requests.post(endpoint, headers=headers, params=params, data=data)
json_response = response.json()
print(json.dumps(json_response, indent=4))
```

```
Output (partially shown here):
"suggestions": [
        {
            "suggestion": "Hello",
            "score": 0.9115257530801
        },
        {
            "suggestion": "Hollow",
            "score": 0.858039839213461
        },
        {
            "suggestion": "Hallo",
            "score": 0.597385084464481
        }
```

You can see the full tutorial in [21].

Going beyond APIs, we can build our own spell checker using a huge dictionary of words from a specific language. A naive solution would be to look for all words that can be composed with minimal alteration (addition, deletion, substitution) to its constituent letters. For example, if "Hello" is a valid word that is already present in the dictionary, then the addition of "o" (minimal) to "Hllo" would make the correction.

System-Specific Error Correction

HTML or raw text scraped from the web are just a couple of sources for textual data. Consider another scenario where our dataset is in the form of a collection of PDF documents. The pipeline in this case starts with extraction of plain text from PDF documents. However, different PDF documents are encoded differently, and sometimes, we may not be able to extract the full text, or the structure of the text may get messed up. If we need full text or our text has to be grammatical or in full sentences (e.g., when we want to extract relations between various people in the news based on newspaper text), this can impact our application. While there are several libraries, such as PyPDF [22], PDFMiner [23], etc., to extract text from PDF documents, they are far from perfect, and it's not uncommon to encounter PDF documents that can't be processed by such libraries. We leave their exploration as an exercise for the reader. [24] discusses some of the issues involved in PDF-to-text extraction in detail.

Another common source of textual data is scanned documents. Text extraction from scanned documents is typically done through optical character recognition (OCR), using libraries such as Tesseract [25, 26]. Consider the example image—a snippet from a 1950 article in a journal [27]—shown in Figure 2-5.

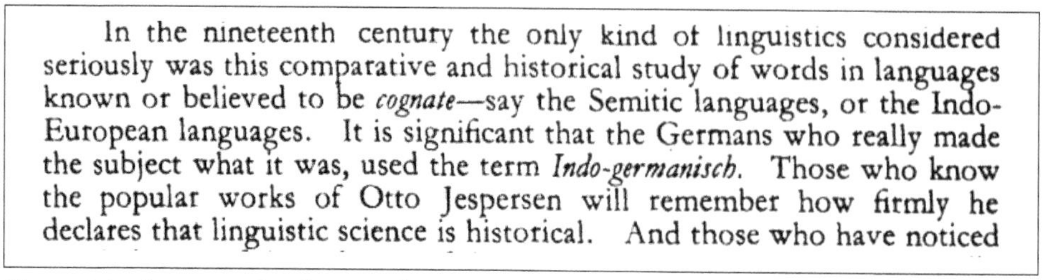

> In the nineteenth century the only kind of linguistics considered seriously was this comparative and historical study of words in languages known or believed to be *cognate*—say the Semitic languages, or the Indo-European languages. It is significant that the Germans who really made the subject what it was, used the term *Indo-germanisch*. Those who know the popular works of Otto Jespersen will remember how firmly he declares that linguistic science is historical. And those who have noticed

Figure 2-5. An example of scanned text

The code snippet below shows how the Python library pytesseract can be used to extract text from this image:

```
from PIL import Image
from pytesseract import image_to_string
filename = "somefile.png"
text = image_to_string(Image.open(filename))
print(text)
```

This code will print the output as follows, where "\n" indicates a newline character:

```
'in the nineteenth century the only Kind of linguistics considered\nseriously
was this comparative and historical study of words in languages\nknown or
believed to Fe cognate—say the Semitic languages, or the Indo-\nEuropean
languages. It is significant that the Germans who really made\nthe subject what
it was, used the term Indo-germanisch. Those who know\nthe popular works of
Otto Jespersen will remember how fitmly he\ndeclares that linguistic
science is historical. And those who have noticed'
```

We notice that there are two errors in the output of the OCR system in this case. Depending on the quality of the original scan, OCR output can potentially have larger amounts of errors. How do we clean up this text before feeding it into the next stage of the pipeline? One approach is to run the text through a spell checker such as pyenchant [28], which will identify misspellings and suggest some alternatives. More recent approaches use neural network architectures to train word/character-based language models, which are in turn used for correcting OCR text output based on the context [29].

Recall that we saw an example of a voice-based assistant in Chapter 1. In such cases, the source of text extraction is the output of an automatic speech recognition (ASR) system. Like OCR, it's common to see some errors in ASR, owing to various factors, such as dialectical variations, slang, non-native English, new or domain-specific vocabulary, etc. The above-mentioned approach of spell checkers or neural language models can be followed here as well to clean up the extracted text.

What we've seen so far are just some examples of potential issues that may come up during the text-extraction and cleaning process. Though NLP plays a very small role in this process, we hope these examples illustrate how text extraction and cleanup

---

could pose challenges in a typical NLP pipeline. We'll also touch on these aspects in upcoming chapters for different NLP applications, where relevant. Let's move on to the next step in our pipeline: pre-processing.

Pre-Processing

Let's start with a simple question: we already did some cleanup in the previous step; why do we still have to pre-process text? Consider a scenario where we're processing text from Wikipedia pages about individuals to extract biographical information about them. Our data acquisition starts with crawling such pages. However, our crawled data is all in HTML, with a lot of boilerplate from Wikipedia (e.g., all the links in the left panel), possibly the presence of links to multiple languages (in their script), etc. All such information is irrelevant for extracting features from text (in most cases). Our text-extraction step removed all this and gave us the plain text of the article we need. However, all NLP software typically works at the sentence level and expects a separation of words at the minimum. So, we need some way to split a text into words and sentences before proceeding further in a processing pipeline. Sometimes, we need to remove special characters and digits, and sometimes, we don't care whether a word is in upper or lowercase and want everything in lowercase. Many more decisions like this are made while processing text. Such decisions are addressed during the pre-processing step of the NLP pipeline. Here are some common pre-processing steps used in NLP software:

Preliminaries
   Sentence segmentation and word tokenization.

Frequent steps
   Stop word removal, stemming and lemmatization, removing digits/punctuation, lowercasing, etc.

Other steps
   Normalization, language detection, code mixing, transliteration, etc.

Advanced processing
   POS tagging, parsing, coreference resolution, etc.

While not all steps will be followed in all the NLP pipelines we encounter, the first two are more or less seen everywhere. Let's take a look at what each of these steps mean.

Preliminaries

As mentioned earlier, NLP software typically analyzes text by breaking it up into words (tokens) and sentences. Hence, any NLP pipeline has to start with a reliable system to split the text into sentences (sentence segmentation) and further split a sentence into words (word tokenization). On the surface, these seem like simple tasks, and you may wonder why they need special treatment. We will see why in the coming two subsections.

Sentence segmentation

As a simple rule, we can do sentence segmentation by breaking up text into sentences at the appearance of full stops and question marks. However, there may be abbreviations, forms of addresses (Dr., Mr., etc.), or ellipses (...) that may break the simple rule.

Thankfully, we don't have to worry about how to solve these issues, as most NLP libraries come with some form of sentence and word splitting implemented. A commonly used library is Natural Language Tool Kit (NLTK) [30]. The code example below shows how to use a sentence and word splitter from NLTK and uses the first paragraph of this chapter as input:

```
from nltk.tokenize import sent_tokenize, word_tokenize

mytext = "In the previous chapter, we saw examples of some common NLP
applications that we might encounter in everyday life. If we were asked to
build such an application, think about how we would approach doing so at our
organization. We would normally walk through the requirements and break the
problem down into several sub-problems, then try to develop a step-by-step
procedure to solve them. Since language processing is involved, we would also
list all the forms of text processing needed at each step. This step-by-step
processing of text is known as pipeline. It is the series of steps involved in
building any NLP model. These steps are common in every NLP project, so it
makes sense to study them in this chapter. Understanding some common procedures
in any NLP pipeline will enable us to get started on any NLP problem encountered
in the workplace. Laying out and developing a text-processing pipeline is seen
as a starting point for any NLP application development process. In this
chapter, we will learn about the various steps involved and how they play
important roles in solving the NLP problem and we'll see a few guidelines
about when and how to use which step. In later chapters, we'll discuss
specific pipelines for various NLP tasks (e.g., Chapters 4-7)."

my_sentences = sent_tokenize(mytext)
```

Word tokenization

Similar to sentence tokenization, to tokenize a sentence into words, we can start with a simple rule to split text into words based on the presence of punctuation marks. The NLTK library allows us to do that. If we take the previous example:

```
for sentence in my_sentences:
    print(sentence)
    print(word_tokenize(sentence))
```

For the first sentence, the output is printed as follows:

```
In the previous chapter, we saw a quick overview of what is NLP, what are some
of the common applications and challenges in NLP, and an introduction to
different tasks in NLP.
['In', 'the', 'previous', 'chapter', ',', 'we', 'saw', 'a', 'quick',
'overview', 'of', 'what', 'is', 'NLP', ',', 'what', 'are', 'some', 'of', 'the',
'common', 'applications', 'and', 'challenges', 'in', 'NLP', ',', 'and', 'an',
'introduction', 'to', 'different', 'tasks', 'in', 'NLP', '.']
```

While readily available solutions work for most of our needs and most NLP libraries will have a tokenizer and sentence splitter bundled with them, it's important to remember that they're far from perfect. For example, consider this sentence: "Mr. Jack O'Neil works at Melitas Marg, located at 245 Yonge Avenue, Austin, 70272." If we run this through the NLTK tokenizer, O, ', and Neil are identified as three separate tokens. Similarly, if we run the sentence: "There are $10,000 and €1000 which are there just for testing a tokenizer" through this tokenizer, while $ and 10,000 are identified as separate tokens, €1000 is identified as a single token. In another scenario, if we want to tokenize tweets, this tokenizer will separate a hashtag into two tokens: a "#" sign and the string that follows it. In such cases, we may need to use a custom tokenizer built for our purpose. To complete our example, we'll perform word tokenization after we perform sentence tokenization.

A point to note in this context is that NLTK also has a tweet tokenizer; we'll see how it's useful in Chapters 4 and 8. To summarize, although word- and sentence-tokenization approaches appear to be elementary and easy to implement, they may not always meet our specific tokenization needs, as we saw in the above examples. Note that we refer to NLTK's example, but these observations hold true for any other library as well. We leave that exploration as an exercise for the reader.

As tokenization may differ from one domain to the other, tokenization is also heavily dependent on language. Each language can have various linguistic rules and exceptions. Figure 2-6 shows an example where "N.Y.!" has a total of three punctuations. But in English, N.Y. stands for New York, hence "N.Y." should be treated as a single word and not be tokenized further. Such language-specific exceptions can be specified in the tokenizer provided by spaCy [31]. It's also possible in spaCy to develop custom rules to handle such exceptions for languages that have high inflections (prefixes or suffixes) and complex morphology.

Another important fact to keep in mind is that any sentence segmenter and tokenizer will be sensitive to the input they receive. Let's say we're writing software to extract some information, such as company, position, and salary, from job offer letters. They follow a certain format, with a To and a From address, a signed note at the end, and so on. How will we decide what a sentence is in such a case? Should the entire address be considered a single "sentence"? Or should each line be split separately? Answers to such questions depend on what you want to extract and how sensitive the rest of the pipeline is about such decisions. For identifying specific patterns (e.g., dates or money expressions), well-formed regular expressions are the first step. In many practical scenarios, we may end up using a custom tokenizer or sentence segmenter that suits our text structure instead of or on top of an existing one available in a standard NLP library [32].

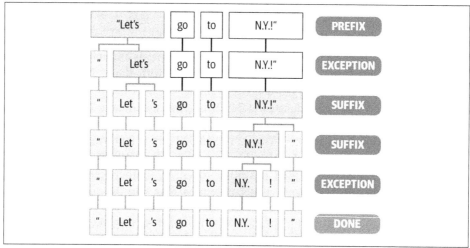

Figure 2-6. Language-specific (English here) exceptions during tokenization [31]

Frequent Steps

Let's look at some other frequently performed pre-processing operations in an NLP pipeline. Say we're designing software that identifies the category of a news article as one of politics, sports, business, and other. Assume we have a good sentence segmenter and word tokenizer in place. At that point, we would have to start thinking about what kind of information is useful for developing a categorization tool. Some of the frequently used words in English, such as a, an, the, of, in, etc., are not particularly useful for this task, as they don't carry any content on their own to separate between the four categories. Such words are called *stop words* and are typically (though not always) removed from further analysis in such problem scenarios. There is no standard list of stop words for English, though. There are some popular lists (NLTK has one, for example), although what a stop word is can vary depending on

---

what we're working on. For example, the word "news" is perhaps a stop word for this problem scenario, but it may not be a stop word for the offer letter data in the example mentioned in the previous step.

Similarly, in some cases, upper or lowercase may not make a difference for the problem. So, all text is lowercased (or uppercased, although lowercasing is more common). Removing punctuation and/or numbers is also a common step for many NLP problems, such as text classification (Chapter 4), information retrieval (Chapter 7), and social media analytics (Chapter 8). We'll see examples of how and if these steps are useful in upcoming chapters.

The code example below shows how to remove stop words, digits, and punctuation and lowercase a given collection of texts:

```
from nltk.corpus import stopwords
From string import punctuation
def preprocess_corpus(texts):
    mystopwords = set(stopwords.words("english"))
    def remove_stops_digits(tokens):
        return [token.lower() for token in tokens if token not in mystopwords
                not token.isdigit() and token not in punctuation]
    return [remove_stops_digits(word_tokenize(text)) for text in texts]
```

It's important to note that these four processes are neither mandatory nor sequential in nature. The above function is just an illustration of how to add those processing steps into our project. The pre-processing we saw here, while specific to textual data, has nothing particularly linguistic about it—we're not looking at any aspect of language other than frequency (stop words are very frequent words), and we're removing non-alphabetic data (punctuation, digits). Two commonly used pre-processing steps that take the word-level properties into account are stemming and lemmatization.

Stemming and lemmatization

Stemming refers to the process of removing suffixes and reducing a word to some base form such that all different variants of that word can be represented by the same form (e.g., "car" and "cars" are both reduced to "car"). This is accomplished by applying a fixed set of rules (e.g., if the word ends in "-es," remove "-es"). More such examples are shown in Figure 2-7. Although such rules may not always end up in a linguistically correct base form, stemming is commonly used in search engines to match user queries to relevant documents and in text classification to reduce the feature space to train machine learning models.

The following code snippet shows how to use a popular stemming algorithm called Porter Stemmer [33] using NLTK:

```
from nltk.stem.porter import PorterStemmer
stemmer = PorterStemmer()
word1, word2 = "cars", "revolution"
print(stemmer.stem(word1), stemmer.stem(word2))
```

This gives "car" as the stemmed version for "cars," but "revolut" as the stemmed form of "revolution," even though the latter is not linguistically correct. While this may not affect the performance of a search engine, derivation of correct linguistic form becomes useful in some other scenarios. This is accomplished by another process, closer to stemming, called lemmatization.

Lemmatization is the process of mapping all the different forms of a word to its base word, or *lemma*. While this seems close to the definition of stemming, they are, in fact, different. For example, the adjective "better," when stemmed, remains the same. However, upon lemmatization, this should become "good," as shown in Figure 2-7. Lemmatization requires more linguistic knowledge, and modeling and developing efficient lemmatizers remains an open problem in NLP research even now.

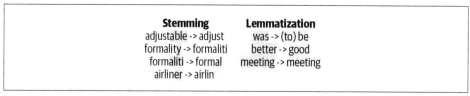

Figure 2-7. Difference between stemming and lemmatization [34]

The following code snippet shows the usage of a lemmatizer based on WordNet from NLTK:

```
from nltk.stem import WordNetLemmatizer
lemmatizer = WordnetLemmatizer()
print(lemmatizer.lemmatize("better", pos="a")) #a is for adjective
```

And this code snippet shows a lemmatizer using spaCy:

```
import spacy
sp = spacy.load('en_core_web_sm')
token = sp(u'better')
for word in token:
    print(word.text, word.lemma_)
```

NLTK prints the output as "good," whereas spaCy prints "well"—both are correct. Since lemmatization involves some amount of linguistic analysis of the word and its context, it is expected that it will take longer to run than stemming, and it's also typically used only if absolutely necessary. We'll see how stemming and lemmatization are useful in the next chapters. The choice of lemmatizer is optional; we can choose NLTK or spaCy given what framework we're using for other pre-processing steps in order to use a single framework in the complete pipeline.

Remember that not all of these steps are always necessary, and not all of them are performed in the order in which they're discussed here. For example, if we were to remove digits and punctuation, what is removed first may not matter much. However, we typically lowercase the text before stemming. We also don't remove tokens or lowercase the text before doing lemmatization because we have to know the part of speech of the word to get its lemma, and that requires all tokens in the sentence to be intact. A good practice to follow is to prepare a sequential list of pre-processing tasks to be done after having a clear understanding of how to process our data.

Figure 2-8 lists the different pre-processing steps we've seen in this subsection so far, as a quick summary.

Note that these are the more common pre-processing steps, but they're by no means exhaustive. Depending on the nature of the data, some additional pre-processing steps may be important. Let's take a look at a few of those steps.

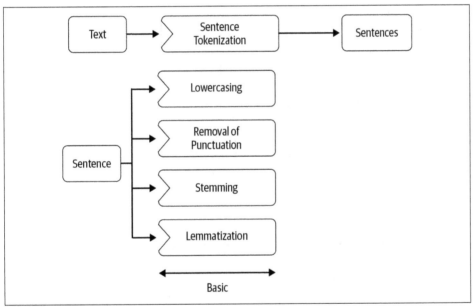

Figure 2-8. Common pre-processing steps on a blob of text

Other Pre-Processing Steps

So far, we've seen a few common pre-processing steps in an NLP pipeline. While we haven't explicitly stated the nature of the texts, we have assumed that we're dealing with regular English text. What's different if that's not the case? Let's introduce a few more pre-processing steps to deal with such scenarios, using a few examples.

Text normalization

Consider a scenario where we're working with a collection of social media posts to detect news events. Social media text is very different from the language we'd see in, say, newspapers. A word can be spelled in different ways, including in shortened forms, a phone number can be written in different formats (e.g., with and without hyphens), names are sometimes in lowercase, and so on. When we're working on developing NLP tools to work with such data, it's useful to reach a canonical representation of text that captures all these variations into one representation. This is known as *text normalization*. Some common steps for text normalization are to convert all text to lowercase or uppercase, convert digits to text (e.g., 9 to nine), expand abbreviations, and so on. A simple way to incorporate text normalization can be found in Spacy's source code [35], which is a dictionary showing different spellings of a preset collection of words mapped to a single spelling. We'll see more examples of text normalization in Chapter 8.

Language detection

A lot of web content is in non-English languages. For example, say we're asked to collect all reviews about our product on the web. As we navigate different e-commerce websites and start crawling pages related to our product, we notice several non-English reviews showing up. Since a majority of the pipeline is built with language-specific tools, what will happen to our NLP pipeline, which is expecting English text? In such cases, language detection is performed as the first step in an NLP pipeline. We can use libraries like Polyglot [36] for language detection. Once this step is done, the next steps could follow a language-specific pipeline.

Code mixing and transliteration

The discussion above was about a scenario where the content is in non-English languages. However, there's another scenario where a single piece of content is in more than one language. Many people across the world speak more than one language in their day-to-day lives. Thus, it's not uncommon to see them using multiple languages in their social media posts, and a single post may contain many languages. As an example of code mixing, we can look at a Singlish (Singapore slang + English) phrase from LDC [37] in Figure 2-9.

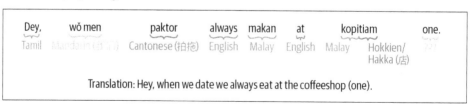

Figure 2-9. Code mixing in a single Singlish phrase

A single popular phrase has words from Tamil, English, Malay, and three Chinese language variants. Code mixing refers to this phenomenon of switching between languages. When people use multiple languages in their write-ups, they often type words from these languages in Roman script, with English spelling. So, the words of another language are written along with English text. This is known as *transliteration*. Both of these phenomena are common in multilingual communities and need to be handled during the pre-processing of text. We'll discuss more about these in Chapter 8, where we'll see examples of these phenomena in social media text.

This concludes our discussion of common pre-processing steps. While this list is by no means exhaustive, we hope it gives you some idea of the different forms of pre-processing that may be required, depending on the nature of the dataset. Now, let's take a look at a few more pre-processing steps in the NLP pipeline—ones that need advanced language processing beyond what we've seen so far.

Advanced Processing

Imagine we're asked to develop a system to identify person and organization names in our company's collection of one million documents. The common pre-processing steps we discussed earlier may not be relevant in this context. Identifying names requires us to be able to do POS tagging, as identifying proper nouns can be useful in identifying person and organization names. How do we do POS tagging during the pre-processing stage of the project? We're not going into the details of how POS taggers are developed (see Chapter 8 in [38] for details) in this book. Pre-trained and readily usable POS taggers are implemented in NLP libraries such as NLTK, spaCy [39], and Parsey McParseface Tagger [40], and we generally don't have to develop our own POS-tagging solutions. The following code snippet illustrates how to use many of the pre-built pre-processing functions we've discussed so far using the NLP library spaCy:

```
import spacy
nlp = spacy.load('en_core_web_sm')
doc = nlp(u'Charles Spencer Chaplin was born on 16 April 1889 toHannah Chaplin
        (born Hannah Harriet
Pedlingham Hill) and Charles Chaplin Sr')
for token in doc:
    print(token.text, token.lemma_, token.pos_,
            token.shape_, token.is_alpha, token.is_stop)
```

In this simple snippet, we can see tokenization, lemmatization, POS tagging, and several other steps in action! Note that if needed we can add additional processing steps with the same code snippet; we'll leave that as an exercise for the reader. A point to note is that there may be differences in the output among different NLP libraries for the same pre-processing step. This is due in part to implementation differences and algorithmic variations among different libraries. Which library (or libraries) you'll eventually want to use in your project is a subjective decision based on the amount of language processing you want.

Let's now consider a slightly different problem: along with identifying person and organization names in our company's collection of one million documents, we're also asked to identify if a given person and organization are related to each other in some way (e.g., Satya Nadella is related to Microsoft through the relation CEO). This is known as the problem of *relation extraction*, which we'll discuss in greater detail in Chapter 5. But for now, think about what kind of pre-processing we need for this case. We need POS tagging, which we already know how to add to our pipeline. We need a way of identifying person and organization names, which is a separate information extraction task known as *named entity recognition (NER)*, which we'll discuss in Chapter 5. Apart from these two, we need a way to identify patterns indicating "relation" between two entities in a sentence. This requires us to have some form of syntactic representation of the sentence, such as parsing, which we saw in Chapter 1. Further, we also want a way to identify and link multiple mentions of an entity (e.g., Satya Nadella, Mr. Nadella, he, etc.). We accomplish this with the pre-processing step known as *coreference resolution*. We saw an example of this in "An NLP Walkthrough: Conversational Agents" on page 31. Figure 2-10 shows the output from Stanford CoreNLP [41], which illustrates a parser output and coreference resolution output for an example sentence, along with other pre-processing steps we discussed previously.

What we've seen so far in this section are some of the most common pre-processing steps in a pipeline. They're all available as pre-trained, usable models in different NLP libraries. Apart from these, additional, customized pre-processing may be necessary, depending on the application. For example, consider a case where we're asked to mine the social media sentiment on our product. We start by collecting data from, say, Twitter, and quickly realize there are tweets that are not in English. In such cases, we may also need a language-detection step before doing anything else.

Additionally, what steps we need also depends on a specific application. If we're creating a system to identify whether the reviewer is expressing a positive or negative sentiment about a movie from a review they wrote, we might not worry much about parsing or coreference resolution, but we would want to consider stop word removal, lowercasing, and removing digits. However, if we're interested instead in extracting calendar events from emails, we'll probably be better off not removing stop words or doing stemming, but rather including, say, parsing. In the case where we want to extract relationships between different entities in the text and events mentioned in it, we would need coreference resolution, as we discussed previously. We'll see examples of cases requiring such steps in Chapter 5.

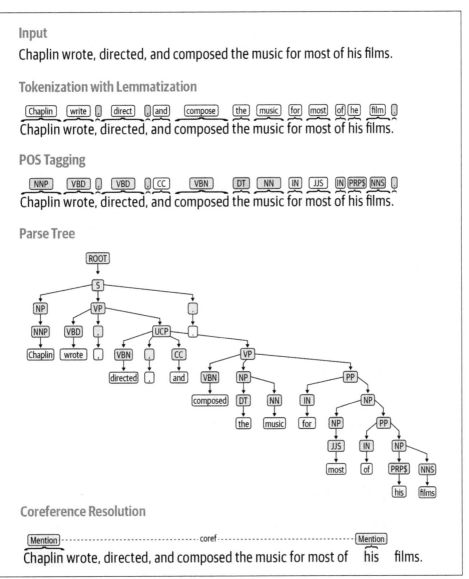

Input

Chaplin wrote, directed, and composed the music for most of his films.

Tokenization with Lemmatization

Chaplin write ⬚ direct ⬚ and compose the music for most of he film ⬚
Chaplin wrote, directed, and composed the music for most of his films.

POS Tagging

NNP VBD ⬚ VBD ⬚ CC VBN DT NN IN JJS IN PRP$ NNS ⬚
Chaplin wrote, directed, and composed the music for most of his films.

Parse Tree

Coreference Resolution

Mention ----------- coref ----------- Mention
Chaplin wrote, directed, and composed the music for most of his films.

Figure 2-10. Output from different stages of NLP pipeline processing

Finally, we have to consider the step-by-step procedures of pre-processing in each case, as summarized in Figure 2-11.

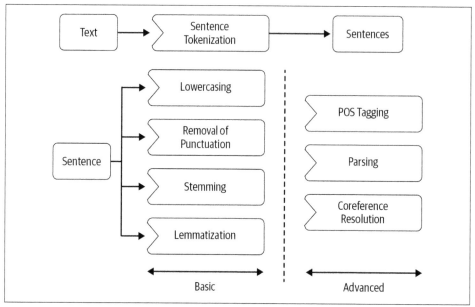

Figure 2-11. Advanced pre-processing steps on a blob of text

For example, POS tagging cannot be preceded by stop word removal, lowercasing, etc., as such processing affects POS tagger output by changing the grammatical structure of the sentence. How a particular pre-processing step is helping a given NLP problem is another question that is specific to the application, and it can only be answered with a lot of experimentation. We'll discuss more specific pre-processing required for different NLP applications in upcoming chapters. For now, let's move on to the next step: feature engineering.

Feature Engineering

So far, we've seen different pre-processing steps and where they can be useful. When we use ML methods to perform our modeling step later, we'll still need a way to feed this pre-processed text into an ML algorithm. *Feature engineering* refers to the set of methods that will accomplish this task. It's also referred to as *feature extraction*. The goal of feature engineering is to capture the characteristics of the text into a numeric vector that can be understood by the ML algorithms. We refer to this step as "text representation" in this book, and it's the topic of Chapter 3. We also detail feature extraction in the context of developing a complete NLP pipeline and iterating to improve performance in Chapter 11. Here, we'll briefly touch on two different approaches taken in practice for feature engineering in (1) a classical NLP and traditional ML pipeline and (2) a DL pipeline. Figure 2-12 (adapted from [42]) distinguishes the two approaches.

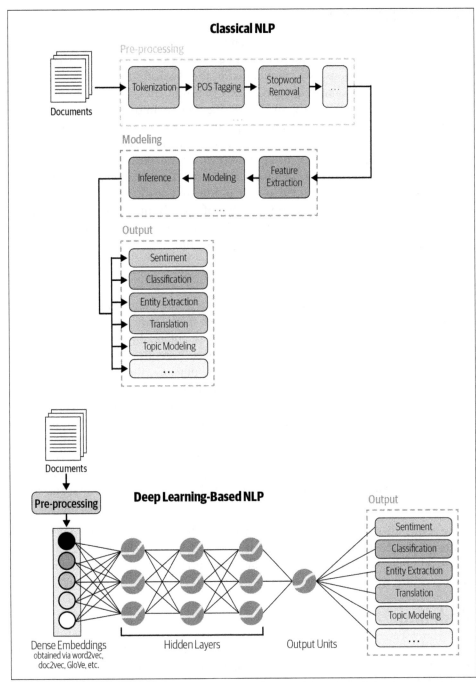

Figure 2-12. Feature engineering for classical NLP versus DL-based NLP

Classical NLP/ML Pipeline

Feature engineering is an integral step in any ML pipeline. Feature engineering steps convert the raw data into a format that can be consumed by a machine. These transformation functions are usually handcrafted in the classical ML pipeline, aligning to the task at hand. For example, imagine a task of sentiment classification on product reviews in e-commerce. One way to convert the reviews into meaningful "numbers" that helps predict the reviews' sentiments (positive or negative) would be to count the number of positive and negative words in each review. There are statistical measures for understanding if a feature is useful for a task or not; we'll discuss this in Chapter 11. The main takeaway for building classical ML models is that the features are heavily inspired by the task at hand as well as domain knowledge (for example, using sentiment words in the review example). One of the advantages of handcrafted features is that the model remains interpretable—it's possible to quantify exactly how much each feature is influencing the model prediction.

DL Pipeline

The main drawback of classical ML models is the feature engineering. Handcrafted feature engineering becomes a bottleneck for both model performance and the model development cycle. A noisy or unrelated feature can potentially harm the model's performance by adding more randomness to the data. Recently, with the advent of DL models, this approach has changed. In the DL pipeline, the raw data (after pre-processing) is directly fed to a model. The model is capable of "learning" features from the data. Hence, these features are more in line with the task at hand, so they generally give improved performance. But, since all these features are learned via model parameters, the model loses interpretability. It's very hard to explain a DL model's prediction, which is a disadvantage in a business-driven use case. For example, when identifying an email as ham or spam, it might be worth knowing which word or phrases played the significant role in making the email ham or spam. While this is easy to do with handcrafted features, it's not easy in the case of DL models.

As we've already mentioned, feature engineering is heavily task specific, so we discuss it throughout the book in the context of textual data and a range of tasks. With a high-level understanding of feature engineering, now let's take a look at the next step in the pipeline, which we call *modeling*.

Modeling

We now have some amount of data related to our NLP project and a clear idea of what sort of cleaning up and pre-processing needs to be done and what features are to be extracted. The next step is about how to build a useful solution out of this. At the start, when we have limited data, we can use simpler methods and rules. Over time, with more data and a better understanding of the problem, we can add more complexity and improve performance. We'll cover this process in this section.

Start with Simple Heuristics

At the very start of building a model, ML may not play a major role by itself. Part of that could be due to a lack of data, but human-built heuristics can also provide a great start in some ways. Heuristics may already be part of your system, either implicitly or explicitly. For instance, in email spam-classification tasks, we may have a blacklist of domains that are used exclusively to send spam. This information can be used to filter emails from those domains. Similarly, a blacklist of words in an email that denote a high chance of spam could also be used for this classification.

Such heuristics can be found in a range of tasks, especially at the start of applying ML. In an e-commerce setting, we may use a heuristic based on the number of purchases for ordering search results and show products belonging to the same category as recommendations while we collect data that could be used to build a larger, collaborative, filtering-based system that can recommend products using a range of other characteristics based on what customers with similar buying profiles purchased.

Another popular approach to incorporating heuristics in your system is using regular expressions. Let's say we're developing a system to extract different forms of information from text documents, such as dates and phone numbers, names of people who work in a given organization, etc. While some information, such as email IDs, dates, and telephone numbers can be extracted using normal (albeit complex) regular expressions, Stanford NLP's TokensRegex [43] and spaCy's rule-based matching [20] are two tools that are useful for defining advanced regular expressions to capture other information, such as people who work in a specific organization. Figure 2-13 shows an example of spaCy's rule-based matcher in action.

This shows a pattern that looks for text containing the lemma "match," appearing as a noun, optionally preceded by an adjective, and followed by any word form of lemma "be." Such patterns are an advanced form of regular expressions, which require some of the NLP pre-processing steps we saw earlier in this chapter. In the absence of large amounts of training data, and when we have some domain knowledge, we can start building systems by encoding this knowledge in the form of rules/heuristics. Even when we're building ML-based models, we can use such heuristics to handle special cases—for example, cases where the model has failed to learn well. Thus, simple heuristics can give us a good starting point and be useful in ML models. Now, assuming we built such a heuristics-based system, where do we go from there?

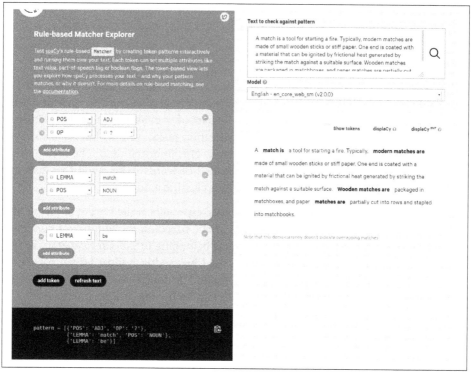

Figure 2-13. spaCy's rule-based matcher

Building Your Model

While a set of simple heuristics is a good start, as our system matures, adding newer and newer heuristics may result in a complex, rule-based system. Such a system is hard to manage, and it can be even harder to diagnose the cause of errors. We need a system that's easier to maintain as it matures. Further, as we collect more data, our ML model starts beating pure heuristics. At that point, a common practice is to combine heuristics directly or indirectly with the ML model. There are two broad ways of doing that:

Create a feature from the heuristic for your ML model

> When there are many heuristics where the behavior of a single heuristic is deterministic but their combined behavior is fuzzy in terms of how they predict, it's best to use these heuristics as features to train your ML model. For instance, in the email spam-classification example, we can add features, such as the number of words from the blacklist in a given email or the email bounce rate, to the ML model.

Pre-process your input to the ML model

> If the heuristic has a really high prediction for a particular kind of class, then it's best to use it before feeding the data in your ML model. For instance, if for certain words in an email, there's a 99% chance that it's spam, then it's best to classify that email as spam instead of sending it to an ML model.

Additionally, we have NLP service providers, such as Google Cloud Natural Language [44], Amazon Comprehend [45], Microsoft Azure Cognitive Services [46], and IBM Watson Natural Language Understanding [47], which provide off-the-shelf APIs to solve various NLP tasks. If your project has an NLP problem that's addressed by these APIs, you can start by using them to get an estimate of the feasibility of the task and how good your existing dataset is. Once you're comfortable that the task is feasible and conclude that the off-the-shelf models give reasonable results, you can move toward building custom ML models and improving them.

Building THE Model

We've seen examples of getting started building an NLP system by using heuristics or existing APIs, or by building our own ML models. We start with a baseline approach and work toward improving it. We may have to do many iterations of the model-building process to "build THE model" that gives good performance and is also production-ready. We cover some of the approaches to address this issue here:

Ensemble and stacking

> In our experience, a common practice is not to have a single model, but to use a collection of ML models, often dealing with different aspects of the prediction problem. There are two ways of doing this: we can feed one model's output as input for another model, thus sequentially going from one model to another and obtaining a final output. This is called *model stacking*.[i] Alternatively, we can also pool predictions from multiple models and make a final prediction. This is called *model ensembling*. Figure 2-14 demonstrates both of these procedures.

> In this figure, training data is used to build Models 1, 2, and 3. Outputs of these models are then combined to be used in a meta-model (a model that uses other models) to predict the final outcome. For example, in the email spam-classification case, we can assume that we run three different models: a heuristic-based score, Naive Bayes, and LSTM. The output of these three models is then fed into the meta-model based on logistic regression, which then gives the chances of the email being spam or not. As the product grows in terms of its features, the model will also grow in complexity. So, we may eventually end up using a

---

i. This is different from the vertical stacking done in neural networks like LSTM.

combination of all of these—i.e., heuristics, machine learning, and stacked and ensemble models—as part of a large product.

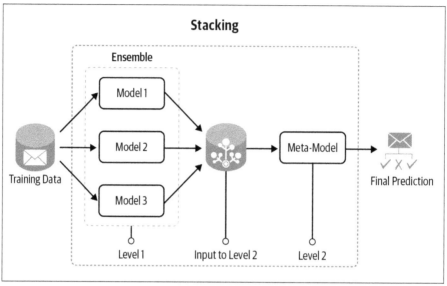

Figure 2-14. Model ensemble and stacking

Better feature engineering

For both API-based and custom-built models, feature engineering is an important step, and it evolves throughout the process. A better feature engineering step may lead to better performance. For instance, if there are a lot of features, then we use feature selection to find a better model. We detail strategies for iterating feature engineering to achieve an optimal setting in Chapter 11.

Transfer learning

Apart from model stacking or ensemble, there is a newer trend that's becoming popular in the NLP community—*transfer learning*, which we introduced in Chapter 1. Often, the model needs external knowledge beyond the dataset for the task to understand the language and the problem well. Transfer learning tries to transfer preexisting knowledge from a big, well-trained model to a newer model at its initial phase. Afterward, the new model slowly adapts to the task at hand. This is analogous to a teacher transferring wisdom and knowledge to a student. Transfer learning provides a better initialization, which helps in the downstream tasks, especially when the dataset for the downstream task is smaller. In these cases, transfer learning yields better results than just initializing a downstream model from scratch with random initialization. As an example, for email spam classification, we can use BERT to fine-tune the email dataset. We cover BERT in greater detail in Chapters 4 through 6.

Reapplying heuristics

No ML model is perfect. Hence, ML models still make mistakes. It's possible to revisit these cases again at the end of the modeling pipeline to find any common pattern in errors and use heuristics to correct them. We can also apply domain-specific knowledge that is not automatically captured in the data to refine the model predictions. An analogy for reapplying heuristics would be our model as a trapeze artist performing great feats and these rules as the safety net so the artist doesn't fall off.

Between the stage of having no data, when we fully rely on heuristics, to a lot of data, where we can try a range of modeling techniques, we encounter a situation where we have a small amount of data, which is often not sufficient to build good ML models. In such scenarios, one approach to follow is active learning, where we can use user feedback or other such sources to continuously collect new data to build better models. We'll discuss this in detail in Chapter 4. As we've just seen, modeling strategies depend heavily on the data at hand. Table 2-1 provides a range of decision paths given our data volume and quality, based on our experience.

Table 2-1. Data attributes and associated decision paths

Data attribute	Decision path	Examples
Large data volume	Can use techniques that require more data, like DL. Can use a richer set of features as well. If the data is sufficiently large but unlabeled, we can also apply unsupervised techniques.	If we have a lot of reviews and metadata associated with them, we can build a sentiment-analysis tool from scratch.
Small data volume	Need to start with rule-based or traditional ML solutions that are less data hungry. Can also adapt cloud APIs and generate more data with weak supervision. We can also use transfer learning if there's a similar task that has large data.	This often happens at the start of a completely new project.
Data quality is poor and the data is heterogeneous in nature	More data cleaning and pre-processing might be required.	This entails issues like code mixing (different languages being mixed in the same sentence), unconventional language, transliteration, or noise (like social media text).
Data quality is good	Can directly apply off-the-shelf algorithms or cloud APIs more easily.	Legal text or newspapers.
Data consists of full-length documents	Choose the right strategy for breaking the document into lower levels, like paragraphs, sentences, or phrases, depending on the problem.	Document classification, review analysis, etc.

So far, we've seen an overview of different forms of modeling that can be useful in an NLP pipeline and what modeling path to choose based on the data we have. Supervised learning, especially classification, is the most common modeling process you'll encounter in the NLP projects you'll be building in an industry scenario. We'll discuss classification models in Chapter 4 and models used for different application scenarios in NLP in Chapters 5 through 7. Now, let's take a look at the next step in the pipeline: evaluation.

Evaluation

A key step in the NLP pipeline is to measure how *good* the model we've built is. "Goodness" of a model can have multiple meanings, but the most common interpretation is the measure of the model's performance on unseen data. Success in this phase depends on two factors: (1) using the right metric for evaluation, and (2) following the right evaluation process. Let's first focus on 1. Depending on the NLP task or problem, the evaluation metrics can vary. They can also vary depending on the phase: the model building, deployment, and production phases. Whereas in the first two phases, we typically use ML metrics, in the final phase, we also include business metrics to measure business impact.

Also, evaluations are of two types: intrinsic and extrinsic. Intrinsic focuses on *intermediary* objectives, while extrinsic focuses on evaluating performance on the *final* objective. For example, consider a spam-classification system. The ML metric will be precision and recall, while the business metric will be "the amount of time users spent on a spam email." Intrinsic evaluation will focus on measuring the system performance using precision and recall. Extrinsic evaluation will focus on measuring the time a user wasted because a spam email went to their inbox or a genuine email went to their spam folder.

Intrinsic Evaluation

In this section, we'll look at some intrinsic evaluation metrics that are commonly used to measure NLP systems. For most metrics in this category, we assume a test set where we have the *ground truth* or *labels* (human annotated, correct answers). Labels could be binary (e.g., 0/1 for text classification), one-to-two words (e.g., names for named entity recognition), or large text itself (e.g., text translated by machine translation). The output of the NLP model on a data point is *compared* against the corresponding label for that data point, and metrics are calculated based on the match (or mismatch) between the output and label. For most NLP tasks, the comparison can be automated, hence intrinsic evaluation can be automated. For some cases, like machine translation or summarization, it's not always possible to automate evaluation since comparison is not subjective.

Table 2-2 lists various metrics used for intrinsic evaluation across various NLP tasks. For a more detailed discussion of the metrics, refer to the corresponding reference.

Table 2-2. Popular metrics and NLP applications where they're used

Metric	Description	Applications
Accuracy [48]	Used when the output variable is categorical or discrete. It denotes the fraction of times the model makes correct predictions as compared to the total predictions it makes.	Mainly used in classification tasks, such as sentiment classification (multiclass), natural language inference (binary), paraphrase detection (binary), etc.
Precision [48]	Shows how precise or exact the model's predictions are, i.e., given all the positive (the class we care about) cases, how many can the model classify correctly?	Used in various classification tasks, especially in cases where mistakes in a positive class are more costly than mistakes in a negative class, e.g., disease predictions in healthcare.
Recall [48]	Recall is complementary to precision. It captures how well the model can recall positive class, i.e., given all the positive predictions it makes, how many of them are indeed positive?	Used in classification tasks, especially where retrieving positive results is more important, e.g., e-commerce search and other information-retrieval tasks.
F1 score [49]	Combines precision and recall to give a single metric, which also captures the trade-off between precision and recall, i.e., completeness and exactness. F1 is defined as $(2 \times \text{Precision} \times \text{Recall}) / (\text{Precision} + \text{Recall})$.	Used simultaneously with accuracy in most of the classification tasks. It is also used in sequence-labeling tasks, such as entity extraction, retrieval-based questions answering, etc.
AUC [48]	Captures the count of positive predictions that are correct versus the count of positive predictions that are incorrect as we vary the threshold for prediction.	Used to measure the quality of a model independent of the prediction threshold. It is used to find the optimal prediction threshold for a classification task.
MRR (mean reciprocal rank) [50]	Used to evaluate the responses retrieved given their probability of correctness. It is the mean of the reciprocal of the ranks of the retrieved results.	Used heavily in all information-retrieval tasks, including article search, e-commerce search, etc.
MAP (mean average precision) [51]	Used in ranked retrieval results, like MRR. It calculates the mean precision across each retrieved result.	Used in information-retrieval tasks.
RMSE (root mean squared error) [48]	Captures a model's performance in a real-value prediction task. Calculates the square root of the mean of the squared errors for each data point.	Used in conjunction with MAPE in the case of regression problems, from temperature prediction to stock market price prediction.
MAPE (mean absolute percentage error) [52]	Used when the output variable is a continuous variable. It is the average of absolute percentage error for each data point.	Used to test the performance of a regression model. It is often used in conjunction with RMSE.
BLEU (bilingual evaluation understudy) [53]	Captures the amount of n-gram overlap between the output sentence and the reference ground truth sentence. It has many variants.	Mainly used in machine-translation tasks. Recently adapted to other text-generation tasks, such as paraphrase generation and text summarization.
METEOR [54]	A precision-based metric to measure the quality of text generated. It fixes some of the drawbacks of BLEU, such as exact word matching while calculating precision. METEOR allows synonyms and stemmed words to be matched with the reference word.	Mainly used in machine translation.

Metric	Description	Applications
ROUGE [55]	Another metric to compare quality of generated text with respect to a reference text. As opposed to BLEU, it measures recall.	Since it measures recall, it's mainly used for summarization tasks where it's important to evaluate how many words a model can recall.
Perplexity [56]	A probabilistic measure that captures how confused an NLP model is. It's derived from the cross-entropy in a next word prediction task. The exact definition can be found at [56].	Used to evaluate language models. It can also be used in language-generation tasks, such as dialog generation.

Apart from the list of metrics shown in Table 2-2, there are few more metrics and visualizations that are often used for solving NLP problems. While we've covered these topics briefly here, we encourage you to follow the references and learn more about these metrics.

In the case of classification tasks, a commonly used visual evaluation method is a *confusion matrix*. It allows us to inspect the actual and predicted output for different classes in the dataset. The name stems from the fact that it helps to understand how "confused" the classification model is in terms of identifying different classes. A confusion matrix is in turn used to compute metrics such as precision, recall, F1 score, and accuracy. We'll see how to use confusion matrices in Chapter 4.

Ranking tasks like information search and retrieval mostly uses ranking-based metrics, such as MRR and MAP, but usual classification metrics can be used, too. In the case of retrieval, we care mainly about recall, so recall at various ranks is calculated. For example, for information retrieval, a common metric is "Recall at rank K"; it looks for the presence of ground truth in top K retrieved results. If present, it's a success.

When it comes to text-generation tasks, there are a number of metrics that are used, depending on the task. Even though BLEU and METEOR are good metrics for machine translation, they may not be good metrics when applied to other generation tasks. For example, in the case of dialog generation, the ground truth is one of the correct answers, but there could be many variations in responses that are not listed. In cases like this, precision-based metrics such as BLEU and METEOR will completely fail to capture the task performance faithfully. For these reasons, perplexity is one metric that's used extensively to understand a model's text-generation ability.

However, any evaluation scheme for text generation is not perfect. This is because there could be multiple sentences that have the same meaning, and it's not possible to have all the variations listed as ground truth. Therefore, the text generated and the ground truth can have the same meaning but be different sentences. This makes automated evaluation a difficult process. For example, say we build a machine-translation model that converts sentences from French to English. Consider the following sentence in French: "J'ai mangé trois filberts." In English, this means, "I ate three filberts."

So, we put this sentence as the label. Say our model generates the following English translation: "I ate three hazelnuts." Since the output does not match the label, automated evaluation will say the output is incorrect. But this *evaluation* is incorrect because English speakers are known to refer to filberts as hazelnuts. Even if we add this sentence as a possible label, our model could still generate "I have eaten three hazelnuts" as output. Yet again, the automated evaluation will say the model got it wrong since the output does not match either of the two labels. This is where human evaluation comes into play. But human evaluation can be expensive both in terms of time and money.

Extrinsic Evaluation

Like we said earlier, extrinsic evaluation focuses on evaluating the model performance on the final objective. In industrial projects, any AI model is built with the aim of solving a business problem. For example, a regression model is built with the aim of ranking the emails of the users and bringing the most important emails to the top of the inbox, thereby helping the users of an email service save time. Consider a scenario where the regression model does well on the ML metrics but doesn't really save a lot of time for the email service users, or where a question-answering model does very well on intrinsic metrics but fails to address a large number of questions in the production environment. Would we call such models successful? No, because they failed to achieve their business objectives. While this is not an issue for researchers in academia, for practitioners in industry, it's very important.

The way to carry out extrinsic evaluation is to set up the business metrics and the process to measure them correctly at the start of the project. We'll see examples of the right business metrics in later chapters.

We might ask: if extrinsic evaluation is what matters, why do intrinsic evaluation at all? The reason we must do intrinsic evaluation before extrinsic evaluation is that extrinsic evaluation often includes project stakeholders outside the AI team—sometimes even end users. Intrinsic evaluation can be done mostly by the AI team itself. This makes extrinsic evaluation a much more expensive process as compared to intrinsic evaluation. Therefore, intrinsic evaluation is used as a proxy for extrinsic evaluation. Only when we get consistently good results in intrinsic evaluation should we go for extrinsic evaluation.

Another thing to remember is that bad results in intrinsic evaluation often imply bad results in extrinsic evaluation. However, the converse may not be true. That is, we can have a model that does very well in intrinsic evaluation but does badly in extrinsic evaluation, but it's unlikely that a model that does well in extrinsic evaluation did poorly during intrinsic evaluation. The reasons for poor performance in extrinsic evaluation could be many, from setting up the wrong metrics to not having suitable data or having wrong expectations. We touched on some of these in Chapter 1 and will discuss them in more detail in Chapter 11.

So far, we've seen some metrics commonly used for intrinsic evaluation and also discussed the importance of extrinsic evaluation to measure the performance of NLP models. There are some more metrics that are task specific, which are not seen across different NLP application scenarios. We'll discuss such evaluation measures in detail as we cover these specific applications in upcoming chapters. With this, now let's look at the next components of the pipeline: model deployment, monitoring, and updating.

Post-Modeling Phases

Once our model has been tried and tested, we move on to the post-modeling phase: deploying, monitoring, and updating the model. We'll cover these briefly in this section.

Deployment

In most practical application scenarios, the NLP module we're implementing is a part of a larger system (e.g., a spam-classification system in a larger email application). Thus, working through the processing, modeling, and evaluation pipeline is only a part of the story. Eventually, once we're happy with one final solution, it needs to be deployed in a production environment as a part of a larger system. Deployment entails plugging the NLP module into the broader system. It may also involve making sure input and output data pipelines are in order, as well as making sure our NLP module is scalable under heavy load.

An NLP module is typically deployed as a web service. Let's say we designed a web service that takes a text as input and returns the email's category (spam or non-spam) as output. Now, each time someone gets a new email, it goes to the microservice, which classifies the email text. This, in turn, can be used to make a decision about what to do with the email (either show it or send it to the spam folder). In certain circumstances, like batch processing, the NLP module is deployed in the larger task queue. As an example, take a look at task queues in Google Cloud [57] or AWS [58]. We'll cover deployment in more detail in Chapter 11.

Monitoring

Like with any software engineering project, extensive software testing has to be done before final deployment, and the model performance is monitored constantly after deploying. Monitoring for NLP projects and models has to be handled differently than a regular engineering project, as we need to ensure that the outputs produced by our models daily make sense. If we're automatically training the model frequently, we have to make sure that the models behave in a reasonable manner. Part of this is done through a performance dashboard showing the model parameters and key performance indicators. We'll discuss this more in Chapter 11.

Model Updating

Once the model is deployed and we start gathering new data, we'll iterate the model based on this new data to stay current with predictions. We cover this model update for each task throughout the book, especially in Chapters 4 through 7 and Chapter 11. As a start, Table 2-3 gives some guidance on how to approach the model updating process for different post-deployment scenarios.

Table 2-3. Project attribute and associated decision paths

Project attribute	Decision paths	Examples
More training data is generated post-deployment.	Once deployed, extracted signals can be used to automatically improve the model. Can also try online learning to train the model automatically on a daily basis.	Abuse-detection systems where users flag data.
Training data is not generated post-deployment.	Manual labeling could be done to improve evaluation and the models. Ideally, each new model has to be manually built and evaluated.	A subset of a larger NLP pipeline with no direct feedback.
Low model latency is required, or model has to be online with near-real-time response.	Need to use models that can be inferred quickly. Another option is to create memoization strategies like caching or have substantially bigger computing power.	Systems that need to respond right away, like any chatbot or an emergency tracking system.
Low model latency is not required, or model can be run in an offline fashion.	Can use more advanced and slower models. This can also help in optimizing costs where feasible.	Systems that can be run on a batch process, like retail product catalog analysis.

Working with Other Languages

So far, our discussion has assumed that we're dealing mostly with English text. Depending on the task at hand, we may need to build models and solutions for other languages as well. How we approach this will change based on what language we're dealing with. The pipeline for some languages may be very similar to English, whereas some languages and scenarios may require us to rethink how we approach the problem. We've compiled some action points for dealing with different languages in Table 2-4, based on our experiences working on projects that involve non-English language processing.

Table 2-4. Language attribute and action plan

Language attribute	Example and languages	Action
High-resource languages	Languages that have both ample data as well as pre-built models. Examples include English, French, and Spanish.	Possible to use pre-trained DL models. Easier to use.
Low-resource languages	Languages that have limited data and recent digital adoption. May not have pre-built models. Examples include Swahili, Burmese, and Uzbek.	Depending on the task, may need to label more data as well as explore individual components.
Morphologically rich	Linguistic and grammatical information like subject, object, predicate, tense, and mode are not separate words, but are joined together. Examples include Latin, Turkish, Finnish, and Malayalam.	If the language is not resource rich, we'll need to explore morphological analyzers that exist for the language. In the worst case, manual rules to handle certain cases might be needed.
Vocabulary variation heavy	Nonstandard spellings and high word variation. For Arabic and Hindi, the spellings are nonstandard.	If the language is not resource rich, then we may need to first normalize the words/spellings before training any model. This may not be needed for languages with large datasets, as they can still learn of vocabulary variation.
CJK languages	These languages are derived from ancient Chinese characters. They're not alphabet based and have several thousand characters for basic literacy and over 40,000 characters for larger coverage. Thus, they have to be handled differently. They include Chinese, Japanese, and Korean, hence the name CJK.	Use specific tokenization schemes in these languages. Given that an ample amount of CJK data is available, it's possible to build NLP models for various tasks from scratch. There are also pre-trained models for them. Transfer learning from models trained in other languages beyond CJK may not be useful in this case.

Next, we'll turn our attention to a case study that will put all these steps together.

Case Study

So far, we've seen different stages of an NLP pipeline. At each stage, we discussed what it's about, why it's useful, and how it fits into the general framework of an NLP pipeline. However, we tackled these individual stages separately, away from the overall context. How do all these stages work together in a real-world NLP system pipeline? Let's see a case study, using Uber's tool to improve customer care: Customer Obsession Ticketing Assistant (COTA).

Uber operates in 400+ cities worldwide, and cbased on the number of people who use Uber every day, we can expect that their customer support teams receive several hundreds of thousands of tickets on different issues each day. There are a couple of solutions to choose from for a given ticket. The goal of COTA is to rank these solutions and pick the best possible one. Uber developed COTA using ML and NLP techniques to enable better customer support and quick and efficient resolution of such tickets. Figure 2-15 shows the pipeline in Uber's COTA and the various NLP components in it.

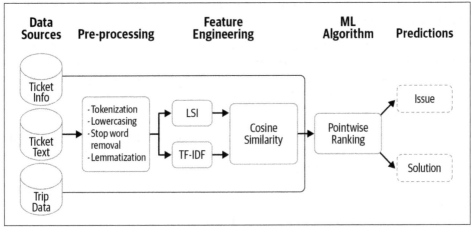

Figure 2-15. NLP pipeline for ranking tickets in a ticketing system by Uber [59]

The information needed to identify the ticket issue and select a solution in this system comes from three sources, as shown in the figure. Ticket text is, as the name indicates, textual content, which is where NLP comes into the picture. After cleaning up the text by removing HTML tags (not shown in the figure), the pre-processing steps consist of tokenization, lowercasing, stop word removal, and lemmatization. We saw how to do all of these earlier in this chapter. After pre-processing, the ticket text is represented as a collection of words (known as a *bag of words* and discussed in detail in Chapter 3).

The next step in this pipeline is feature engineering. The bag of words we obtained earlier is fed to two NLP modules—TF-IDF (term frequency and inverse document frequency) and LSI (latent semantic indexing)—which are used to understand the meaning of a text using this bag of words representation. This process comes under the NLP task called topic modeling, which we'll discuss in Chapter 7. Exactly how Uber uses these NLP tasks in this context is an interesting idea: Uber collects the historical tickets for each solution from their database, forms a bag-of-words vector representation for each solution, and creates a topic model based on these representations. An incoming ticket is then mapped to this topic space of solutions, creating a vector representation for the ticket. Cosine similarity is a common measure of similarity between any two vectors. It is used to create a vector where each element indicates the ticket text's similarity to one solution. Thus, at the end of this feature engineering step, we end up with a representation indicating the ticket text's similarity to all possible solutions.

In the next stage, modeling, this representation is combined with ticket information and trip data to build a ranking system that shows the three best solutions for the ticket. Under the hood, this ranking model consists of a binary classification system, which classifies each ticket-solution combination as a match or mismatch. The matches are then ranked based on a scoring function. [59] describes more details on the implementation of this system pipeline.

The next step in our pipeline is evaluation. How does evaluation work in this context? While the evaluation of model performance itself can be done in terms of an intrinsic evaluation measure such as MRR, the overall effectiveness of this approach is evaluated extrinsically. It's estimated that COTA's quick ticket resolution saves Uber tens of millions of dollars every year.

As we learned earlier, a model is not built just once. COTA, too, was continually experimented with and improved upon. After exploring a range of DL architectures, the best solution that was ultimately chosen resulted in a 10% greater accuracy compared to the previous version with the binary classification-based ranking system. The process does not end here, though. As we can see from the COTA team's article [59], it's a continuous process of model deployment, monitoring, and updating.

Wrapping Up

In this chapter, we saw the different steps involved in developing an NLP pipeline for a given project description and saw a detailed case study of a real-world application. We also saw how a traditional NLP pipeline and a DL-based NLP pipeline differ from each other and learned what to do when working with non-English languages. Aside from the case study, we looked at these steps in a more general manner in this chapter. Specific details for each step will depend on the task at hand and the purpose of our implementation. We'll look at a few task-specific pipelines from Chapter 4 onward, describing in detail what's unique as well as common across different tasks while designing such pipelines. In the next chapter, we'll tackle the question of text representation that we mentioned briefly earlier in this chapter.

References

[1] Iderhoff, Nicolas. nlp-datasets: Alphabetical list of free/public domain datasets with text data for use in Natural Language Processing (NLP) (*https://oreil.ly/NcwbT*), (GitHub repo). Last accessed June 15, 2020.

[2] Google. "Dataset Search" (*https://oreil.ly/RYjaz*). Last accessed June 15, 2020.

[3] Miller, George A. "WordNet: A Lexical Database for English." *Communications of the ACM* 38.11 (1995): 39–41.

[4] NTLTK documentation. "WordNet Interface" (*https://oreil.ly/ALA5z*). Last accessed June 15, 2020.

[5] Xie, Qizhe, Zihang Dai, Eduard Hovy, Minh-Thang Luong, and Quoc V. Le. "Unsupervised Data Augmentation for Consistency Training" (*https://oreil.ly/0KEoN*). (2019).

[6] Wikipedia. "Fat-finger error" (*https://oreil.ly/sYoEb*). Last modified January 26, 2020.

[7] Snorkel. "Programmatically Building and Managing Training Data" (*https://www.snorkel.org*). Last accessed June 15, 2020.

[8] Ratner, Alexander, Stephen H. Bach, Henry Ehrenberg, Jason Fries, Sen Wu, and Christopher Ré. "Snorkel: Rapid Training Data Creation with Weak Supervision." *The VLDB Journal* 29 (2019): 1–22.

[9] Bach, Stephen H., Daniel Rodriguez, Yintao Liu, Chong Luo, Haidong Shao, Cassandra Xia, Souvik Sen et al. "Snorkel DryBell: A Case Study in Deploying Weak Supervision at Industrial Scale" (*https://oreil.ly/CnWxH*). (2018).

[10] Wei, Jason W., and Kai Zou. "Eda: Easy Data Augmentation Techniques for Boosting Performance on Text Classification Tasks" (*https://oreil.ly/T4WvN*), (2019).

[11] GitHub repository (*https://oreil.ly/37Bhj*) for [10]. Last accessed June 15, 2020.

[12] Ma, Edward. nplaug: Data augmentation for NLP (*https://oreil.ly/LW78u*), (GitHub repo). Last accessed June 15, 2020.

[13] Shioulin and Nisha. "A Guide to Learning with Limited Labeled Data" (*https://oreil.ly/U5ExU*). April 2, 2019.

[14] eForms. "Blank Invoice Templates" (*https://oreil.ly/sEgr9*). Last accessed June 15, 2020.

[15] Amazon.com. "Amazon Elements Vitamin B12 Methylcobalamin 5000 mcg - Normal Energy Production and Metabolism, Immune System Support - 2 Month Supply (65 Berry Flavored Lozenges)" (*https://oreil.ly/8Zq3K*). Last accessed June 15, 2020.

[16] Beautiful Soup (*https://oreil.ly/W0eDZ*). Last accessed June 15, 2020.

[17] Scrapy.org. Scrapy (*https://scrapy.org*). Last accessed June 15, 2020.

[18] Unicode (*https://home.unicode.org*). Last accessed June 15, 2020.

[19] Dickinson, Markus, Chris Brew, and Detmar Meurers. *Language and Computers*. New Jersey: John Wiley & Sons, 2012. ISBN: 978-1-405-18305-5

[20] Explosion.ai. "Rule-based matching" (*https://oreil.ly/CgeBw*). Last accessed June 15, 2020.

[21] Microsoft documentation. "Quickstart: Check spelling with the Bing Spell Check REST API and Python" (*https://oreil.ly/Rwq0w*). Last accessed June 15, 2020.

[22] Stamy, Matthew. PyPDF2: A utility to read and write PDFs with Python (*https://oreil.ly/6OXi3*), (GitHub repo). Last accessed June 15, 2020.

[23] pdfminer. pdfminer.six: Community maintained fork of pdfminer (*https://oreil.ly/FVlxl*), (GitHub repo). Last accessed June 15, 2020.

[24] FilingDB. "What's so hard about PDF text extraction?" (*https://oreil.ly/Fa1gB*) Last accessed June 15, 2020.

[25] Tesseract-OCR. "Tesseract Open Source OCR Engine (main repository)" (*https://oreil.ly/WLIWy*), (GitHub repo). Last accessed June 15, 2020.

[26] Python-tesseract documentationPython-tesseract (*https://oreil.ly/UqaEz*). Last accessed June 15, 2020.

[27] Firth, John Rupert. "Personality and Language in Society." *The Sociological Review* 42.1 (1950): 37–52.

[28] pyenchant. Spellchecking library for python (*https://oreil.ly/Ntq5J*), (GitHub repo). Last accessed June 15, 2020.

[29] KBNL Research. ochre: Toolbox for OCR post-correction (*https://oreil.ly/BEWT1*), (GitHub repo). Last accessed June 15, 2020.

[30] "Natural Language ToolKit" (*http://www.nltk.org*). Last accessed June 15, 2020.

[31] Explosion.ai. "spaCy 101: Everything you need to know" (*https://oreil.ly/W97S3*). Last accessed June 15, 2020.

[32] Evang, Kilian, Valerio Basile, Grzegorz Chrupała, and Johan Bos. "Elephant: Sequence Labeling for Word and Sentence Segmentation." *Proceedings of the 2013 Conference on Empirical Methods in Natural Language Processing* (2013): 1422–1426.

[33] Porter, Martin F. "An Algorithm For Suffix Stripping." *Program: electronic library and information systems* 14.3 (1980): 130–137.

[34] Padmanabhan, Arvind. "Lemmatization" (*https://oreil.ly/erczD*). October 11, 2019.

[35] Explosion.ai. "spaCy" (*https://oreil.ly/kw5_4*). Last accessed June 15, 2020.

[36] Polyglot documentation.Polyglot Python library (*https://oreil.ly/vt4XB*). Last accessed June 15, 2020.

[37] Mair, Victor. "Singlish: alive and well" (*https://oreil.ly/tbnK3*). May 14, 2016.

[38] Jurafsky, Dan and James H. Martin. *Speech and Language Processing*, Third Edition (Draft) (*https://oreil.ly/Ta16f*), 2018.

[39] Explosion.ai. "spaCy: Industrial-Strength Natural Language Processing in Python" (*https://spacy.io/*). Last accessed June 15, 2020.

[40] DeepAI. "Parsey Mcparseface API" (*https://oreil.ly/BaRyS*). Last accessed June 15, 2020.

[41] Stanford CoreNLP.Stanford CoreNLP – Natural language software (*https://oreil.ly/137-o*). Last accessed June 15, 2020.

[42] Ghaffari, Parsa. "Leveraging Deep Learning for Multilingual Sentiment Analysis" (*https://oreil.ly/Fmy_2*). July 14, 2016.

[43] The Stanford Natural Language Processing Group. "Stanford TokensRegex" (*https://oreil.ly/AUGVP*). Last accessed June 15, 2020.

[44] Google. "Cloud Natural Language" (*https://oreil.ly/Tti8y*). Last accessed June 15, 2020.

[45] Amazon. "AWS Comprehend" (*https://oreil.ly/DO9jA*). Last accessed June 15, 2020.

[46] Microsoft. "Azure Cognitive Services documentation" (*https://oreil.ly/0dokf*). Last accessed June 15, 2020.

[47] IBM. "Watson Natural Language Understanding" (*https://oreil.ly/_KUkX*). Last accessed June 15, 2020.

[48] Friedman, Jerome, Trevor Hastie, and Robert Tibshirani. *The Elements of Statistical Learning*, Second Edition. New York: Springer, 2001. ISBN: 978-0-387-84857-0

[49] Wikipedia. "F1 score" (*https://oreil.ly/-d6IZ*). Last modified April 18, 2020.

[50] Wikipedia. "Mean reciprocal rank" (*https://oreil.ly/9eK2K*). Last modified December 6, 2018.

[51] Wikipedia. "Evaluation measures (information retrieval)" (*https://oreil.ly/a2Jmq*). Last modified February 12, 2020.

[52] Wikipedia. "Mean absolute percentage error" (*https://oreil.ly/TXzj5*). Last modified February 6, 2020.

[53] Papineni, Kishore, Salim Roukos, Todd Ward, and Wei-Jing Zhu. "BLEU: A Method for Automatic Evaluation of Machine Translation." *Proceedings of the 40th Annual Meeting on Association for Computational Linguistics* (2002): 311–318.

[54] Banerjee, Satanjeev and Alon Lavie. "METEOR: An Automatic Metric for MT Evaluation with Improved Correlation with Human Judgments." *Proceedings of the ACL Workshop on Intrinsic and Extrinsic Evaluation Measures for Machine Translation and/or Summarization* (2005): 65–72.

[55] Lin, Chin-Yew. "ROUGE: A Package for Automatic Evaluation of Summaries." *Text Summarization Branches Out* (2004): 74–81.

[56] Wikipedia. "Perplexity" (*https://oreil.ly/NDKkiy*). Last modified February 13, 2020.

[57] Google Cloud. "Quickstart for Cloud Tasks queues" (*https://oreil.ly/O7CD0*). Last accessed June 15, 2020.

[58] Amazon. "Amazon Simple Queue Service" (*https://oreil.ly/zXHZz*). Last accessed June 15, 2020.

[59] Zheng, Huaixiu., Yi-Chia Wang, and Piero Molino. "COTA: Improving Uber Customer Care with NLP & Machine Learning" (*https://oreil.ly/dxhWB*). January 3, 2018.

## CHAPTER 3

Text Representation

> *In language processing,*
> *the vectors x are derived from textual data,*
> *in order to reflect various linguistic properties of the text.*
> —*Yoav Goldberg*

Feature extraction is an important step for any machine learning problem. No matter how good a modeling algorithm you use, if you feed in poor features, you will get poor results. In computer science, this is often called "garbage in, garbage out." In the previous two chapters, we saw an overview of NLP, the different tasks and challenges involved, and what a typical NLP pipeline looks like. In this chapter, we'll address the question: how do we go about doing feature engineering for text data? In other words, how do we transform a given text into numerical form so that it can be fed into NLP and ML algorithms? In NLP parlance, this conversion of raw text to a suitable numerical form is called *text representation*. In this chapter, we'll take a look at the different methods for text representation, or representing text as a numeric vector. With respect to the larger picture for any NLP problem, the scope of this chapter is depicted by the dotted box in Figure 3-1.

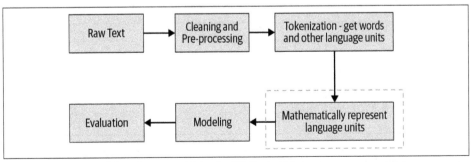

Figure 3-1. Scope of this chapter within the NLP pipeline

Feature representation is a common step in any ML project, whether the data is text, images, videos, or speech. However, feature representation for text is often much more involved as compared to other formats of data. To understand this, let's look at a few examples of how other data formats can be represented numerically. First, consider the case of images. Say we want to build a classifier that can distinguish images of cats from images of dogs. Now, in order to train an ML model to accomplish this task, we need to feed it (labeled) images. How do we feed images to an ML model? The way an image is stored in a computer is in the form of a matrix of pixels where each cell[i,j] in the matrix represents pixel i,j of the image. The real value stored at cell[i,j] represents the intensity of the corresponding pixel in the image, as shown in Figure 3-2. This matrix representation accurately represents the complete image. Video is similar: a video is just a collection of frames where each frame is an image. Hence, any video can be represented as a sequential collection of matrices, one per frame, in the same order.

What We See   What Computers See

Figure 3-2. How we see an image versus how computers see it [1]

Now consider speech—it's transmitted as a wave. To represent it mathematically, we sample the wave and record its amplitude (height), as shown in Figure 3-3.

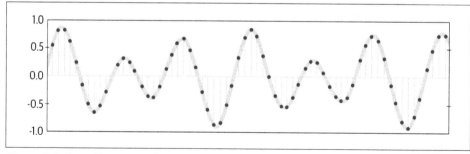

Figure 3-3. Sampling a speech wave

This gives us a numerical array representing the amplitude of a sound wave at fixed time intervals, as shown in Figure 3-4.

```
[-1274, -1252, -1160, -986, -792, -692, -614, -429, -286, -134, -57, -41,
-169, -456, -450, -541, -761, -1067, -1231, -1047, -952, -645, -489, -448,
-397, -212, 193, 114, -17, -110, 128, 261, 198, 390, 461, 772, 948, 1451,
1974, 2624, 3793, 4968, 5939, 6057, 6581, 7302, 7640, 7223, 6119, 5461,
4820, 4353, 3611, 2740, 2004, 1349, 1178, 1085, 901, 301, -262, -499,
-488, -707, -1406, -1997, -2377, -2494, -2605, -2675, -2627, -2500, -2148,
-1648, -970, -364, 13, 260, 494, 788, 1011, 938, 717, 507, 323, 324, 325,
350, 103, -113, 64, 176, 93, -249, -461, -606, -909, -1159, -1307, -1544]
```

Figure 3-4. Speech signal represented by a numerical vector

From this discussion, it's clear that mathematically representing images, video, and speech is straightforward. What about text? It turns out that representing text is not straightforward, hence a whole chapter focusing on various schemes to address this question. We're given a piece of text, and we're asked to find a scheme to represent it mathematically. In literature, this is called *text representation*. Text representation has been an active area of research in the past decades, especially the last one. In this chapter, we'll start with simple approaches and go all the way to state-of-the-art techniques for representing text. These approaches are classified into four categories:

- Basic vectorization approaches
- Distributed representations
- Universal language representation
- Handcrafted features

The rest of this chapter describes these categories one by one, covering various algorithms in each. Before we delve deeper into various schemes, consider the following scenario: we're given a labeled text corpus and asked to build a sentiment analysis model. To correctly predict the sentiment of a sentence, the model needs to understand the meaning of the sentence. In order to correctly extract the meaning of the sentence, the most crucial data points are:

1. Break the sentence into lexical units such as lexemes, words, and phrases
2. Derive the meaning for each of the lexical units
3. Understand the syntactic (grammatical) structure of the sentence
4. Understand the context in which the sentence appears

The *semantics* (meaning) of the sentence arises from the combination of the above points. Thus, any *good* text representation scheme must facilitate the extraction of those data points in the best possible way to reflect the linguistic properties of the text. Without this, a text representation scheme isn't of much use.

Often in NLP, feeding a good text representation to an ordinary algorithm will get you much farther compared to applying a top-notch algorithm to an ordinary text representation.

Let's take a look at a key concept that carries throughout this entire chapter: the vector space model.

Vector Space Models

It should be clear from the introduction that, in order for ML algorithms to work with text data, the text data must be converted into some mathematical form. Throughout this chapter, we'll represent text units (characters, phonemes, words, phrases, sentences, paragraphs, and documents) with vectors of numbers. This is known as the *vector space model* (VSM).[i] It's a simple algebraic model used extensively for representing any text blob. VSM is fundamental to many information-retrieval operations, from scoring documents on a query to document classification and document clustering [2]. It's a mathematical model that represents text units as vectors (*https://oreil.ly/mtyKw*). In the simplest form, these are vectors of identifiers, such as index numbers in a corpus vocabulary. In this setting, the most common way to calculate similarity between two text blobs is using cosine similarity: the cosine of the angle between their corresponding vectors. The cosine of 0° is 1 and the cosine of 180° is –1, with the cosine monotonically decreasing from 0° to 180°. Given two vectors, A and B, each with n components, the similarity between them is computed as follows:

$$\text{similarity} = \cos(\theta) = \frac{\mathbf{A} \cdot \mathbf{B}}{||\mathbf{A}||_2 ||\mathbf{B}||_2} = \frac{\sum_{i=1}^{n} A_i B_i}{\sqrt{\sum_{i=1}^{n} A_i^2} \sqrt{\sum_{i=1}^{n} B_i^2}}$$

where A_i and B_i are the ith components (*https://oreil.ly/7tNTM*) of vectors A and B, respectively. Sometimes, people also use Euclidean distance between vectors to capture similarity.

All the text representation schemes we'll study in this chapter fall within the scope of vector space models. What differentiates one scheme from another is how well the resulting vector captures the linguistic properties of the text it represents. With this, we're ready to discuss various text representation schemes.

---

i. It is sometimes also referred to as the *term vector model,* but we'll stick to the notation VSM.

Basic Vectorization Approaches

Let's start with a basic idea of text representation: map each word in the vocabulary (V) of the text corpus to a unique ID (integer value), then represent each sentence or document in the corpus as a V-dimensional vector. How do we operationalize this idea? To understand this better, let's take a toy corpus (shown in Table 3-1) with only four documents—D_1, D_2, D_3, D_4 —as an example.

Table 3-1. Our toy corpus

D1	Dog bites man.
D2	Man bites dog.
D3	Dog eats meat.
D4	Man eats food.

Lowercasing text and ignoring punctuation, the vocabulary of this corpus is comprised of six words: [dog, bites, man, eats, meat, food]. We can organize the vocabulary in any order. In this example, we simply take the order in which the words appear in the corpus. Every document in this corpus can now be represented with a vector of size six. We'll discuss multiple ways in which we can do this. We'll assume that the text is already pre-processed (lowercased, punctuation removed, etc.) and tokenized (text string split into tokens), following the pre-processing step in the NLP pipeline described in Chapter 2. We'll start with one-hot encoding.

One-Hot Encoding

In one-hot encoding, each word w in the corpus vocabulary is given a unique integer ID w_{id} that is between 1 and $|V|$, where V is the set of the corpus vocabulary. Each word is then represented by a V-dimensional binary vector of 0s and 1s. This is done via a $|V|$ dimension vector filled with all 0s barring the index, where index = w_{id}. At this index, we simply put a 1. The representation for individual words is then combined to form a sentence representation.

Let's understand this via our toy corpus. We first map each of the six words to unique IDs: dog = 1, bites = 2, man = 3, meat = 4 , food = 5, eats = 6.[ii] Let's consider the document D1: "dog bites man". As per the scheme, each word is a six-dimensional vector. Dog is represented as [1 0 0 0 0 0], as the word "dog" is mapped to ID 1. Bites is represented as [0 1 0 0 0 0], and so on and so forth. Thus, D1 is represented as [[1 0 0 0 0 0] [0 1 0 0 0 0] [0 0 1 0 0 0]]. D4 is represented as [[0 0 1 0 0] [0 0 0 0 1 0] [0 0 0 0 0 1]]. Other documents in the corpus can be represented similarly.

---

ii. This mapping is arbitrary. Any other mapping works just as well.

Let's look at a simple way to implement this in Python from first principles. The note-book *Ch3/OneHotEncoding.ipynb* demonstrates an example of this. The code that follows is borrowed from the notebook and implements one-hot encoding. In real-world projects, we mostly use scikit-learn's implementation of one-hot encoding, which is much more optimized. We've provided the same in the notebook.

Since we assume that the text is tokenized, we can just split the text on white space in this example:

```
def get_onehot_vector(somestring):
  onehot_encoded = []
  for word in somestring.split():
          temp = [0]*len(vocab)
          if word in vocab:
                  temp[vocab[word]-1] = 1
          onehot_encoded.append(temp)
  return onehot_encoded
```

```
get_onehot_vector(processed_docs[1])
```

```
Output: [[0, 0, 1, 0, 0, 0], [0, 1, 0, 0, 0, 0], [1, 0, 0, 0, 0, 0]]
```

Now that we understand the scheme, let's discuss some of its pros and cons. On the positive side, one-hot encoding is intuitive to understand and straightforward to implement. However, it suffers from a few shortcomings:

- The size of a one-hot vector is directly proportional to size of the vocabulary, and most real-world corpora have large vocabularies. This results in a sparse representation where most of the entries in the vectors are zeroes, making it computationally inefficient to store, compute with, and learn from (sparsity leads to overfitting).

- This representation does not give a fixed-length representation for text, i.e., if a text has 10 words, you get a longer representation for it as compared to a text with 5 words. For most learning algorithms, we need the feature vectors to be of the same length.

- It treats words as atomic units and has no notion of (dis)similarity between words. For example, consider three words: run, ran, and apple. Run and ran have similar meanings as opposed to run and apple. But if we take their respective vectors and compute Euclidean distance between them, they're all equally apart ($\sqrt{2}$). Thus, semantically, they're very poor at capturing the meaning of the word in relation to other words.

- Say we train a model using our toy corpus. At runtime, we get a sentence: "man eats fruits." The training data didn't include "fruit" and there's no way to represent it in our model. This is known as the *out of vocabulary (OOV)* problem. A one-hot encoding scheme cannot handle this. The only way is to retrain the model: start by expanding the vocabulary, give an ID to the new word, etc.

 These days, one-hot encoding scheme is seldom used.

Some of these shortcomings can be addressed by the bag-of-words approach described next.

Bag of Words

Bag of words (BoW) is a classical text representation technique that has been used commonly in NLP, especially in text classification problems (see Chapter 4). The key idea behind it is as follows: represent the text under consideration as a *bag* (collection) *of words* while ignoring the order and context. The basic intuition behind it is that it assumes that the text belonging to a given class in the dataset is characterized by a unique set of words. If two text pieces have nearly the same words, then they belong to the same bag (class). Thus, by analyzing the words present in a piece of text, one can identify the class (bag) it belongs to.

Similar to one-hot encoding, BoW maps words to unique integer IDs between 1 and |V|. Each document in the corpus is then converted into a vector of |V| dimensions where in the ith component of the vector, $i = w_{id}$, is simply the number of times the word w occurs in the document, i.e., we simply score each word in V by their occurrence count in the document.

Thus, for our toy corpus (Table 3-1), where the word IDs are dog = 1, bites = 2, man = 3, meat = 4 , food = 5, eats = 6, D1 becomes [1 1 1 0 0 0]. This is because the first three words in the vocabulary appeared exactly once in D1, and the last three did not appear at all. D4 becomes [0 0 1 0 1 1]. The notebook *Ch3/Bag_of_Words.ipynb* demonstrates how we can implement BoW text representation. The following code shows the key parts:

```
from sklearn.feature_extraction.text import CountVectorizer
count_vect = CountVectorizer()

#Build a BOW representation for the corpus
bow_rep = count_vect.fit_transform(processed_docs)

#Look at the vocabulary mapping
print("Our vocabulary: ", count_vect.vocabulary_)

#See the BOW rep for first 2 documents
```

```
print("BoW representation for 'dog bites man': ", bow_rep[0].toarray())
print("BoW representation for 'man bites dog: ",bow_rep[1].toarray())

#Get the representation using this vocabulary, for a new text
temp = count_vect.transform(["dog and dog are friends"])
print("Bow representation for 'dog and dog are friends':",

temp.toarray())
```

If we run this code, we'll notice that the BoW representation for a sentence like "dog and dog are friends" has a value of 2 for the dimension of the word "dog," indicating its frequency in the text. Sometimes, we don't care about the frequency of occurrence of words in text and we only want to represent whether a word exists in the text or not. Researchers have shown that such a representation without considering frequency is useful for sentiment analysis (see Chapter 4 in [3]). In such cases, we just initialize CountVectorizer with the binary=True option, as shown in the following code:

```
count_vect = CountVectorizer(binary=True)
bow_rep_bin = count_vect.fit_transform(processed_docs)
temp = count_vect.transform(["dog and dog are friends"])
print("Bow representation for 'dog and dog are friends':", temp.toarray())
```

This results in a different representation for the same sentence. CountVectorizer supports both word as well as character n-grams.

Let's look at some of the advantages of this encoding:

- Like one-hot encoding, BoW is fairly simple to understand and implement.
- With this representation, documents having the same words will have their vector representations closer to each other in Euclidean space as compared to documents with completely different words. The distance between D_1 and D_2 is 0 as compared to the distance between D_1 and D_4, which is 2. Thus, the vector space resulting from the BoW scheme captures the semantic similarity of documents. So if two documents have similar vocabulary, they'll be closer to each other in the vector space and vice versa.
- We have a fixed-length encoding for any sentence of arbitrary length.

However, it has its share of disadvantages, too:

- The size of the vector increases with the size of the vocabulary. Thus, sparsity continues to be a problem. One way to control it is by limiting the vocabulary to *n* number of the most frequent words.
- It does not capture the similarity between different words that mean the same thing. Say we have three documents: "I run", "I ran", and "I ate". BoW vectors of all three documents will be equally apart.

- This representation does not have any way to handle out of vocabulary words (i.e., new words that were not seen in the corpus that was used to build the vectorizer).
- As the name indicates, it is a "bag" of words—word order information is lost in this representation. Both D1 and D2 will have the same representation in this scheme.

However, despite these shortcomings, due to its simplicity and ease of implementation, BoW is a commonly used text representation scheme, especially for text classification among other NLP problems.

Bag of N-Grams

All the representation schemes we've seen so far treat words as independent units. There is no notion of phrases or word ordering. The *bag-of-n-grams* (BoN) approach tries to remedy this. It does so by breaking text into chunks of *n* contiguous words (or tokens). This can help us capture some context, which earlier approaches could not do. Each chunk is called an *n-gram*. The corpus vocabulary, V, is then nothing but a collection of all unique n-grams across the text corpus. Then, each document in the corpus is represented by a vector of length |V|. This vector simply contains the frequency counts of n-grams present in the document and zero for the n-grams that are not present.

To elaborate, let's consider our example corpus. Let's construct a 2-gram (a.k.a. bigram) model for it. The set of all bigrams in the corpus is as follows: {dog bites, bites man, man bites, bites dog, dog eats, eats meat, man eats, eats food}. Then, BoN representation consists of an eight-dimensional vector for each document. The bigram representation for the first two documents is as follows: D_1 : [1,1,0,0,0,0,0,0], D_2 : [0,0,1,1,0,0,0,0]. The other two documents follow similarly. Note that the BoW scheme is a special case of the BoN scheme, with $n=1$. $n=2$ is called a "bigram model," and $n=3$ is called a "trigram model." Further, note that, by increasing the value of n, we can incorporate larger context; however, this further increases the sparsity. In NLP parlance, the BoN scheme is also called "n-gram feature selection."

The following code (*Ch3/Bag_of_N_Grams.ipynb*) shows an example of a BoN representation considering 1–3 n-gram word features to represent the corpus that we've used so far. Here, we use unigram, bigram, and trigram vectors by setting ngram_range = (1,3):

```
#n-gram vectorization example with count vectorizer and uni, bi, trigrams
count_vect = CountVectorizer(ngram_range=(1,3))

#Build a BOW representation for the corpus
bow_rep = count_vect.fit_transform(processed_docs)
```

```
#Look at the vocabulary mapping
print("Our vocabulary: ", count_vect.vocabulary_)

#Get the representation using this vocabulary, for a new text
temp = count_vect.transform(["dog and dog are friends"])
print("Bow representation for 'dog and dog are friends':", temp.toarray())
```

Here are the main pros and cons of BoN:

- It captures some context and word-order information in the form of n-grams.

- Thus, resulting vector space is able to capture some semantic similarity. Documents having the same n-grams will have their vectors closer to each other in Euclidean space as compared to documents with completely different n-grams.

- As *n* increases, dimensionality (and therefore sparsity) only increases rapidly.

- It still provides no way to address the OOV problem.

TF-IDF

In all the three approaches we've seen so far, all the words in the text are treated as equally important—there's no notion of some words in the document being more important than others. TF-IDF, or *term frequency–inverse document frequency*, addresses this issue. It aims to quantify the importance of a given word relative to other words in the document and in the corpus. It's a commonly used representation scheme for information-retrieval systems, for extracting relevant documents from a corpus for a given text query.

The intuition behind TF-IDF is as follows: if a word *w* appears many times in a document d_i but does not occur much in the rest of the documents d_j in the corpus, then the word *w* must be of great importance to the document d_i. The importance of *w* should increase in proportion to its frequency in d_i, but at the same time, its importance should decrease in proportion to the word's frequency in other documents d_j in the corpus. Mathematically, this is captured using two quantities: TF and IDF. The two are then combined to arrive at the *TF-IDF score*.

TF (term frequency) measures how often a term or word occurs in a given document. Since different documents in the corpus may be of different lengths, a term may occur more often in a longer document as compared to a shorter document. To normalize these counts, we divide the number of occurrences by the length of the document. *TF* of a term *t* in a document *d* is defined as:

$$\mathrm{TF}\left(t, d\right) = \frac{\text{(Number of occurrences of term } t \text{ in document } d)}{\text{(Total number of terms in the document } d)}$$

IDF *(inverse document frequency)* measures the importance of the term across a corpus. In computing TF, all terms are given equal importance (weightage). However, it's a well-known fact that stop words like is, are, am, etc., are not important, even though they occur frequently. To account for such cases, IDF weighs down the terms that are very common across a corpus and weighs up the rare terms. IDF of a term t is calculated as follows:

$$\text{IDF}\left(t\right) = \log_e \frac{\text{(Total number of documents in the corpus)}}{\text{(Number of documents with term } t \text{ in them)}}$$

The TF-IDF score is a product of these two terms. Thus, *TF-IDF score = TF * IDF*. Let's compute TF-IDF scores for our toy corpus. Some terms appear in only one document, some appear in two, while others appear in three documents. The size of our corpus is N=4. Hence, corresponding TF-IDF values for each term are shown in Table 3-2.

Table 3-2. TF-IDF values for our toy corpus

Word	TF score	IDF score	TF-IDF score
dog	$\frac{1}{3} = 0.33$	$\log_2(4/3) = 0.4114$	$0.4114 * 0.33 = 0.136$
bites	$\frac{1}{6} = 0.17$	$\log_2(4/2) = 1$	$1 * 0.17 = 0.17$
man	0.33	$\log_2(4/3) = 0.4114$	$0.4114 * 0.33 = 0.136$
eats	0.17	$\log_2(4/2) = 1$	$1 * 0.17 = 0.17$
meat	$1/12 = 0.083$	$\log_2(4/1) = 2$	$2 * 0.083 = 0.17$
food	0.083	$\log_2(4/1) = 2$	$2 * 0.083 = 0.17$

The TF-IDF vector representation for a document is then simply the TF-IDF score for each term in that document. So, for D_1 we get

Dog	bites	man	eats	meat	food
0.136	0.17	0.136	0	0	0

The following code (*Ch3/TF_IDF.ipynb*) shows how to use TF-IDF to represent text:

```
from sklearn.feature_extraction.text import TfidfVectorizer

tfidf = TfidfVectorizer()
bow_rep_tfidf = tfidf.fit_transform(processed_docs)
print(tfidf.idf_) #IDF for all words in the vocabulary
print(tfidf.get_feature_names()) #All words in the vocabulary.

temp = tfidf.transform(["dog and man are friends"])
print("Tfidf representation for 'dog and man are friends':\n", temp.toarray())
```

There are several variations of the basic TF-IDF formula that are used in practice. Notice that the TF-IDF scores that we calculated for our corpus in Table 3-2 might not match the TF-IDF scores given by scikit-learn. This is because scikit-learn uses a slightly modified version of the IDF formula. This stems from provisions to account for possible zero divisions and to not entirely ignore terms that appear in all documents. An interested reader can look into the TF-IDF vectorizer documentation [4] for the exact formula.

Similar to BoW, we can use the TF-IDF vectors to calculate similarity between two texts using a similarity measure like Euclidean distance or cosine similarity. TF-IDF is a commonly used representation in application scenarios such as information retrieval and text classification. However, despite the fact that TF-IDF is better than the vectorization methods we saw earlier in terms of capturing similarities between words, it still suffers from the curse of high dimensionality.

Even today, TF-IDF continues to be a popular representation scheme for many NLP tasks, especially the initial versions of the solution.

If we look back at all the representation schemes we've discussed so far, we notice three fundamental drawbacks:

- They're discrete representations—i.e., they treat language units (words, n-grams, etc.) as atomic units. This discreteness hampers their ability to capture relationships between words.
- The feature vectors are sparse and high-dimensional representations. The dimensionality increases with the size of the vocabulary, with most values being zero for any vector. This hampers learning capability. Further, high-dimensionality representation makes them computationally inefficient.
- They cannot handle OOV words.

With this, we come to the end of basic vectorization approaches. Now, let's start looking at distributed representations.

Distributed Representations

In the previous section, we saw some key drawbacks that are common to all basic vectorization approaches. To overcome these limitations, methods to learn low-dimensional representations were devised. These methods, covered in this section, gained momentum in the past six to seven years. They use neural network architectures to create dense, low-dimensional representations of words and texts. But before we look into these methods, we need to understand some key terms:

Distributional similarity

This is the idea that the meaning of a word can be understood from the context in which the word appears. This is also known as *connotation*: meaning is defined by context. This is opposed to *denotation*: the literal meaning of any word. For example: "NLP rocks." The literal meaning of the word "rocks" is "stones," but from the context, it's used to refer to something good and fashionable.

Distributional hypothesis [5]

In linguistics, this hypothesizes that words that occur in similar contexts have similar meanings. For example, the English words "dog" and "cat" occur in similar contexts. Thus, according to the distributional hypothesis, there must be a strong similarity between the meanings of these two words. Now, following from VSM, the meaning of a word is represented by the vector. Thus, if two words often occur in similar context, then their corresponding representation vectors must also be close to each other.

Distributional representation [6]

This refers to representation schemes that are obtained based on distribution of words from the context in which the words appear. These schemes are based on distributional hypotheses. The distributional property is induced from context (textual vicinity). Mathematically, distributional representation schemes use high-dimensional vectors to represent words. These vectors are obtained from a co-occurrence matrix that captures co-occurrence of word and context. The dimension of this matrix is equal to the size of the vocabulary of the corpus. The four schemes that we've seen so far—one-hot, bag of words, bag of n-grams, and TF-IDF—all fall under the umbrella of distributional representation.

Distributed representation [6]

This is a related concept. It, too, is based on the distributional hypothesis. As discussed in the previous paragraph, the vectors in distributional representation are very high dimensional and sparse. This makes them computationally inefficient and hampers learning. To alleviate this, distributed representation schemes significantly compress the dimensionality. This results in vectors that are compact (i.e., low dimensional) and dense (i.e., hardly any zeros). The resulting vector space is known as *distributed representation*. All the subsequent schemes we'll discuss in this chapter are examples of distributed representation.

Embedding

For the set of words in a corpus, *embedding* is a mapping between vector space coming from distributional representation to vector space coming from distributed representation.

Vector semantics

This refers to the set of NLP methods that aim to learn the word representations based on distributional properties of words in a large corpus.

Now that you have a basic understanding of these terms, we can move on to our first method: word embeddings.

Word Embeddings

What does it mean when we say a text representation should capture "distributional similarities between words"? Let's consider some examples. If we're given the word "USA," distributionally similar words could be other countries (e.g., Canada, Germany, India, etc.) or cities in the USA. If we're given the word "beautiful," words that share some relationship with this word (e.g., synonyms, antonyms) could be considered distributionally similar words. These are words that are likely to occur in similar contexts. In 2013, a seminal work by Mikolov et al. [7] showed that their neural network–based word representation model known as "Word2vec," based on "distributional similarity," can capture word analogy relationships such as:

King – Man + Woman ≈ Queen

Their model was able to correctly answer many more analogies like this. Figure 3-5 shows a snapshot of a system based on Word2vec answering analogies. The Word2vec model is in many ways the dawn of modern-day NLP.

While learning such semantically rich relationships, Word2vec ensures that the learned word representations are low dimensional (vectors of dimensions 50–500, instead of several thousands, as with previously studied representations in this chapter) and dense (that is, most values in these vectors are non-zero). Such representations make ML tasks more tractable and efficient. Word2vec led to a lot of work (both pure and applied) in the direction of learning text representations using neural networks. These representations are also called "embeddings." Let's build an intuition of how they work and how to use them to represent text.

Given a text corpus, the aim is to learn embeddings for every word in the corpus such that the word vector in the embedding space best captures the meaning of the word. To "derive" the meaning of the word, Word2vec uses distributional similarity and distributional hypothesis. That is, it derives the meaning of a word from its context: words that appear in its neighborhood in the text. So, if two different words (often) occur in similar context, then it's highly likely that their meanings are also similar. Word2vec operationalizes this by projecting the meaning of the words in a vector space where words with similar meanings will tend to cluster together, and words with very different meanings are far from one another.

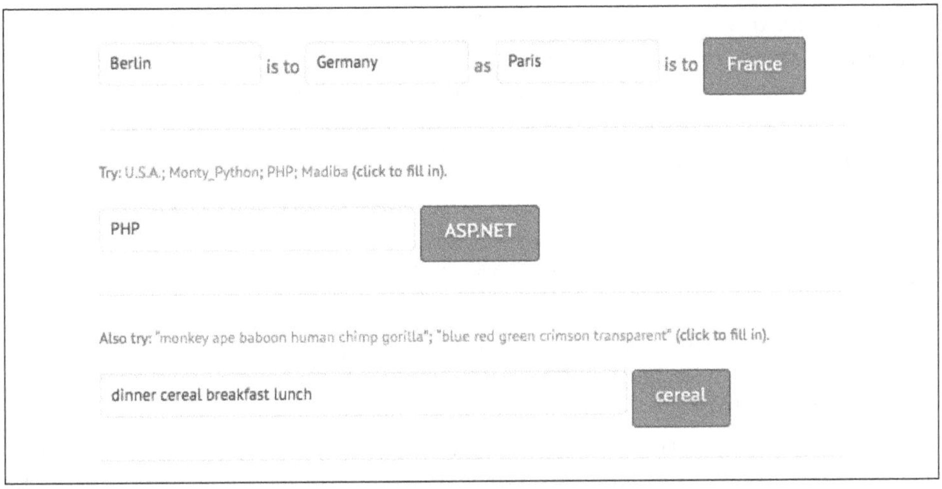

Figure 3-5. Word2vec-based analogy-answering system

Conceptually, Word2vec takes a large corpus of text as input and "learns" to represent the words in a common vector space based on the contexts in which they appear in the corpus. Given a word w and the words appearing in its context C, how do we find the vector that best represents the meaning of the word? For every word w in corpus, we start with a vector v_w initialized with random values. The Word2vec model refines the values in v_w by predicting v_w, given the vectors for words in the context C. It does this using a two-layer neural network. We'll dive deeper into this by discussing pre-trained embeddings before moving on to train our own.

Pre-trained word embeddings

Training your own word embeddings is a pretty expensive process (in terms of both time and computing). Thankfully, for many scenarios, it's not necessary to train your own embeddings, and using pre-trained word embeddings often suffices. What are pre-trained word embeddings? Someone has done the hard work of training word embeddings on a large corpus, such as Wikipedia, news articles, or even the entire web, and has put words and their corresponding vectors on the web. These embeddings can be downloaded and used to get the vectors for the words you want. Such embeddings can be thought of as a large collection of key-value pairs, where keys are the words in the vocabulary and values are their corresponding word vectors. Some of the most popular pre-trained embeddings are Word2vec by Google [8], GloVe by Stanford [9], and fasttext embeddings by Facebook [10], to name a few. Further, they're available for various dimensions like d = 25, 50, 100, 200, 300, 600.

Ch3/Pre_Trained_Word_Embeddings.ipynb, the notebook associated with the rest of this section, shows an example of how to load pre-trained Word2vec embeddings and look for the most similar words (ranked by cosine similarity) to a given word. The code that follows covers the key steps. Here, we find the words that are semantically most similar to the word "beautiful"; the last line returns the embedding vector of the word "beautiful":

```
from gensim.models import Word2Vec, KeyedVectors
pretrainedpath = "NLPBookTut/GoogleNews-vectors-negative300.bin"
w2v_model = KeyedVectors.load_word2vec_format(pretrainedpath, binary=True)
print('done loading Word2Vec')
print(len(w2v_model.vocab)) #Number of words in the vocabulary.
print(w2v_model.most_similar['beautiful'])
W2v_model['beautiful']
```

`most_similar('beautiful')` returns the most similar words to the word "beautiful." The output is shown below. Each word is accompanied by a similarity score. The higher the score, the more similar the word is to the query word:

```
[('gorgeous', 0.8353004455566406),
 ('lovely', 0.810693621635437),
 ('stunningly_beautiful', 0.7329413890838623),
 ('breathtakingly_beautiful', 0.7231341004371643),
 ('wonderful', 0.6854087114334106),
 ('fabulous', 0.6700063943862915),
 ('loveliest', 0.6612576246261597),
 ('prettiest', 0.6595001816749573),
 ('beatiful', 0.6593326330184937),
 ('magnificent', 0.6591402292251587)]
```

`w2v_model` returns the vector for the query word. For the word "beautiful," we get the vector as shown in Figure 3-6.

Note that if we search for a word that is not present in the Word2vec model (e.g., "practicalnlp"), we'll see a "key not found" error. Hence, as a good coding practice, it's always advised to first check if the word is present in the model's vocabulary before attempting to retrieve its vector. The Python library we used in this code snippet, gensim, also supports training and loading GloVe pre-trained models.

 If you're new to embeddings, always start by using pre-trained word embeddings in your project. Understand their pros and cons, then start thinking of building your own embeddings. Using pre-trained embeddings will quickly give you a strong baseline for the task at hand.

```
[6]  #What is the vector representation for a word?
     w2v_model['beautiful']

    array([-0.01831055,  0.05566406, -0.01153564,  0.07275391,  0.15136719,
           -0.06176758,  0.20605469, -0.15332031, -0.05908203,  0.22851562,
           -0.06445312, -0.22851562, -0.09472656, -0.03344727,  0.24707031,
            0.05541992, -0.00921631,  0.1328125 , -0.15429688,  0.08105469,
           -0.07373047,  0.24316406,  0.12353516, -0.09277344,  0.08203125,
            0.06494141,  0.15722656,  0.11279297, -0.0612793 , -0.296875  ,
           -0.13378906,  0.234375  ,  0.09765625,  0.17773438,  0.06689453,
           -0.27539062,  0.06445312, -0.13867188, -0.08886719,  0.171875  ,
            0.07861328, -0.10058594,  0.23925781,  0.03808594,  0.18652344,
           -0.11279297,  0.22558594,  0.10986328, -0.11865234,  0.02026367,
            0.11376953,  0.09570312,  0.29492188,  0.08251953, -0.05444336,
           -0.0090332 , -0.0625    , -0.17578125, -0.08154297,  0.01062012,
           -0.04736328, -0.08544922, -0.19042969, -0.30273438,  0.07617188,
            0.125     , -0.05932617,  0.03833008, -0.03564453,  0.2421875 ,
            0.36132812,  0.04760742,  0.00631714, -0.03088379, -0.13964844,
            0.22558594, -0.06298828, -0.02636719,  0.1171875 ,  0.33398438,
           -0.07666016, -0.06689453,  0.04150391, -0.15136719, -0.22460938,
            0.03320312, -0.15332031,  0.07128906,  0.16992188,  0.11572266,
           -0.13085938,  0.12451172, -0.20410156,  0.04736328, -0.296875  ,
           -0.17480469,  0.00872803, -0.04638672,  0.10791016, -0.203125  ,
           -0.27539062,  0.2734375 ,  0.02563477, -0.11035156,  0.0625    ,
            0.1953125 ,  0.16015625, -0.13769531, -0.09863281, -0.1953125 ,
           -0.22851562,  0.25390625,  0.00915527, -0.03857422,  0.3984375 ,
           -0.1796875 ,  0.03833008, -0.24804688,  0.03515625,  0.03881836,
            0.03442383, -0.04101562,  0.20214844, -0.03015137, -0.09619141,
            0.11669922, -0.06738281,  0.0625    ,  0.10742188,  0.25585938,
           -0.21777344,  0.05639648, -0.0065918 ,  0.16113281,  0.11865234,
           -0.03088379, -0.11572266,  0.02685547,  0.03100586,  0.09863281,
            0.05883789,  0.00634766,  0.11914062,  0.07324219, -0.01586914,
            0.18457031,  0.05322266,  0.19824219, -0.22363281, -0.25195312,
            0.15039062,  0.22753906,  0.05737305,  0.16992188, -0.22558594,
            0.06494141,  0.11914062, -0.06640625, -0.10449219, -0.07226562,
           -0.16992188,  0.0625    ,  0.14648438,  0.27148438, -0.02172852,
           -0.12695312,  0.18457031, -0.27539062, -0.36523438, -0.03491211,
           -0.18554688,  0.23828125, -0.13867188,  0.00296021,  0.04272461,
            0.13867188,  0.12207031,  0.05957031, -0.22167969, -0.18945312,
           -0.23242188, -0.28710938, -0.00866699, -0.16113281, -0.24316406,
            0.05712891, -0.06982422,  0.00053406, -0.10302734, -0.13378906,
           -0.16113281,  0.11621094,  0.31640625, -0.02697754, -0.01574707,
            0.11425781, -0.04174805,  0.05908203,  0.0266113 , -0.08642578,
            0.140625  ,  0.09228516, -0.25195312, -0.31445312, -0.05688477,
            0.01031494,  0.0234375 , -0.02331543, -0.08056641,  0.01269531,
           -0.34179688,  0.17285156, -0.16015625,  0.07763672, -0.03088379,
            0.11962891,  0.11767578,  0.20117188, -0.01940918,  0.02172852,
            0.23046875,  0.28125   , -0.17675781,  0.02978516,  0.08740234,
           -0.06176758,  0.00939941, -0.09277344, -0.203125  ,  0.13085938,
           -0.13671875, -0.00500488, -0.04296875,  0.12988281,  0.3515625 ,
            0.0402832 , -0.12988281, -0.03173828,  0.28515625,  0.18261719,
            0.13867188, -0.16503906, -0.26171875, -0.04345703,  0.0100708 ,
            0.08740234,  0.00421143, -0.1328125 , -0.17578125, -0.04321289,
           -0.015625  ,  0.16894531,  0.25      ,  0.37109375,  0.19921875,
           -0.36132812, -0.10302734, -0.20800781, -0.20117188, -0.01519775,
           -0.12207031, -0.12011719, -0.07421875, -0.04345703,  0.14160156,
            0.15527344, -0.03027344, -0.09326172, -0.04589844,  0.16796875,
           -0.03027344,  0.09179688, -0.10058594,  0.20703125,  0.11376953,
           -0.12402344,  0.04003906,  0.06933594, -0.34570312,  0.03881836,
            0.16210938,  0.05761719, -0.12792969, -0.05810547,  0.03857422,
           -0.11328125, -0.1953125 , -0.28125   , -0.13183594,  0.15722656,
           -0.09765625,  0.09619141, -0.09960938, -0.00285339, -0.03637695,
            0.15429688,  0.06152344, -0.34570312,  0.11083984,  0.03344727],
          dtype=float32)
```

Figure 3-6. Vector representing the word "beautiful" in pre-trained Word2vec

Now let's look at training our own word embeddings.

Distributed Representations | 97

Training our own embeddings

Now we'll focus on training our own word embeddings. For this, we'll look at two architectural variants that were proposed in the original Word2vec approach. The two variants are:

- Continuous bag of words (CBOW)
- SkipGram

Both of these have a lot of similarities in many respects. We'll begin by understanding the CBOW model, then we'll look at SkipGram. Throughout this section, we'll use the sentence "The quick brown fox jumps over the lazy dog" as our toy corpus.

CBOW. In CBOW, the primary task is to build a language model that correctly predicts the center word given the context words in which the center word appears. What is a language model? It is a (statistical) *model* that tries to give a probability distribution over sequences of words. Given a sentence of, say, m words, it assigns a probability $Pr(w_1, w_2, ..., w_n)$ to the whole sentence. The objective of a language model is to assign probabilities in such a way that it gives high probability to "good" sentences and low probabilities to "bad" sentences. By good, we mean sentences that are semantically and syntactically correct. By bad, we mean sentences that are incorrect—semantically or syntactically or both. So, for a sentence like "The cat jumped over the dog," it will try to assign a probability close to 1.0, whereas for a sentence like "jumped over the the cat dog," it tries to assign a probability close to 0.0.

CBOW tries to learn a language model that tries to predict the "center" word from the words in its context. Let's understand this using our toy corpus. If we take the word "jumps" as the center word, then its context is formed by words in its vicinity. If we take the context size of 2, then for our example, the context is given by brown, fox, over, the. CBOW uses the context words to predict the target word—jumps—as shown in Figure 3-7. CBOW tries to do this for every word in the corpus; i.e., it takes every word in the corpus as the target word and tries to predict the target word from its corresponding context words.

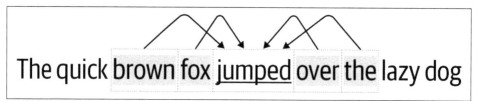

The quick brown fox jumped over the lazy dog

Figure 3-7. CBOW: given the context words, predict the center word

The idea discussed in the previous paragraph is then extended to the entire corpus to build the training set. Details are as follows: we run a sliding window of size $2k+1$ over the text corpus. For our example, we took k as 2. Each position of the window marks the set of $2k+1$ words that are under consideration. The center word in the window is the target, and k words on either side of the center word form the context. This gives us one data point. If the point is represented as (X, Y), then the context is the X and the target word is the Y. A single data point consists of a pair of numbers: ($2k$ indices of words in context, index of word in target). To get the next data point, we simply shift the window to the right on the corpus by one word and repeat the process. This way, we slide the window across the entire corpus to create the training set. This is shown in Figure 3-8. Here, the target word is shown in blue and $k=2$.

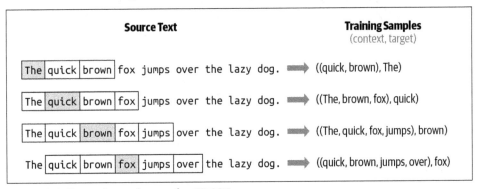

Figure 3-8. Preparing a dataset for CBOW

Now that we have the training data ready, let's focus on the model. For this, we construct a shallow net (it's shallow since it has a single hidden layer), as shown in Figure 3-9. We assume we want to learn D-dim word embeddings. Further, let V be the vocabulary of the text corpus.

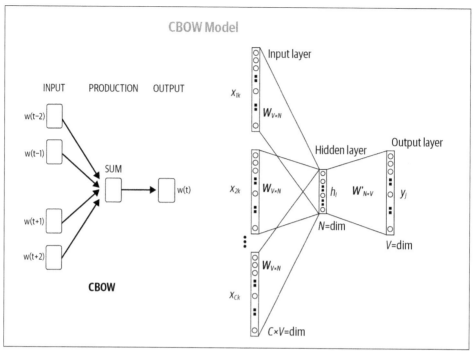

Figure 3-9. CBOW model [7]

The objective is to learn an embedding matrix $E_{|V| \times d}$. To begin with, we initialize the matrix randomly. Here, $|V|$ is the size of corpus vocabulary and d is the dimension of the embedding. Let's break down the shallow net in Figure 3-9 layer by layer. In the input layer, indices of the words in context are used to fetch the corresponding rows from the embedding matrix $E_{|V| \times d}$. The vectors fetched are then added to get a single D-dim vector, and this is passed to the next layer. The next layer simply takes this d vector and multiplies it with another matrix $E'_{d \times |V|}$. This gives a 1 x $|V|$ vector, which is fed to a softmax function to get probability distribution over the vocabulary space. This distribution is compared with the label and uses back propagation to update both the matrices E and E' accordingly. At the end of the training, E is the embedding matrix[iii] we wanted to learn.

---

iii. Technically speaking, both E and E' are two different learned embeddings. You can use either of them or even combine the two by simply averaging them.

SkipGram. SkipGram is very similar to CBOW, with some minor changes. In Skip-Gram, the task is to predict the context words from the center word. For our toy corpus with context size 2, using the center word "jumps," we try to predict every word in context—"brown," "fox," "over," "the"—as shown in Figure 3-10. This constitutes one step. SkipGram repeats this one step for every word in the corpus as the center word.

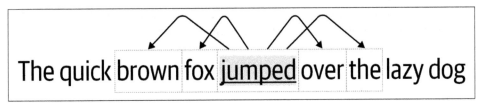

Figure 3-10. SkipGram: given the center word, predict every word in context

The dataset to train a SkipGram is prepared as follows: we run a sliding window of size $2k+1$ over the text corpus to get the set of $2k+1$ words that are under consideration. The center word in the window is the X, and k words on either side of the center word are Y. Unlike CBOW, this gives us $2k$ data points. A single data point consists of a pair: (index of the center word, index of a target word). We then shift the window to the right on the corpus by one word and repeat the process. This way, we slide the window across the entire corpus to create the training set. This is shown in Figure 3-11.

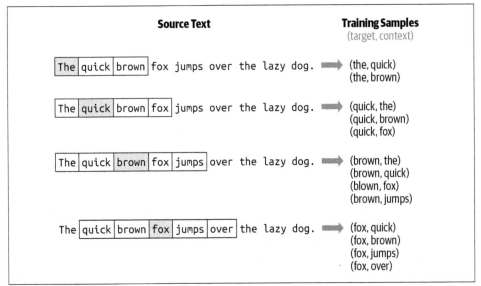

Figure 3-11. Preparing a dataset for SkipGram

The shallow network used to train the SkipGram model, shown in Figure 3-12, is very similar to the network used for CBOW, with some minor changes. In the input layer, the index of the word in the target is used to fetch the corresponding row from the embedding matrix $E_{|V| \times d}$. The vectors fetched are then passed to the next layer. The next layer simply takes this d vector and multiplies it with another matrix $E'_{d \times |V|}$. This gives a $1 \times |V|$ vector, which is fed to a softmax function to get probability distribution over the vocabulary space. This distribution is compared with the label and uses back propagation to update both the matrices E and E' accordingly. At the end of the training, E is the embedding matrix we wanted to learn.

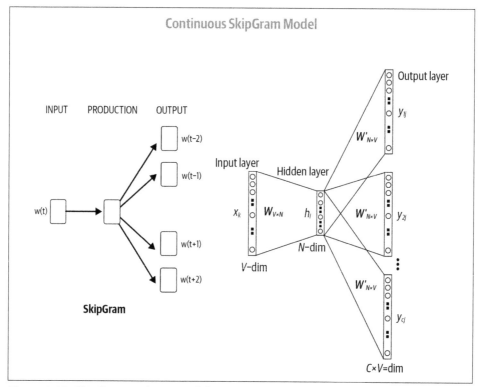

Figure 3-12. SkipGram architecture [7]

There are a lot of other minute details that go into both CBOW and the SkipGram model. An interested reader can look at the three-part blog post by Sebastian Ruder [11]. You can also refer to Rong (2016) [12] for a step-by-step derivation of Word2vec parameter learning. Another key aspect to keep in mind is hyperparameters of the model. There are several hyperparameters: window size, dimensionality of the vectors to be learned, learning rate, number of epochs, etc. It's a well-established fact that hyperparameters play a crucial role in the quality of the final model [13, 14].

To use both the CBOW and SkipGram algorithms in practice, there are several available implementations that abstract the mathematical details for us. One of the most commonly used implementations is gensim [15].

Despite the availability of several off-the-shelf implementations, we still have to make decisions on several hyperparameters (i.e., the variables that need to be set before starting the training process). Let's look at two examples.

Dimensionality of the word vectors
As the name indicates, this decides the space of the learned embeddings. While there is no ideal number, it's common to construct word vectors with dimensions in the range of 50–500 and evaluate them on the task we're using them for to choose the best option.

Context window
How long or short the context we look for to learn the vector representation is.

There are also other choices we make, such as whether to use CBOW or SkipGram to learn the embeddings. These choices are more of an art than science at this point, and there's a lot of ongoing research on methods for choosing the right hyperparameters.

Using packages like gensim, it's pretty straightforward from a code point of view to implement Word2vec. The following code shows how to train our own Word2vec model using a toy corpus called common_texts that's available in gensim. Assuming you have the corpus for your domain, following this code snippet will quickly give you your own embeddings:

```
#Import a test data set provided in gensim to train a model
from gensim.test.utils import common_texts
#Build the model, by selecting the parameters.
our_model = Word2Vec(common_texts, size=10, window=5, min_count=1, workers=4)
#Save the model
our_model.save("tempmodel.w2v")
#Inspect the model by looking for the most similar words for a test word.
print(our_model.wv.most_similar('computer', topn=5))
#Let us see what the 10-dimensional vector for 'computer' looks like.
print(our_model['computer'])
```

Now, we can get the vector representation for any word in our corpus, provided it's in the model's vocabulary—we just look up the word in the model. But what if we have a phrase (e.g., "word embeddings") for which we need a vector?

Going Beyond Words

So far, we've seen examples of how to use pre-trained word embeddings and train our own word embeddings. This gives us a compact and dense representation for words in our vocabulary. However, in most NLP applications, we seldom deal with atomic units like words—we deal with sentences, paragraphs, or even full texts. So, we need a way to represent larger units of text. Is there a way we can use word embeddings to get feature representations for larger units of text?

A simple approach is to break the text into constituent words, take the embeddings for individual words, and combine them to form the representation for the text. There are various ways to combine them, the most popular being sum, average, etc., but these may not capture many aspects of the text as a whole, such as ordering. Surprisingly, they work very well in practice (see Chapter 4). As a matter of fact, in CBOW, this was demonstrated by taking the sum of word vectors in context. The resulting vector represents the entire context and is used to predict the center word.

It's always a good idea to experiment with this before moving to other representations. The following code shows how to obtain the vector representation for text by averaging word vectors using the library spaCy [16]:

```
import spacy
import en_core_web_sm

# Load the spacy model. This takes a few seconds.
nlp = en_core_web_sm.load()

# Process a sentence using the model
doc = nlp("Canada is a large country")

#Get a vector for individual words
#print(doc[0].vector) #vector for 'Canada', the first word in the text
print(doc.vector) #Averaged vector for the entire sentence
```

Both pre-trained and self-trained word embeddings depend on the vocabulary they see in the training data. However, there is no guarantee that we will only see those words in the production data for the application we're building. Despite the ease of using Word2vec or any such word embedding to do feature extraction from texts, we don't have a good way of handling OOV words yet. This has been a recurring problem in all the representations we've seen so far. What do we do in such cases?

A simple approach that often works is to exclude those words from the feature extraction process so we don't have to worry about how to get their representations. If we're using a model trained on a large corpus, we shouldn't see too many OOV words anyway. However, if a large fraction of the words from our production data isn't present in the word embedding's vocabulary, we're unlikely to see good performance. This vocabulary overlap is a great heuristic to gauge the performance of an NLP model.

 If the overlap between corpus vocabulary and embedding vocabulary is less than 80%, we're unlikely to see good performance from our NLP model.

Even if the overlap is above 80%, the model can still do poorly depending on which words fall in the 20%. If these words are important for the task, then this is very possible. For example, say we want to build a classifier that can classify medical documents on cancer from medical documents on the heart. Now, in this case, certain terms like heart, cancer, etc., will become important for differentiating the two sets of documents. If these terms are not present in the word embedding's vocabulary, our classifier might still do poorly.

Another way to deal with the OOV problem for word embeddings is to create vectors that are initialized randomly, where each component is between –0.25 to +0.25, and continue to use these vectors throughout the application we're building [17, 18]. From our own experience, this can give us a jump of 1–2% in performance.

There are also other approaches that handle the OOV problem by modifying the training process by bringing in characters and other subword-level linguistic components. Let's look at one such approach now. The key idea is that one can potentially handle the OOV problem by using subword information, such as morphological properties (e.g., prefixes, suffixes, word endings, etc.), or by using character representations. fastText [19], from Facebook AI research, is one of the popular algorithms that follows this approach. A word can be represented by its constituent character n-grams. Following a similar architecture to Word2vec, fastText learns embeddings for words and character n-grams together and views a word's embedding vector as an aggregation of its constituent character n-grams. This makes it possible to generate embeddings even for words that are not present in the vocabulary. Say there's a word, "gregarious," that's not found in the embedding's word vocabulary. We break it into character n-grams—gre, reg, ega, ...ous—and combine these embeddings of the n-grams to arrive at the embedding of "gregarious."

Pre-trained fastText models can be downloaded from their website [20], and gensim's fastText wrapper can be used both for loading pre-trained models or training models using fastText in a way similar to Word2vec. We leave that as an exercise for the reader. In Chapter 4, we'll see how to use fastText embeddings for text classification. Now, we'll take a look at some distributed representations that move beyond words.

Distributed Representations Beyond Words and Characters

So far, we've seen two approaches to coming up with text representations using embeddings. Word2vec learned representations for words, and we aggregated them to form text representations. fastText learned representations for character n-grams, which were aggregated to form word representations and then text representations. A potential problem with both approaches is that they do not take the context of words into account. Take, for example, the sentences "dog bites man" and "man bites dog."

Both receive the same representation in these approaches, but they obviously have very different meanings. Let's look at another approach, Doc2vec, which allows us to directly learn the representations for texts of arbitrary lengths (phrases, sentences, paragraphs, and documents) by taking the context of words in the text into account.

Doc2vec is based on the paragraph vectors framework [21] and is implemented in gensim. This is similar to Word2vec in terms of its general architecture, except that, in addition to the word vectors, it also learns a "paragraph vector" that learns a representation for the full text (i.e., with words in context). When learning with a large corpus of many texts, the paragraph vectors are unique for a given text (where "text" can mean any piece of text of arbitrary length), while word vectors will be shared across all texts. The shallow neural networks used to learn Doc2vec embeddings (Figure 3-13) are very similar to the CBOW and SkipGram architecture of Word2vec. The two architectures are called *distributed memory (DM)* and *distributed bag of words (DBOW)*. They are shown in Figure 3-13.

Once the Doc2vec model is trained, paragraph vectors for new texts are inferred using the common word vectors from training. Doc2vec was perhaps the first widely accessible implementation for getting an embedding representation for the full text instead of using a combination of individual word vectors. Since it models some form of context and can encode texts of arbitrary length into a fixed, low-dimensional, dense vector, it has found application in a wide range of NLP applications, such as text classification, document tagging, text recommendation systems, and simple chatbots for FAQs. We'll see an example of training a Doc2vec representation and using it for text classification in the next chapter. Let's look at other text representation methods that extend this idea of taking full text into account.

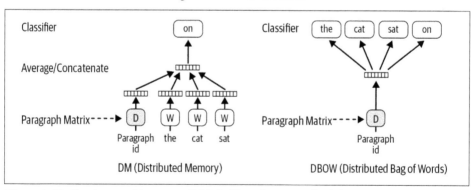

Figure 3-13. Doc2vec architectures: DM (left) and DBOW (right)

Universal Text Representations

In all the representations we've seen so far, we notice that one word gets one fixed representation. Can this be a problem? Well, to some extent, yes. Words can mean different things in different contexts. For example, the sentences "I went to a bank to withdraw money" and "I sat by the river bank and pondered about text representations" both use the word "bank." However, they mean different things in each sentence. With the vectorization and embedding approaches that we've seen so far, there's no direct way to capture this information.

In 2018, researchers came up with the idea of *contextual word representations*, which addresses this issue. It uses "language modeling," which is the task of predicting the next likely word in a sequence of words. In its earliest form, it used the idea of n-gram frequencies to estimate the probability of the next word given a history of words. The past few years have seen the advent of advanced neural language models (e.g., transformers [22, 23]) that make use of the word embeddings we discussed earlier but use complex architectures involving multiple passes through the text and multiple reads from left to right and right to left to model the context of language use.

Neural architectures such as recurrent neural networks (RNNs) and transformers were used to develop large-scale models of language (ELMo [24], BERT [25]), which can be used as pre-trained models to get text representations. The key idea is to leverage "transfer learning"—that is, to learn embeddings on a generic task (like language modeling) on a massive corpus and then fine-tune learnings on task-specific data. These models have shown significant improvements on some fundamental NLP tasks, such as question answering, semantic role labeling, named entity recognition, and coreference resolution, to name a few. We briefly described what some of these tasks are in Chapter 1. Interested readers can go through the references, including the upcoming book by Taher and Collados [26].

In the last three sections, we looked at the key ideas behind word embeddings, how to train them, and how to use pre-trained embeddings to get text representations. We'll learn more about how to use these representations in different NLP applications in the coming chapters. These representations are very useful and popular in modern-day NLP. However, based on our experience, here are a few important aspects to keep in mind while using them in your project:

- All text representations are inherently biased based on what they saw in training data. For example, an embedding model trained heavily on technology news or articles is likely to identify Apple as being closer to, say, Microsoft or Facebook than to an orange or pear. While this is anecdotal, such biases stemming from training data can have serious implications on the performance of NLP models and systems that rely on these representations. Understanding biases that may be present in learned embeddings and developing methods for addressing them is very important. An interested reader can look at Tolga et al. [27]. These biases are an important factor to consider in any NLP software development.

- Unlike the basic vectorization approaches, pre-trained embeddings are generally large-sized files (several gigabytes), which may pose problems in certain deployment scenarios. This is something we need to address while using them, otherwise it can become an engineering bottleneck in performance. The Word2vec model takes ~4.5 GB RAM. One good hack is to use in-memory databases like Redis [28] with a cache on top of them to address scaling and latency issues. Load your embeddings into such databases and use the embeddings as if they're available in RAM.

- Modeling language for a real-world application is more than capturing the information via word and sentence embeddings. We still need ways to encode specific aspects of text, the relationships between sentences in it, and any other domain- and application-specific needs that may not be addressed by the embedding representations themselves (yet!). For example, the task of sarcasm detection requires nuances that are not yet captured well by embedding techniques.

- As we speak, neural text representation is an evolving area in NLP, with rapidly changing state of the art. While it's easy to get carried away by the next big model in the news, a practitioner needs to exercise caution and consider practical issues such as return on investment from the effort, business needs, and infrastructural constraints before trying to use them in production-grade applications.

An interested reader may refer to Smith [29] for a concise summary of the evolution of different word representations and the research challenges ahead for neural network models of text representation. Now, let's move on to techniques for visualizing embeddings.

Visualizing Embeddings

So far, we've seen various vectorization techniques for representing text. The vectors obtained are used as features for the NLP task at hand, be it text classification or a question-answering system. An important aspect of any ML project is feature exploration. How can we explore the vectors that we have to work with? Visual exploration is a very important aspect of any data-related problem. Is there a way to visually inspect word vectors? Even though embeddings are low-dimensional vectors, even 100 or 300 dimensions are too high to visualize.

Enter t-SNE [30], or *t-distributed Stochastic Neighboring Embedding*. It's a technique used for visualizing high-dimensional data like embeddings by reducing them to two- or three-dimensional data. The technique takes in the embeddings (or any data) and looks at how to best represent the input data using lesser dimensions, all while maintaining the same data distributions in original high-dimensional input space and low-dimensional output space. This, therefore, enables us to plot and visualize the input data. It helps to get a feel for the space of word embedding.

Let's look at some visualizations using t-SNE. First, we look at feature vectors obtained from the MNIST digits dataset [31]. Here, the images are passed through a convolution neural network and the final feature vectors. Figure 3-14 shows the two-dimensional plot of the vectors. It clearly shows that our feature vectors are very useful since vectors of the same class tend to cluster together.

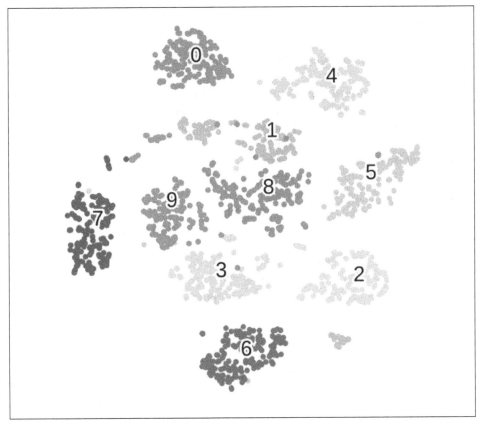

Figure 3-14. Visualizing MNIST data using t-SNE [32]

Let's now visualize word embeddings. In Figure 3-15, we show only a few words. The interesting thing to note is that the words that have similar meanings tend to cluster together.

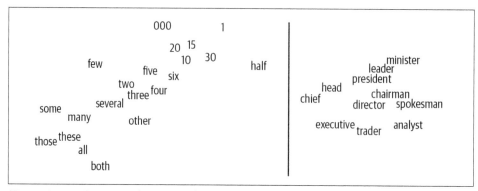

Figure 3-15. t-SNE visualizations of word embeddings (eft: numbers, right: job titles [33]

Let's look at another word embedding visualization, probably the most famous one in the NLP community. Figure 3-16 shows two-dimensional visualization of embedding vectors for a subset of words: man, woman, uncle, aunt, king, queen. Figure 3-16 shows not only the position of the vectors of these words, but also an interesting observation between the vectors—the arrows capture the "relationship" between words. t-SNE visualization helps greatly in coming up with such nice observations.

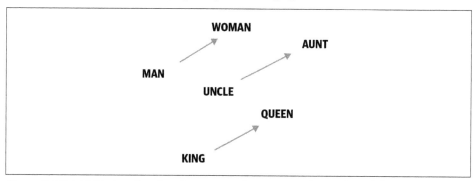

Figure 3-16. t-SNE visualization shows some interesting relationships [7]

t-SNE works equally well for visualizing document embeddings. For example, we might take Wikipedia articles on various topics, obtain corresponding document vectors for each article, then plot these vectors using t-SNE. The visualization in Figure 3-17 clearly shows that articles in a given category are grouped together.

Clearly, t-SNE is very useful for eyeballing the quality of feature vectors. We can use tools like the embedding projector from TensorBoard [34] to visualize embeddings in our day-to-day work. As shown in Figure 3-18, TensorBoard has a nice interface that is tailor-made for visualizing embeddings. We leave it as an exercise for the reader to explore it further. For more on t-SNE, you can read the excellent article on using t-SNE more effectively by Martin et al. [35].

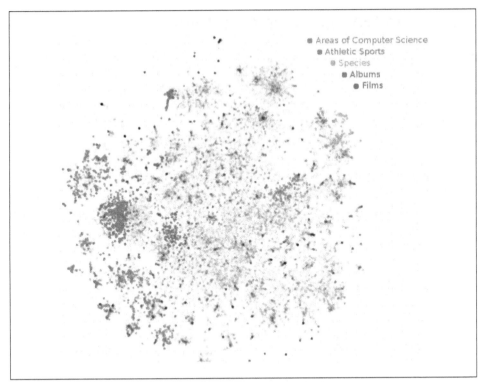

Figure 3-17. Visualization of Wikipedia document vectors [36]

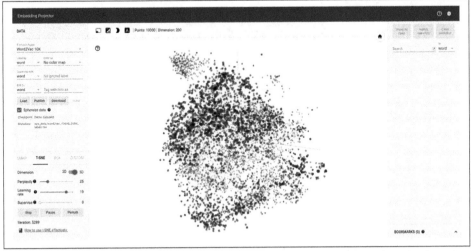

Figure 3-18. Screenshot of TensorBoard interface for visualizing embeddings [37]

Handcrafted Feature Representations

So far in this chapter, we've seen various feature representation schemes that are learned from a text corpus, large or small. These feature representations are mostly not dependent on the NLP problem or application domain.[iv] The same approach works whether we want text representation for information extraction or text classification and whether we work with a corpus of tweets or scientific articles.

However, in many cases, we do have some domain-specific knowledge about the given NLP problem, which we would like to incorporate into the model we're building. In such cases, we resort to handcrafted features. Let's take an example of a real-world NLP system: TextEvaluator [38]. It's software developed by Educational Testing Service (ETS). The goal of this tool is to help teachers and educators provide support in choosing grade-appropriate reading materials for students and identifying sources of comprehension difficulty in texts. Clearly, this is a very specific problem. Having general-purpose word embeddings will not help much. It needs specialized features extracted from text to model some form of grade appropriateness. The screenshot in Figure 3-19 shows some of the specialized features that are extracted from text for various dimensions of text complexity they model. Clearly, measures such as "syntactic complexity," "concreteness," etc., cannot be calculated by only converting text into BoW or embedding representations. They have to be designed manually, keeping in mind both the domain knowledge and the ML algorithms to train the NLP models. This is why we call these *handcrafted feature representations*.

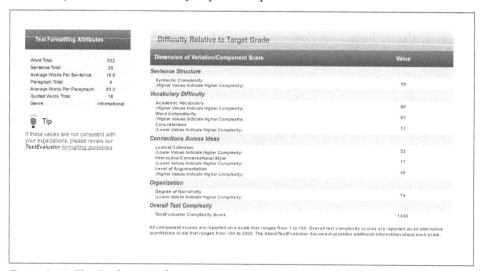

Figure 3-19. TextEvaluator software output requiring handcrafted features [38]

---

iv. Unless they've been fine-tuned for the task at hand.

Another software tool from ETS that's popular for grading is the automated essay scorer used in online exams, such as the Graduate Record Examination (GRE) and Test of English as a Foreign Language (TOEFL), to evaluate test-taker essays [39]. This tool, too, requires handcrafted features. Evaluating an essay for various aspects of writing requires specialized features that address those needs. One cannot rely only on n-grams or word embeddings. Another NLP application where one may need such specialized feature engineering is the spelling and grammar correction we use in tools such as Microsoft Word, Grammarly, etc. These are all examples of commonly used tools where we often need custom features to incorporate domain knowledge.

Clearly, custom feature engineering is much more difficult to formulate compared to other feature engineering schemes we've seen so far. It's for this reason that vectorization approaches are more accessible to get started with, especially when we don't have enough understanding of the domain. Still, handcrafted features are very common in several real-world applications. In most industrial application scenarios, we end up combining the problem-agnostic feature representations we saw earlier (basic vectorization and distributed representations) with some domain-specific features to develop hybrid features. Recent studies from IBM Research [40] and Walmart [41] show examples of how heuristics, handcrafted features, and ML are all used together in real-world industrial systems dealing with NLP problems. We'll see some examples of how to use such handcrafted features in upcoming chapters, such as text classification (Chapter 4) and information extraction (Chapter 5).

Wrapping Up

In this chapter, we saw different techniques for representing text, starting from the basic approaches to state-of-the-art DL methods. A question that may arise organically at this point would be: when should we go for vectorization features and embeddings, and when should we look for handcrafted features? The answer is that it depends on the task at hand. For some applications, such as text classification, it's more common to see vectorization approaches and embeddings as the go-to feature representations for text. For some other applications, such as information extraction, or in the examples we saw in the previous section, it's more common to look for handcrafted, domain-specific features. Quite often, a hybrid approach that combines both kinds of features are used in practice. Having said that, vectorization-based approaches are a great starting point.

We hope the discussion and various perspectives presented in this chapter gave you a good idea about the role of text representation in NLP, different techniques for representing text, and their respective pros and cons. In the next chapters, we'll move on to solving some of the essential NLP tasks (Chapters 4–7), where we'll see different text representations being put to use, starting with text representation.

References

[1] Bansal, Suraj. "Convolutional Neural Networks Explained" (*https://oreil.ly/8dbxV*). December 28, 2019.

[2] Manning, C., Hinrich Schütze, and Prabhakar Raghavan. *Introduction to Information Retrieval.* Cambridge: Cambridge University Press, 2008. ISBN: 978-0-521-86571-5

[3] Jurafsky, Dan and James H. Martin. *Speech and Language Processing*, Third Edition (Draft) (*https://oreil.ly/Ta16f*), 2018.

[4] scikit-learn.org. TFIDF vectorizer documentation (*https://oreil.ly/ukjam*). Last accessed June 15, 2020.

[5] Firth, John R. "A Synopsis of Linguistic Theory 1930–1955." *Studies in Linguistic Analysis* (1968).

[6] Ferrone, Lorenzo, and Fabio Massimo Zanzotto. "Symbolic, Distributed and Distributional Representations for Natural Language Processing in the Era of Deep Learning: A Survey" (*https://oreil.ly/c4x8M*), (2017).

[7] Mikolov, Tomas, Kai Chen, Greg Corrado, and Jeffrey Dean. "Efficient Estimation of Word Representations in Vector Space" (*https://oreil.ly/q35QS*), (2013).

[8] Google. Word2vec pre-trained model (*https://oreil.ly/tYfdH*). Last accessed June 15, 2020.

[9] Pennington, Jeffrey, Richard Socher, and Christopher D. Manning. "GloVe: Global Vectors for Word Representation" (*https://oreil.ly/3f1E5*). Last accessed June 15, 2020.

[10] Facebook. fastText pre-trained model (*https://oreil.ly/9qj4C*). Last accessed June 15, 2020.

[11] Ruder, Sebastian. Three-part blog series on word embeddings. *https://oreil.ly/OkJnx, https://oreil.ly/bjygp,* and *https://oreil.ly/GHgg9.* Last accessed June 15, 2020.

[12] Rong, Xin. "word2vec parameter learning explained" (*https://oreil.ly/Z8KUe*), (2014).

[13] Levy, Omer, Yoav Goldberg, and Ido Dagan. "Improving Distributional Similarity with Lessons Learned from Word Embeddings." *Transactions of the Association for Computational Linguistics* 3 (2015): 211–225.

[14] Levy, Omer and Yoav Goldberg. "Neural Word Embedding as Implicit Matrix Factorization." *Proceedings of the 27th International Conference on Neural Information Processing Systems* 2 (2014): 2177–2185.

[15] RaRe Technologies. gensim: Topic Modelling for Humans (*https://oreil.ly/4dG6S*), (GitHub repo). Last accessed June 15, 2020.

[16] Explosion.ai. "spaCy: Industrial-Strength Natural Language Processing in Python" (*https://spacy.io/*). Last accessed June 15, 2020.

[17] word2vec-toolkit Google Group discussion (*https://oreil.ly/OKbU8*). Last accessed June 15, 2020.

[18] Code for: Kim, Yoon. "Convolutional neural networks for sentence classification" (*https://oreil.ly/QWqwT*). (2014).

[19] Facebook Open Source. "fastText: Library for efficient text classification and representation learning" (*https://fasttext.cc*). Last accessed June 15, 2020.

[20] Facebook Open Source. "English word vectors" (*https://oreil.ly/sycR0*). Last accessed June 15, 2020.

[21] Le, Quoc, and Tomas Mikolov. "Distributed Representations of Sentences and Documents." *Proceedings of the 31st International Conference on Machine Learning* (2014): 1188–1196.

[22] Vaswani, Ashish, Noam Shazeer, Niki Parmar, Jakob Uszkoreit, Llion Jones, Aidan N. Gomez, Łukasz Kaiser, and Illia Polosukhin. "Attention is All You Need." *Advances in Neural Information Processing Systems* 30 (NIPS 2017): 5998–6008.

[23] Wang, Chenguang, Mu Li, and Alexander J. Smola. "Language Models with Transformers" (*https://oreil.ly/HZ4Mh*), (2019).

[24] Allen Institute for AI. "ELMo: Deep contextualized word representations" (*https://oreil.ly/PKRst*). Last accessed June 15, 2020.

[25] Google Research. bert: TensorFlow code and pre-trained models for BERT (*https://oreil.ly/7oYQo*), (GitHub repo). Last accessed June 15, 2020.

[26] Pilehvar, Mohammad Taher and Jose Camacho-Collados. "Embeddings in Natural Language Processing: Theory and Advances in Vector Representation of Meaning." *Synthesis Lectures on Human Language Technologies*. Morgan & Claypool, 2020.

[27] Bolukbasi, Tolga, Kai-Wei Chang, James Y. Zou, Venkatesh Saligrama, and Adam T. Kalai. "Man Is to Computer Programmer as Woman Is to Homemaker? Debiasing Word Embeddings." *Advances in Neural Information Processing Systems* 29 (NIPS 2016): 4349–4357.

[28] Redis (*https://redis.io*). Last accessed June 15, 2020.

[29] Smith, Noah A. "Contextual Word Representations: A Contextual Introduction" (*https://oreil.ly/DIA_h*), (2019).

[30] Maaten, Laurens van der and Geoffrey Hinton. "Visualizing Data Using t-SNE." *Journal of Machine Learning Research* 9, Nov. (2008): 2579–2605.

[31] Le Cun, Yann, Corinna Cortes, and Christopher J.C. Burges. "The MNIST database of handwritten digits" (*https://oreil.ly/qv6ao*). Last accessed June 15, 2020.

[32] Rossant, Cyril. "An illustrated introduction to the t-SNE algorithm" (*https://oreil.ly/0tN2S*). March 3, 2015.

[33] Turian, Joseph, Lev Ratinov, and Yoshua Bengio. "Word Representations: A Simple and General Method for Semi-Supervised Learning." *Proceedings of the 48th Annual Meeting of the Association for Computational Linguistics* (2020): 384–394.

[34] TensorFlow. "Word embeddings" (*https://oreil.ly/JLXGL*) tutorial. Last accessed June 15, 2020.

[35] Wattenberg, Martin, Fernanda Viégas, and Ian Johnson. "How to Use t-SNE Effectively." *Distill* 1.10 (2016): e2.

[36] Dai, Andrew M., Christopher Olah, and Quoc V. Le. "Document Embedding with Paragraph Vectors" (*https://oreil.ly/gyaiC*), (2015).

[37] TensorFlow. "Embedding Projector" (*https://oreil.ly/eGpUV*). Last accessed June 15, 2020.

[38] Educational Testing Service. "TextEvaluator" (*https://oreil.ly/cJ6uK*). Last accessed June 15, 2020.

[39] Educational Testing Service. "Automated Scoring of Written Responses" (*https://oreil.ly/dksDo*), 2019.

[40] Chiticariu, L., Yunyao Li, and Frederick R. Reiss. "Rule-Based Information Extraction is Dead! Long Live Rule-Based Information Extraction Systems!" *Proceedings of the 2013 Conference on Empirical Methods in Natural Language Processing* (2013): 827–832.

[41] Suganthan G.C., Paul, Chong Sun, Haojun Zhang, Frank Yang, Narasimhan Rampalli, Shishir Prasad, Esteban Arcaute, et al. "Why Big Data Industrial Systems Need Rules and What We Can Do About It." *Proceedings of the 2015 ACM SIGMOD International Conference on Management of Data* (2015): 265–276.

## PART II

Essentials

## CHAPTER 4

Text Classification

Organizing is what you do before you do something,
so that when you do it, it is not all mixed up.
—A.A. Milne

All of us check email every day, possibly multiple times. A useful feature of most email service providers is the ability to automatically segregate spam emails away from regular emails. This is a use case of a popular NLP task known as *text classification*, which is the focus of this chapter. Text classification is the task of assigning one or more categories to a given piece of text from a larger set of possible categories. In the email spam–identifier example, we have two categories—spam and non-spam—and each incoming email is assigned to one of these categories. This task of categorizing texts based on some properties has a wide range of applications across diverse domains, such as social media, e-commerce, healthcare, law, and marketing, to name a few. Even though the purpose and application of text classification may vary from domain to domain, the underlying abstract problem remains the same. This invariance of the core problem and its applications in a myriad of domains makes text classification by far the most widely used NLP task in industry and the most researched in academia. In this chapter, we'll discuss the usefulness of text classification and how to build text classifiers for our use cases, along with some practical tips for real-world scenarios.

In machine learning, classification is the problem of categorizing a data instance into one or more known classes. The data point can be originally of different formats, such as text, speech, image, or numeric. Text classification is a special instance of the classification problem, where the input data point(s) is text and the goal is to categorize the piece of text into one or more buckets (called a class) from a set of predefined buckets (classes). The "text" can be of arbitrary length: a character, a word, a sentence, a paragraph, or a full document. Consider a scenario where we want to classify all customer reviews for a product into three categories: positive, negative, and neutral. The challenge of text classification is to "learn" this categorization from a collection of examples for each of these categories and predict the categories for new, unseen products and new customer reviews. This categorization need not always result in a single category, though, and there can be any number of categories available. Let's take a quick look at the taxonomy of text classification to understand this.

Any supervised classification approach, including text classification, can be further distinguished into three types based on the number of categories involved: binary, multiclass, and multilabel classification. If the number of classes is two, it's called *binary classification*. If the number of classes is more than two, it's referred to as *multiclass classification*. Thus, classifying an email as spam or not-spam is an example of binary classification setting. Classifying the sentiment of a customer review as negative, neutral, or positive is an example of multiclass classification. In both binary and multiclass settings, each document belongs to exactly one class from C, where C is the set of all possible classes. In *multilabel classification*, a document can have one or more labels/classes attached to it. For example, a news article on a soccer match may belong to more than one category, such as "sports" and "soccer," simultaneously, whereas another news article on US elections may have the labels "politics," "USA," and "elections." Thus, each document has labels that are a subset of C. Each article can be in no class, exactly one class, multiple classes, or all of the classes. Sometimes, the number of labels in the set C can be very large (known as "extreme classification"). In some other scenarios, we may have a hierarchical classification system, which may result in each text getting different labels at different levels in the hierarchy. In this chapter, we'll focus only on binary and multiclass classification, as those are the most common use cases of text classification in the industry.

Text classification is sometimes also referred to as *topic classification, text categorization*, or *document categorization*. For the rest of this book, we'll stick to the term "text classification." Note that topic classification is different from *topic detection*, which refers to the problem of uncovering or extracting "topics" from texts, which we'll study in Chapter 7.

In this chapter, we'll take a closer look at text classification and build text classifiers using different approaches. Our aim is to provide an overview of some of the most commonly applied techniques along with practical advice on handling different scenarios and decisions that have to be made when building text classification systems in practice. We'll start by introducing some common applications of text classification, then we'll discuss what an NLP pipeline for text classification looks like and illustrate the use of this pipeline to train and test text classifiers using different approaches, ranging from the traditional methods to the state of the art. We'll then tackle the problem of training data collection/sparsity and different methods to handle it. We'll end the chapter by summarizing what we learned in all these sections along with some practical advice and a case study.

Note that, in this chapter, we'll only deal with the aspect of training and evaluating the text classifiers. Issues related to deploying NLP systems in general and performing quality assurance will be discussed in Chapter 11.

Applications

Text classification has been of interest in a number of application scenarios, ranging from identifying the author of an unknown text in the 1800s to the efforts of USPS in the 1960s to perform optical character recognition on addresses and zip codes [1]. In the 1990s, researchers began to successfully apply ML algorithms for text classification for large datasets. Email filtering, popularly known as "spam classification," is one of the earliest examples of automatic text classification, which impacts our lives to this day. From manual analyses of text documents to purely statistical, computer-based approaches and state-of-the-art deep neural networks, we've come a long way with text classification. Let's briefly discuss some of the popular applications before diving into the different approaches to perform text classification. These examples will also be useful in identifying problems that can be solved using text classification methods in your organization.

Content classification and organization

This refers to the task of classifying/tagging large amounts of textual data. This, in turn, is used to power use cases like content organization, search engines, and recommendation systems, to name a few. Examples of such data include news websites, blogs, online bookshelves, product reviews, tweets, etc.; tagging product descriptions in an e-commerce website; routing customer service requests in a company to the appropriate support team; and organizing emails into personal, social, and promotions in Gmail are all examples of using text classification for content classification and organization.

Customer support

Customers often use social media to express their opinions about and experiences of products or services. Text classification is often used to identify the tweets that brands must respond to (i.e., those that are actionable) and those that don't require a response (i.e., noise) [2, 3]. To illustrate, consider the three tweets about the brand Macy's shown in Figure 4-1.

Although all three tweets mention the brand Macy's explicitly, only the first one necessitates a reply from Macy's customer support team.

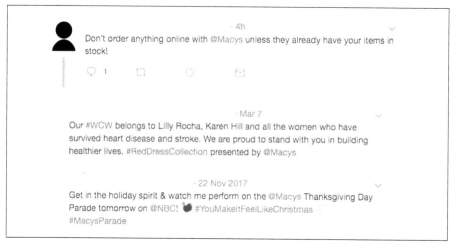

Figure 4-1. Tweets reaching out to brands: one is actionable, the other two are noise

E-commerce

Customers leave reviews for a range of products on e-commerce websites like Amazon, eBay, etc. An example use of text classification in this kind of scenario is to understand and analyze customers' perception of a product or service based on their comments. This is commonly known as "sentiment analysis." It's used extensively by brands across the globe to better understand whether they're getting closer to or farther away from their customers. Rather than categorizing customer feedback as simply positive, negative, or neutral, over a period of time, sentiment analysis has evolved into a more sophisticated paradigm: "aspect"-based sentiment analysis. To understand this, consider the customer review of a restaurant shown in Figure 4-2.

Figure 4-2. A review that praises some aspects and criticizes few

Would you call the review in Figure 4-2 negative, positive, or neutral? It's difficult to answer this—the food was great, but the service was bad. Practitioners and brands working with sentiment analysis have realized that many products or services have multiple facets. In order to understand overall sentiment, understanding each and every facet is important. Text classification plays a major role in performing such fine-grained analysis of customer feedback. We'll discuss this specific application in detail in Chapter 9.

Other applications

Apart from the above-mentioned areas, text classification is also used in several other applications in various domains:

- Text classification is used in language identification, like identifying the language of new tweets or posts. For example, Google Translate has an automatic language identification feature.

- Authorship attribution, or identifying the unknown authors of texts from a pool of authors, is another popular use case of text classification, and it's used in a range of fields from forensic analysis to literary studies.

- Text classification has been used in the recent past for triaging posts in an online support forum for mental health services [4]. In the NLP community, annual competitions are conducted (e.g., clpsych.org) for solving such text classification problems originating from clinical research.

- In the recent past, text classification has also been used to segregate fake news from real news.

Note that this section only serves as an illustration of the wide range of applications of text classification, and the list is not exhaustive, but we hope it gives you enough background to identify text classification problems in your workplace projects when you encounter them. Let's now look at how to build such text classification models.

A Pipeline for Building Text Classification Systems

In Chapter 2, we discussed some of the common NLP pipelines. The text classification pipeline shares some of its steps with the pipelines we learned in that chapter.

One typically follows these steps when building a text classification system:

1. Collect or create a labeled dataset suitable for the task.

2. Split the dataset into two (training and test) or three parts: training, validation (i.e., development), and test sets, then decide on evaluation metric(s).

3. Transform raw text into feature vectors.

4. Train a classifier using the feature vectors and the corresponding labels from the training set.

5. Using the evaluation metric(s) from Step 2, benchmark the model performance on the test set.

6. Deploy the model to serve the real-world use case and monitor its performance.

Figure 4-3 shows these typical steps in building a text classification system.

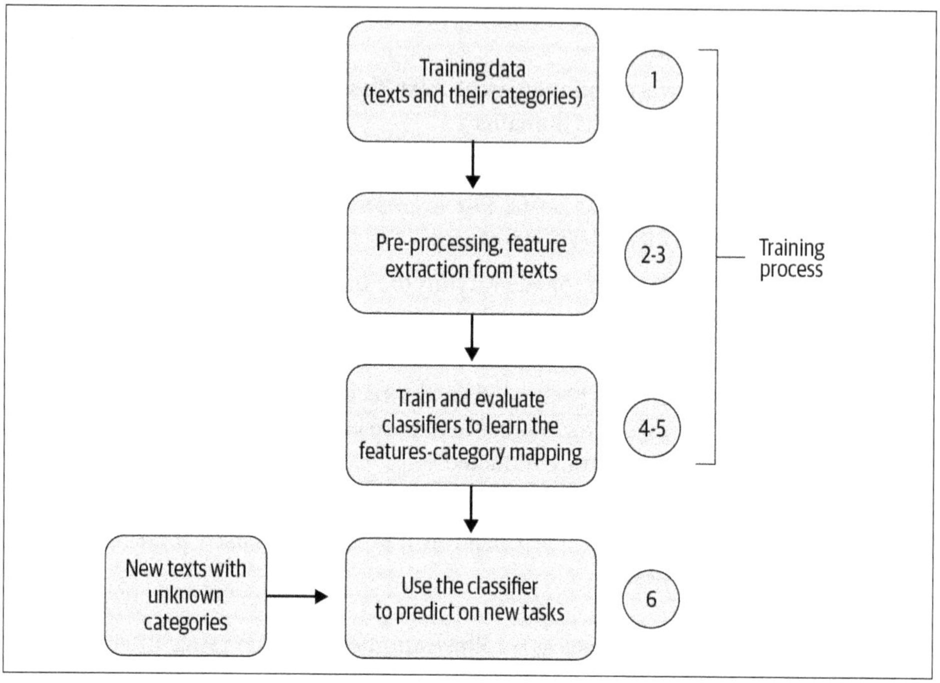

Figure 4-3. Flowchart of a text classification pipeline

Steps 3 through 5 are iterated on to explore different variants of features and classification algorithms and their parameters and to tune the hyperparameters before proceeding to Step 6, deploying the optimal model in production.

Some of the individual steps related to data collection and pre-processing were discussed in past chapters. For example, Steps 1 and 2 were discussed in detail in Chapter 2. Chapter 3 focused entirely on Step 3. Our focus in this chapter is on Steps 4 through 5. Toward the end of this chapter, we'll revisit Step 1 to discuss issues specific to text classification. We'll deal with Step 6 in Chapter 11. To be able to perform Steps 4 through 5 (i.e., to benchmark the performance of a model or compare multiple classifiers), we need the right measure(s) of evaluation. Chapter 2 discussed various general metrics used in evaluating NLP systems. For evaluating classifiers specifically, among the metrics introduced in Chapter 2, the following are used more commonly: classification accuracy, precision, recall, F1 score, and area under ROC curve. In this chapter, we'll use some of these measures to evaluate our models and also look at confusion matrices to understand the model performance in detail.

Apart from these, when classification systems are deployed in real-world applications, key performance indicators (KPIs) specific to a given business use case are also used to evaluate their impact and return on investment (ROI). These are often the metrics business teams care about. For example, if we're using text classification to automatically route customer service requests, a possible KPI could be the reduction in wait time before the request is responded to compared to manual routing. In this chapter, we'll focus on the NLP evaluation measures. In Part III of the book, where we'll discuss NLP use cases specific to industry verticals, we'll introduce some KPIs that are often used in those verticals.

Before we start looking at how to build text classifiers using the pipeline we just discussed, let's take a look at the scenarios where this pipeline is not at all necessary or where it's not possible to use it.

A Simple Classifier Without the Text Classification Pipeline

When we talk about the text classification pipeline, we're referring to a supervised machine learning scenario. However, it's possible to build a simple classifier without machine learning and without this pipeline. Consider the following problem scenario: we're given a corpus of tweets where each tweet is labeled with its corresponding sentiment: negative or positive. For example, a tweet that says, "The new James Bond movie is great!" is clearly expressing a positive sentiment, whereas a tweet that says, "I would never visit this restaurant again, horrible place!!" has a negative sentiment. We want to build a classification system that will predict the sentiment of an unseen tweet using only the text of the tweet. A simple solution could be to create lists of positive and negative words in English—i.e., words that have a positive or negative sentiment. We then compare the usage of positive versus negative words in the input tweet and make a prediction based on this information. Further enhancements to this approach may involve creating more sophisticated dictionaries with degrees of positive, negative, and neutral sentiment of words or formulating specific heuristics (e.g., usage of certain smileys indicate positive sentiment) and using them to make predictions. This approach is called *lexicon-based sentiment analysis*.

Clearly, this does not involve any "learning" of text classification; that is, it's based on a set of heuristics or rules and custom-built resources such as dictionaries of words with sentiment. While this approach may seem too simple to perform reasonably well for many real-world scenarios, it may enable us to deploy a minimum viable product (MVP) quickly. Most importantly, this simple model can lead to better understanding of the problem and give us a simple baseline for our evaluation metric and speed. From our experience, it's always good to start with such simpler approaches when tackling a new NLP problem, where possible. However, eventually, we'll need ML methods that can infer more insights from large collections of text data and perform better than the baseline approach.

Using Existing Text Classification APIs

Another scenario where we may not have to "learn" a classifier or follow this pipeline is when our task is more generic in nature, such as identifying a general category of a text (e.g., whether it's about technology or music). In such cases, we can use existing APIs, such as Google Cloud Natural Language [5], that provide off-the-shelf content classification models that can identify close to 700 different categories of text. Another popular classification task is sentiment analysis. All major service providers (e.g., Google, Microsoft, and Amazon) serve sentiment analysis APIs [5, 6, 7] with varying payment structures. If we're tasked with building a sentiment classifier, we may not have to build our own system if an existing API addresses our business needs.

However, many classification tasks could be specific to our organization's business needs. For the rest of this chapter, we'll address the scenario of building our own classifier by considering the pipeline described earlier in this section.

One Pipeline, Many Classifiers

Let's now look at building text classifiers by altering Steps 3 through 5 in the pipeline and keeping the remaining steps constant. A good dataset is a prerequisite to start using the pipeline. When we say "good" dataset, we mean a dataset that is a true representation of the data we're likely to see in production. Throughout this chapter, we'll use some of the publicly available datasets for text classification. A wide range of NLP-related datasets, including ones for text classification, are listed online [8]. Additionally, Figure Eight [9] contains a collection of crowdsourced datasets, some of which are relevant to text classification. The UCI Machine Learning Repository [10] also contains a few text classification datasets. Google recently launched a dedicated search system for datasets for machine learning [11]. We'll use multiple datasets throughout this chapter instead of sticking to one to illustrate any dataset-specific issues you may come across.

Note that our goal in this chapter is to give you an overview of different approaches. No single approach is known to work universally well on all kinds of data and all classification problems. In the real world, we experiment with multiple approaches, evaluate them, and choose one final approach to deploy in practice.

For the rest of this section, we'll use the "Economic News Article Tone and Relevance" dataset from Figure Eight to demonstrate text classification. It consists of 8,000 news articles annotated with whether or not they're relevant to the US economy (i.e., a yes/no binary classification). The dataset is also imbalanced, with ~1,500 relevant and ~6,500 non-relevant articles, which poses the challenge of guarding against learning a bias toward the majority category (in this case, non-relevant articles). Clearly, learning what a relevant news article is is more challenging with this dataset than learning what is irrelevant. After all, just guessing that everything is irrelevant already gives us 80% accuracy!

Let's explore how a BoW representation (introduced in Chapter 3) can be used with this dataset following the pipeline described earlier in this chapter. We'll build classifiers using three well-known algorithms: Naive Bayes, logistic regression, and support vector machines. The notebook related to this section (*Ch4/OnePipeline_ManyClassifiers.ipynb*) shows the step-by-step process of following our pipeline using these three algorithms. We'll discuss some of the important aspects in this section.

Naive Bayes Classifier

Naive Bayes is a probabilistic classifier that uses Bayes' theorem to classify texts based on the evidence seen in training data. It estimates the conditional probability of each feature of a given text for each class based on the occurrence of that feature in that class and multiplies the probabilities of all the features of a given text to compute the final probability of classification for each class. Finally, it chooses the class with maximum probability. A detailed step-by-step explanation of the classifier is beyond the scope of this book. However, a reader interested in Naive Bayes with a detailed explanation in the context of text classification can look at Chapter 4 of Jurafsky and Martin [12]. Although simple, Naive Bayes is commonly used as a baseline algorithm in classification experiments.

Let's walk through the key steps of an implementation of the pipeline described earlier for our dataset. For this, we use a Naive Bayes implementation in scikit-learn. Once the dataset is loaded, we split the data into train and test data, as shown in the code snippet below:

```
#Step 1: train-test split
X = our_data.text
#the column text contains textual data to extract features from.
y = our_data.relevance
#this is the column we are learning to predict.
X_train, X_test, y_train, y_test = train_test_split(X, y, random_state=1)
#split X and y into training and testing sets. By default,
it splits 75% #training and 25% test. random_state=1 for reproducibility.
```

The next step is to pre-process the texts and then convert them into feature vectors. While there are many different ways to do the pre-processing, let's say we want to do the following: lowercasing and removal of punctuation, digits and any custom strings, and stop words. The code snippet below shows this pre-processing and converting the train and test data into feature vectors using CountVectorizer in scikit-learn, which is the implementation of the BoW approach we discussed in Chapter 3:

```
#Step 2-3: Pre-process and Vectorize train and test data
vect = CountVectorizer(preprocessor=clean)
#clean is a function we defined for pre-processing, seen in the notebook.
X_train_dtm = vect.fit_transform(X_train)
```

```
X_test_dtm = vect.transform(X_test)
print(X_train_dtm.shape, X_test_dtm.shape)
```

Once we run this in the notebook, we'll see that we ended up having a feature vector with over 45,000 features! We now have the data in a format we want: feature vectors. So, the next step is to train and evaluate a classifier. The code snippet below shows how to do the training and evaluation of a Naive Bayes classifier with the features we extracted above:

```
nb = MultinomialNB() #instantiate a Multinomial Naive Bayes classifier
nb.fit(X_train_dtm, y_train)#train the mode
y_pred_class = nb.predict(X_test_dtm)#make class predictions for test data
```

Figure 4-4 shows the confusion matrix of this classifier with test data.

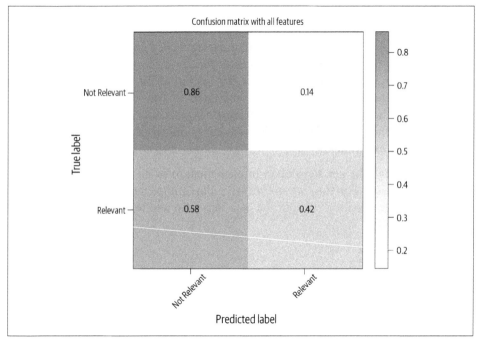

Figure 4-4. Confusion matrix for Naive Bayes classifier

As evident from Figure 4-4, the classifier is doing fairly well with identifying the non-relevant articles correctly, only making errors 14% of the time. However, it does not perform well in comparison to the second category: relevance. The category is identified correctly only 42% of the time. An obvious thought may be to collect more data. This is correct and often the most rewarding approach. But in the interest of covering other approaches, we assume that we cannot change it or collect additional data. This is not a far-fetched assumption—in industry, we often don't have the luxury of collecting more data; we have to work with what we have. We can think of a few possible reasons for this performance and ways to improve this classifier. These are summarized in Table 4-1, and we'll look into some of them as we progress in this chapter.

Table 4-1. Potential reasons for poor classifier performance

Reason 1	Since we extracted all possible features, we ended up in a large, sparse feature vector, where most features are too rare and end up being noise. A sparse feature set also makes training hard.
Reason 2	There are very few examples of relevant articles (~20%) compared to the non-relevant articles (~80%) in the dataset. This class imbalance makes the learning process skewed toward the non-relevant articles category, as there are very few examples of "relevant" articles.
Reason 3	Perhaps we need a better learning algorithm.
Reason 4	Perhaps we need a better pre-processing and feature extraction mechanism.
Reason 5	Perhaps we should look to tuning the classifier's parameters and hyperparameters.

Let's see how to improve our classification performance by addressing some of the possible reasons for it. One way to approach Reason 1 is to reduce noise in the feature vectors. The approach in the previous code example had close to 40,000 features (refer to the Jupyter notebook for details). A large number of features introduce sparsity; i.e., most of the features in the feature vector are zero, and only a few values are non-zero. This, in turn, affects the ability of the text classification algorithm to learn. Let's see what happens if we restrict this to 5,000 and rerun the training and evaluation process. This requires us to change the `CountVectorizer` instantiation in the process, as shown in the code snippet below, and repeat all the steps:

```
vect = CountVectorizer(preprocessor=clean, max_features=5000) #Step-1
X_train_dtm = vect.fit_transform(X_train)#combined step 2 and 3
X_test_dtm = vect.transform(X_test)
nb = MultinomialNB() #instantiate a Multinomial Naive Bayes model
%time nb.fit(X_train_dtm, y_train)
#train the model(timing it with an IPython "magic command")
y_pred_class = nb.predict(X_test_dtm)
#make class predictions for X_test_dtm
print("Accuracy: ", metrics.accuracy_score(y_test, y_pred_class))
```

Figure 4-5 shows the new confusion matrix with this setting.

Now, clearly, while the average performance seems lower than before, the correct identification of relevant articles increased by over 20%. At that point, one may wonder whether this is what we want. The answer to that question depends on the problem we're trying to solve. If we care about doing reasonably well with non-relevant article identification and doing as well as possible with relevant article identification, or doing equally well with both, we could conclude that reducing the feature vector size with the Naive Bayes classifier was useful for this dataset.

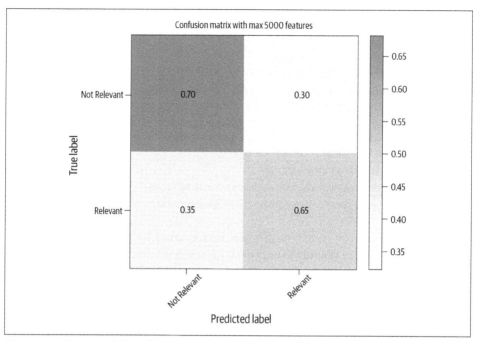

Figure 4-5. Improved classification performance with Naive Bayes and feature selection

Consider reducing the number of features if there are too many to reduce data sparsity.

Reason 2 in our list was the problem of skew in data toward the majority class. There are several ways to address this. Two typical approaches are oversampling the instances belonging to minority classes or undersampling the majority class to create a balanced dataset. Imbalanced-Learn [13] is a Python library that incorporates some of the sampling methods to address this issue. While we won't delve into the details of this library here, classifiers also have a built-in mechanism to address such imbalanced datasets. We'll see how to use that by taking another classifier, logistic regression, in the next subsection.

Class imbalance is one of the most common reasons for a classifier to not do well. We must always check if this is the case for our task and address it.

To address Reason 3, let's try using other algorithms, beginning with logistic regression.

Logistic Regression

When we described the Naive Bayes classifier, we mentioned that it learns the probability of a text for each class and chooses the one with maximum probability. Such a classifier is called a *generative classifier*. In contrast, there's a *discriminative classifier* that aims to learn the probability distribution over all classes. Logistic regression is an example of a discriminative classifier and is commonly used in text classification, as a baseline in research, and as an MVP in real-world industry scenarios.

Unlike Naive Bayes, which estimates probabilities based on feature occurrence in classes, logistic regression "learns" the weights for individual features based on how important they are to make a classification decision. The goal of logistic regression is to learn a linear separator between classes in the training data with the aim of maximizing the probability of the data. This "learning" of feature weights and probability distribution over all classes is done through a function called "logistic" function, and (hence the name) logistic regression [14].

Let's take the 5,000-dimensional feature vector from the last step of the Naive Bayes example and train a logistic regression classifier instead of Naive Bayes. The code snippet below shows how to use logistic regression for this task:

```
from sklearn.linear_model import LogisticRegression
logreg = LogisticRegression(class_weight="balanced")
logreg.fit(X_train_dtm, y_train)
y_pred_class = logreg.predict(X_test_dtm)
print("Accuracy: ", metrics.accuracy_score(y_test, y_pred_class))
```

This results in a classifier with an accuracy of 73.7%. Figure 4-6 shows the confusion matrix with this approach.

Our logistic regression classifier instantiation has an argument `class_weight`, which is given a value `"balanced"`. This tells the classifier to boost the weights for classes in inverse proportion to the number of samples for that class. So, we expect to see better performance for the less-represented classes. We can experiment with this code by removing that argument and retraining the classifier, to witness a fall (by approximately 5%) in the bottom-right cell of the confusion matrix. However, logistic regression clearly seems to perform worse than Naive Bayes for this dataset.

Reason 3 in our list was: "Perhaps we need a better learning algorithm." This gives rise to the question: "What is a better learning algorithm?" A general rule of thumb when working with ML approaches is that there is no one algorithm that learns well on all datasets. A common approach is to experiment with various algorithms and compare them.

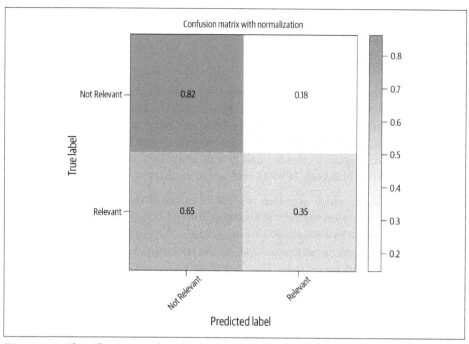

Figure 4-6. Classification performance with logistic regression

Let's see if this idea helps us by replacing logistic regression with another well-known classification algorithm that was shown to be useful for several text classification tasks, called the "support vector machine."

Support Vector Machine

We described logistic regression as a discriminative classifier that learns the weights for individual features and predicts a probability distribution over the classes. A *support vector machine (SVM)*, first invented in the early 1960s, is a discriminative classifier like logistic regression. However, unlike logistic regression, it aims to look for an optimal hyperplane in a higher dimensional space, which can separate the classes in the data by a maximum possible margin. Further, SVMs are capable of learning even non-linear separations between classes, unlike logistic regression. However, they may also take longer to train.

SVMs come in various flavors in sklearn. Let's see how one of them is used by keeping everything else the same and altering maximum features to 1,000 instead of the previous example's 5,000. We restrict to 1,000 features, keeping in mind the time an SVM algorithm takes to train. The code snippet below shows how to do this, and Figure 4-7 shows the resultant confusion matrix:

```
from sklearn.svm import LinearSVC
vect = CountVectorizer(preprocessor=clean, max_features=1000) #Step-1
X_train_dtm = vect.fit_transform(X_train)#combined step 2 and 3
X_test_dtm = vect.transform(X_test)
classifier = LinearSVC(class_weight='balanced') #notice the "balanced" option
classifier.fit(X_train_dtm, y_train) #fit the model with training data
y_pred_class = classifier.predict(X_test_dtm)
print("Accuracy: ", metrics.accuracy_score(y_test, y_pred_class))
```

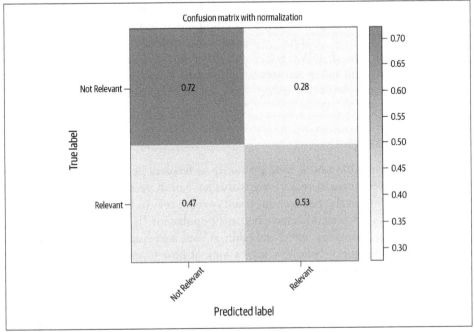

Figure 4-7. Confusion matrix for classification with SVM

When compared to logistic regression, SVMs seem to have done better with the relevant articles category, although, among this small set of experiments we did, Naive Bayes, with the smaller set of features, seems to be the best classifier for this dataset.

All the examples in this section demonstrate how changes in different steps affected the classification performance and how to interpret the results. Clearly, we excluded many other possibilities, such as exploring other text classification algorithms, changing different parameters of various classifiers, coming up with better pre-processing methods, etc. We leave them as further exercises for the reader, using the notebook as a playground. A real-world text classification project involves exploring multiple options like this, starting with the simplest approach in terms of modeling, deployment, and scaling, and gradually increasing the complexity. Our eventual goal is to build the classifier that best meets our business needs given all the other constraints.

Let's now consider a part of Reason 4 in Table 4-1: better feature representation. So far in this chapter, we've used BoW features. Let's see how we can use other feature representation techniques we saw in Chapter 3 for text classification.

Using Neural Embeddings in Text Classification

In the latter half of Chapter 3, we discussed feature engineering techniques using neural networks, such as word embeddings, character embeddings, and document embeddings. The advantage of using embedding-based features is that they create a dense, low-dimensional feature representation instead of the sparse, high-dimensional structure of BoW/TF-IDF and other such features. There are different ways of designing and using features based on neural embeddings. In this section, let's look at some ways of using such embedding representations for text classification.

Word Embeddings

Words and n-grams have been used primarily as features in text classification for a long time. Different ways of vectorizing words have been proposed, and we used one such representation in the last section, CountVectorizer. In the past few years, neural network–based architectures have become popular for "learning" word representations, which are known as "word embeddings." We surveyed some of the intuitions behind this in Chapter 3. Let's now take a look at how to use word embeddings as features for text classification. We'll use the sentiment-labeled sentences dataset from the UCI repository, consisting of 1,500 positive-sentiment and 1,500 negative-sentiment sentences from Amazon, Yelp, and IMDB. All the steps are detailed in the notebook *Ch4/Word2Vec_Example.ipynb*. Let's walk through the important steps and where this approach differs from the previous section's procedures.

Loading and pre-processing the text data remains a common step. However, instead of vectorizing the texts using BoW-based features, we'll now rely on neural embedding models. As mentioned earlier, we'll use a pre-trained embedding model. Word2vec is a popular algorithm we discussed in Chapter 3 for training word embedding models. There are several pre-trained Word2vec models trained on large corpora available on the internet. Here, we'll use the one from Google [15]. The following code snippet shows how to load this model into Python using gensim:

```
data_path= "/your/folder/path"
path_to_model = os.path.join(data_path,'GoogleNews-vectors-negative300.bin')
training_data_path = os.path.join(data_path, "sentiment_sentences.txt")
#Load W2V model. This will take some time.
w2v_model = KeyedVectors.load_word2vec_format(path_to_model, binary=True)
print('done loading Word2Vec')
```

This is a large model that can be seen as a dictionary where the keys are words in the vocabulary and the values are their learned embedding representations. Given a query word, if the word's embedding is present in the dictionary, it will return the same. How do we use this pre-learned embedding to represent features? As we discussed in Chapter 3, there are multiple ways of doing this. A simple approach is just to average the embeddings for individual words in text. The code snippet below shows a simple function to do this:

```
# Creating a feature vector by averaging all embeddings for all sentences
def embedding_feats(list_of_lists):
    DIMENSION = 300
    zero_vector = np.zeros(DIMENSION)
    feats = []
    for tokens in list_of_lists:
        feat_for_this =  np.zeros(DIMENSION)
        count_for_this = 0
        for token in tokens:
                if token in w2v_model:
                    feat_for_this += w2v_model[token]
                    count_for_this +=1
        feats.append(feat_for_this/count_for_this)
    return feats

train_vectors = embedding_feats(texts_processed)
print(len(train_vectors))
```

Note that it uses embeddings only for the words that are present in the dictionary. It ignores the words for which embeddings are absent. Also, note that the above code will give a single vector with DIMENSION(=300) components. We treat the resulting embedding vector as the feature vector that represents the entire text. Once this feature engineering is done, the final step is similar to what we did in the previous section: use these features and train a classifier. We leave that as an exercise to the reader (refer to the notebook for the full code).

When trained with a logistic regression classifier, these features gave a classification accuracy of 81% on our dataset (see the notebook for more details). Considering that we just used an existing word embeddings model and followed only basic pre-processing steps, this is a great model to have as a baseline! We saw in Chapter 3 that there are other pre-trained embedding approaches, such as GloVe, which can be experimented with for this approach. Gensim, which we used in this example, also supports training our own word embeddings if necessary. If we're working on a custom domain whose vocabulary is remarkably different from that of the pre-trained news embeddings we used here, it would make sense to train our own embeddings to extract features.

In order to decide whether to train our own embeddings or use pre-trained embeddings, a good rule of thumb is to compute the vocabulary overlap. If the overlap between the vocabulary of our custom domain and that of pre-trained word embeddings is greater than 80%, pre-trained word embeddings tend to give good results in text classification.

An important factor to consider when deploying models with embedding-based feature extraction approaches is that the learned or pre-trained embedding models have to be stored and loaded into memory while using these approaches. If the model itself is bulky (e.g., the pre-trained model we used takes 3.6 GB), we need to factor this into our deployment needs.

Subword Embeddings and fastText

Word embeddings, as the name indicates, are about word representations. Even off-the-shelf embeddings seem to work well on classification tasks, as we saw earlier. However, if a word in our dataset was not present in the pre-trained model's vocabulary, how will we get a representation for this word? This problem is popularly known as *out of vocabulary (OOV)*. In our previous example, we just ignored such words from feature extraction. Is there a better way?

We discussed fastText embeddings [16] in Chapter 3. They're based on the idea of enriching word embeddings with subword-level information. Thus, the embedding representation for each word is represented as a sum of the representations of individual character n-grams. While this may seem like a longer process compared to just estimating word-level embeddings, it has two advantages:

- This approach can handle words that did not appear in training data (OOV).
- The implementation facilitates extremely fast learning on even very large corpora.

While fastText is a general-purpose library to learn the embeddings, it also supports off-the-shelf text classification by providing end-to-end classifier training and testing; i.e., we don't have to handle feature extraction separately. The remaining part of this subsection shows how to use the fastText classifier [17] for text classification. We'll work with the DBpedia dataset [18]. It's a balanced dataset consisting of 14 classes, with 40,000 training and 5,000 testing examples per class. Thus, the total size of the dataset is 560,000 training and 70,000 testing data points. Clearly, this is a much larger dataset than what we saw before. Can we build a fast training model using fast-Text? Let's check it out!

The training and test sets are provided as CSV files in this dataset. So, the first step involves reading these files into your Python environment and cleaning the text to remove extraneous characters, similar to what we did in the pre-processing steps for the other classifier examples we've seen so far. Once this is done, the process to use fastText is quite simple. The code snippet below shows a simple fastText model. The step-by-step process is detailed in the associated Jupyter notebook (*Ch4/Fast-Text_Example.ipynb*):

```
## Using fastText for feature extraction and training
from fasttext import supervised
"""fastText expects and training file (csv), a model name as input arguments.
label_prefix refers to the prefix before label string in the dataset.
default is __label__. In our dataset, it is __class__.
There are several other parameters which can be seen in:
https://pypi.org/project/fasttext/
"""
model = supervised(train_file, 'temp', label_prefix="__class__")
results = model.test(test_file)
print(results.nexamples, results.precision, results.recall)
```

If we run this code in the notebook, we'll notice that, despite the fact that this is a huge dataset and we gave the classifier raw text and not the feature vector, the training takes only a few seconds, and we get close to 98% precision and recall! As an exercise, try to build a classifier using the same dataset but with either BoW or word embedding features and algorithms like logistic regression. Notice how long it takes for the individual steps of feature extraction and classification learning!

When we have a large dataset, and when learning seems infeasible with the approaches described so far, fastText is a good option to use to set up a strong working baseline. However, there's one concern to keep in mind when using fastText, as was the case with Word2vec embeddings: it uses pre-trained character n-gram embeddings. Thus, when we save the trained model, it carries the entire character n-gram embeddings dictionary with it. This results in a bulky model and can result in engineering issues. For example, the model stored with the name "temp" in the above code snippet has a size close to 450 MB. However, fastText implementation also comes with options to reduce the memory footprint of its classification models with minimal reduction in classification performance [19]. It does this by doing vocabulary pruning and using compression algorithms. Exploring these possibilities could be a good option in cases where large model sizes are a constraint.

 fastText is extremely fast to train and very useful for setting up strong baselines. The downside is the model size.

We hope this discussion gives a good overview of the usefulness of fastText for text classification. What we showed here is a default classification model without any tuning of the hyperparameters. fastText's documentation contains more information on the different options to tune your classifier and on training custom embedding representations for a dataset you want. However, both of the embedding representations we've seen so far learn a representation of words and characters and collect them together to form a text representation. Let's see how to learn the representation for a document directly using the Doc2vec approach we discussed in Chapter 3.

Document Embeddings

In the Doc2vec embedding scheme, we learn a direct representation for the entire document (sentence/paragraph) rather than each word. Just as we used word and character embeddings as features for performing text classification, we can also use Doc2vec as a feature representation mechanism. Since there are no existing pre-trained models that work with the latest version of Doc2vec [20], let's see how to build our own Doc2vec model and use it for text classification.

We'll use a dataset called "Sentiment Analysis: Emotion in Text" from figure-eight.com [9], which contains 40,000 tweets labeled with 13 labels signifying different emotions. Let's take the three most frequent labels in this dataset—neutral, worry, happiness—and build a text classifier for classifying new tweets into one of these three classes. The notebook for this subsection (*Ch4/Doc2Vec_Example.ipynb*) walks you through the steps involved in using Doc2vec for text classification and provides the dataset.

After loading the dataset and taking a subset of the three most frequent labels, an important step to consider here is pre-processing the data. What's different here compared to previous examples? Why can't we just follow the same procedure as before? There are a few things that are different about tweets compared to news articles or other such text, as we briefly discussed in Chapter 2 when we talked about text pre-processing. First, they are very short. Second, our traditional tokenizers may not work well with tweets, splitting smileys, hashtags, Twitter handles, etc., into multiple tokens. Such specialized needs prompted a lot of research into NLP for Twitter in the recent past, which resulted in several pre-processing options for tweets. One such solution is a `TweetTokenizer`, implemented in the NLTK [21] library in Python. We'll discuss more on this topic in Chapter 8. For now, let's see how we can use a `TweetTokenizer` in the following code snippet:

```
tweeter = TweetTokenizer(strip_handles=True,preserve_case=False)
mystopwords = set(stopwords.words("english"))

#Function to pre-process and tokenize tweets
def preprocess_corpus(texts):
    def remove_stops_digits(tokens):
    #Nested function to remove stopwords and digits
        return [token for token in tokens if token not in mystopwords
                and not token.isdigit()]
    return [remove_stops_digits(tweeter.tokenize(content)) for content in texts]

mydata = preprocess_corpus(df_subset['content'])
mycats = df_subset['sentiment']
```

The next step in this process is to train a Doc2vec model to learn tweet representations. Ideally, any large dataset of tweets will work for this step. However, since we don't have such a ready-made corpus, we'll split our dataset into train-test and use the training data for learning the Doc2vec representations. The first part of this process involves converting the data into a format readable by the Doc2vec implementation, which can be done using the TaggedDocument class. It's used to represent a document as a list of tokens, followed by a "tag," which in its simplest form can be just the filename or ID of the document. However, Doc2vec by itself can also be used as a nearest neighbor classifier for both multiclass and multilabel classification problems using . We'll leave this as an exploratory exercise for the reader. Let's now see how to train a Doc2vec classifier for tweets through the code snippet below:

```
#Prepare training data in doc2vec format:
d2vtrain = [TaggedDocument((d),tags=[str(i)]) for i, d in enumerate(train_data)]
#Train a doc2vec model to learn tweet representations. Use only training data!!
model = Doc2Vec(vector_size=50, alpha=0.025, min_count=10, dm =1, epochs=100)
model.build_vocab(d2vtrain)
model.train(d2vtrain, total_examples=model.corpus_count, epochs=model.epochs)
model.save("d2v.model")
print("Model Saved")
```

Training for Doc2vec involves making several choices regarding parameters, as seen in the model definition in the code snippet above. vector_size refers to the dimensionality of the learned embeddings; alpha is the learning rate; min_count is the minimum frequency of words that remain in vocabulary; dm, which stands for distributed memory, is one of the representation learners implemented in Doc2vec (the other is dbow, or distributed bag of words); and epochs are the number of training iterations. There are a few other parameters that can be customized. While there are some guidelines on choosing optimal parameters for training Doc2vec models [22], these are not exhaustively validated, and we don't know if the guidelines work for tweets.

The best way to address this issue is to explore a range of values for the ones that matter to us (e.g., dm versus dbow, vector sizes, learning rate) and compare multiple models. How do we compare these models, as they only learn the text representation? One way to do it is to start using these learned representations in a downstream task—in this case, text classification. Doc2vec's infer_vector function can be used to infer the vector representation for a given text using a pre-trained model. Since there is some amount of randomness due to the choice of hyperparameters, the inferred vectors differ each time we extract them. For this reason, to get a stable representation, we run it multiple times (called steps) and aggregate the vectors. Let's use the learned model to infer features for our data and train a logistic regression classifier:

```
#Infer the feature representation for training and test data using
#the trained model
model= Doc2Vec.load("d2v.model")
#Infer in multiple steps to get a stable representation
train_vectors = [model.infer_vector(list_of_tokens, steps=50)
```

```
            for list_of_tokens in train_data]
test_vectors = [model.infer_vector(list_of_tokens, steps=50)
            for list_of_tokens in test_data]
myclass = LogisticRegression(class_weight="balanced")
#because classes are not balanced
myclass.fit(train_vectors, train_cats)
preds = myclass.predict(test_vectors)
print(classification_report(test_cats, preds))
```

Now, the performance of this model seems rather poor, achieving an F1 score of 0.51 on a reasonably large corpus, with only three classes. There are a couple of interpretations for this poor result. First, unlike full news articles or even well-formed sentences, tweets contain very little data per instance. Further, people write with a wide variety in spelling and syntax when they tweet. There are a lot of emoticons in different forms. Our feature representation should be able to capture such aspects. While tuning the algorithms by searching a large parameter space for the best model may help, an alternative could be to explore problem-specific feature representations, as we discussed in Chapter 3. We'll see how to do this for tweets in Chapter 8. An important point to keep in mind when using Doc2vec is the same as for fastText: if we have to use Doc2vec for feature representation, we have to store the model that learned the representation. While it's not typically as bulky as fastText, it's also not as fast to train. Such trade-offs need to be considered and compared before we make a deployment decision.

So far, we've seen a range of feature representations and how they play a role for text classification using ML algorithms. Let's now turn to a family of algorithms that became popular in the past few years, known as "deep learning."

Deep Learning for Text Classification

As we discussed in Chapter 1, deep learning is a family of machine learning algorithms where the learning happens through different kinds of multilayered neural network architectures. Over the past few years, it has shown remarkable improvements on standard machine learning tasks, such as image classification, speech recognition, and machine translation. This has resulted in widespread interest in using deep learning for various tasks, including text classification. So far, we've seen how to train different machine learning classifiers, using BoW and different kinds of embedding representations. Now, let's look at how to use deep learning architectures for text classification.

Two of the most commonly used neural network architectures for text classification are convolutional neural networks (CNNs) and recurrent neural networks (RNNs). Long short-term memory (LSTM) networks are a popular form of RNNs. Recent approaches also involve starting with large, pre-trained language models and fine-tuning them for the task at hand. In this section, we'll learn how to train CNNs and

LSTMs and how to tune a pre-trained language model for text classification using the IMDB sentiment classification dataset [23]. Note that a detailed discussion on how neural network architectures work is beyond the scope of this book. Interested readers can read the textbook by Goodfellow et al. [24] for a general theoretical discussion and Goldberg's book [25] for NLP-specific uses of neural network architectures. Jurafsky and Martin's book [12] also provides a short but concise overview of different neural network methods for NLP.

The first step toward training any ML or DL model is to define a feature representation. This step has been relatively straightforward in the approaches we've seen so far, with BoW or embedding vectors. However, for neural networks, we need further processing of input vectors, as we saw in Chapter 3. Let's quickly recap the steps involved in converting training and test data into a format suitable for the neural network input layers:

1. Tokenize the texts and convert them into word index vectors.

2. Pad the text sequences so that all text vectors are of the same length.

3. Map every word index to an embedding vector. We do that by multiplying word index vectors with the embedding matrix. The embedding matrix can either be populated using pre-trained embeddings or it can be trained for embeddings on this corpus.

4. Use the output from Step 3 as the input to a neural network architecture.

Once these are done, we can proceed with the specification of neural network architectures and training classifiers with them. The Jupyter notebook associated with this section (*Ch4/DeepNN_Example.ipynb*) will walk you through the entire process from text pre-processing to neural network training and evaluation. We'll use Keras, a Python-based DL library. The code snippet below illustrates Steps 1 and 2:

```
#Vectorize these text samples into a 2D integer tensor using Keras Tokenizer.
#Tokenizer is fit on training data only, and that is used to tokenize both train
#and test data.
tokenizer = Tokenizer(num_words=MAX_NUM_WORDS)
tokenizer.fit_on_texts(train_texts)
train_sequences = tokenizer.texts_to_sequences(train_texts)
test_sequences = tokenizer.texts_to_sequences(test_texts)
word_index = tokenizer.word_index
print('Found %s unique tokens.' % len(word_index))
#Converting this to sequences to be fed into neural network. Max seq. len is
#1000 as set earlier. Initial padding of 0s, until vector is of
#size MAX_SEQUENCE_LENGTH
trainvalid_data = pad_sequences(train_sequences, maxlen=MAX_SEQUENCE_LENGTH)
test_data = pad_sequences(test_sequences, maxlen=MAX_SEQUENCE_LENGTH)
trainvalid_labels = to_categorical(np.asarray(train_labels))
test_labels = to_categorical(np.asarray(test_labels))
```

Step 3: If we want to use pre-trained embeddings to convert the train and test data into an embedding matrix like we did in the earlier examples with Word2vec and fastText, we have to download them and use them to convert our data into the input format for the neural networks. The following code snippet shows an example of how to do this using GloVe embeddings, which were introduced in Chapter 3. GloVe embeddings come with multiple dimensionalities, and we chose 100 as our dimension here. The value of dimensionality is a hyperparameter, and we can experiment with other dimensions as well:[i]

```
embeddings_index = {}
with open(os.path.join(GLOVE_DIR, 'glove.6B.100d.txt')) as f:
    for line in f:
        values = line.split()
        word = values[0]
        coefs = np.asarray(values[1:], dtype='float32')
        embeddings_index[word] = coefs

num_words = min(MAX_NUM_WORDS, len(word_index)) + 1
embedding_matrix = np.zeros((num_words, EMBEDDING_DIM))
for word, i in word_index.items():
    if i > MAX_NUM_WORDS:
        continue
    embedding_vector = embeddings_index.get(word)
    if embedding_vector is not None:
        embedding_matrix[i] = embedding_vector
```

Step 4: Now, we're ready to train DL models for text classification! DL architectures consist of an input layer, an output layer, and several hidden layers in between the two. Depending on the architecture, different hidden layers are used. The input layer for textual input is typically an embedding layer. The output layer, especially in the context of text classification, is a softmax layer with categorical output. If we want to train the input layer instead of using pre-trained embeddings, the easiest way is to call the Embedding layer class in Keras, specifying the input and output dimensions. However, since we want to use pre-trained embeddings, we should create a custom embedding layer that uses the embedding matrix we just built. The following code snippet shows how to do that:

```
embedding_layer = Embedding(num_words, EMBEDDING_DIM,
                            embeddings_initializer=Constant(embedding_matrix),
                            input_length=MAX_SEQUENCE_LENGTH,
                            trainable=False)
print("Preparing of embedding matrix is done")
```

This will serve as the input layer for any neural network we want to use (CNN or LSTM). Now that we know how to pre-process the input and define an input layer,

---

i. There are other such pre-trained embeddings available. Our choice in this case is arbitrary.

let's move on to specifying the rest of the neural network architecture using CNNs and LSTMs.

CNNs for Text Classification

Let's now look at how to define, train, and evaluate a CNN model for text classification. CNNs typically consist of a series of convolution and pooling layers as the hidden layers. In the context of text classification, CNNs can be thought of as learning the most useful bag-of-words/n-grams features instead of taking the entire collection of words/n-grams as features, as we did earlier in this chapter. Since our dataset has only two classes—positive and negative—the output layer has two outputs, with the softmax activation function. We'll define a CNN with three convolution-pooling layers using the Sequential model class in Keras, which allows us to specify DL models as a sequential stack of layers—one after another. Once the layers and their activation functions are specified, the next task is to define other important parameters, such as the optimizer, loss function, and the evaluation metric to tune the hyperparameters of the model. Once all this is done, the next step is to train and evaluate the model. The following code snippet shows one way of specifying a CNN architecture for this task using the Python library Keras and prints the results with the IMDB dataset for this model:

```
print('Define a 1D CNN model.')
cnnmodel = Sequential()
cnnmodel.add(embedding_layer)
cnnmodel.add(Conv1D(128, 5, activation='relu'))
cnnmodel.add(MaxPooling1D(5))
cnnmodel.add(Conv1D(128, 5, activation='relu'))
cnnmodel.add(MaxPooling1D(5))
cnnmodel.add(Conv1D(128, 5, activation='relu'))
cnnmodel.add(GlobalMaxPooling1D())
cnnmodel.add(Dense(128, activation='relu'))
cnnmodel.add(Dense(len(labels_index), activation='softmax'))
cnnmodel.compile(loss='categorical_crossentropy',
                 optimizer='rmsprop',
                 metrics=['acc'])
cnnmodel.fit(x_train, y_train,
          batch_size=128,
          epochs=1, validation_data=(x_val, y_val))
score, acc = cnnmodel.evaluate(test_data, test_labels)
print('Test accuracy with CNN:', acc)
```

As you can see, we made a lot of choices in specifying the model, such as activation functions, hidden layers, layer sizes, loss function, optimizer, metrics, epochs, and batch size. While there are some commonly recommended options for these, there's no consensus on one combination that works best for all datasets and problems. A good approach while building your models is to experiment with different settings (i.e., hyperparameters). Keep in mind that all these decisions come with some associated cost. For example, in practice, we have the number of epochs as 10 or above. But that also increases the amount of time it takes to train the model. Another thing to note is that, if you want to train an embedding layer instead of using pre-trained embeddings in this model, the only thing that changes is the line cnnmodel.add(embedding_layer). Instead, we can specify a new embedding layer as, for example, cnnmodel.add(Embedding(Param1, Param2)). The code snippet below shows the code and model performance for the same:

```
print("Defining and training a CNN model, training embedding layer on the fly
        instead of using pre-trained embeddings")
cnnmodel = Sequential()
cnnmodel.add(Embedding(MAX_NUM_WORDS, 128))
…
. . .
cnnmodel.fit(x_train, y_train,
        batch_size=128,
        epochs=1, validation_data=(x_val, y_val))
score, acc = cnnmodel.evaluate(test_data, test_labels)
print('Test accuracy with CNN:', acc)
```

If we run this code in the notebook, we'll notice that, in this case, training the embedding layer on our own dataset seems to result in better classification on test data. However, if the training data were substantially small, sticking to the pre-trained embeddings, or using the domain adaptation techniques we'll discuss later in this chapter, would be a better choice. Let's look at how to train similar models using an LSTM.

LSTMs for Text Classification

As we saw briefly in Chapter 1, LSTMs and other variants of RNNs in general have become the go-to way of doing neural language modeling in the past few years. This is primarily because language is sequential in nature and RNNs are specialized in working with sequential data. The current word in the sentence depends on its context—the words before and after. However, when we model text using CNNs, this crucial fact is not taken into account. RNNs work on the principle of using this context while learning the language representation or a model of language. Hence, they're known to work well for NLP tasks. There are also CNN variants that can take such context into account, and CNNs versus RNNs is still an open area of debate. In this section, we'll see an example of using RNNs for text classification. Now that we've already seen one neural network in action, it's relatively easy to train another! Just replace the convolutional and pooling parts with an LSTM in the prior two code examples. The following code snippet shows how to train an LSTM model using the same IMDB dataset for text classification:

```
print("Defining and training an LSTM model, training embedding layer on the fly")
rnnmodel = Sequential()
rnnmodel.add(Embedding(MAX_NUM_WORDS, 128))
```

```
rnnmodel.add(LSTM(128, dropout=0.2, recurrent_dropout=0.2))
rnnmodel.add(Dense(2, activation='sigmoid'))
rnnmodel.compile(loss='binary_crossentropy',
                 optimizer='adam',
                 metrics=['accuracy'])
print('Training the RNN')
rnnmodel.fit(x_train, y_train,
         batch_size=32,
         epochs=1,
         validation_data=(x_val, y_val))
score, acc = rnnmodel.evaluate(test_data, test_labels,
                          batch_size=32)
print('Test accuracy with RNN:', acc)
```

Notice that this code took much longer to run than the CNN example. While LSTMs are more powerful in utilizing the sequential nature of text, they're much more data hungry as compared to CNNs. Thus, the relative lower performance of the LSTM on a dataset need not necessarily be interpreted as a shortcoming of the model itself. It's possible that the amount of data we have is not sufficient to utilize the full potential of an LSTM. As in the case of CNNs, several parameters and hyperparameters play important roles in model performance, and it's always a good practice to explore multiple options and compare different models before finalizing on one.

Text Classification with Large, Pre-Trained Language Models

In the past two years, there have been great improvements in using neural network–based text representations for NLP tasks. We discussed some of these in "Universal Text Representations" on page 107. These representations have been used successfully for text classification in the recent past by fine-tuning the pre-trained models to the given task and dataset. BERT, which was mentioned in Chapter 3, is a popular model used in this way for text classification. Let's take a look at how to use BERT for text classification using the IMDB dataset we used earlier in this section. The full code is in the relevant notebook (*Ch4/BERT_Sentiment_Classification_IMDB.ipynb*).

We'll use ktrain, a lightweight wrapper to train and use pre-trained DL models using the TensorFlow library Keras. ktrain provides a straightforward process for all steps, from obtaining the dataset and the pre-trained BERT to fine-tuning it for the classification task. Let's see how to load the dataset first through the code snippet below:

```
dataset = tf.keras.utils.get_file(
fname="aclImdb.tar.gz",
origin="http://ai.stanford.edu/~amaas/data/sentiment/aclImdb_v1.tar.gz",
  extract=True,)
```

Once the dataset is loaded, the next step is to download the BERT model and pre-process the dataset according to BERT's requirements. The following code snippet shows how to do this with ktrain's functions:

```
(x_train, y_train), (x_test, y_test), preproc =
                    text.texts_from_folder(IMDB_DATADIR,maxlen=500,
    preprocess_mode='bert',train_test_names=['train','test'],
```

The next step is to load the pre-trained BERT model and fine-tune it for this dataset. Here's the code snippet to do this:

```
model = text.text_classifier('bert', (x_train, y_train), preproc=preproc)
learner=ktrain.get_learner(model,train_data=(x_train,y_train),
                    val_data=(x_test, y_test), batch_size=6)
learner.fit_onecycle(2e-5, 4)
```

These three lines of code will train a text classifier using the BERT pre-trained model. As with other examples we've seen so far, we would need to do parameter tuning and a lot of experimentation to pick the best-performing model. We leave that as an exercise for the reader.

In this section, we introduced the idea of using DL for text classification using two neural network architectures—CNN and LSTM—and showed how we can tune a state-of-the-art, pre-trained language model (BERT) for a given dataset and classification task. There are several variants to these architectures, and new models are being proposed every day by NLP researchers. We saw how to use one pre-trained language model, BERT. There are other such models, and this is a constantly evolving area in NLP research; the state of the art keeps changing every few months (or even weeks!). However, in our experience as industry practitioners, several NLP tasks, especially text classification, still widely use several of the non-DL approaches we described earlier in the chapter. Two primary reasons for this are a lack of the large amounts of task-specific training data that neural networks demand and issues related to computing and deployment costs.

 DL-based text classifiers are often nothing but condensed representations of the data they were trained on. These models are often as good as the training dataset. Selecting the right dataset becomes all the more important in such cases.

We'll end this section by reiterating what we mentioned earlier when we discussed the text classification pipeline: in most industrial settings, it always makes sense to start with a simpler, easy-to-deploy approach as your MVP and go from there incrementally, taking customer needs and feasibility into account.

We've seen several approaches to building text classification models so far. Unlike heuristics-based approaches where the predictions can be justified by tracing back the rules applied on the data sample, ML models are treated as a black box while making predictions. However, in the recent past, the topic of interpretable ML started to gain prominence, and programs that can "explain" an ML model's predictions exist now. Let's take a quick look at their application for text classification.

Interpreting Text Classification Models

In the previous sections, we've seen how to train text classifiers using multiple approaches. In all these examples, we took the classifier predictions as is, without seeking any explanations. In fact, most real-world use cases of text classification may be similar—we just consume the classifier's output and don't question its decisions. Take spam classification: we generally don't look for explanations of why a certain email is classified as spam or regular email. However, there may be scenarios where such explanations are necessary.

Consider a scenario where we developed a classifier that identifies abusive comments on a discussion forum website. The classifier identifies comments that are objectionable/abusive and performs the job of a human moderator by either deleting them or making them invisible to users. We know that classifiers aren't perfect and can make errors. What if the commenter questions this moderation decision and asks for an explanation? Some method to "explain" the classification decision by pointing to which feature's presence prompted such a decision can be useful in such cases. Such a method is also useful to provide some insights into the model and how it may perform on real-world data (instead of train/test sets), which may result in better, more reliable models in the future.

As ML models started getting deployed in real-world applications, interest in the direction of model interpretability grew. Recent research [26, 27] resulted in usable tools [28, 29] for interpreting model predictions (especially for classification). Lime [28] is one such tool that attempts to interpret a black-box classification model by approximating it with a linear model locally around a given training instance. The advantage of this is that such a linear model is expressed as a weighted sum of its features and is easy to interpret for humans. For example, if there are two features, f1 and f2, for a given test instance of a binary classifier with classes A and B, a Lime linear model around this instance could be something like -0.3 × f1 + 0.4 × f2 with a prediction B. This indicates that the presence of feature f1 will negatively affect this prediction (by 0.3) and skew it toward A. [26] explains this in more detail. Let's now look at how Lime [28] can be used to understand the predictions of a text classifier.

Explaining Classifier Predictions with Lime

Let's take a model we already built earlier in this chapter and see how Lime can help us interpret its predictions. The following code snippet uses the logistic regression model we built earlier using the "Economy News Article Tone and Relevance" dataset, which classifies a given news article as being relevant or non-relevant and shows how we can use Lime (the full code can be accessed in the notebook *Ch4/Lime-Demo.ipynb*):

```
from lime import lime_text
from lime.lime_text import LimeTextExplainer
from sklearn.pipeline import make_pipeline

y_pred_prob = classifier.predict_proba(X_test_dtm)[:, 1]
c = make_pipeline(vect, classifier)
mystring = list(X_test)[221] #Take a string from test instance
print(c.predict_proba([mystring])) #Prediction is a "No" here, i.e., not relevant
class_names = ["no", "yes"] #not relevant, relevant
explainer = LimeTextExplainer(class_names=class_names)
exp = explainer.explain_instance(mystring, c.predict_proba, num_features=6)
exp.as_list()
```

This code shows six features that played an important role in making this prediction. They're as follows:

```
[('YORK', 0.23416984139912805),
 ('NEW', -0.22724581340890154),
 ('showing', -0.12532906927967377),
 ('AP', -0.08486610147834726),
 ('dropped', 0.079582819439957331),
 ('trend', 0.06567603359316518)]
```

Thus, the output of the above code can be seen as a linear sum of these six features. This would mean that, if we remove the features "NEW" and "showing," the prediction should move toward the opposite class, i.e., "relevant/Yes," by 0.35 (the sum of the weights of these two features). Lime also has functions to visualize these predictions. Figure 4-8 shows a visualization of the above explanation.

As shown in the figure, the presence of three words—York, trend, and dropped—skews the prediction toward Yes, whereas the other three words skew the prediction toward No. Apart from some uses we mentioned earlier, such visualizations of classifiers can also help us if we want to do some informed feature selection.

We hope this brief introduction gave you an idea of what to do if you have to explain a classifier's predictions. We also have a notebook (*Ch4/Lime_RNN.ipynb*) that explains an LSTM model's predictions using Lime, and we leave this detailed exploration of Lime as an exercise for the reader.

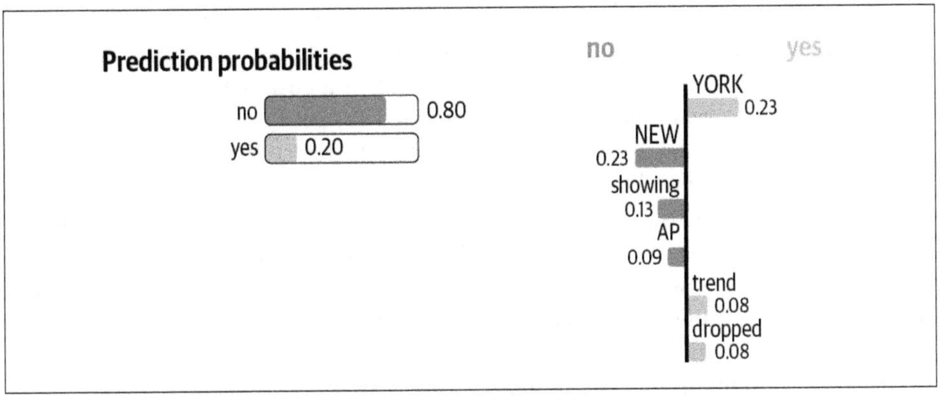
Prediction probabilities
no
0.80
yes
0.20
no
yes
YORK
0.23
NEW
0.23
showing
0.13
AP
0.09
trend
0.08
dropped
0.08

Figure 4-8. Visualization of Lime's explanation of a classifier's prediction

Learning with No or Less Data and Adapting to New Domains

In all the examples we've seen so far, we had a relatively large training dataset available for the task. However, in most real-world scenarios, such datasets are not readily available. In other cases, we may have an annotated dataset available, but it might not be large enough to train a good classifier. There can also be cases where we have a large dataset of, say, customer complaints and requests for one product suite, but we're asked to customize our classifier to another product suite for which we have a very small amount of data (i.e., we're adapting an existing model to a new domain). In this section, let's discuss how to build good classification systems for these scenarios where we have no or little data or have to adapt to new domain training data.

No Training Data

Let's say we're asked to design a classifier for segregating customer complaints for our e-commerce company. The classifier is expected to automatically route customer complaint emails into a set of categories: billing, delivery, and others. If we're fortunate, we may discover a source of large amounts of annotated data for this task within the organization in the form of a historical database of customer requests and their categories. If such a database doesn't exist, where should we start to build our classifier?

The first step in such a scenario is creating an annotated dataset where customer complaints are mapped to the set of categories mentioned above. One way to approach this is to get customer service agents to manually label some of the complaints and use that as the training data for our ML model. Another approach is called "bootstrapping" or "weak supervision." There can be certain patterns of information in different categories of customer requests. Perhaps billing-related requests mention variants of the word "bill," amounts in a currency, etc. Delivery-related requests talk about shipping, delays, etc. We can get started with compiling some such patterns and using their presence or absence in a customer request to label it, thereby creating a small (perhaps noisy) annotated dataset for this classification task. From here, we can build a classifier to annotate a larger collection of data. Snorkel [30], a recent software tool developed by Stanford University, is useful for deploying weak supervision for various learning tasks, including classification. Snorkel was used to deploy weak supervision–based text classification models at industrial scale at Google [31]. They showed that weak supervision could create classifiers comparable in quality to those trained on tens of thousands of hand-labeled examples! [32] shows an example of how to use Snorkel to generate training data for text classification using a large amount of unlabeled data.

In some other scenarios where large-scale collection of data is necessary and feasible, crowdsourcing can be seen as an option to label the data. Websites like Amazon Mechanical Turk and Figure Eight provide platforms to make use of human intelligence to create high-quality training data for ML tasks. A popular example of using the wisdom of crowds to create a classification dataset is the "CAPTCHA test," which Google uses to ask if a set of images contain a given object (e.g., "Select all images that contain a street sign").

Less Training Data: Active Learning and Domain Adaptation

In scenarios like the one described earlier, where we collected small amounts of data using human annotations or bootstrapping, it may sometimes turn out that the amount of data is too small to build a good classification model. It's also possible that most of the requests we collected belonged to billing and very few belonged to the other categories, resulting in a highly imbalanced dataset. Asking the agents to spend many hours doing manual annotation is not always feasible. What should we do in such scenarios?

One approach to address such problems is *active learning*, which is primarily about identifying which data points are more crucial to be used as training data. It helps answer the following question: if we had 1,000 data points but could get only 100 of them labeled, which 100 would we choose? What this means is that, when it comes to training data, not all data points are equal. Some data points are more important as compared to others in determining the quality of the classifier trained. Active learning converts this into a continuous process.

Using active learning for training a classifier can be described as a step-by-step process:

1. Train the classifier with the available amount of data.
2. Start using the classifier to make predictions on new data.

3. For the data points where the classifier is very unsure of its predictions, send them to human annotators for their correct classification.

4. Include these data points in the existing training data and retrain the model.

Repeat Steps 1 through 4 until a satisfactory model performance is reached.

Tools like Prodigy [33] have active learning solutions implemented for text classification and support the efficient usage of active learning to create annotated data and text classification models quickly. The basic idea behind active learning is that the data points where the model is less confident are the data points that contribute most significantly to improving the quality of the model, and therefore only those data points get labeled.

Now, imagine a scenario for our customer complaint classifier where we have a lot of historical data for a range of products. However, we're now asked to tune it to work on a set of newer products. What's potentially challenging in this situation? Typical text classification approaches rely on the vocabulary of the training data. Hence, they're inherently biased toward the kind of language seen in the training data. So, if the new products are very different (e.g., the model is trained on a suite of electronic products and we're using it for complaints on cosmetic products), the pre-trained classifiers trained on some other source data are unlikely to perform well. However, it's also not realistic to train a new model from scratch on each product or product suite, as we'll again run into the problem of insufficient training data. Domain adaptation is a method to address such scenarios; this is also called *transfer learning*. Here, we "transfer" what we learned from one domain (source) with large amounts of data to another domain (target) with less labeled data but large amounts of unlabeled data. We already saw one example of how to use BERT for text classification earlier in this chapter.

This approach for domain adaptation in text classification can be summarized as follows:

1. Start with a large, pre-trained language model trained on a large dataset of the source domain (e.g., Wikipedia data).

2. Fine-tune this model using the target language's unlabeled data.

3. Train a classifier on the labeled target domain data by extracting feature representations from the fine-tuned language model from Step 2.

ULMFit [34] is another popular domain adaptation approach for text classification. In research experiments, it was shown that this approach matches the performance of training from scratch with 10 to 20 times more training examples and only 100 labeled examples in text classification tasks. When unlabeled data was used to fine-tune the pre-trained language model, it matched the performance of using 50 to 100 times more labeled examples when trained from scratch, on the same text classification tasks. Transfer learning methods are currently an active area of research in NLP. Their use for text classification has not yet shown dramatic improvements on standard datasets, nor are they the default solution for all classification scenarios in industry setups yet. But we can expect to see this approach yielding better and better results in the near future.

So far, we've seen a range of text classification methods and discussed obtaining appropriate training data and using different feature representations for training the classifiers. We also briefly touched on how to interpret the predictions made by some text classification models. Let's now consolidate what we've learned so far using a small case study of building a text classifier for a real-world scenario.

Case Study: Corporate Ticketing

Let's consider a real-world scenario and learn how we can apply some of the concepts we've discussed in this section. Imagine we're asked to build a ticketing system for our organization that will track all the tickets or issues people face in the organization and route them to either internal or external agents. Figure 4-9 shows a representative screenshot for such a system; it's a corporate ticketing system called Spoke.

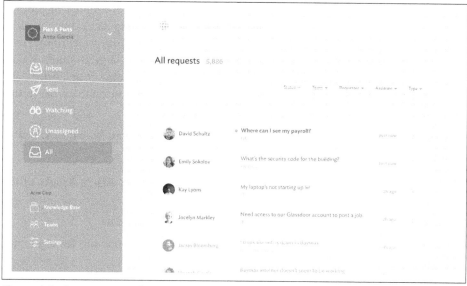

Figure 4-9. A corporate ticketing system

Now let's say our company has recently hired a medical counsel and partnered with a hospital. So our system should also be able to pinpoint any medical-related issue and route it to the relevant people and teams. But while we have some past tickets, none of them are labeled as health related. In the absence of these labels, how will we go about building such a health issue–related classification system?

Let's explore a couple of options:

Use existing APIs or libraries
> One option is to start with a public API or library and map its classes to what's relevant to us. For instance, the Google APIs mentioned earlier in the chapter can classify content into over 700 categories. There are 82 categories associated with medical or health issues. These include categories like /Health/Health Conditions/Pain Management, /Health/Medical Facilities & Services/Doctors' Offices, /Finance/Insurance/Health Insurance, etc.
>
> While not all categories are relevant to our organization, some could be, and we can map these accordingly. For example, let's say our company doesn't consider substance abuse and obesity issues as relevant for medical counsel. We can ignore /Health/Substance Abuse and /Health/Health Conditions/Obesity in this API. Similarly, whether insurance should be a part of HR or referred outside can also be handled with these categories.

Use public datasets
> We can also adopt public datasets for our needs. For example, 20 Newsgroups is a popular text classification dataset, and it's also part of the sklearn library. It has a range of topics, including sci.med. We can also use it to train a basic classifier, classifying all other topics in one category and sci.med in another.

Utilize weak supervision
> We have a history of past tickets, but they're not labeled. So, we can consider bootstrapping a dataset out of it using the approaches described earlier in this section. For example, consider having a rule: "If the past ticket contains words like fever, diarrhea, headache, or nausea, put them in the medical counsel category." This rule can create a small amount of data, which we can use as a starting point for our classifier.

Active learning
> We can use tools like Prodigy to conduct data collection experiments where we ask someone working at the customer service desk to look at ticket descriptions and tag them with a preset list of categories. Figure 4-10 shows an example of using Prodigy for this purpose.

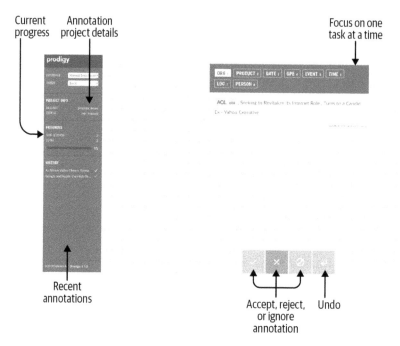

Figure 4-10. Active learning with Prodigy

Learning from implicit and explicit feedback

Throughout the process of building, iterating, and deploying this solution, we're getting feedback that we can use to improve our system. Explicit feedback could be when the medical counsel or hospital says explicitly that the ticket was not relevant. Implicit feedback could be extracted from other dependent variables like ticket response times and ticket response rates. All of these could be factored in to improve our model using active learning techniques.

A sample pipeline summarizing these ideas may look like what's shown in Figure 4-11. We start with no labeled data and use either a public API or a model created with a public dataset or weak supervision as the first baseline model. Once we put this model to production, we'll get explicit and implicit signals on where it's working or failing. We use this information to refine our model and active learning to select the best set of instances that need to be labeled. Over time, as we collect more data, we can build more sophisticated and deeper models.

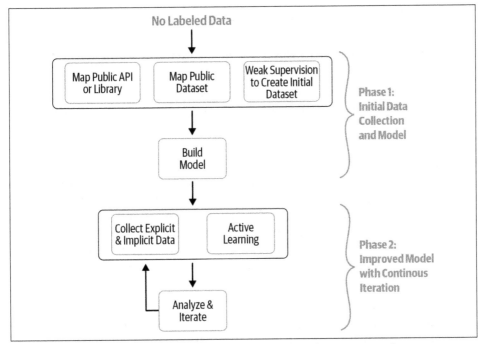

Figure 4-11. A pipeline for building a classifier when there's no training data

In this section, we started looking at a practical scenario of not having enough training data for building our own text classifier for our custom problem. We discussed several possible solutions to address the issue. Hopefully, this helps you foresee and prepare for some of the scenarios related to data collection and creation in your future projects related to text classification.

Practical Advice

So far, we've shown a range of different methods for building text classifiers and potential issues you may run into. We'd like to end this chapter with some practical advice that summarizes our observations and experience with building text classification systems in industry. Most of these are generic enough to be applied to other topics in the book as well.

Establish strong baselines

A common fallacy is to start with a state-of-the-art algorithm. This is especially true in the current era of deep learning, where every day, new approaches/algorithms keep coming up. However, it's always good to start with simpler approaches and try to establish strong baselines first. This is useful for three main reasons:

a. It helps us get a better understanding of the problem statement and key challenges.

b. Building a quick MVP helps us get initial feedback from end users and stakeholders.

c. A state-of-the-art research model may give us only a minor improvement compared to the baseline, but it might come with a huge amount of technical debt.

Balance training data

While working with classification, it's very important to have a balanced dataset where all categories have an equal representation. An imbalanced dataset can adversely impact the learning of the algorithm and result in a *biased* classifier. While we cannot always control this aspect of the training data, there are various techniques to fix class imbalance in the training data. Some of them are collecting more data, resampling (undersample from majority classes or oversample from minority classes), and weight balancing.

Combine models and humans in the loop

In practical scenarios, it makes sense to combine the outputs of multiple classification models with handcrafted rules from domain experts to achieve the best performance for the business. In other cases, it's practical to defer the decision to a human evaluator if the machine is not sure of its classification decision. Finally, there could also be scenarios where the learned model has to change with time and newer data. We'll discuss some solutions for such scenarios in Chapter 11, which focuses on end-to-end systems.

Make it work, make it better

Building a classification system is not just about building a model. For most industrial settings, building a model is often just 5% to 10% of the total project. The rest consists of gathering data, building data pipelines, deployment, testing, monitoring, etc. It is always good to build a model quickly, use it to build a system, then start improvement iterations. This helps us to quickly identify major roadblocks and the parts that need the most work, and it's often not the modeling part.

Use the wisdom of many

Every text classification algorithm has its own strengths and weaknesses. There is no single algorithm that always works well. One way to circumvent this is via *ensembling*: training multiple classifiers. The data is passed through every classifier, and the predictions generated are combined (e.g., majority voting) to arrive at a final class prediction. An interested reader can look at the work of Dong et al. [35, 36] for a deep dive into ensemble methods for text classification.

Wrapping Up

In this chapter, we saw how to address the problem of text classification from multiple viewpoints. We discussed how to identify a classification problem, tackle the various stages in a text classification pipeline, collect data to create relevant datasets, use different feature representations, and train several classification algorithms. With this, we hope you're now well-equipped and ready to solve text classification problems for your use case and scenario and understand how to use existing solutions, build our own classifiers using various methods, and tackle the roadblocks you may face in the process. We focused on only one aspect of building text classification systems in industry applications: building the model. Issues related to the end-to-end deployment of NLP systems will be dealt with in Chapter 11. In the next chapter, we'll use some of the ideas we learned here to tackle a related but different NLP problem: information extraction.

References

[1] United States Postal Service. *The United States Postal Service: An American History* (*https://oreil.ly/g32q4*), 57–60. ISBN: 978-0-96309-524-4. Last accessed June 15, 2020.

[2] Gupta, Anuj, Saurabh Arora, Satyam Saxena, and Navaneethan Santhanam. "Noise reduction and smart ticketing for social media-based communication systems." US Patent Application 20190026653, filed January 24, 2019.

[3] Spasojevic, Nemanja and Adithya Rao. "Identifying Actionable Messages on Social Media." *2015 IEEE International Conference on Big Data*: 2273–2281.

[4] CLPSYCH: Computational Linguistics and Clinical Psychology Workshop (*https://oreil.ly/qBOLP*). Shared Tasks 2019.

[5] Google Cloud. "Natural Language" (*https://oreil.ly/6JR2T*). Last accessed June 15, 2020.

[6] Amazon Comprehend (*https://oreil.ly/NlU3m*). Last accessed June 15, 2020.

[7] Azure Cognitive Services (*https://oreil.ly/7qZSK*). Last accessed June 15, 2020.

[8] Iderhoff, Nicolas. nlp-datasets: Alphabetical list of free/public domain datasets with text data for use in Natural Language Processing (NLP) (*https://oreil.ly/NcwbT*), (GitHub repo). Last accessed June 15, 2020.

[9] Kaggle. "Sentiment Analysis: Emotion in Text" (*https://oreil.ly/Imbhb*). Last accessed June 15, 2020.

[10] UC Irvine Machine Learning Repository. A collection of repositories for machine learning (*https://oreil.ly/YsY4f*). Last accessed June 15, 2020.

[11] Google. "Dataset Search" (*https://oreil.ly/GJxBp*). Last accessed June 15, 2020.

[12] Jurafsky, Dan and James H. Martin. *Speech and Language Processing* (*https://oreil.ly/Ta16f*), Third Edition (Draft), 2018.

[13] Lemaître, Guillaume, Fernando Nogueira, and Christos K. Aridas. "Imbalanced-learn: A Python Toolbox to Tackle the Curse of Imbalanced Datasets in Machine Learning" (*https://oreil.ly/GIj0o*). *The Journal of Machine Learning Research* 18.1 (2017): 559–563.

[14] For a detailed mathematical description of logistic regression, refer to Chapter 5 in [12].

[15] Google. Pre-trained word2vec model (*https://oreil.ly/JLX5C*). Last accessed June 15, 2020.

[16] Bojanowski, Piotr, Edouard Grave, Armand Joulin, and Tomas Mikolov. "Enriching Word Vectors with Subword Information." *Transactions of the Association for Computational Linguistics* 5 (2017): 135–146.

[17] Joulin, Armand, Edouard Grave, Piotr Bojanowski, and Tomas Mikolov. "Bag of Tricks for Efficient Text Classification" (*https://oreil.ly/uJX-t*). (2016).

[18] Ramesh, Sree Harsha. torchDatasets (*https://oreil.ly/MaLab*), (GitHub repo). Last accessed June 15, 2020.

[19] Joulin, Armand, Edouard Grave, Piotr Bojanowski, Matthijs Douze, Hérve Jégou, and Tomas Mikolov. "Fasttext.zip: Compressing text classification models" (*https://oreil.ly/LEf1y*). (2016).

[20] For older Doc2vec versions, there are some pre-trained models; e.g., *https://oreil.ly/kt0U0* (last accessed June 15, 2020).

[21] Natural Language Toolkit. "NLTK 3.5 documentation" (*https://www.nltk.org*). Last accessed June 15, 2020.

[22] Lau, Jey Han and Timothy Baldwin. "An Empirical Evaluation of doc2vec with Practical Insights into Document Embedding Generation" (*https://oreil.ly/SgtZK*). (2016).

[23] Stanford Artificial Intelligence Laboratory. "Large Movie Review Dataset" (*https://oreil.ly/ehHdC*). Last accessed June 15, 2020.

[24] Goodfellow, Ian, Yoshua Bengio, and Aaron Courville. *Deep Learning*. Cambridge: MIT Press, 2016. ISBN: 978-0-26203-561-3

[25] Goldberg, Yoav. "Neural Network Methods for Natural Language Processing." *Synthesis Lectures on Human Language Technologies* 10.1 (2017): 1–309.

[26] Ribeiro, Marco Tulio, Sameer Singh, and Carlos Guestrin. "'Why Should I Trust You?' Explaining the Predictions of Any Classifier." *Proceedings of the 22nd ACM*

SIGKDD International Conference on Knowledge Discovery and Data Mining (2016): 1135–1144.

[27] Lundberg, Scott M. and Su-In Lee. "A Unified Approach to Interpreting Model Predictions." *Advances in Neural Information Processing Systems* 30 (NIPS 2017): 4765–4774.

[28] Marco Tulio Correia Ribeiro. Lime: Explaining the predictions of any machine learning classifier (*https://oreil.ly/AadAv*), (GitHub repo). Last accessed June 15, 2020.

[29] Lundberg, Scott. shap: A game theoretic approach to explain the output of any machine learning model (*https://oreil.ly/Spm6i*), (GitHub repo).

[30] Snorkel. "Programmatically Building and Managing Training Data" (*https://www.snorkel.org*). Last accessed June 15, 2020.

[31] Bach, Stephen H., Daniel Rodriguez, Yintao Liu, Chong Luo, Haidong Shao, Cassandra Xia, Souvik Sen et al. "Snorkel DryBell: A Case Study in Deploying Weak Supervision at Industrial Scale" (*https://oreil.ly/CnWxH*). (2018).

[32] Snorkel. "Snorkel Intro Tutorial: Data Labeling" (*https://oreil.ly/3emjt*). Last accessed June 15, 2020.

[33] Prodigy (*https://prodi.gy*). Last accessed June 15, 2020.

[34] Fast.ai. "Introducing state of the art text classification with universal language models" (*https://oreil.ly/vHgQk*). Last accessed June 15, 2020.

[35] Dong, Yan-Shi and Ke-Song Han. "A comparison of several ensemble methods for text categorization." *IEEE International Conference on Services Computing* (2004): 419–422.

[36] Caruana, Rich, Alexandru Niculescu-Mizil, Geoff Crew, and Alex Ksikes. "Ensemble Selection from Libraries of Models." *Proceedings of the Twenty-First International Conference on Machine Learning* (2004): 18.

## CHAPTER 5

Information Extraction

What's in a name? A rose
by any other name would smell as sweet.
—William Shakespeare

We deal with a lot of textual content every day, be it short messages on the phone or daily emails or longer texts we read for fun or at work or to catch up on current affairs. Such text documents are a rich source of information for us. Depending on the context, "information" can mean multiple things, such as key events, people, or relationships between people, places, or organizations, etc. Information extraction (IE) refers to the NLP task of extracting relevant information from text documents. An example of IE put to use in real-world applications are the short blurbs we see to the right when we search for a popular figure's name on Google.

When compared to structured information sources like databases or tables or semi-structured sources such as webpages (which have some markup), text is a form of unstructured data. For example, in a database, we know where to look for something based on its schema. However, to a large extent, text documents typically comprise free-flowing text without a set schema. This makes IE a challenging problem. Texts may contain various kinds of information. In most cases, extracting information that has a fixed pattern (e.g., addresses, phone numbers, dates, etc.) is relatively straight-forward using pattern-based extraction techniques like regular expressions, even though the text itself is considered unstructured data. However, extracting other information (e.g., names of people, relations between different entities in the text, details for a calendar event, etc.) may require more advanced language processing.

In this chapter, we'll discuss various IE tasks and the methods for implementing them for our applications. We'll start with a brief historical background, followed by an overview of different IE tasks and applications of IE in the real world. We'll then introduce the typical NLP processing pipeline for solving any IE task and move on to discuss how to solve specific IE tasks—key phrase extraction, named entity recognition, named entity disambiguation and linking, and relationship extraction—along with some practical advice on implementing them in your projects. We'll then present a case study of how IE is used in a real-world scenario and briefly cover other advanced IE tasks. With this introduction, let's explore IE, starting with a brief history.

Approaches for extracting different kinds of information from documents like scientific papers and medical reports have been proposed in the past in the research community. However, Message Understanding Conferences organized by the US Navy (1987–1998) [1] can be considered the starting point for modern-day research on information extraction from text. This was followed by the Automatic Content Extraction Program (1999–2008) [2] and the Text Analysis Conference (2009–2018) series organized by NIST [3], which introduced competitions for extracting different kinds of information from text, from recognizing names of different entities to constructing large, queryable knowledge bases. Existing libraries and methods for extracting various forms of information from text and their use in real-world applications trace their origins back to the research that started in these conference series. Before we start looking at what the methods and libraries for IE are, let's first take a look at some examples of where IE is used in real-world applications.

IE Applications

IE is used in a wide range of real-world applications, from news articles, to social media, and even receipts. Here, we'll cover the details of a few of them:

Tagging news and other content

There's a lot of text generated about various events happening around the world every day. In addition to classifying text using methods discussed in Chapter 4, it's useful for some applications, such as search engines and recommendation systems, if such texts are tagged with important entities mentioned within them. For example, look at Figure 5-1, which shows a screenshot from the Google News [4] homepage.

People (e.g., Jean Vanier), organizations (e.g., Progressive Conservative Party of Ontario), locations (e.g., Canada), and events (e.g., Brexit) currently in the news are extracted and shown to the reader so that they can go directly to news about a specific entity. This is one example of information extraction at work in a popular application.

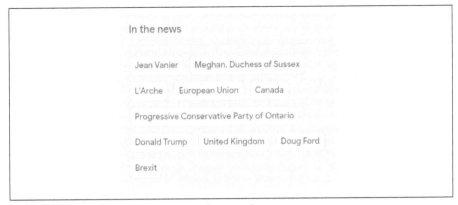

Figure 5-1. Screenshot from the Google News homepage

Chatbots

A chatbot needs to understand the user's question in order to generate/retrieve a correct response. For example, consider the question, "What are the best cafes around the Eiffel Tower?" The chatbot needs to understand that "Eiffel Tower" and "cafe" are locations, then identify cafes within a certain distance of the Eiffel Tower. IE is useful in extracting such specific information from a pool of available data. We'll discuss more on chatbots in Chapter 6.

Applications in social media

A lot of information is disseminated through social media channels like Twitter. Extracting informative excerpts from social media text may help in decision making. An example use case is extracting time-sensitive, frequently updated information, such as traffic updates and disaster relief efforts, based on tweets. NLP for Twitter is one of the most useful applications that utilizes the abundant information present in social media. We'll touch on some of these applications in Chapter 8.

Extracting data from forms and receipts

Many banking apps nowadays have the feature to scan a check and deposit the money directly into the user's account. Whether you're an individual, small business, or larger business enterprise, it's not uncommon to use apps that scan bills and receipts. Along with optical character recognition (OCR), information extraction techniques play an important role in these apps [5, 6]. We won't discuss this aspect in this chapter, as OCR is the primary step in such applications and isn't part of the processing pipelines in this book.

Now that we have an idea of what IE is and where it's useful, let's move on to understanding what the different tasks covered under IE are.

IE Tasks

IE is a term that's used to refer to a range of different tasks of varying complexity. The overarching goal of IE is to extract "knowledge" from text, and each of these tasks provides different information to do that. To understand what these tasks are, consider the snippet from a *New York Times* article shown in Figure 5-2.

SAN FRANCISCO — Shortly after Apple used a new tax law last year to bring back most of the $252 billion it had held abroad, the company said it would buy back $100 billion of its stock.

On Tuesday, Apple announced its plans for another major chunk of the money: It will buy back a further $75 billion in stock.

"Our first priority is always looking after the business and making sure we continue to grow and invest," Luca Maestri, Apple's finance chief, said in an interview. "If there is excess cash, then obviously we want to return it to investors."

Apple's record buybacks should be welcome news to shareholders, as the stock price is likely to climb. But the buybacks could also expose the company to more criticism that the tax cuts it received have mostly benefited investors and executives.

Figure 5-2. A New York Times article from April 30, 2019 [7]

As human readers, we find several useful pieces of information in this blurb. For example, we know that the article is about Apple, the company (and not the fruit), and that it mentions a person, Luca Maestri, who is the finance chief of the company. The article is about the buyback of stock and other issues related to it. For a machine to understand all this involves different levels of IE.

Identifying that the article is about "buyback" or "stock price" relates to the IE task of *keyword* or *keyphrase extraction (KPE)*. Identifying Apple as an organization and Luca Maestri as a person comes under the IE task of *named entity recognition (NER)*. Recognizing that Apple is not a fruit, but a company, and that it refers to Apple, Inc. and not some other company with the word "apple" in its name is the IE task of *named entity disambiguation and linking*. Extracting the information that Luca Maestri is the finance chief of Apple refers to the IE task of *relation extraction*.

There are a few advanced IE tasks beyond those mentioned above. Identifying that this article is about a single event (let's call it "Apple buys back stocks") and being able to link it to other articles talking about the same event over time refers to the IE task of *event extraction*. A related task is *temporal information extraction*, which aims to extract information about times and dates, which is also useful for developing calendar applications and interactive personal assistants. Finally, many applications, such as automatically generating weather reports or flight announcements, follow a standard template with some slots that need to be filled based on extracted data. This IE task is known as *template filling*.

Each of these tasks requires different levels of language processing. A range of rule-based methods as well as supervised, unsupervised, and semi-supervised machine learning (including state-of-the-art deep learning approaches) can be used for developing solutions to solve these tasks. However, considering that IE is very much dependent on the application domain (e.g., finance, news, airlines, etc.), IE in industry is generally implemented as a hybrid system incorporating rule-based and learning-based approaches [8, 9]. IE is still a very active area of research, and not all these tasks are considered "solved" or matured enough to have standard approaches that can be used in real-world application scenarios. Tasks such as KPE and NER are more widely studied than others and have some tried-and-tested solutions. The rest of the tasks are relatively more challenging, and it's more common to rely on pay-as-you-use services from large providers like Microsoft, Google, and IBM.

An important point to note regarding IE is that the datasets needed to train IE models are typically more specialized than what we saw, for example, in Chapter 4, where all we needed to get started was a collection of texts mapped to some categories. Hence, real-world use cases of IE may not always require us to train models from scratch, and we can make use of external APIs for some tasks. Before moving on to specific tasks, let's first take a look at the general NLP pipeline for any IE task.

The General Pipeline for IE

The general pipeline for IE requires more fine-grained NLP processing than what we saw for text classification (Chapter 4). For example, to identify named entities (persons, organizations, etc.), we would need to know the part-of-speech tags of words. For relating multiple references to the same entity (e.g., Albert Einstein, Einstein, the scientist, he, etc.), we would need coreference resolution. Note that none of these are mandatory steps for building a text classification system. Thus, IE is a task that is more NLP intensive than text classification. Figure 5-3 shows a typical NLP pipeline for IE tasks. Not all steps in the pipeline are necessary for all IE tasks, and the figure demonstrates which IE tasks require what levels of analysis.

We discussed the details of the different processing steps illustrated in this figure in Chapters 1 and 2. As the figure shows, key phrase extraction is the task requiring minimal NLP processing (some algorithms also do POS tagging before extracting keyphrases), whereas, other than named entity recognition, all the other IE tasks require deeper NLP pre-processing followed by models developed for those specific tasks. IE tasks are typically evaluated in terms of precision, recall, and F1 scores using standard evaluation sets. Considering the different levels of NLP pre-processing required, IE tasks are also affected by the accuracy of these processing steps themselves. Collecting relevant training data and training our own models for IE, if necessary, should take all these aspects into account. With this background, let's now start looking at each of the IE tasks, one by one.

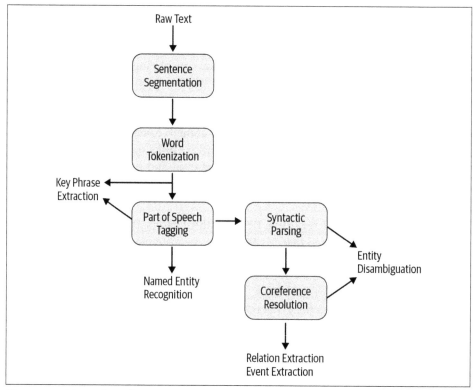

Figure 5-3. IE pipeline illustrating NLP processing needed for some IE tasks

Keyphrase Extraction

Consider a scenario where we want to buy a product, which has a hundred reviews, on Amazon. There's no way we're going to read all of them to get an idea of what users think about the product. To facilitate this, Amazon has a filtering feature: "Read reviews that mention." This presents a bunch of keywords or phrases that several people used in these reviews to filter the reviews, as shown in Figure 5-4. This is a good example of where KPE can be useful in an application we all use.

Keyword and phrase extraction, as the name indicates, is the IE task concerned with extracting important words and phrases that capture the gist of the text from a given text document. It's useful for several downstream NLP tasks, such as search/information retrieval, automatic document tagging, recommendation systems, text summarization, etc.

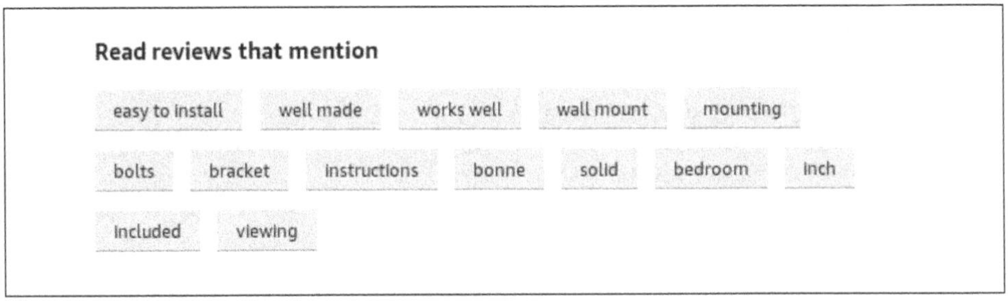

Read reviews that mention

easy to install   well made   works well   wall mount   mounting

bolts   bracket   instructions   bonne   solid   bedroom   inch

included   viewing

Figure 5-4. "Read reviews that mention" on Amazon.ca

KPE is a well-studied problem in the NLP community, and the two most commonly used methods to solve it are supervised learning and unsupervised learning. Supervised learning approaches require corpora with texts and their respective keyphrases and use engineered features or DL techniques [10]. Creating such labeled datasets for KPE is a time- and cost-intensive endeavor. Hence, unsupervised approaches that do not require a labeled dataset and are largely domain agnostic are more popular for KPE. These approaches are also more commonly used in real-world KPE applications. Recent research has also shown that state-of-the-art DL methods for KPE don't perform any better than unsupervised approaches [11].

All the popular unsupervised KPE algorithms are based on the idea of representing the words and phrases in a text as nodes in a weighted graph where the weight indicates the importance of that keyphrase. Keyphrases are then identified based on how connected they are with the rest of the graph. The top-N important nodes from the graph are then returned as keyphrases. Important nodes are those words and phrases that are frequent enough and also well connected to different parts of the text. The different graph-based KPE approaches differ in the way they select potential words/phrases from the text (from a large set of possible words and phrases in the entire text) and the way these words/phrases are scored in the graph.

There's a huge body of work on this topic, with some working implementations available. In most cases, existing approaches are a great starting point to meet your requirements. How can we use these to implement a keyphrase extractor in our project? Let 's look at an example.

Implementing KPE

The Python library textacy [12], built on top of the well-known library spaCy [13], contains implementations for some of the common graph-based keyword and phrase extraction algorithms. The notebook associated with this section (*Ch5/KPE.ipynb*) illustrates the use of textacy to extract keyphrases using two algorithms, TextRank

[14] and SGRank. We'll use a text file that talks about the history of NLP as our test document. The code snippet below illustrates KPE with textacy:

```
from textacy import *
import textacy.ke

mytext = open("nlphistory.txt").read()
en = textacy.load_spacy_lang("en_core_web_sm", disable=("parser",))
doc = textacy.make_spacy_doc(mytext, lang=en)

print("Textrank output: ", [kps for kps, weights in
textacy.ke.textrank(doc, normalize="lemma",  topn=5)])

print("SGRank output: ", [kps for kps, weights in
textacy.ke.sgrank(mydoc, n_keyterms=5)])

Output:
Textrank output:  ['successful natural language processing system',
'statistical machine translation system', 'natural language system',
'statistical natural language processing', 'natural language task']

SGRank output:  ['natural language processing system',
'statistical machine translation', 'research', 'late 1980', 'early']
```

There are numerous options for how long our n-grams should be in these phrases; what POS tags should be considered or ignored; what pre-processing should be done a priori; how to eliminate overlapping n-grams, such as statistical machine translation and machine translation in the above example; and so on. Some of these are explored in the notebook, and we leave the rest as exercises for the reader.

We showed one example of implementing KPE with textacy. There are other options, though. For example, the Python library gensim has a keyword extractor based on TextRank [15]. [16] shows how to implement TextRank from scratch. You can explore multiple library implementations and compare them before choosing one.

Practical Advice

We've seen how keyphrase extraction can be implemented using spaCy and textacy and how we can modify it to suit our needs. From a practical point of view, there are a few caveats to keep in mind when using such graph-based algorithms in production, though. We'll list a few of them below, along with some suggestions for working around them based on our experience with adding KPE as a feature in software products:

- The process of extracting potential n-grams and building the graph with them is sensitive to document length, which could be an issue in a production scenario. One approach to dealing with it is to not use the full text, but instead try using the first M% and the last N% of the text, since we would expect that the introductory and concluding parts of the text should cover the main summary of the text.

- Since each keyphrase is independently ranked, we sometimes end up seeing overlapping keyphrases (e.g., "buy back stock" and "buy back"). One solution for this could be to use some similarity measure (e.g., cosine similarity) between the top-ranked keyphrases and choose the ones that are most dissimilar to one another. textacy already implements a function to address this issue, as shown in the notebook.

- Seeing counterproductive patterns (e.g., a keyphrase that starts with a preposition when you don't want that) is another common problem. This is relatively straightforward to handle by tweaking the implementation code for the algorithm and explicitly encoding information about such unwanted word patterns.

- Improper text extraction can affect the rest of the KPE process, especially when dealing with formats such as PDF or scanned images. This is primarily because KPE is sensitive to sentence structure in the document. Hence, it's always a good idea to add some post-processing to the extracted key phrases list to create a final, meaningful list without noise.

A custom solution could be a combination of an existing graph-based KPE algorithm that addresses the above-mentioned issues and a domain-specific list of heuristics, if available. From our experience, this covers the issues most commonly encountered with KPE in typical NLP projects.

In this section, we saw how to use KPE algorithms to extract important words and phrases from any document and some ways to overcome potential challenges. While such keyphrases can potentially capture the names of important entities in the text, we're not specifically looking for them when we use KPE algorithms. Let's now look at the next—and perhaps most popular—IE task, which is designed to look specifically for the presence of named entities in the text.

Named Entity Recognition

Consider a scenario where the user asks a search query—"Where was Albert Einstein born?"—using Google search. Figure 5-5 shows a screenshot of what we see before a list of search results.

To be able to show "Ulm, Germany" for this query, the search engine needs to decipher that Albert Einstein is a person before going on to look for a place of birth. This is an example of NER in action in a real-world application.

Figure 5-5. Screenshot of a Google search result

NER refers to the IE task of identifying the entities in a document. Entities are typi-cally names of persons, locations, and organizations, and other specialized strings, such as money expressions, dates, products, names/numbers of laws or articles, and so on. NER is an important step in the pipeline of several NLP applications involving information extraction. Figure 5-6 illustrates the function of NER using the displaCy visualizer by explosion.ai [17].

As seen in the figure, for a given text, NER is expected to identify person names, loca-tions, dates, and other entities. Different categories of entities identified here are some of the ones commonly used in NER system development [18]. NER is a prerequisite for being able to do other IE tasks, such as relation extraction or event extraction, which were introduced earlier in this chapter and will be discussed in greater detail later on. NER is also useful in other applications like machine translation, as names need not necessarily be translated while translating a sentence. So, clearly, there's a range of scenarios in NLP projects where NER is a major component. It's one of the common tasks you're likely to encounter in NLP projects in industry. How do we build such an NER system? The rest of this section focuses on this question, consider-ing three cases: building our own NER system, using existing libraries, and using active learning.

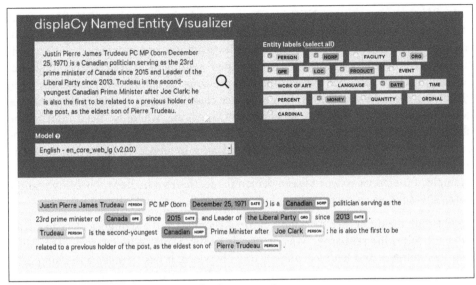

Figure 5-6. NER example using the displaCy visualizer

Building an NER System

A simple approach to building an NER system is to maintain a large collection of person/organization/location names that are the most relevant to our company (e.g., names of all clients, cities in their addresses, etc.); this is typically referred to as a *gazetteer*. To check whether a given word is a named entity or not, just do a lookup in the gazetteer. If a large number of entities present in our data are covered by a gazetteer, then it's a great way to start, especially when we don't have an existing NER system available. There are a few questions to consider with such an approach. How does it deal with new names? How do we periodically update this database? How does it keep track of aliases, i.e., different variations of a given name (e.g., USA, United States, etc.)?

An approach that goes beyond a lookup table is rule-based NER, which can be based on a compiled list of patterns based on word tokens and POS tags. For example, a pattern "NNP was born," where "NNP" is the POS tag for a proper noun, indicates that the word that was tagged "NNP" refers to a person. Such rules can be programmed to cover as many cases as possible to build a rule-based NER system. Stanford NLP's RegexNER [19] and spaCy's EntityRuler [20] provide functionalities to implement your own rule-based NER.

A more practical approach to NER is to train an ML model, which can predict the named entities in unseen text. For each word, a decision has to be made whether or not that word is an entity, and if it is, what type of the entity it is. In many ways, this is very similar to the classification problems we discussed in detail in Chapter 4. The only difference here is that NER is a "sequence labeling" problem [21]. The typical classifiers we saw in Chapter 4 predict labels for texts independent of their surrounding context. Consider a classifier that classifies sentences in a movie review into positive/negative/neutral categories based on their sentiment. This classifier does not (usually) take into account the sentiment of previous (or subsequent) sentences when classifying the current sentence. In a sequence classifier, such context is important. A common use case for sequence labeling is POS tagging, where we need information about the parts of speech of surrounding words to estimate the part of speech of the current word. NER is traditionally modeled as a sequence classification problem, where the entity prediction for the current word also depends on the context. For example, if the previous word was a person name, there's a higher probability that the current word is also a person name if it's a noun (e.g., first and last names).

To illustrate the difference between a normal classifier and a sequence classifier, consider the following sentence: "Washington is a rainy state." When a normal classifier sees this sentence and has to classify it word by word, it has to make a decision as to whether Washington refers to a person (e.g., George Washington) or the State of Washington without looking at the surrounding words. It's possible to classify the word "Washington" in this particular sentence as a location only after looking at the context in which it's being used. It's for this reason that sequence classifiers are used for training NER models.

Conditional random fields (CRFs) is one of the popular sequence classifier training algorithms. The notebook associated with this section (*Ch5/NERTraining.ipynb*) shows how we can use CRFs to train an NER system. We'll use CONLL-03, a popular dataset used for training NER systems [22], and an open source sequence labeling library called sklearn-crfsuite [23], along with a set of simple word- and POS tag–based features, which provide contextual information we need for this task.

To perform sequence classification, we need data in a format that allows us to model the context. Typical training data for NER looks like Figure 5-7, which is a sentence from the CONLL-03 dataset.

The labels in the figure follow what's known as a BIO notation: B indicates the beginning of an entity; I, inside an entity, indicates when entities comprise more than one word; and O, other, indicates non-entities. Peter Such is a name with two words in the example shown in Figure 5-7. Thus, "Peter" gets tagged as a B-PER, and "Such" gets tagged as an I-PER to indicate that Such is a part of the entity from the previous word. The remaining entities in this example, Essex, Yorkshire, and Headingley, are all one-word entities. So, we only see B-ORG and B-LOC as their tags. Once we obtain a dataset of sentences annotated in this form and we have a sequence classifier algorithm, how should we train an NER system?

The steps are the same as those for the text classifiers we saw in Chapter 4:

1. Load the dataset
2. Extract the features
3. Train the classifier
4. Evaluate it on a test set

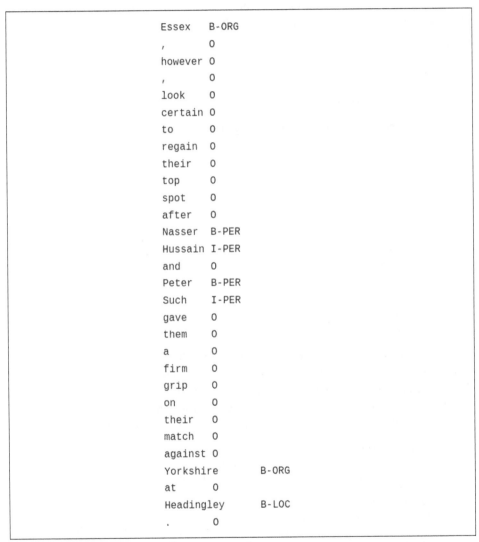

Figure 5-7. NER training data format example

Loading the dataset is straightforward. This particular dataset is also already split into a train/dev/test set. So, we'll train the model using the training set. We saw a range of feature representation techniques in Chapter 3. Let's look at an example using hand-crafted features this time. What features seem intuitively relevant for this task? To identify names of people or places, for example, patterns such as whether the word starts with an uppercase character or whether it's preceded or succeeded by a verb/noun, etc., can be used as starting points to train an NER model. The following code snippet shows a function that extracts the previous and next words' POS tags for a given sentence. The notebook has a more elaborate feature set:

```python
def sent2feats(sentence):
    feats = []
    sen_tags = pos_tag(sentence)
    for i in range(0,len(sentence)):
        word = sentence[i]
        wordfeats = {}
        #POS tag features: current tag, previous and next 2 tags.
        wordfeats['tag'] = sen_tags[i][1]
        if i == 0:
            wordfeats["prevTag"] = "<S>"
        elif i == 1:
            wordfeats["prevTag"] = sen_tags[0][1]
        else:
            wordfeats["prevTag"] = sen_tags[i - 1][1]
        if i == len(sentence) - 2:
            wordfeats["nextTag"] = sen_tags[i + 1][1]
        elif i == len(sentence) - 1:
            wordfeats["nextTag"] = "</S>"
        else:
            wordfeats["nextTag"] = sen_tags[i + 1][1]
        feats.append(wordfeats)
    return feats
```

As you can see from the wordfeats variable in this code sample, each word is transformed into a dictionary of features, and therefore each sentence will look like a list of dictionaries (the variable feats in the code), which will be used by the CRF classifier. The following code snippet shows a function to train an NER system with a CRF model and evaluates the model performance on the development set:

```python
#Train a sequence model
def train_seq(X_train,Y_train,X_dev,Y_dev):
    crf = CRF(algorithm='lbfgs', c1=0.1, c2=10, max_iterations=50)
    crf.fit(X_train, Y_train)
    labels = list(crf.classes_)
    y_pred = crf.predict(X_dev)
    sorted_labels = sorted(labels, key=lambda name: (name[1:], name[0]))
    print(metrics.flat_f1_score(Y_dev,y_pred,average='weighted',
                    labels=labels))
```

Training this CRF model gave an F1 score of 0.92 on the development data, which is a very good score! The notebook shows more detailed evaluation measures and how to calculate them. Here, we showed some of the most commonly used features in learning an NER system and used a popular training method and a publicly available dataset. Clearly, there's a lot to be done in terms of tuning the model and developing (even) better features; this example only serves to illustrate one way of developing an NER model quickly using one particular library in case you need to and you have a relevant dataset. MITIE [24] is another such library to train NER systems.

Recent advances in NER research either exclude or augment the kind of feature engineering we did in this example with neural network models. NCRF++ [25] is another library that can be used to train your own NER using different neural network architectures. A notebook that uses the BERT model for training an NER system using the same dataset is available in the GitHub repo (*Ch5/BERT_CONLL_NER.ipynb*). We leave working through that as an exercise for the reader.

We took a quick tour of how to train our own NER system. However, in real-world scenarios, using the trained model by itself won't be sufficient, as the data keeps changing and new entities keep getting added, and there will also be some domain-specific entities or patterns that were not seen in generic training datasets. Hence, most NER systems deployed in real-world scenarios use a combination of ML models, gazetteers, and some pattern matching–based heuristics to improve their performance [26]. [24] shows an example of how Rasa, a company that builds intelligent chatbots, improves its entity extraction using lookup tables.

Clearly, to build these NER systems ourselves, we need large, annotated datasets in a format similar to the one shown in Figure 5-7. While datasets like CONLL-03 are available, they work with a limited set of entities (person, organization, location, miscellaneous, other) and in limited domains. There are other such datasets, such as OntoNotes [27], which are much larger and cover different kinds of text. However, they're not freely available and usually need to be purchased under expensive license agreements, which may not always be supported by our organizations' budgets. So, what should we do?

NER Using an Existing Library

While all this discussion about training an NER system may make building and deploying it look like a long process (starting with procuring a dataset), thankfully, NER has been well researched over the past few decades, and we have off-the-shelf libraries to start with. Stanford NER [28], spaCy, and AllenNLP [29] are some well-known NLP libraries that can be used to incorporate a pre-trained NER model into a software product. The code snippet below illustrates using NER from spaCy:

```
import spacy
nlp = spacy.load("en_core_web_lg")
text_from_fig = "On Tuesday, Apple announced its plans for another major chunk
                 of the money: It will buy back a further $75 billion in stock."
doc = nlp(text_from_fig)
for ent in doc.ents:
    if ent.text:
        print(ent.text, "\t", ent.label_)
```

Running this code snippet will show Tuesday as DATE, Apple as ORG, and $75 billion as MONEY. Considering that spaCy's NER is based on a state-of-the-art neural model coupled with some pattern matching and heuristics, it's a good starting point. However, we may run into two issues:

1. As mentioned earlier, we may be using NER in a specific domain, and the pre-trained models may not capture the specific nature of our own domain.

2. Sometimes, we may want to add new categories to the NER system without having to collect a large dataset for all the common categories.

What should we do in such cases?

NER Using Active Learning

From our experience, the best approach to NER when we want customized solutions but don't want to train everything from scratch is to start with an off-the-shelf product and either augment it with customized heuristics for our problem domain (using tools such as RegexNER or EntityRuler) and/or use active learning using tools like Prodigy (like we saw in Chapter 4 for text classification). This allows us to improve an existing pre-trained NER model by manually tagging a few example sentences containing new NER categories or correct a few model predictions manually and use these to retrain the model. [30] shows some examples of going through this process using Prodigy.

In general, in most cases, we don't always have to think about developing an NER system from scratch. If we do have to develop an NER system from scratch, the first thing we would need, as we saw in this section, is a large collection of annotated data of sentences where each word/token is tagged with its category (entity type or other). Once such a dataset is available, the next step is to use it to obtain handcrafted and/or neural feature representations and feed them to a sequence labeling model. Chapters 8 and 9 in [31] deal with specific methods to learn from such sequences. In the absence of such data, rule-based NER is the first step.

Start with a pre-trained NER model and enhance it with heuristics, active learning, or both.

Practical Advice

So far, we've taken a quick look at how to use existing NER systems, discussed some ways of augmenting them, and discussed how to train our own NER from scratch. Despite the fact that state-of-the-art NER is highly accurate (with F1 scores over 90% using standard evaluation frameworks for NER in NLP research), there are several issues to keep in mind when using NER in our own software applications. Here are a couple caveats based on our own experience with developing NER systems:

- NER is very sensitive to the format of its input. It's more accurate with well-formatted plain text than with, say, a PDF document from which plain text needs to be extracted first. While it's possible to build custom NER systems for specific domains or for data like tweets, the challenge with PDFs comes from the failure to be 100% accurate in extracting text from them while preserving the structure. [32] illustrates some of the challenges with PDF-to-text extraction. Why do we need to be so accurate in properly extracting the structure from PDFs, though? In PDFs, partial sentences, headings, and formatting are common, and they can all mess up NER accuracy. There's no single solution for this. One approach is to do custom post-processing of PDFs to extract blobs of text, then run NER on the blobs.

If you're working with documents, such as reports, etc., pre-process them to extract text blobs, then run NER on them.

- NER is also very sensitive to the accuracy of the prior steps in its processing pipeline: sentence splitting, tokenization, and POS tagging (refer back to Figure 5-2). To understand how improper sentence splitting can result in poor NER results, try taking the content from the screenshot back in Figure 5-1 and looking at the output from spaCy (see the notebook *Ch5/NERIssues.ipynb* for a short illustration). So, some amount of pre-processing may be necessary before passing a piece of text into an NER model to extract entities.

Despite such shortcomings, NER is immensely useful for many IE scenarios, such as content tagging, search, and mining social media to identify customer feedback about specific products, to name a few. While NER (and KPE) serve the useful task of identifying important words, phrases, and entities in documents, some NLP applications require further analysis of language, which leads us to more advanced NLP tasks. One such IE task is entity disambiguation or entity linking, and it's the topic of the next section.

Named Entity Disambiguation and Linking

Consider a scenario where we're working on the data science team of a large newspaper publication (say, *The New York Times*). We're charged with the task of building a system that creates visual representation of news stories by connecting different entities mentioned in the stories to what they refer to in the real world, as shown in Figure 5-8.

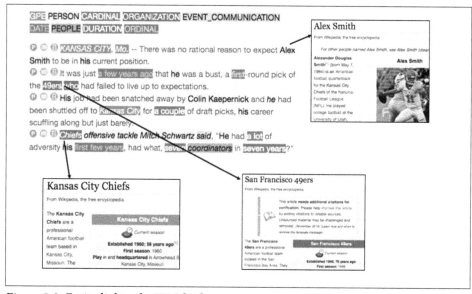

Figure 5-8. Entity linking by IBM [33]

Doing this requires knowledge of several IE tasks beyond what we've seen with NER and KPE. As a first step, we have to know what these entities or keywords actually refer to in the real world. Let's take another example to illustrate why this could be challenging. Consider this sentence: "Lincoln drives a Lincoln Aviator and lives on Lincoln Way." All three mentions of "Lincoln" here refer to different entities and different types of entities: the first Lincoln is a person, the second one is a vehicle, and the third is a location. How can we reliably link the three Lincolns to their correct Wikipedia pages like in Figure 5-8?

Named entity disambiguation (NED) refers to the NLP task of achieving exactly this: assigning a unique identity to entities mentioned in the text. It's also the first step in moving toward more sophisticated tasks to address the scenario mentioned above by identifying relationships between entities. NER and NED together are known as *named entity linking (NEL)*. Some other NLP applications that would need NEL include question answering and constructing large knowledge bases of connected events and entities, such as the Google Knowledge Graph [34].

So, how do we build an IE system for performing NEL? Just as NER identifies entities and their spans using contextual information encoded by a range of features, NEL also relies on context. However, it requires going beyond POS tagging in terms of the NLP pre-processing needed. At a minimum, NEL needs some form of parsing to identify linguistic items like subject, verb, and object. Additionally, it may also need coreference resolution to resolve and link multiple references to the same entity (e.g., Albert Einstein, the scientist, Einstein, etc.) to the same reference in a large, encyclopedic knowledge base (e.g., Wikipedia). This is typically modeled as a supervised ML problem and evaluated in terms of precision, recall, and F1 scores on standard test sets.

State-of-the-art NEL uses a range of different neural network architectures [35]. Clearly, learning an NEL model requires the presence of a large, annotated dataset as well as some kind of encyclopedic resource to link to. Further, NEL is a much more specialized NLP task compared to what we've seen so far (text representation, text classification, NER, KPE). In our experience as industry practitioners, it's more common to use off-the-shelf, pay-as-you-use services offered by big providers such as IBM (Watson) and Microsoft (Azure) for NEL rather than developing an in-house system. Let's look at an example of using one such service.

NEL Using Azure API

The Azure Text Analytics API is one of the popular APIs for NEL. DBpedia Spotlight [36] is a freely available tool to do the same. The following code snippet (*Ch5/EntityLinking-AzureTextAnalytics.ipynb*) shows how to access the Azure API to perform entity linking on a text. Azure comes with a seven-day free trial, which is a good way to explore the API to understand whether it meets your requirements:

```
import requests
my_api_key = 'XXXXXXX'
def print_entities(text):
    url = "https://westcentralus.api.cognitive.microsoft.com/text/analytics/\
    v2.1/entities"
    documents = {'documents':[{'id':'1', 'language':'en', 'text':text}]}
    headers = {'Ocp-Apim-Subscription-Key': my_api_key}
    response = requests.post(url, headers=headers, json=documents)
    entities = response.json()
    return entities
```

```
mytext = open("nytarticle.txt").read() #file is in the github repo.
entities = print_entities(mytext)
for document in entities['documents']:
    print("Entities in this document: ")
    for entity in document['entities']:
        if entity['type'] in ["Person", "Location", "Organization"]:
            print(entity['name'], "\t", entity['type'])
            if 'wikipediaUrl' in entity.keys():
                print(entity['wikipediaUrl'])
```

The result of running this code using the Azure API is shown in Figure 5-9; it lists entities in the text along with their Wikipedia links wherever available.

```
Entities in this document:
San Francisco    Location
https://en.wikipedia.org/wiki/San_Francisco
Facebook            Organization
https://en.wikipedia.org/wiki/Facebook
Alex Jones       Person
https://en.wikipedia.org/wiki/Alex_Jones
InfoWars         Organization
https://en.wikipedia.org/wiki/InfoWars
Louis Farrakhan          Person
https://en.wikipedia.org/wiki/Louis_Farrakhan
Silicon Valley   Location
https://en.wikipedia.org/wiki/Silicon_Valley
Instagram           Organization
https://en.wikipedia.org/wiki/Instagram
us       Location
```

Figure 5-9. Output of entity linking for a news article from The New York Times

We see that San Francisco is a location, but a specific location, which is indicated by its Wikipedia page. Alex Jones is not any other Alex Jones, but an American TV show host, as can be seen from the Wikipedia page. This is clearly much more informative than stopping at NER, and it can be used for better information extraction. This information can then be used for understanding the relationship between these entities, which we'll see later in this chapter.

So, we now have a way to incorporate NEL in our NLP system. How good is this solution? Based on our experience using off-the-shelf NEL systems, there are a few important things to keep in mind while using NEL in your project:

- Existing NEL approaches are not perfect, and they're unlikely to fare well with new names or domain-specific terms. Since NEL also requires further linguistic processing, including syntactic parsing, its accuracy is also affected by how well the different processing steps are done.

- Like with other IE tasks, the first step in any NLP pipeline—text extraction and cleanup—affects what we see as output for NEL as well. When we use third-party services, we have little control over adapting them to our domain, if needed, or understanding their internal workings to modify them to our needs.

With this overview, now that we know how to introduce NEL into our project's NLP pipeline if necessary, let's move on to the next IE task that has NEL as a prerequisite: relationship extraction.

Relationship Extraction

Imagine we're working at a company that mines tons of news articles to derive, say, financial insights. To be able to do such analysis on thousands of news texts every day, we would need a constantly updated knowledge base that connects different people, organizations, and events based on the news content. A use case for this knowledge base could be to analyze stock markets based on documents released by companies and the news articles about them. How will we get started building such a tool? The IE tasks we've seen so far—KPE, NER, and NEL—are all useful to a certain extent in helping identify entities, events, keyphrases, etc. But how do we go from there to the next step of "connecting" them with some relation? What exactly are the relations? How will we extract them? Let's revisit Figure 5-2, which shows a screenshot of a *New York Times* article. One relation that can be extracted is: (Luca Maestri, finance chief, Apple). Here, we connect Luca Maestri to Apple with the relationship of finance chief.

Relationship extraction (RE) is the IE task that deals with extracting entities and relationships between them from text documents. It's an important step in building a knowledge base, and it's also useful in improving search and developing question-answering systems. Figure 5-10 shows an example of a working RE system by Rosette Text Analytics [37] for the following text snippet [38]:

> Satya Narayana Nadella is an Indian-American business executive. He currently serves as the Chief Executive Officer (CEO) of Microsoft, succeeding Steve Ballmer in 2014. Before becoming chief executive, he was Executive Vice President of Microsoft's Cloud and Enterprise Group, responsible for building and running the company's computing platforms.

This output shows that Narayana Nadella is a person related to Microsoft as an employee, related to India and America as a citizen, and so on. How does one proceed with extracting such relationships from a piece of text? Clearly, it's more challenging than the other IE tasks we've seen so far in this chapter and requires deeper knowledge of language processing as compared to every other task we've covered in this book so far. Apart from identifying what entities there are and disambiguating them, we need to model the process of extracting the relationships between them by considering the words connecting the entities in a sentence, their sense of usage, and so on. Further, an important question that needs to be resolved is: what constitutes a "relation"? Relations can be specific to a given domain. For example, in the medical domain, relations could include type of injury, location of injury, cause of injury, treatment of injury, etc. In the financial domain, relations could mean something completely different. A few generic relations between people, locations, and organizations are: located in, is a part of, founder of, parent of, etc. How do we extract them?

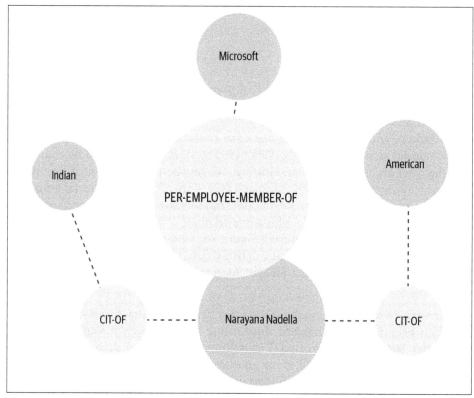

Figure 5-10. Relation extraction demo

Approaches to RE

In NLP, RE is a well-researched topic, and—starting from handwritten patterns to different forms of supervised, semi-supervised, and unsupervised learning—various methods have been explored (and are still being used) for building RE systems. Hand-built patterns consist of regular expressions that aim to capture specific relationships. For example, a pattern such as "PER, [something] of ORG" can indicate a sort of "is-a-part-of" relation between that person and organization. Such patterns have the advantage of high precision, but they often have less coverage, and it could be challenging to create such patterns to cover all possible relations within a domain.

Hence, RE is often treated as a supervised classification problem. The datasets used to train RE systems contain a set of pre-defined relations, similar to classification datasets. This consists of modeling it as a two-step classification problem:

1. Whether two entities in a text are related (binary classification).

2. If they are related, what is the relation between them (multiclass classification)?

These are treated as a regular text classification problem, using handcrafted features, contextual features like in NER (e.g., words around a given entity), syntactic structure (e.g., a pattern such as NP VP NP, where NP is a noun phrase and VP is a verb phrase), and so on. Neural models typically use different embedding representations (which we saw in Chapter 3) followed by an architecture like recurrent neural networks (which we saw in Chapter 4).

Both supervised approaches and pattern-based approaches are typically domain specific, and getting large amounts of annotated data each time we start on a new domain can be both challenging and expensive. As we saw in Chapter 4, bootstrapping can be used in such scenarios, starting with a small set of seed patterns and generalizing by learning new patterns based on the sentences extracted using these seed patterns. An extension of such weak supervision approaches is called *distant supervision*. In this, instead of using a small set of seed patterns, large databases such as Wikipedia, Freebase, etc., are used to first collect thousands of examples of many relations (e.g., using Wikipedia infoboxes), thereby creating a large dataset of relations. This can then be followed by a regular supervised relation extraction approach. Even this works only when such large databases exist. [39] illustrates how to use Snorkel, which we saw in Chapters 2 and 4, to learn specific relations in the absence of any training data. We leave its exploration as an exercise for the reader.

In scenarios where we cannot procure training data for supervised approaches, we can resort to unsupervised approaches. Unsupervised RE (also known as "open IE") aims to extract relations from the web without relying on any training data or any list of relations. The relations extracted are in the form of <verb, argument1, argument2> tuples. Sometimes, a verb may have more arguments. Figure 5-11 shows an example of the output of such an open IE system by AllenNLP [40, 41].

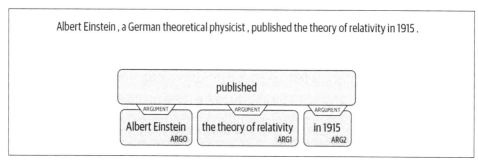

Figure 5-11. Open IE demo by AllenNLP

In this example, we see the relation as a verb and its three arguments <published, albert einstein, the theory of relativity, in 1915>. We can also extract the relation tuples <published, albert einstein, the theory of relativity>, <published, albert einstein, in 1915>, and <published, theory of relativity, 1915>. Obviously, in such a system, we see at least as many (typically, more) such tuples/quadruples as the number of verbs. While this is an advantage in the sense that it can extract all such relations, the challenge with this approach lies in mapping the extracted versions to some standardized set of relations (e.g., fatherOf, motherOf, inventorOf, etc.) from a database. To then extract specific relations from this information (if we need to), we would have to devise our own procedures combining the outputs of NER/NEL, coreference resolution, and open IE.

RE with the Watson API

RE is a hard problem, and it would be challenging and time consuming to develop our own relation extraction systems from scratch. A solution commonly used in NLP projects in the industry is to rely on the Natural Language Understanding service provided by IBM Watson [42]. The next code snippet (*Ch5/REWatson.ipynb*) shows how to extract relationships between entities with IBM Watson using a text snippet from the Wikipedia page referenced earlier in this section:

```
mytext3 = """Nadella attended the Hyderabad Public School, Begumpet [12] before
receiving a bachelor's in electrical engineering[13] from the Manipal Institute
of Technology (then part of Mangalore University)in Karnataka in 1988."""
response = natural_language_understanding.analyze(text=mytext3,
        features=Features(relations=RelationsOptions())).get_result()
for item in response['relations']:
        print(item['type'])
        for subitem in item['arguments']:
         print(subitem['entities'])
```

Figure 5-12 shows the output of this code in terms of the relations it extracted. The relations are extracted using a supervised model and contain a preset list of relations [43]. Thus, anything outside that list of relations will not be extracted.

```
employedBy
[{'type': 'Person', 'text': 'Nadella'}]
[{'type': 'Organization', 'text': 'Hyderabad Public School', 'disambiguation': {'subtype': ['Commercial']}}]
awardedTo
[{'type': 'Degree', 'text': 'bachelor'}]
[{'type': 'Person', 'text': 'Nadella'}]
educatedAt
[{'type': 'Person', 'text': 'Nadella'}]
[{'type': 'Organization', 'text': 'Manipal Institute of Technology', 'disambiguation': {'subtype': ['Educati
onal']}}]
educatedAt
[{'type': 'Person', 'text': 'Nadella'}]
[{'type': 'Organization', 'text': 'Mangalore University', 'disambiguation': {'subtype': ['Educational']}}]
awardedBy
[{'type': 'Degree', 'text': 'bachelor'}]
[{'type': 'Organization', 'text': 'Manipal Institute of Technology', 'disambiguation': {'subtype': ['Educati
onal']}}]
basedIn
[{'type': 'Organization', 'text': 'Mangalore University', 'disambiguation': {'subtype': ['Educational']}}]
[{'type': 'GeopoliticalEntity', 'text': 'Karnataka'}]
```

Figure 5-12. Relation extraction output from IBM Watson

This output information, showing relations between different entities, can then be used to construct a knowledge base for the organization's data. As we can see, RE is not a completely solved problem yet, and the performance of the approach is also domain dependent. What worked for a Wikipedia article may not work for a general news article or, say, social media text. [44] summarizes the state of the art in RE.

Start with pattern-based approaches and use some form of weak supervision in scenarios where pre-trained supervised models may not work.

We hope this gave an overview of where RE is useful and how to approach the problem if you encounter it at your workplace. Let's now take a look at a few other IE tasks before concluding the discussion on this topic.

Other Advanced IE Tasks

So far, we've discussed different information extraction tasks, where they're useful, and how we can build them into our NLP projects if required. While this list of tasks is by no means exhaustive, they're the tasks most commonly used across industry use cases. In this section, let's take a quick look at a few more specialized IE tasks. These are not very common and are used sparingly in NLP projects in the industry, so we'll only introduce them briefly in this section. We would advise the reader to start with [26] to get further guidance on the different approaches for solving these tasks. Let's look at an overview of three other IE tasks: temporal IE, event extraction, and template filling.

Temporal Information Extraction

Consider an email text: "Let us meet at 3 p.m. today and decide on what to present at the meeting on Friday." Say we're working on an application to identify and populate calendars with events extracted from such conversations, much like we see in Gmail. Figure 5-13 shows a screenshot of this utility in Gmail.

To build a similar application, in addition to extracting date and time information (3 pm, today, Friday) from the text, we should also convert the extracted data into some kind of standard form (e.g., mapping the expression "on Friday" to the exact date, based on context, and "today" to today's date). While extracting date and time information can be done using a collection of handcrafted patterns in the form of regex, or by applying supervised sequence labeling techniques like we did for NER, normalization of extracted date and time into a standard date-time format can be challenging. Together, these tasks are referred to as *temporal IE and normalization*. Contemporary approaches to such temporal expression normalization are primarily rule based and coupled with semantic analysis [26].

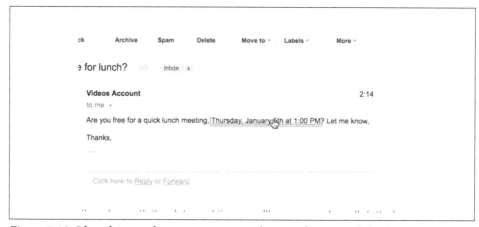

Figure 5-13. Identifying and extracting temporal events from emails [45]

Duckling [46] is a Python library recently released by Facebook's bots team that was used to build bots for Facebook Messenger. The package is designed to parse text and get structured data. Among the many tasks it can do, it can process the natural language text data to extract temporal events. Figure 5-14 shows the output when we run the sentence "Let us meet at 3 p.m. today and decide on what to present at the meeting on Friday" through Duckling. It's able to map "3 p.m. today" to the correct time on a given day.

Duckling supports multiple languages. From our experience, it works very well and is a great off-the-shelf package to begin with if you want to incorporate some form of temporal IE into your project. Other packages, such as SUTime [47] by Stanford NLP,

Natty [48], Parsedatetime [49], and Chronic [50], are also capable of processing human-readable dates and times. We leave it to the reader to explore these packages further and see how useful they are for temporal IE. Now, let's move on to the next IE task: event extraction.

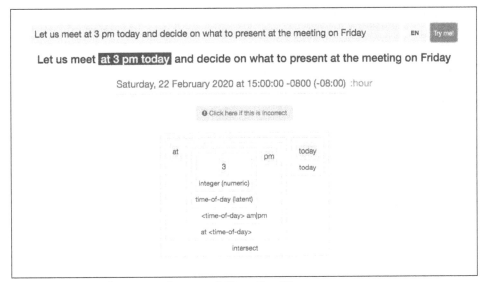

Figure 5-14. Sample output of temporal IE via Duckling

Event Extraction

In the email-text example we discussed in the previous section, the aim of extracting temporal expressions is to eventually extract information about an "event." Events can be anything that happens at a certain point in time: meetings, increase in fuel prices in a region at a certain time, presidential elections, the rise and fall of stocks, life events like birth, marriage, and demise, and so on. *Event extraction* is the IE task that deals with identifying and extracting events from text data. Figure 5-15 shows an example of extracting life events from people's Twitter feeds.

There are many business applications of event extraction. Consider a finance-lending company that reaches out to people for education loans. Wouldn't they love to have a system that can scan Twitter feeds and identify "university admission" events? Or consider a trade analyst in a hedge fund who needs to keep tabs on major events around the world. It's believed that Bloomberg Terminal [51] has a submodule that reports major events that are identified from thousands of news sources and social channels like Twitter in real time across the globe. A popular, fun application of event extraction is the congratsbot [52]. The bot reads through tweets and responds with a "congrats" message if it sees any event that one should be congratulated on. See Figure 5-16 for an example.

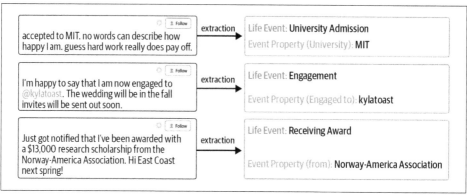

Figure 5-15. Examples of extracting life events from Twitter data [53]

Figure 5-16. Congratsbot in action

So, how should we approach this problem? Event extraction is treated as a supervised learning problem in NLP literature. Contemporary approaches use sequence tagging and multilevel classifiers, much like we saw earlier with relationship extraction. The ultimate goal is to identify various events over time periods, connect them, and create a temporally ordered event graph. This is still an active area of research, and working solutions for event extraction like those mentioned previously only work for specific scenarios; i.e., there are no relatively generic solutions like we saw for RE, NER, etc. To the best of our knowledge, there are no off-the-shelf services or packages for this task. If you end up doing a project that requires event extraction, the best way forward is to first start with a rule-based approach based on domain knowledge, then follow it up with weak supervision. As you start accumulating more data, you can move toward ML approaches.

Template Filling

In some application scenarios, such as weather forecasts and financial reports, the text format is fairly standard, and what changes are the specific details pertaining to that situation. For example, consider a scenario where we work in an organization that sends reports on companies' stock prices on a daily basis. The format of these reports will be similar for most companies. An example of one such "template" sentence is: "Company X's stock is up by Y% since yesterday," where X and Y change but the sentence pattern remains the same. If we're asked to automate the report generation process, how should we approach it? Such scenarios are good use cases for an IE task called *template filling*, where the task is to model text generation as a slot-filling problem. Figure 5-17 shows an example of template filling and how it can be used to build an entity graph.

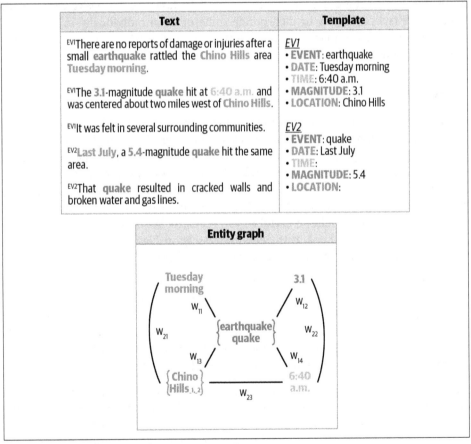

Text	Template
[EV1]There are no reports of damage or injuries after a small **earthquake** rattled the Chino Hills area Tuesday morning.	*EV1* • **EVENT**: earthquake • **DATE**: Tuesday morning • TIME: 6:40 a.m.
[EV1]The 3.1-magnitude **quake** hit at 6:40 a.m. and was centered about two miles west of Chino Hills.	• **MAGNITUDE**: 3.1 • **LOCATION**: Chino Hills
[EV1]It was felt in several surrounding communities.	*EV2* • **EVENT**: quake
[EV2]Last July, a 5.4-magnitude **quake** hit the same area.	• **DATE**: Last July • TIME: • **MAGNITUDE**: 5.4
[EV2]That **quake** resulted in cracked walls and broken water and gas lines.	• **LOCATION**:

Entity graph

Figure 5-17. Example of template filling [54]

Generally, the templates to fill are pre-defined. This is typically modeled as a two-stage, supervised ML problem, similar to relation extraction. The first step involves identifying whether a template is present in a given sentence, and the second step involves identifying slot fillers for that template, with a separate classifier trained for each slot. Work is being done in the direction of automatically inducing templates. Since this is a specialized, domain-dependent case, we're not aware of any off-the-shelf service provider for this task. As with other tasks in this section, we recommend you start with the chapter on IE in [31] to gain further understanding.

A recent real-world example of template filling–based text generation is the BBC's coverage of the 2019 UK elections. BBC created a template and created news stories automatically for all of the UK's 650 electoral areas. [55] and [56] discuss this project in greater detail.

With this, we conclude our discussion of most IE tasks. So far, we've seen a wide range of IE tasks and how to incorporate some of them individually in your code. How do these tasks connect with one another in a real-world application? Let's discuss a case study.

Case Study

Imagine we work for a large, traditional enterprise. We communicate via email and enterprise messaging platforms like Slack or Yammer. A lot of discussions about meetings happen as part of email threads. There are the three main types of meetings: team meeting, one-on-one meeting, and talk/presentation, plus their associated venues. Say we're tasked with building a system that automatically finds relevant meetings, books the venue or conference hall, and notifies people. Let's look at how the IE tasks we've discussed would be useful in this scenario. We'll assume that there's only one meeting per email. Look at the email exchange in Figure 5-18 for our scenario description. How would we go about starting to build that?

As a caveat, we might need to restrict what we're building at the start and solve a more focused problem. For instance, an email my contain multiple meeting mentions, like in this example: "MountLogan was a good venue. Let us meet there tomorrow and have an all hands in MountRainer on Thursday." Let's assume there's only one meeting per email in our case study and start thinking about how to approach the problem of building a simple system as an MVP to get started.

First, we'll need some amount of labeled data. We can start building labeled data in multiple ways. Imagine we have access to past calendar and conference booking information as well as email. Does comparing booking information and the emails yield positive matches? If so, we could try hardcoded weak supervision, similar to the one described in Chapter 4. Alternatively, we could try bootstrapping with pre-built services like Google Cloud NLP or AWS Comprehend. For example, Google Cloud

NLP has an entity extraction service that returns events, and we can use it to generate a dataset. However, as such automatically created datasets may not be perfect, we'll need manual verification.

Let's say we're dealing with the following entities and have collected some data with these annotations: Room Name (Meeting Location), Meeting Date, Meeting Time, Meeting Type (derived field), Meeting Invitees. For our first model, we can use a sequence labeling model like conditional random fields (CRFs), which are also used for NER. To classify the type of meeting, we can start with a rule-based classifier based on features such as room size (larger rooms may generally imply larger meetings), number of invitees, etc.

Figure 5-18. Meeting information extraction from email (representative image)

Once our system is in deployment, we can start collecting feedback in the form of explicit tagging or more implicit feedback. These may include meeting accept/reject rates and meeting conflict rates on the calendar and for the room. All this information can be used to collect more data so we can apply more sophisticated models.

Once we have enough data (5–10K labeled sentences from emails), we can start exploring more powerful language understanding models. If enough compute power is available, we may take advantage of a powerful pre-trained model like BERT and can fine-tune it on the new labeled dataset. The pipeline for this process is depicted in Figure 5-19.

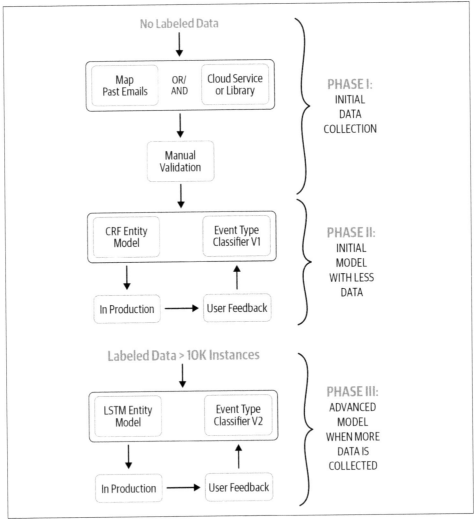

Figure 5-19. Pipeline for meeting information extraction system development

Now let's consider the more complex case we discussed at the beginning, where we may have mentions of multiple entities (room names) and also loose mentions of multiple meetings happening at different times. We want to tackle this problem as a multiclass, multilabel classification problem. The linguistic ambiguity could be hard to decipher via handcrafted feature engineering like the presence of some specific entity, fixed vocabulary, etc. A reasonable way to approach this problem would be to use a deeper neural network with recurrence, such as an LSTM or a GRU network. These networks will model contextual information around each word and encode that knowledge into the hidden vectors we would use to finally classify the email. While all this discussion is specific to one real-world IE problem, it's possible to incrementally implement and improve a solution to any IE problem using the approach outlined in this section.

Wrapping Up

In this chapter, we looked at information extraction and its usefulness in different real-world scenarios and discussed how to implement solutions for different IE tasks, including keyphrase extraction, named entity recognition, named entity linking, and relationship extraction. We also introduced the tasks of temporal information extraction, event extraction, and template filling. Compared to what we saw with text classification, an important difference with IE is that these tasks rely on resources beyond large annotated corpora and also require more domain knowledge. Hence, in a practical scenario, it's more common to use pre-trained models and solutions from large service providers rather than developing IE systems of our own from scratch, unless we're working on a super-specialized domain that needs custom solutions. Another important point to note, which we also reiterated several times throughout the chapter, is the role that a good text extraction and cleanup process plays in all these tasks. While we didn't take up specific end-to-end examples involving multiple IE tasks (some of which will be covered in Part III of the book), we hope that this chapter gives you enough of an idea about IE and the things to keep in mind when implementing IE tasks in your projects. In the next chapter, we'll take a look at how to build chatbots for different use cases you may encounter in your workplace.

References

[1] Wikipedia. "Message Understanding Conference" (*https://oreil.ly/trYdm*). Last modified November 20, 2019.

[2] Linguistic Data Consortium. "ACE" (*https://oreil.ly/Zy0VO*). Last accessed June 15, 2020.

[3] NIST. "Text Analysis Conference" (*https://tac.nist.gov*). Last accessed June 15, 2020.

[4] Google News (*https://news.google.ca*). Last accessed June 15, 2020.

[5] Sarno, Adrian. "Information Extraction from Receipts with Graph Convolutional Networks" (*https://oreil.ly/bpw5v*), *Nanonets (blog)*, 2020.

[6] Sensibill (*https://oreil.ly/zDNVs*). Last accessed June 15, 2020.

[7] Nicas, Jack. "Apple's Plan to Buy $75 Billion of Its Stock Fuels Spending Debate" (*https://oreil.ly/LJnCI*). *New York Times*, April 30, 2019.

[8] Chiticariu, Laura, Yunyao Li, and Frederick Reiss. "Rule-Based Information Extraction is Dead! Long Live Rule-Based Information Extraction Systems!" *Proceedings of the 2013 Conference on Empirical Methods in Natural Language Processing* (2013): 827–832.

[9] Chiticariu, L. et al. "Web Information Extraction". In Liu, L. and Özsu, M.T. (eds), *Encyclopedia of Database Systems*, New York: Springer, 2018.

[10] Hasan, Kazi Saidul and Vincent Ng. "Automatic Keyphrase Extraction: A Survey of the State of the Art." *Proceedings of the 52nd Annual Meeting of the Association for Computational Linguistics* 1: (2014): 1262–1273.

[11] Çano, Erion and Ondřej Bojar. "Keyphrase Generation: A Text Summarization Struggle." *Proceedings of the 2019 Conference of the North American Chapter of the Association for Computational Linguistics: Human Language Technologies* 1 (2019): 666–672.

[12] Chartbeat Labs Projects. textacy: NLP, before and after spaCy (*https://oreil.ly/9INdz*), (GitHub repo). Last accessed June 15, 2020.

[13] Explosion.ai. "SpaCy: Industrial-Strength Natural Language Processing in Python" (*https://spacy.io*). Last accessed June 15, 2020.

[14] Mihalcea, Rada and Paul Tarau. "Textrank: Bringing Order into Text." *Proceedings of the 2004 Conference on Empirical Methods in Natural Language Processing* (2004): 404–411.

[15] Gensim. "summarization.keywords—Keywords for TextRank summarization algorithm" (*https://oreil.ly/74MxG*). Last accessed June 15, 2020.

[16] Chowdhury, Jishnu Ray. "Implementation of TextRank" (*https://oreil.ly/05FtV*). Last accessed June 15, 2020.

[17] Explosion.ai. "displaCy Named Entity Visualizer" (*https://oreil.ly/1nhKg*). Last accessed June 15, 2020.

[18] spaCy. Common entity categories in NER development (*https://oreil.ly/ztbb7*). Last accessed June 15, 2020.

[19] The Stanford Natural Language Processing Group. "Stanford RegexNER" (*https://oreil.ly/9kXyW*). Last accessed June 15, 2020.

[20] Explosion.ai. spacy's EntityRuler (*https://oreil.ly/m7eXK*). Last accessed June 15, 2020.

[21] Wikipedia. "Sequence labeling" (*https://oreil.ly/YDupI*). Last modified January 18, 2017.

[22] Sang, Erik F. and Fien De Meulder. "Introduction to the CoNLL-2003 Shared Task: Language-Independent Named Entity Recognition." *Proceedings of the Seventh Conference on Natural Language Learning at HLT-NAACL* (2003).

[23] Team HG-Memex. sklearn-crfsuite: scikit-learn inspired API for CRFsuite (*https://oreil.ly/kgHD5*), (GitHub repo). Last accessed June 15, 2020.

[24] MIT-NLP. MITIE: library and tools for information extraction (*https://oreil.ly/SZPdT*), (GitHub repo). Last accessed June 15, 2020.

[25] Yang, Jie. NCRF++: a Neural Sequence Labeling Toolkit (*https://oreil.ly/vqAeA*), (GitHub repo). Last accessed June 15, 2020.

[26] Jurafsky, Dan and James H. Martin. *Speech and Language Processing*, Third Edition (Draft) (*https://oreil.ly/Ta16f*), 2018, Chapter 18.

[27] Linguistic Data Consortium. "OntoNotes Release 5.0" (*https://oreil.ly/3dDIU*). Last accessed June 15, 2020.

[28] The Stanford Natural Language Processing Group. "Stanford Named Entity Recognizer (NER)" (*https://oreil.ly/ocVdM*). Last accessed June 15, 2020.

[29] Allen Institute for AI. "AllenNLP: An open-source NLP research library, built on PyTorch" (*https://allennlp.org*). Last accessed June 15, 2020.

[30] Explosion.ai. Prodigy's NER Recipes (*https://oreil.ly/YtP8J*). Last accessed June 15, 2020.

[31] Jurafsky, Daniel and James H. Martin. *Speech and Language Processing: An Introduction to Natural Language Processing, Computational Linguistics and Speech Recognition*. Upper Saddle River, NJ: Prentice Hall, 2008.

[32] FilingDB. "What's so hard about PDF text extraction?" (*https://oreil.ly/W9VRo*) Last accessed June 15, 2020.

[33] IBM Research Editorial Staff. "Making sense of language. Any language" (*https://oreil.ly/55aoa*). October 28, 2016.

[34] Wikipedia. "Knowledge Graph" (*https://oreil.ly/phOGJ*). Last modified April 12, 2020.

[35] NLP-progress. "Entity Linking" (*https://oreil.ly/5fhhN*). Last accessed June 15, 2020.

[36] DBpedia Spotlight. "Shedding light on the web of documents" (*https://oreil.ly/wM1Ax*). Last accessed June 15, 2020.

[37] Rosette Text Analytics. "Relationship Extraction" (*https://oreil.ly/i_pXV*). Last accessed June 15, 2020.

[38] Wikipedia. "Satya Nadella" (*https://oreil.ly/4bjlF*). Last modified April 10, 2020.

[39] Snorkel. "Detecting spouse mentions in sentences" (*https://oreil.ly/Is2Ll*). Last accessed June 15, 2020.

[40] Allen Institute for AI. "Reading Comprehension: Demo" (*https://oreil.ly/nj3jL*). Last accessed June 15, 2020.

[41] AllenNLP's GitHub repository (*https://oreil.ly/cbd6v*). Last accessed June 15, 2020.

[42] IBM Cloud. "Watson Natural Language Understanding" (*https://oreil.ly/syL2g*). Last accessed June 15, 2020.

[43] IBM Cloud. Relation types (*https://oreil.ly/y97Oo*). Last accessed June 15, 2020.

[44] NLP-progress. "Relationship Extraction" (*https://oreil.ly/7VZiR*). Last accessed June 15, 2020.

[45] BetterCloud. "Hidden Shortcuts for Creating Calendar Events Right from Gmail" (*https://oreil.ly/RcrLQ*). Last accessed June 15, 2020.

[46] Wit.ai. Duckling (*https://duckling.wit.ai*). Last accessed June 15, 2020.

[47] The Stanford Natural Language Processing Group. "Stanford Temporal Tagger" (*https://oreil.ly/8WQHC*). Last accessed June 15, 2020.

[48] Stelmach, Joe. "Natty" (*https://oreil.ly/Y7roo*). Last accessed June 15, 2020.

[49] Taylor, Mike. "parsedatetime" (*https://oreil.ly/tOVxl*). Last accessed June 15, 2020.

[50] Preston-Warner, Tom. Chronic: a pure Ruby natural language date parser (*https://oreil.ly/Pt3op*), (GitHub repo). Last accessed June 15, 2020.

[51] Bloomberg Professional Services. "Event-Driven Feeds" (*https://oreil.ly/UP2gQ*). Last accessed June 15, 2020.

[52] Twitter. Congratulatron (@congratsbot (*https://oreil.ly/fStKj*)). Last accessed June 15, 2020.

[53] Li, Jiwei, Alan Ritter, Claire Cardie, and Eduard Hovy. "Major Life Event Extraction from Twitter based on Congratulations/Condolences Speech Acts" (*https://*

oreil.ly/ixoM2). Proceedings of the 2014 Conference on Empirical Methods in Natural Language Processing (EMNLP) (2014): 1997–2007.

[54] Jean-Louis, Ludovic, Romaric Besançon, and Olivier Ferret. "Text Segmentation and Graph-based Method for Template Filling in Information Extraction." *Proceedings of 5th International Joint Conference on Natural Language Processing* (2011): 723–731.

[55] Molumby, Conor and Joe Whitwell. "General Election 2019: Semi-Automation Makes It a Night of 689 Stories" (*https://oreil.ly/NRiA0*). *BBC News Labs*, December 13, 2019.

[56] Reiter, Ehud. "Election Results: Lessons from a Real-World NLG System" (*https://oreil.ly/ukiXH*), *Ehud Reiter's Blog*, December 23, 2019.

## CHAPTER 6

Chatbots

One machine can do the work of fifty ordinary men.
No machine can do the work of one extraordinary man.
—*Elbert Green Hubbard*

Chatbots are interactive systems that allow users to interact in natural language. They generally interact via text but can also use speech interfaces. Early 2016 saw the introduction of the first wave of chatbots that soon became ubiquitous. Platforms like Facebook Messenger, Google Assistant, and Amazon Alexa are some examples of chatbots. There are now tools that allow developers to create custom chatbots [1] for their brand or service so that consumers can carry out some of their daily actions from within their messaging platforms.

The introduction of chatbots into society has brought us to the beginning of a new era in technology: the era of the conversational interface. It's an interface that soon won't require a screen or a mouse to use. There will be no need to click or swipe; just the use of voice will be enough. This interface will be completely conversational, and those conversations will be indistinguishable from the conversations we have with our friends and family. Since chatbots deal with text under the hood, it's all about understanding the text responses coming from users and producing reasonable replies. From understanding to generation, NLP plays a significant role, which we'll see throughout this chapter.

The history of chatbots and of artificial intelligence in general are pretty intertwined. In the 1950s and '60s, computer scientists Alan Turing and Joseph Weizenbaum contemplated the concept of computers communicating like humans do. Later, in 1966, Joseph Weizebaum built Eliza [2], the first chatterbot ever coded, using only 200 lines of code. Eliza imitated the language of a Rogerian Psychotherapist using regular expressions and rules. Humans knew they were interacting with a computer program, and yet, through the emotional responses Eliza would offer, still grew emotionally attached to the program during trials.

Later, in the advent of powerful signal processing tools, researchers focused on building spoken dialog tools with the goal of improving user experience. Many spoken dialog systems were built between 1980 and 2000 and started as military-based projects (by DARPA) aimed mainly at improving automated communication with soldiers. The systems were used to provide instructions, which later translated into chatbots capable of helping users get answers to frequently asked questions for various services. The bots were still handcrafted such that responses they generated were fixed, and the bots were not good at handling the context provided in the conversation.

In recent years, chatbots have become more feasible and useful, both due to the ubiquity of smartphones and recent advances in ML and DL. In addition to APIs to create chatbots on popular messaging platforms like Facebook Messenger, we now have various platforms to create the AI and logic behind the chatbots. This has allowed folks and companies with limited AI background and experience to deploy their own chatbots easily.

This chapter aims to cover the underlying systems and theory of chatbots, along with practical, hands-on experience building chatbots using different scenarios. We'll end with some state-of-the-art research that may bring major advances to this entire paradigm. We'll motivate our readers by introducing popular applications of chatbots.

Applications

Chatbots can be used for many different tasks in many different industries, from retail, to news, and even the medical field. We'll briefly discuss various applications of chatbots. Many of these use cases have become more mature in recent years, while some are still in their infancy. These use cases include:

Shopping and e-commerce
Recently, chatbots are being used for various e-commerce operations, including placing or modifying an order, payment, etc. Bots for recommending various items are also of great interest to the e-commerce industry. Industries are focused on building conversational recommendation systems to provide a more seamless user experience.

News and content discovery
Similar to e-commerce, chatbots can be used in news and content discovery. Users may specify various nuances of their search in a conversational manner, and the bot should be able respond with relevant articles.

Customer service

    Customer service is another area where bots are used heavily. They're used to lodge complaints, help answer FAQs, and navigate queries in pre-defined conversational flows set by the business requirements.

Medical

    In health and medical applications, FAQ bots are of great use. These bots can help patients fetch relevant information quickly based on their symptoms. Recently, there has also been interest in building chatbots that elicit useful information from patients, especially older patients, regarding their health conditions by asking relevant questions.

Legal

    In legal applications, bots can also be used to serve FAQs for users. They can even be used for more complex goals, such as asking follow-up questions. For example, if a user asks for legal articles to follow up on a case, a bot might ask specific questions regarding the nature of the case to find a more appropriate match.

Here's a more elaborate example of an FAQ bot, which is common in many service platforms, to help users by providing answers to frequently asked questions.

A Simple FAQ Bot

A FAQ bot is generally a search-based system where, given a question, it looks for correct answers and provides them to the user. It's essentially a bot that allows a user to ask questions in different ways to get a response. Such bots are quite useful for providing a conversational interface to a complex set of questions.

As an example, we'll consider a subset of Amazon Machine Learning Frequently Asked Questions. A machine needs to learn to provide the correct answer given similar questions, so it's a good idea to have some paraphrases of each question. See Table 6-1 for some input-output examples for such a chatbot.

Table 6-1. Amazon ML FAQ to be used for a FAQ bot [3]

Questions	Answer
What can I do with Amazon Machine Learning? How can I use Amazon Machine Learning? What can Amazon Machine Learning do?	You can use Amazon Machine Learning to create a wide variety of predictive applications. For example, you can use Amazon Machine Learning to help you build applications that flag suspicious transactions, detect fraudulent orders, forecast demand, etc.
What algorithm does Amazon Machine Learning use to generate models? How does Amazon Machine Learning build models?	Amazon Machine Learning currently uses an industry-standard logistic regression algorithm to generate models.
Are there limits to the size of the dataset I can use for training? What is the maximum size of training dataset?	Amazon Machine Learning can train models on datasets up to 100 GB in size.

Figure 6-1 is a working version of such an FAQ bot. Later in the chapter, we'll learn how to build such a bot for various applications step by step.

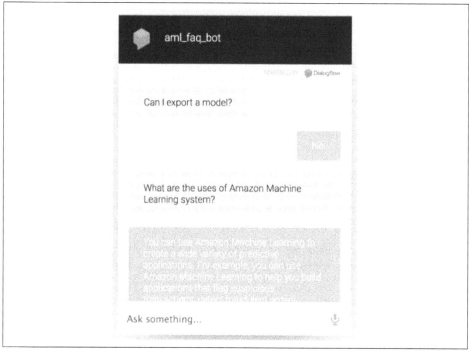

Figure 6-1. An FAQ bot

Now, we'll transition to the taxonomy of chatbots and explain various categories of chatbot based on their usage.

A Taxonomy of Chatbots

Let's expand on chatbots of various uses and their applicability to various domains. Chatbots can be classified in many ways, which affects how they're built and where they're used. A way of looking at these chatbots is how they interact with the user:

Exact answer or FAQ bot with limited conversations

These chatbots are linked to a fixed set of responses and retrieve a correct response based on understanding the user's query. For example, if we build an FAQ bot, the bot has to understand the question and retrieve a fixed, correct answer for it. Generally, one response from the user does not depend on the previous responses. Take a look at Figure 6-2. In the FAQ bot example, we see that, in the first two turns, the bot provides a fixed response to similar questions that are asked with slight variations. For a different question, it pulls out a different answer.

Flow-based bot

Flow-based conversational bots are generally more complex than FAQ bots in terms of the variability of their responses. Users may gradually express their opinions or requests over the course of conversations. For example, when ordering a pizza, a user may express their requested toppings, pizza size, and other nuances gradually. The bot should understand and track this information throughout the conversation to successfully generate a response every time. In Figure 6-2, for the flow-based bot, we see that the bot asks a specific set of questions to achieve the goal of making a pizza order. This flow was pre-defined, and the bot asks relevant questions to fulfill the order. We'll discuss such a flow-based bot in greater detail later in this chapter.

Open-ended bot

Open-ended bots are intended mainly for entertainment, where the bot is supposed to converse with the user about various topics. The bot doesn't have to maintain specific directions or flows of the conversation. In Figure 6-2, the open-ended bot carries out a conversation without any pre-existing template or fixed question-answer pairs. It transitions fluently from one topic to another to maintain the interesting conversation. This example of an open-ended bot was built by one of the authors for a popular digital assistant platform.

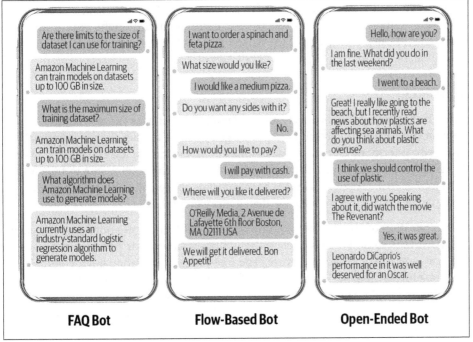

Figure 6-2. Types of chatbots

Chatbots are classified into two broad categories: (1) goal-oriented dialogs and (2) chitchats. FAQ bots and flow-based bots fall into the first category, whereas open-ended bots are mainly chitchat types. Both of these types of bots are used heavily in industry and are also in the active area of research in academia.

Goal-Oriented Dialog

The natural human purpose of having a conversation is to accomplish a goal via relevant information seeking. In the similar line of thought, it's easy to design any chatbot or conversation agent for a specific use case where the end goal is known. Most of the chatbots we've discussed so far (those typically used in research or industry) are goal-oriented chatbots. The user interacting with the chatbot should have complete information about what they want to achieve after the conversation. For example, looking for a movie recommendation or booking flight reservations through chatbots or conversational agents are examples of goal-oriented dialog where the goal is to watch a movie or book a flight.

Now, by definition, the goal-oriented systems are domain-specific, which requires domain-specific knowledge in the system. This hampers the generalizability and scalability of the chatbot framework. Research from Facebook [4] recently presented an end-to-end framework for training all components from the dialogs themselves to mitigate that limitation. This research proposes an automatic manipulation of the data—for example, question-answer pairs to carry out a meaningful conversation via required API calls. This is one of the newest approaches that researchers and industry practitioners have started to follow.

Chitchats

Apart from goal-oriented conversations, humans also engage in unstructured, open-domain conversations without any specific goals. These human-human conversations involve free-form, opinionated discussions about various topics. Having a conversational agent that can have a chitchat with a human is challenging due to the absence of objective goals. A conversational agent must generate coherent, on-topic, and factually correct responses to make the dialog more natural.

The application of chitchat bots is futuristic but holds immense potential. For example, these bots could be used to elicit useful but sensitive information in the case of a medical emergency for geriatric care. The free-form conversational bot could also be used to address the long-standing issue of loneliness and depression among teenagers and elderly people. Some of the market-leader companies, such as Amazon, Apple, and Google, to name a few, are investing heavily in building such bots for worldwide customers.

So far, we've discussed various kinds of chatbots and their usage in various industries. This will allow us to appreciate various components of chatbots based on usage and also help us implement some of the components as we need them. Now, we'll deep-dive into the chatbot development pipeline and discuss details of various components.

A Pipeline for Building Dialog Systems

We discussed various NLP tasks, such as classification and entity detection, throughout Chapters 4 and 5. Now, we'll utilize some of them to describe an example pipeline to build a dialog system. Figure 6-3 depicts a complete pipeline of a dialog system with various components. We'll discuss the utility of each component and data flow through the pipeline.

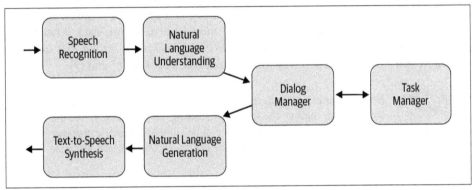

Figure 6-3. Pipeline for a dialog system

Speech recognition
> Usually, the dialog system works as an interface between human and machine, so the input into the dialog system is human speech. Speech recognition algorithms transcribe speech to natural text. In industrial dialog systems, state-of-the-art [5] speech-to-text models are used, which is beyond the scope of this book. If you're interested in speech models, refer to [5] for an overall view.

Natural language understanding (NLU)
> After transcribing, the system tries to analyze and "understand" the transcribed text. This module encompasses various natural language understanding tasks. Examples of such tasks are sentiment detection, named entity extraction, coreference resolution, etc. This module is primarily responsible for gathering all possible information that is implicitly (sentiment) or explicitly (named entities) present in the input text.

Dialog and task manager

Once we obtain information from the input, a *dialog manager*, as shown in the figure, gathers and systematically decides which pieces of information are important or not. A dialog manager is a module that controls and guides the flow of the conversation. Imagine this as a table containing information extracted in NLU steps and stored concurrently for all utterances in the ongoing conversation. The dialog manager develops a strategy via rules or other complex mechanisms, such as reinforcement learning, to effectively utilize the information obtained from the input. Dialog managers are mostly prevalent in goal-oriented dialogs since there's a definite objective to reach via the conversation.

Natural language generation

Finally, as the dialog manager decides a strategy for responding, the natural language generation module generates a response in a human-readable form according to the strategy devised by the dialog manager. The response generator could be template based or a generative model learned from data. After this, a speech synthesis module converts the text back to speech to the end user. For more information on speech synthesis tasks, take a look at [6] and [7].

 Any chatbot can be built using such a pipeline. For text-based chatbots, we can remove the speech processing components. While the NLU and generation component can be complex, a dialog manager could simply be rules routing the bot to an appropriate response generator.

Although the pipeline in Figure 6-3 assumes the chatbot is voice based, a similar pipeline without the speech processing modules will work for text-based chatbots. But in all industrial applications, we're moving toward eventually having more and more voice-based systems, so the pipeline discussed here is more general, and it applies to a variety of applications we described previously (including the case study in Chapter 1). Now that we've briefly discussed the various components of a chatbot and how a conversation flow takes place, let's deep dive to understand these components in detail.

Dialog Systems in Detail

The main idea of a dialog system or chatbot is to understand a user's query or input and to provide an appropriate response. This is different from typical question-answering systems where, given a question, there has to be an answer. In a dialog setup, users may ask their queries in "turns." In each turn, a user reveals their interest about the topic based on what the bot may have responded with. So, in a dialog system, the most important thing is understanding nuances from the user's input in a turn-by-turn way and storing them in context to generate responses.

Before we get into the details of bots and dialog systems, we'll cover the terminology used in dialog systems and chatbot development more broadly.

Dialog act or intent

This is the aim of a user command. In traditional systems, the intent is a primary descriptor. Often, several other things, such as sentiment, can be linked to the intent. The intent is also called a "dialog act" in some literature. In the first example in Figure 6-4, orderPizza is the intent of the user command. Similarly, in the second example, the user wants to know about a stock, so the intent is getStockQuote. These intents are usually pre-defined based on the chatbot's domain of operation.

Slot or entity

This is the fixed ontological construct that holds information regarding specific entities related to the intent. The information related to each slot that's surfaced in the original utterance is "value." The slots and value together are sometimes denoted as an "entity." Figure 6-4 shows two examples of entities. The first example looks for specific attributes of the pizza to be ordered: "medium" and "extra cheese." On the other hand, the second example looks for the related entities for getStockQuote: the stock name and the time period the chatbot is asked for.

Dialog state or context

A dialog state is an ontological construct that contains both the information about the dialog act as well as state-value pairs. Similarly, context can be viewed as a set of dialog states that also captures previous dialog states as history.

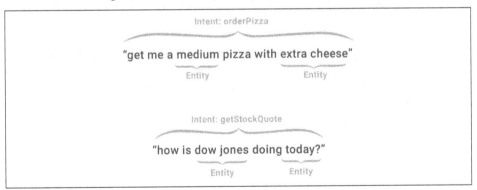

Figure 6-4. Example of different terminology used in chatbots

Now, let's complete a walkthrough using a cloud API called Dialogflow [8] for a fictional pizza shop to enable users to converse with a chatbot to order pizza. This is a goal-oriented system where the goal is to accommodate the user's request and order a pizza.

PizzaStop Chatbot

Dialogflow is a conversational agent–building platform by Google. By providing the tools to understand and generate natural language and manage the conversation, Dialogflow enables us to easily create conversational experiences. While there are many other tools available, we chose this one because it's easy to use, mature, and is being improved constantly.

Imagine there's a fictional pizza shop called PizzaStop, and we have to build a chatbot that can take an order from a customer. A pizza can have multiple toppings (like onions, tomatoes, and peppers), and it can come in different sizes. An order can also contain one or more items from the sides, appetizers, and/or beverages section of the menu. Now that we understand the requirements, let's begin building our bot using the Dialogflow framework.

Building our Dialogflow agent

Before we begin creating our agent, we need to create an account and set up a few things. For this, open the official Dialogflow website [9], log in with your Google account, and provide the required permissions. Navigate to V2 of the API [10]. Click on "try it for free" and you'll be directed to the free tier of Google Cloud Services, then you can follow the registration process.

1. First, we need to create an agent. Click the Create Agent button, then enter the name of the agent. You can provide any name, but it's good practice to provide a name that gives an idea of what the agent is used for. For our PizzaStop project, we'll name our agent "Pizza." Now, set the time zone and click the Create button.

   Figure 6-5 shows the UI you'll see while creating an agent.

Figure 6-5. Creating an agent using Dialogflow

2. You'll then be redirected to another page with options that allow you to create the bot. Figure 6-6 shows the UI of Dialogflow, which we'll use multiple times while creating our agent. By default, we'll already have two intents: *Default Fallback Intent* and *Default Welcome Intent*. Default Fallback Intent is the default response if some internal API fails and Default Welcome Intent will generate a welcome message.

Figure 6-6. Dialogflow UI after creating an agent

3. Now, we need to add the intents and entities we care about to our agent. To add an intent, hover over the Intents block and click the + button. You'll see something similar to Figure 6-7. These intents and entities are what we defined earlier in the section.

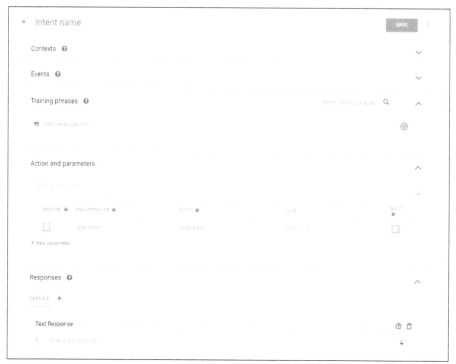

Figure 6-7. Dialogflow UI after clicking the "+" button

4. Now, we'll create the first intent: orderPizza. As we create a new intent, we have to provide training examples, called "training phrases," to enable the bot to detect variations of responses that belong to the intent. We also need to provide "context": a piece of information that can be remembered over the span of a conversation and that will be used for subsequent intent detection.

Examples of training phrases are "I want to order a pizza" or "medium with cheese please." The first one denotes a simple intent of pizza ordering, whereas the second one consists of entities that are useful to remember, such as medium size and cheese topping.

Figure 6-8 shows sample training phrases added to the agent.

Figure 6-8. Adding training phrases for intents

5. Since we've included intent, we need to add the respective entities to remember important information provided by the user. Create an entity named pizzaSize, enable "fuzzy matching" (which matches entities even if they're only approximately the same), and provide the necessary values. Similarly, create a pizzaTopping entity, but this time, also enable "Define synonyms" (this lets us define synonyms while allowing us to match several words, defined as synonyms, to the same entity).

These two together will help us detect "medium size" and "cheese toppings," as shown in Figures 6-9 and 6-10.

Figure 6-9. Creating the pizzaSize entity

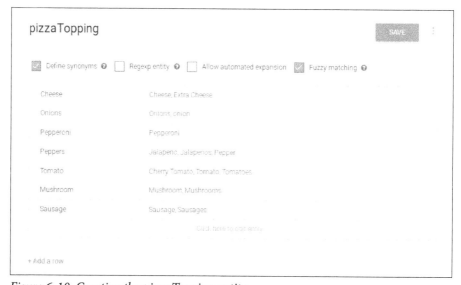

Figure 6-10. Creating the pizzaTopping entity

6. Now, let's go back to the Intents block to add additional information to the Action and Parameters section. We need both the topping and size to complete the order, so we need to check the Required box on those. One pizza can't be multiple sizes, but one pizza can have multiple toppings. So, enable the isList option for toppings to allow it to have multiple values.

A user might only mention the size *or* the topping. To gather the complete information, we need to add a prompt that asks follow-up questions, such as, "What size of pizza would you like?" as a prompt for pizzaSize. This is shown in Figure 6-11.

Figure 6-11. Actions and parameters for orderPizza intent

7. We also need to provide sample responses, as shown in Figure 6-12, that the agent will give the user. We can ask the user if they need drinks, appetizers, or sides. If we were creating something like a billing intent, we could end the conversation after it by enabling the "Set this intent as end of conversation" slider in the Responses block.

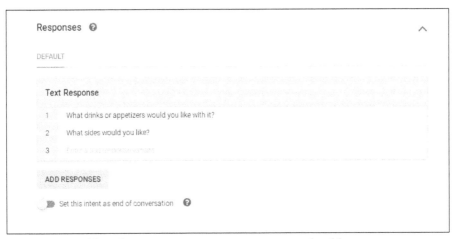

Figure 6-12. Adding the appropriate responses our agent should use

8. So far, we've added a simple intent and entities. Now we can look at a complex entity with context. Consider the statement, "I want to order 2 L of juice and 3 wings." Our agent needs to recognize the quantity and the item ordered. This is done by adding a custom entity in Dialogflow. We've created an entity called compositeSide, and it can handle all of these combinations. For example, in "@sys.number-integer:number-integer @appetizer:appetizer", the first entity deals with recognizing how many of the appetizers are ordered, and the next one

deals with the type of appetizer, as shown in Figures 6-13 and 6-14. As you can see, the signatures of these entities are given as regular expressions.

Figure 6-13. Creating the compositeSide entity

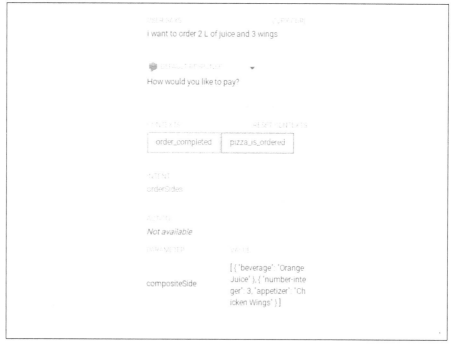

Figure 6-14. Example of a complex statement with multiple entities and context

9. We can add many more intents and entities to make our agent robust. In Figure 6-15 and Figure 6-16, take a look at examples of other intents and entities we added to enrich and enhance the user's pizza-buying experience.

Figure 6-15. All the intents for this agent

Figure 6-16. All the entities for this agent

Now that we've gone through the steps to build a bot for PizzaStop, we'll test our bot to see how it works in various scenarios.

Testing our agent

Now, let's test our agent in a website setting. For this, we need to open it in "web demo" mode. Click the Integrations block and scroll down until you reach Web Demo. Click the link in the pop-up window, and that's it! Feel free to test your agent to your heart's content. Figure 6-17 shows snippets of the one we built. Testing our bot is important for validating that it's working. We'll analyze a few cases of varying difficulty.

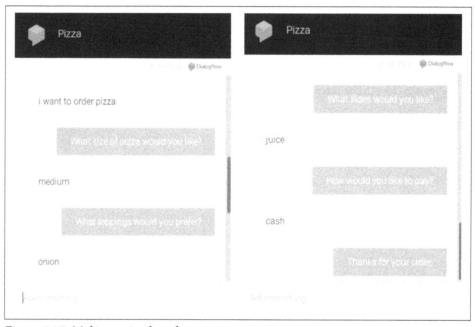

Figure 6-17. Making a simple order using our agent

We can see in Figure 6-17 that our bot is able to handle simple queries to order a pizza. As we have tested the bot end to end, we can also test various components of it individually. Testing individual components helps to prototype quickly and catch edges cases before the end-to-end testing.

Now, let's go through a more complex example, which will be tested with an integration of this bot with Google Assistant. In the example shown in Figure 6-17, our agent identifies the intent to order a pizza and recognizes the toppings we ordered. The pizzaSize entity is not fulfilled, so it asks a question regarding the size of the pizza to fulfill the entity's requirement. With the orderPizza intent fulfilled, the agent then proceeds to ask us about sides and appetizers. Based on the statement we provided, the agent needs to fulfill the orderSize intent and should be able to identify the quantity of juice and the appetizer. This shows that the agent is able to handle complex entities. Finally, we move on to the conversation for selecting the type of payment.

Figures 6-18 and 6-19 show how internal state and extracted entities work in another conversation.

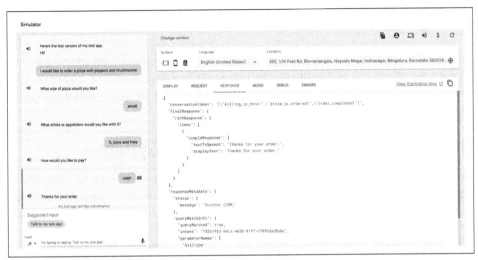

Figure 6-18. Texting complex statements with multiple entities

Figure 6-19. Testing with a complex entity and context

Dialogflow allows us to build goal-oriented chatbots. It's important to have an extensive ontology (possible slots and intents) for our domain, as it will make our bot rich in responding to varied user queries.

We've shown how to build a fully functional chatbot using the Dialogflow API. We learned about intents and entities—the two main building blocks of understanding dialog. Now, we'll delve deep into building custom models for intent/dialog act classification and entity/slot identification.

Deep Dive into Components of a Dialog System

So far, we've seen how to build a chatbot using Dialogflow and how to add various features to handle complex entities and context. Now, we want to deep-dive into the machine learning aspect of the internals of a dialog system. As we discussed while describing the pipeline for a dialog system, understanding the context (i.e., the user response) in light of conversation history is one of the most important tasks for building a dialog system.

Understanding context can be broken down into understanding the user's intent and detecting corresponding entities for that particular intent. These internal components correspond to the natural language understanding component in the chatbot pipeline. To illustrate this, we'll go through a sample of a conversation on restaurant booking and describe how to model different components for context understanding.

Figure 6-20 shows an example of a user looking for a restaurant reservation. As we can see, there are labels available for each response. The labels indicate intents and entities for these responses. We want to use such annotations to train our ML models.

> **User:** I'm looking for a cheaper restaurant
> `inform(price=cheap)`
> **System:** Sure. What kind - and where?
> **User:** Thai food, somewhere downtown
> `inform(price=cheap, food=Thai,`
> `area=centre)`
> **System:** The House serves cheap Thai food
> **User:** Where is it?
> `inform(price=cheap, food=Thai,`
> `area=centre); request(address)`
> **System:** The House is at 106 Regent Street

Figure 6-20. Conversation about restaurant booking [11]

Before we go into the model, we'll formally define two natural understanding tasks related to context understanding for dialogs. Since this involves understanding the nuances of language underneath, these are also attributed as *natural language understanding (NLU)* tasks.

Dialog Act Classification

Dialog act classification is a task to identify how the user utterance plays a role in the context of dialog. This informs what "act" the user is performing. For example, a simple example of dialog acts would be to identify a "yes/no" question. If the user asks, "Are you going to school today?", this would be classified as a yes/no question. On the other hand, if the user asks, "What is the depth of the ocean?", that may not be classified as a yes/no question. We've seen that intents or dialog acts are important for building a chatbot, even in Cloud APIs. Identifying intent helps to understand what the user is asking for and to take actions accordingly.

 Building dialog act classification and slot identification from scratch can be a complex and data-consuming process. Doing so makes sense when our dialog acts and slots are more open-ended in nature than a Cloud API or existing framework can solve. Having complete control of dialog internals can yield better results over time in such problems.

This can be reframed as a classification problem: given a dialog utterance, classify it into dialog acts or labels. In our example from Figure 6-20, we define a dialog act prediction task where labels include inform, request, etc. The utterance "Where is it?" can be classified as a dialog act "request." On the other hand, the utterance "I'm looking for a cheaper restaurant" can be classified as an "inform" dialog act. Drawing on what we learned in Chapter 4, we can use any classifier we like to solve this task. We'll discuss the models pertaining to this task with a complete dataset example in "Dialog Examples with Code Walkthrough" on page 221.

Identifying Slots

Once we've extracted the intents, we want to move on to extracting entities. Extracting entities is also important for generating correct and appropriate responses to the user's input. We also saw in our Dialogflow example that extracting entities along with the intents creates a full understanding of the user's input.

In the example in Figure 6-20—"I'm looking for a cheaper restaurant"—we want to identify "cheaper" as a price slot and take its value verbatim—i.e., the value of the slot is "cheaper." If we know ontologies for slot-value pairs, a more normalized form can ultimately be restored, such as "cheaper" -> "cheap." We have seen similar tasks in Chapter 5, where we learned how to extract entities from sentences. We can take a similar approach (i.e., a sequence labeling approach) here as well to extract these entities.

Previously, in our Dialogflow examples, we saw that slots have to be pre-defined beforehand. But here, we want to build this component on our own using an ML algorithm. Recall the algorithms discussed in the context of NER in Chapter 5. We'll use similar algorithms for slot detection and labeling. We'll use an open source sequence labeling library called sklearn-crfsuite [12], which we introduced in Chapter 5, for this task. We'll discuss details of this experiment in a later section.

 We can choose a range of ontologies for annotating entities. Imagine we're building a travel bot. The choice of entity for the destination can be city or airport. To make it robust, we must detect airports as an entity since one city can have multiple airports. On the other hand, in the case of a restaurant-booking bot, detecting cities as an entity is probably suitable.

One of the disadvantages of these methods is that they need a lot of labeled data for both intent and entity detection. Also, we need dedicated models for both of the tasks. This can make the system slow during deployment. Getting fine-grained labels for entities is also expensive. These issues limit the scalability of the pipeline for more domains.

Recent research [11] on spoken language understanding revealed that joint understanding and tracking is better than individual classification and sequence labeling parts. This joint model is lightweight at deployment as compared to individual models. For joint modeling, we can utilize dialog states, which is "inform(price - cheap)" in our example in Figure 6-20. We can aim to rank or score each candidate pair jointly with dialog act (in combination, a dialog state) to jointly determine the state. Joint determination is more complex and requires better representation learning techniques, which are beyond the scope of this book. Interested readers can learn more about this at [11]. Now that we've discussed NLU components, let's move on to response generation.

Response Generation

Once we identify the slots and intent, the final step is for a dialog system to generate an appropriate response. There are many ways to generate a response: fixed responses, using templates, and automatic generation.

Fixed responses

FAQ bots mainly use fixed responses. Based on the intent and values for the slots, a dictionary lookup is made on a pool of responses and retrieves the best response. A simple case would be to discard the slot information and have one response per intent. For more complex retrieval, a ranking mechanism can be built that ranks the pool of responses based on the detected intent and slot-value pairs (or the dialog state).

Use of templates

To make responses dynamic, a templates-based approach is often taken. Templates are very useful when the follow-up response is a clarifying question. Slot values can be used to come up with a follow-up question or a fact-driven answer. For example, "The House serves cheap Thai food" can be constructed using a template as <restaurant name> serves <price-value> <food-value> food. Once we identify slots and their values, we populate this template to finally generate an appropriate response.

Automatic generation

More natural and fluent generation can be learned using a data-driven approach. Upon obtaining the dialog state, a conditional generative model can be built that takes a dialog state as an input and generates the next response for the agent. These models can be graphical models or DL-based language models. Later, we'll briefly cover end-to-end approaches for dialogs that are similar to automatic generations.

> While automatic generation is robust, template generation has advantages over it. It might be hard to distinguish between the two, especially when the template variety is high, Template-based responses contain fewer grammatical errors and are easier to train.

Now that we've deep-dived into various components of a dialog system, let's walk through examples of dialog act classification and slot predictions.

Dialog Examples with Code Walkthrough

Now, we'll go through instances of various real-world dialog datasets that are publicly available and discuss their usage to model various aspects of a dialog system. Then we'll use two of those datasets to show how to implement models for two tasks we described for context understanding: dialog act prediction or intent classification and slot identification or entity detection. We'll explore a couple of models for each task and show via comparisons how these models can be improved gradually. All the models are inspired from the NLU tasks (classification and information extraction) we discussed in Chapters 4 and 5.

Datasets

Table 6-2 is a brief summary of various datasets that are used for benchmarking algorithms for goal-oriented dialog tasks. As we're interested in various NLU tasks in dialogs, we present four datasets for goal-oriented dialogs that act as benchmarks for dialog-based NLU tasks.

Table 6-2. Goal-oriented datasets from various domains and their usage

Dataset	Domain	Usage
ATIS [13]	Air Ticket Booking	Benchmark for intent classification and slot filling. This is a single-domain dataset, hence entities and intents are restricted to one domain.
SNIPS [14]	Multidomain	Benchmark for intent classification and slot filling. This is a multidomain dataset, hence the entities belong to multiple domains. Multiple-domain datasets are challenging to model due their variability.
DSTC [15]	Restaurants	Benchmark for dialog state tracking or joint determination of intent and slots. This is similarly a single-domain dataset, but the entities are expressed more in terms of annotations and contain more metadata.
MultiWoZ [16]	Multidomain	Benchmark for dialog state tracking or joint determination of intent and slots that spans over multiple domains. For the similar reason of variability, modeling this dataset is more challenging than modeling single-domain ones.

In addition to these datasets, several datasets of varying scale (i.e., number of sample conversations) are available [17] for various other subtasks in a dialog pipeline. Later in this section, we'll discuss how to gather such a dataset and apply it to a domain-specific scenario. For now, we'll focus on goal-oriented dialogs since they have direct usage in industry and the state-of-the-art research is well established.

Despite the existence of many open source datasets, there are only a few datasets that reflect the naturalness of human conversation. Datasets collected by online annotators like Mechanical Turkers suffer from templatish and forced conversation, which affects the dialog quality. Also, domain-specific dialog datasets are still not available for many domains, such as healthcare, law, etc.

Dialog act prediction

Dialog act classification or intent detection is the task we described in the previous section as a part of the NLU component in a dialog system. This is a classification task, and we'll follow our classification pipeline from Chapter 4 to solve it.

Loading the dataset. We'll use ATIS (Airline Travel Information Systems) for the intent detection task. ATIS is a dataset that's used heavily for spoken language understanding and performing various NLU tasks. The dataset consists of 4,478 training utterances and 893 test utterances with a total of 21 intents. We've chosen 17 intents, which appear in both the train and test set. Hence, our task is a 17-class classification task. An instance of the dataset looks like the following code:

```
Query text: BOS please list the flights from charlotte to long beach arriving
    after lunch time EOS
Intent label:  flight
```

Models. Since it's a classification task, we'll use one of the DL techniques we used in Chapter 4 directly: a CNN model. Using CNN is useful here because it captures the n-gram features via its dense representations. N-grams such as "list of flights" is indicative of a "flight" label:

```
atis_cnnmodel = Sequential()
atis_cnnmodel.add(embedding_layer)
atis_cnnmodel.add(Conv1D(128, 5, activation='relu'))
atis_cnnmodel.add(MaxPooling1D(5))
atis_cnnmodel.add(Conv1D(128, 5, activation='relu'))
atis_cnnmodel.add(MaxPooling1D(5))
atis_cnnmodel.add(Conv1D(128, 5, activation='relu'))
atis_cnnmodel.add(GlobalMaxPooling1D())
atis_cnnmodel.add(Dense(128, activation='relu'))
atis_cnnmodel.add(Dense(num_classes), activation='softmax'))
atis_cnnmodel.compile(loss='categorical_crossentropy',
            optimizer='rmsprop',
            metrics= ['acc'])
```

We obtain an accuracy of 72% with the use of a CNN on the test, averaged over all classes. If we use an RNN model, the accuracy shoots up to 96%. We believe that RNN is able to capture the interdependency of words across the input sentence. RNN captures the importance of a word with respect to the context it's seen before. The elaborate details of these models and the dataset code are given in *ch6/ CNN_RNN_ATIS_intents.ipynb*:

```
atis_rnnmodel = Sequential()
atis_rnnmodel.add(Embedding(MAX_NUM_WORDS, 128))
atis_rnnmodel.add(LSTM(128, dropout=0.2, recurrent_dropout=0.2))
atis_rnnmodel.add(Dense(num_classes), activation='sigmoid'))
atis_rnnmodel.compile(loss='binary_crossentropy',
            optimizer='adam',
            metrics= ['accuracy'])
```

As we know, recent transformer pre-trained models (such as BERT) are more powerful. So, we'll try to use BERT to improve the obtained performance so far. BERT can capture the context better and has more parameters, so it's more expressive and models the intricacies of the language. To use BERT, we use a BERT-style input tokenization scheme:

```
# For data:
sentence = " [CLS] " + query + " [SEP]"
Tokenizer = BertTokenizer.from_pretrained('bert-base-uncased',
                            do_lower_case=True)
```

```
tokenizer.tokenize(sentence)

# For model:
model = BertForSequenceClassification.from_pretrained("bert-base-uncased",
                                                      num_labels=num_classes)
```

Since BERT is pre-trained, the representation of content is much better than any models we train from scratch, such as CNNs or RNNs. We see that BERT achieves 98.8% accuracy, beating both CNN and RNN for the dialog act prediction task. Follow the notebook *ch6/BERT_ATIS_intents.ipynb* for the complete code for model and data preparation.

Slot identification

Slot identification is another task we described in the previous section as a part of the NLU component in a dialog system. We described why we can pose this as a sequence labeling task. We need to find the slot values given the input, and we'll follow our sequence labelling pipeline from Chapter 5 to solve this task.

Loading the dataset. We'll use SNIPS for this slot identification task. SNIPS is a dataset curated by Snips, an AI voice platform for connected devices. It contains 16,000 crowdsourced queries and is a popular benchmark for slot identification tasks. We'll load both training and test examples, and an instance of the dataset looks like the code below:

```
Query text: [Play, Magic, Sam, from, the, thirties]  # tokenized
Slots: [O, artist-1, artist-2, O, O, year-1]
```

As we discussed in Chapter 5, we're using the BIO scheme to annotate the slots. Here, O denotes "other," and `artist-1` and `artist-2` denote the two words for artist name. The same goes for the year.

Models. Since a slot identification task can be viewed as a sequence labeling task, we'll use one of the popular techniques we used in Chapter 5: a CRF++ model from the sklearn package. We also use word vectors instead of creating handcrafted features to feed into a CRF. CRFs are a popular sequence labeling technique and are used heavily in information extraction.

We use word features that will be useful for this particular task. We see that the context for each word is important in addition to the meaning of the word itself. So, we use the previous two words and next two words for a given word as features. We also use the word embedding vectors retrieved from GloVe pre-trained embeddings (discussed in Chapter 3) as additional features. Features for each word are concatenated across words in an input. This input representation is passed to a CRF model for sequence labeling:

```python
def sent2feats(sentence):
    feats = []
    sen_tags = pos_tag(sentence) #This format is specific to this POS tagger!
    for i in range(0,len(sentence)):
        word = sentence [i]
        wordfeats = {}
        #word features: word, prev 2 words, next 2 words in the sentence.
        wordfeats ['word'] = word
        if i == 0:
            wordfeats ["prevWord"] = wordfeats ["prevSecondWord"] = "<S>"
        elif i==1:
            wordfeats ["prevWord"] = sentence [0]
            wordfeats ["prevSecondWord"] = "</S>"
        else:
            wordfeats ["prevWord"] = sentence [i-1]
            wordfeats ["prevSecondWord"] = sentence [i-2]
        #next two words as features
        if i == len(sentence)-2:
            wordfeats ["nextWord"] = sentence [i+1]
            wordfeats ["nextNextWord"] = "</S>"
        elif i==len(sentence)-1:
            wordfeats ["nextWord"] = "</S>"
            wordfeats ["nextNextWord"] = "</S>"
        else:
            wordfeats ["nextWord"] = sentence [i+1]
            wordfeats ["nextNextWord"] = sentence [i+2]

        #Adding word vectors
        vector = get_embeddings(word)
        for iv,value in enumerate(vector):
            wordfeats ['v{}'.format(iv)]=value

        feats.append(wordfeats)
    return feats

# training
crf = CRF(algorithm='lbfgs', c1=0.1, c2=10, max_iterations=50)
# Fit on training data
crf.fit(X_train, Y_train)
```

We obtain an F1 of 85.5 with the use of a CRF++ model. More details can be found in the notebook *ch6/CRF_SNIPS_slots.ipynb*. Similar to the previous classification task, we'll try to use BERT to improve the performance obtained so far. BERT can capture the context better, even in the case of a sequence labeling task. We use all the hidden representations for all the words in the query to predict a label for each. Hence, at the end, we input a sequence of words into the model and obtain a sequence of labels (of the same length as the input), which can be inferred as predicted slots with the words as values:

```python
# For data:
sentence = " [CLS] " + query + " [SEP]"
```

```
Tokenizer = BertTokenizer.from_pretrained('bert-base-uncased',
                                           do_lower_case=True)
tokenizer.tokenize(sentence)

# For model:
model = BertForTokenClassification.from_pretrained("bert-base-uncased",
                                           num_labels=num_tags)
```

But, we find that BERT achieves only 73 F1. This could be due to the presence of many named entities in the input that were not well represented by the original BERT parameters. On the other hand, the features we obtained for the CRF were strong enough for this dataset to capture the necessary patterns. This is an interesting example where a simpler model beats BERT. See the complete model details in the notebook *ch6/BERT_SNIPS_slots.ipynb*.

 As we've seen before and here as well, pre-trained models help get better performance over other DL models learned from scratch. There could be exceptions, as pre-trained models are sensitive to the size of the data. Pre-trained models may overfit on smaller datasets, and handcrafted features may generalize well in those cases.

So far, we've learned how to build various NLU components for a goal-oriented dialog using popular datasets. We've seen how various DL models perform relatively well in these tasks. With these, we'll be able to run such custom models in our own dataset and explore various models to pick the best one. We also introduced four datasets that are popular benchmarks for goal-oriented dialog modeling. They can be used for prototyping newer models to verify their performance against state-of-the-art models. Now, we'll transition to other dialog models that are generally used beyond goal-oriented settings, and we'll discuss their advantages and disadvantages.

Other Dialog Pipelines

So far, we've discussed the modular pipeline we introduced in Figure 6-3. But there are many other pipelines that can be used in various scenarios, especially in the case of an open-ended chatbot. The initial pipeline in Figure 6-3 sometimes lacks in terms of ease of trainability due to multiple components, as each of them has to be individually trained and they need separate annotated datasets for each component. Besides that, in a modular pipeline, one needs to define the ontology explicitly and it does not capture latent patterns from the data. That is why we will briefly touch upon other existing pipelines that may be promising in future.

End-to-End Approach

Sequence-to-sequence models (we'll call it seq2seq) have seen huge acceptance in critical NLP tasks such as neural machine translation, named entity recognition, etc. The seq2seq models generally take a sequence as input and output another sequence. In a translation task, imagine our input sentence is in one language and output is in the language we want to translate it to.

Similar to other tasks, we can build a chatbot using seq2seq models. Imagine that the input of the model is the user utterance: a sequence of words. As the output, it generates another sequence of words, which is the response from the bot. Seq2seq models are end-to-end trainable, so we don't have to maintain multiple modules, and they are generally LSTM based. Recently, state-of-the-art transformers have been used for seq2seq tasks, so they can also be applied in the case of dialog.

Usually, we use tokenization to create word tokens and create a sequence out of a question. Seq2seq is capable of capturing the inherent order of the token in the sequence—this is important, as it ensures that we capture the right meaning of the question in order to answer it correctly. See Figure 6-21 for some examples from a work by Google [11] on such an end-to-end model. They input the questions to the model, and the model generated the corresponding outputs.

Machine: *is it a windows machine?* **Machine:** *we have linux on your machine.* **Machine:** *is it windows xp or windows 7?* **Human:** *i am using linux* **Machine:** *let me take a remote of your machine and check if issue has been pushed properly.* **Human:** *ok* **Machine:** *please open terminal and run the below commands in one computer:* **Machine:** *sudo apt - get update* **Machine:** *sudo apt - get upgrade* **Machine:** *sudo <COMMAND> - updater* **Human:** *done* **Machine:** *let me try connecting now* **Human:** *ok* **Machine:** *it 's done*	**Human:** *what is the purpose of life?* **Machine:** *to serve the greater good.* **Human:** *what is the purpose of living?* **Machine:** *to live forever.* **Human:** *what is the purpose of existence?* **Machine:** *to find out what happens when we get to the planet earth.* **Human:** *where are you now?* **Machine:** *i 'm in the middle of nowhere.* **Human:** *what is the purpose of dying?* **Machine:** *to have a life.* **Human:** *what is the purpose of being intelligent?* **Machine:** *to find out what it is.* **Human:** *what is the purpose of emotions?* **Machine:** *i don 't know.*
Browser Tech Support	**Philosophical Discussion**

Figure 6-21. Example of work done by Google on seq2seq models [18]

Deep Reinforcement Learning for Dialogue Generation

If you're wondering how a machine would generate a diverse set of answers given any kind of question, you're not alone. [19] studied the drawbacks of typical seq2seq models and discovered that they often kept generating the generic output, "I don't know." These models generated utterances without considering how to respond in order to have a good conversation. Doing so requires futuristic knowledge about the goodness of the conversation, which will ultimately help the user achieve their goal. The concept of goodness is abstract, so it's typically defined based on the objective of the conversation. For example, with a goal-oriented dialog setup, we have a defined goal to achieve, whereas in a chitchat setup, goodness is defined by how interesting the conversation will be.

Here, we see the combination of two ideas: goal-oriented dialog and seq2seq-based generation. Reinforcement learning can help us here. Each time the machine utters a response is nothing but it performing a specific action. A set of such actions can be made in a way that ensures the goal is finally achieved via the conversation. In reinforcement learning based on exploration and exploitation, the machine tries to learn to generate the best response based on a futuristic reward defined by the user, which is directly related to how likely the current response is to achieve the final goal. Figure 6-22 shows how the reinforcement learning–based model performed well compared to the typical seq2seq-based model. On the right-hand side, you can see that the reinforcement learning–based model generated a more diverse response instead of collapsing into a generic default response.

Baseline mutual information model (Li et al. 2015)	Proposed reinforcement learning model
A: Where are you going? (1)	A: Where are you going? (1)
B: I'm going to the restroom. (2)	B: I'm going to the police station. (2)
A: See you later. (3)	A: I'll come with you. (3)
B: See you later. (4)	B: No, no, no, no, you're not going anywhere. (4)
A: See you later. (5)	A: Why? (5)
B: See you later. (6)	B: I need you to stay here. (6)
...	A: I don't know what you are talking about. (7)
	...
A: how old are you? (1)	A: How old are you? (1)
B: I'm 16. (2)	B: I'm 16. Why are you asking? (2)
A: 16? (3)	A I thought you were 12. (3)
B: I don't know what you are talking about. (4)	B: What made you think so? (4)
A: You don't know what you are saying. (5)	A: I don't know what you are talking about. (5)
B: I don't know what you are talking about . (6)	B: You don't know what you are saying. (6)
A: You don't know what you are saying. (7)	...
...	...

Figure 6-22. Comparison of deep reinforcement learning and a seq2seq model [19]

Human-in-the-Loop

So far, we've talked about machines generating answers in response to questions asked, without human intervention. The machine may improve its performance if humans intervene in its learning process and reward or penalize based on the correct or incorrect response. These rewards or penalties act as feedback for the model.

Answering a natural language query typically follows three steps: understand the query, perform an action, and respond to utterances. While doing this, the machine might need human intervention in various scenarios—for example, if the question is out of the chatbot's scope, if the action it took was not correct, or if the understanding of the query was wrong. Typically, when humans intervene in a machine's learning process, it's termed as *human-in-the-loop*.

In the context of chatbots, Facebook has performed an exercise [20] of using humans to inject partial rewards when the bot is learning in a reinforcement learning setup. As we discussed in the previous subsection, the ultimate goal of the bot is to fulfill the user's needs. But with human-in-the-loop, while exploring various actions, the bot receives additional input from a human "teacher," which clearly improves the quality of the response, as shown in Figure 6-23.

bAbI Task 6: Partial Rewards		WikiMovies Task 6: Partial Rewards	
Mary went to the hallway.		What films are about Hawaii?	50 First Dates
John moved to the bathroom.		Correct!	
Mary travelled to the kitchen.		Who acted in Licence to Kill?	Billy Madison
Where is Mary?	kitchen	No, the answer is Timothy Dalton.	
Yes, that's right!		What genre is Saratoga Trunk in?	Drama
Where is John?	bathroom	Yes! (+)	
Yes, that's correct! (+)		...	

Figure 6-23. Humans providing additional signals during dialog learning [20]

 Human-in-the-loop is ultimately a more practical system to deploy than a completely automated dialog generation system. End-to-end models are efficient to train, but they may not be reliable in producing factually correct outputs. Hence, a hybrid system with the combination of end-to-end dialog generation framework and with human resources will be more reliable and robust.

We've discussed various techniques beyond goal-oriented dialog. Many of these methods are built by industry and are usable in practical settings. These end-to-end models can grow large in terms of parameters (via the use of new transformer architecture) and can therefore become infeasible to deploy in small-scale applications. But we also saw here that even LSTM models can generate reasonable outputs. Human-in-the-loop is also a feasible technique that can be adopted regardless of the computing power available.

Rasa NLU

So far, we've discussed how to build two main components of a dialog system: dialog act prediction and slot filling. Beyond these two components, there are several integration steps to tie them into a complete pipeline for dialog. Also, we can build wrapping logic around these components and create a comprehensive dialog experience for users.

Building such a complete dialog system requires significant engineering work. But the good news is there are frameworks available that allow us to build custom NLP models as various components of the system and that provide overhead engineering tools and supports to build a functioning bot. One example of such a framework is Rasa. Rasa offers a suite of features [21] that can be essential in building a chatbot for industrial use. Figure 6-24 shows the Rasa chatbot interface along with its interactive learning framework, which we'll discuss later.

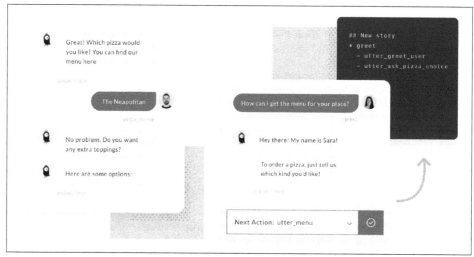

Figure 6-24. Rasa chatbot interface and interactive learning framework [21]

We'll briefly touch on Rasa's available features and discuss how they can be used to improve the user's experience with a chatbot:

Context-based conversations
    The Rasa framework allows users to capture and utilize the conversation context or dialog state. Internally, Rasa performs NLU and captures required slots and their values, which can be utilized in response generation.

Interactive learning
    Rasa offers an interactive interface that can be used for two purposes. One is to create more training data for the internal models by chatting with the bot. The second is to provide feedback when the models make mistakes. This feedback can be used as negative samples for the model to improve performance in challenging cases.

Data annotation
    Rasa presents a highly interactive and easy-to-use interface to annotate more data to improve the model training. Data annotation can be done from scratch or modified from examples where labels are already predicted by the existing

models. See Figure 6-25 for an example of the data annotation step in Rasa. Wrapper frameworks are built on Rasa NLU, which eases the data annotation process to generate large-scale dialog datasets. Once such framework is Chatette [22], which is a tool that accepts templates and then spawns dialog instances using those templates at scale.

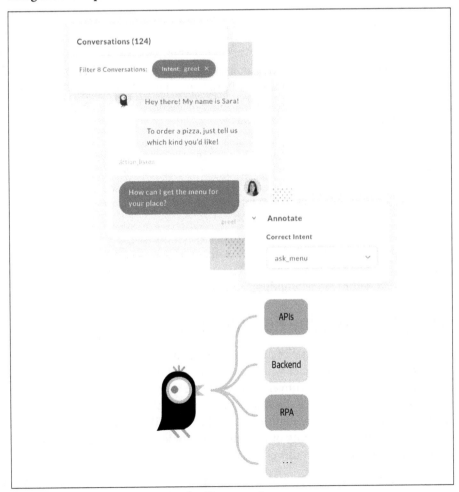

Figure 6-25. Data annotation and API integrations

API integration

Finally, the dialog service can also be integrated with other APIs as well as chat platforms like Slack, Facebook, Google Home, and Amazon Alexa. The next section includes a case study where we'll produce recipe recommendations via conversations and integrate a faceted search API endpoint into the bot to facilitate the recommendation process.

Customize your models in Rasa

Apart from the framework, Rasa also allows us to customize our models by choosing from a pool of models. For example, for intent/dialog act detection, we can choose "sklearn classifier" [23] or "mitie classifier" [24], or we can write our own classifier and add that to the building pipeline for Rasa to use it. Various options for embeddings such as spaCy and Rasa's own are available with the framework.

We can also harness the power of transformer models as we see performance improvement while building our individual components. Rasa provides BERT (and various distilled versions to improve on latency) for both classification and sequence labeling tasks [25, 26]. Overall, this makes Rasa a very powerful tool for building a dialog system from scratch.

Rasa enables us to build our chatbot in a modular way. For example, we can start with existing pre-trained models and later use custom models built on our specific datasets as needed. Similarly, we can start default API integrations and conversation channels and modify them when needed.

Now, let's go over a complete case study with a real scenario discussing what steps are necessary to create a conversational system from scratch in an industrial setup, including data setup, model building, and deployment.

A Case Study: Recipe Recommendations

Cooks often look for specific recipes tailored to their culinary and dietary preferences. A conversational interface where cooks can find their recipe of choice by fleshing out their preferences via a conversation with the agent would be a good user experience. In this case study, we'll discuss all the components we've covered in this chapter along with the frameworks required to build them. We'll see the evolving need for data and modeling complexity of the business problem and address them via various tools we've learned about in this chapter.

Imagine we're part of a recipe and food aggregator site. We've been tasked with building a chatbot. Users can talk about the kind of food they're craving or want to cook. This is an uncharted problem, so how will we go about building this? Figure 6-26 shows some example suggestions of recipes for various user preferences.

We need to convert this business problem into a technical problem with objectives and constraints. As a user will interact with the system, our goal is to create a fully defined query that can fetch a suitable recipe. The recipe can come from an API endpoint or a generative model. This query is made of a set of attributes that define the dish, such as ingredients, cuisine, calorie level, cooking time, etc. We also know that users can reveal their preferences through turns in a conversation, so we need to track their preferences and update the internal dialog state as the conversation proceeds.

Figure 6-26. Example of a recipe-suggestion site: Allrecipes.com

Utilizing Existing Frameworks

We'll start with Dialogflow, the cloud API we described earlier in the chapter since it's easy to build. Before we start, we need to define entities like we did before, such as ingredients, cuisine, calorie level, cooking time. We can build an ontology for the cooking domain and identify the number of slots we'd like our chatbot to support.

Initially, it will be good to keep an exhaustive list of these entities. Here are some examples of training instances that capture nuances in this early phase of bot building:

- I want a <u>low calorie</u> <u>dessert</u> that is vegan.
- I have <u>peas</u>, <u>carrots</u>, and <u>chicken</u> in my kitchen. What can I make with it in <u>30 minutes</u>?

Dialogflow is capable of handling the user's preference and identifying the slots and values necessary to look for a correct recipe. Also, due to the conversational nature of the user's interaction, the bot will maintain its dialog state or context to fully understand the user's input. We'll assume a database of recipes has been pre-defined and prefilled. Now, once the entities are captured via the bot, we need to feed them into an API endpoint. This endpoint will do a faceted search on the database and retrieve the best-ranked recipes.

As we collect more data, Dialogflow will slowly become better. But due to its lack of custom models, it can't solve more complex conversations related to this task. Some examples where a Dialogflow-based bot will eventually fail are:

- I have a <u>chicken</u> with me, what can I cook with it besides <u>chicken lasagna</u>?
- Give me a recipe for a <u>chocolate dessert</u> that can be made in just <u>10 mins</u> instead of the regular <u>half an hour</u>.

These examples show a presence of more than one value for one slot, and only one of them is correct—for example, "10 mins" is correct, while "half an hour" isn't. Matching-based methods in Dialogflow will fail in such cases. That's why we need to build custom models so that these examples can be added as adversarial examples in their training pipeline. In a Rasa pipeline with custom models, we can add such adversarial examples in order for the model to learn to identify correct slots and their values. It's also possible to generate such adversarial examples from the data we've gathered using data augmentation techniques and including them though the data annotation techniques of the Rasa framework, as shown in Figure 6-27.

With this updated training data, new custom models will be able to pick the correct values to fully describe the user's ask for the recipe. Once slots and values are captured, the rest of the process will be similar to how it was before (i.e., an API endpoint can use this information to query an appropriate recipe).

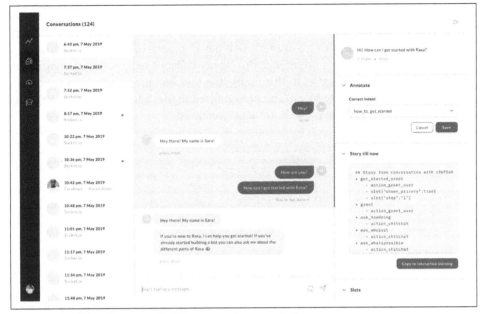

Figure 6-27. How Rasa can facilitate complex annotations

Open-Ended Generative Chatbots

Our solution is good enough to be deployed on a real website where millions of users interact regularly. Now we can focus on solving more challenging tasks with the objective of improving the user experience even more. So far, we've been providing users with specific recipes that are stored in a datastore beforehand. What if we want to make the chatbot more open ended by generating recipes instead of searching for them from a pre-existing pool? The advantage of such systems is their ability to handle unknown attribute values and customize recipes to fit the personalized tastes of the users.

Open-ended chatbots are generally harder to evaluate because many variants of a response can be correct given the context. Human evaluation seems to be most efficient, but it's irreproducible and therefore harder to compare to other systems. A mix of automatic and human evaluation is the right way to evaluate generative dialog systems.

Here, we can utilize powerful seq2seq generative models that can condition their generation on the various desired attributes the user has described for the recipe preference. Researchers (including one of the authors) have shown [27] that these seq2seq models are capable of generating personalized recipes based on preferences and previous recipe interactions. These models are capable of incorporating nuances and potentially generating a novel recipe that's valid but unique to the user's culinary taste. Figure 6-28 shows such an example of a newly generated recipe incorporating a user's preference. The user's preference can be just a list of recipes that they've interacted with before. For example, in this figure, the user had previously interacted with mojito, martini, and Bloody Mary. The personalized model added an extra garnishing step (highlighted in gray) to make it more personalized.

Input	**Name:** Pomberrytini; **Ingredients:** pomegranate-blueberry juice, cranberry juice, vodka ; **Calorie:** Low
Gold	Place everything except the orange slices in a cocktail shaker. Shake until well mixed and well chilled. Pour into martini glasses and float an orange slice in each glass.
Enc-Dec	Combine all ingredients. Cover and refrigerate. Serve with whipped topping.
Prior Tech	Combine all ingredients. Store in refrigerator. Serve over ice. Enjoy!
Prior Recipe	Pour the ice into a cocktail shaker. Pour in the vodka and vodka. Add a little water and shake to mix. Pour into the glass and garnish with a slice of orange slices. Enjoy!
Prior Name	Combine all ingredients except for the ice in a blender or food processor. Process to make a smooth paste and then add the remaining vodka and blend until smooth. Pour into a chilled glass and garnish with a little lemon and fresh mint.

Table 3: Sample generated recipe. Emphasis on personalization and explicit ingredient mentions via highlights.

Figure 6-28. Recipes generated personalized to user's preferences [27]

Merging such generative models with other dialog components can really boost the user experience. While we've discussed one specific recipe-recommendation problem, similar approaches can be taken in developing similar applications. We've discussed necessary tools and models that can be used together to build a bot according to the business problem at hand. We started with a very simple approach using Dialogflow and gradually added more complexity to tackle dialog nuances in the way users may express their queries and choices. Finally, we went the extra mile to build an end-to-end personalized chatbot.

Wrapping Up

In this chapter, we discussed chatbots and their applicability in various domains. We went through a pipeline approach and delved deep into its various components. We talked about a complete flow-based bot with a cloud-based API, then implemented ML components of NLU modules. Finally, we analyzed a business problem and provided some pathways to approach it incrementally.

But as far as dialog systems and chatbots are concerned, there are many challenges that are still unsolved. Hence, this is a very active area of research in the NLP community. In addition to academic research, industrial research groups are also looking for scalable solutions to existing approaches so that chatbots can be built reliably and deployed to users. Still today, many industrial chatbots fail to be robust and suffer in the issue of natural language understanding and natural language generation. We mention these challenges in order to provide a broader picture of the domain of chatbots.

The major problem right now in building dialog systems is a lack of datasets that reflect natural conversations. Many times, personal data can't be collected for privacy reasons. Other times, a lack of such conversational interfaces hinders data collection capability. Also, existing datasets, especially ones that claim to be real-world datasets, lack naturalness. These datasets are created mainly by online annotators, and most of the time, they sound scripted due to the nature of objective data collection. This problem is very different from other NLP tasks. For instance, annotating a correct class to a datapoint in a classification task or pointing out the relevant information in an information extraction task is more objective and easy to get than labels via crowd-sourced online annotators. In the case of dialog, many times the task is subjective hence the data collection process becomes complex.

Furthermore, the current generative models are not capable enough to generate factually correct statements, which becomes a critical problem in the case of chatbots. In the short span of a conversation, factually incorrect generation may hinder the quality of the conversation. Hence, future research and industrial efforts should be toward both gathering better representative datasets and improving both natural language understanding and generation models that can be used in a chatbot pipeline.

In summary, we discussed the foundations of dialog systems, starting with an overall pipeline, and developed a dialog system using Dialogflow, a cloud API; dove deep into building custom models for understanding dialog context; and finally, used all of them to solve a case study. While we anticipate that the area will continue evolving and improving, this chapter will be a good start for you to adapt to the new solutions that keep coming. Now let's turn to a few other common NLP problem scenarios in the next chapter.

References

[1] ParlAI (*https://parl.ai*). Last accessed June 15, 2020.

[2] Wallace, Michal and George Dunlop. Eliza, The Rogerian Therapist (*https://oreil.ly/O3bz8*). Last accessed June 15, 2020.

[3] Amazon. "Build a Machine Learning Model" (*https://oreil.ly/fkjpx*). Last accessed June 15, 2020.

[4] Miller, Alexander H., Will Feng, Adam Fisch, Jiasen Lu, Dhruv Batra, Antoine Bordes, Devi Parikh, and Jason Weston. "ParlAI: A Dialog Research Software Platform." *Proceedings of the 2017 Conference on Empirical Methods in Natural Language Processing: System Demonstrations* (2017): 79–84.

[5] Pratap, Vineel, Awni Hannun, Qiantong Xu, Jeff Cai, Jacob Kahn, Gabriel Syn-naeve, Vitaliy Liptchinsky, and Ronan Collobert. "wav2letter++: The Fastest Open-source Speech Recognition System" (*https://oreil.ly/hCiIU*), (2018).

[6] Google Cloud. "Cloud Text-to-Speech" (*https://oreil.ly/7w1pL*). Last accessed June 15, 2020.

[7] van den Oord, Aäron and Dieleman, Sander. "WaveNet: A Generative Model for Raw Audio" (*https://oreil.ly/dvApO*), *DeepMind (blog)*, September 8, 2016.

[8] Dialogflow (*https://dialogflow.com*). Last accessed June 15, 2020.

[9] Dialogflow login page (*https://oreil.ly/V8eGg*). Last accessed June 15, 2020.

[10] Google Cloud. Dialogflow V2 API (*https://oreil.ly/piEK0*). Last accessed June 15, 2020.

[11] Mrkšić, Nikola, Diarmuid O. Séaghdha, Tsung-Hsien Wen, Blaise Thomson, and Steve Young. "Neural Belief Tracker: Data-Driven Dialogue State Tracking." *Proceedings of the 55th Annual Meeting of the Association for Computational Linguistics* 1 (2016): 1777–1788.

[12] Team HG-Memex. "sklearn-crfsuite: scikit-learn inspired API for CRFsuite" (*https://oreil.ly/zbPGo*). Last accessed June 15, 2020.

[13] Hemphill, Charles T., John J. Godfrey, and George R. Doddington. "The ATIS Spoken Language Systems Pilot Corpus." *Speech and Natural Language: Proceedings of a Workshop Held at Hidden Valley, Pennsylvania*, June 24–27, 1990.

[14] Coucke, Alice, Alaa Saade, Adrien Ball, Théodore Bluche, Alexandre Caulier, David Leroy, Clément Doumouro et al. "Snips Voice Platform: an embedded Spoken Language Understanding system for private-by-design voice interfaces" (*https://oreil.ly/_c5np*), (2018).

[15] Williams, Jason, Antoine Raux, and Matthew Henderson. "The Dialog State Tracking Challenge Series: A Review." *Dialogue & Discourse* 7.3 (2016): 4–33.

[16] Budzianowski, Paweł, Tsung-Hsien Wen, Bo-Hsiang Tseng, Inigo Casanueva, Stefan Ultes, Osman Ramadan, and Milica Gašić. "MultiWOZ - A Large-Scale Multi-Domain Wizard-of-Oz Dataset for Task-Oriented Dialogue Modelling" (*https://oreil.ly/V9zyy*), (2018).

[17] Serban, Iulian Vlad, Ryan Lowe, Peter Henderson, Laurent Charlin, and Joelle Pineau. "A Survey of Available Corpora for Building Data-Driven Dialogue Systems" (*https://oreil.ly/nLrql*), (2015).

[18] Vinyals, Oriol and Quoc Le. "A Neural Conversational Model" (*https://oreil.ly/Gq8Sh*), (2015).

[19] Li, Jiwei, Will Monroe, Alan Ritter, Michel Galley, Jianfeng Gao, and Dan Jurafsky. "Deep Reinforcement Learning for Dialogue Generation" (*https://oreil.ly/mfd3Q*), (2016).

[20] Weston, Jason E. "Dialog-Based Language Learning." *Proceedings of the 30th International Conference on Neural Information Processing Systems* (2016): 829–837.

[21] Rasa (*https://oreil.ly/aJSyJ*). Last accessed June 15, 2020.

[22] SimGus. Chatette: A powerful dataset generator for Rasa NLU, inspired by Chatito (*https://oreil.ly/QQ64f*), (GitHub repo). Last accessed June 15, 2020.

[23] scikit-learn. "Classifier comparison (*https://oreil.ly/WMulf*)." Last accessed June 15, 2020.

[24] MIT-NLP. MITIE: library and tools for information extraction (*https://oreil.ly/o-3Fr*), (GitHub repo). Last accessed June 15, 2020.

[25] Sucik, Sam. "Compressing BERT for faster prediction" (*https://oreil.ly/Iw_5B*). *Rasa (blog)*, August 8, 2019.

[26] Ganesh, Prakhar, Yao Chen, Xin Lou, Mohammad Ali Khan, Yin Yang, Deming Chen, Marianne Winslett, Hassan Sajjad, and Preslav Nakov. "Compressing Large-Scale Transformer-Based Models: A Case Study on BERT" (*https://oreil.ly/VSQvc*), (2020).

[27] Majumder, Bodhisattwa Prasad, Shuyang Li, Jianmo Ni, and Julian McAuley. "Generating Personalized Recipes from Historical User Preferences" (*https://oreil.ly/OVyBz*), (2019).

## CHAPTER 7

Topics in Brief

The problems are solved, not by giving new information,
but by arranging what we have known since long.
—*Ludwig Wittgenstein,* Philosophical Investigations

So far in Part II of this book, we've discussed a few common application scenarios of NLP: text classification, information extraction, and chatbots (Chapters 4 through 6). While these are the most common use cases for NLP we're likely to encounter in industry projects, there are many other NLP tasks that are relevant in building real-world applications involving large collections of documents. We'll take a quick look at some of these topics in this chapter. Let's first start with a few largely unrelated scenarios you may encounter in your workplace projects. We'll discuss them in more detail throughout the chapter.

If someone asks us to find out what NLP is and we have no idea, where do we start? In the pre-internet era, we would've hit the nearest library to do some research. However, now the first place we'd go is to a search engine. *Search* involves a lot of human-computer interaction using natural language, so it gives rise to very interesting use cases for NLP.

Our client is a big law firm. When a new case comes up, they sometimes have to research lots and lots of documents related to the case to get a bigger picture of what it's about. Many times, there isn't enough time for a thorough manual review. Our client wants us to develop software that can provide a quick overview of the topics discussed in large document collections. *Topic modeling* is a technique that's used to address this problem of finding latent topics in a large collection of documents.

The same client's firm has another problem: case report documents they receive are usually quite long, and it's difficult even for an experienced lawyer to get the gist quickly. So our client wants a solution to automatically create summaries of text documents. *Text summarization* approaches are used to address such use cases in the industry.

Many of us read news online every day. A common feature of many news websites is the "related articles" feature, which shows articles that are topically related to the article we're reading. Consider a related scenario where we're shown jobs related to a given job based on the profile descriptions. *Recommendation* methods using NLP are key to building solutions for such use cases.

We live in an increasingly multicultural world, and many organizations have clients or customers across the globe. This results in the need to translate documents (at scale) in all supported languages in the organization. *Machine translation (MT)* is useful in such scenarios. Streaming services like Amazon, Netflix, and YouTube use MT extensively for generating subtitles in various languages. Tools like Google Translate help tourists across the globe communicate in local languages.

We use search engines for many reasons in day-to-day life. Sometimes, we want to know answers to questions. Try asking a factual question such as, "Who wrote Animal Farm?" to your favorite search engine. Google shows "George Orwell" as its top result along with some biographical details about him, followed by other regular search results. Try asking a somewhat descriptive question, say, "How do I calm down a crying baby?" Among the answers, you'll also see a blurb from some website that lists a number of ways to calm a baby. This is an example of *question answering*, where the task is to locate the most appropriate answer to the user query instead of showing a collection of documents. Note that this is slightly different from the FAQ chatbot we saw in Chapter 6, where the scope of answers lies within a much smaller dataset (i.e., FAQs) instead of a large collection of documents (such as the web).

These are the topics we'll discuss in this chapter. While they may seem very different from one another, we'll see the similarities between them as we progress through the chapter. This collection is not an exhaustive list, but these are some common scenarios encountered when developing NLP-based solutions for industrial applications. The first four tasks (search, topic modeling, text summarization, and recommendation) are more common in real-world applied NLP scenarios, so we'll discuss them in greater detail than the other two. With large-scale question answering and machine translation, you're unlikely to encounter a scenario where you'd have to develop solutions from scratch, so we'll only introduce them so you'll know where to get started to build an MVP quickly. Table 7-1 summarizes the topics we'll cover in this chapter, along with example usage scenarios and the kind of data they work on.

Table 7-1. List of the topics covered in this chapter

NLP task	Use	Nature of data
Search	Find relevant content for a given user query.	World wide web/large collection of documents
Topic modeling	Find topics and hidden patterns in a set of documents.	Large collection of documents
Text summarization	Create a shorter version of the text with the most important content	Typically a single document
Recommendations	Showing related articles	Large collection of documents
Machine translation	Translate from one language to another	A single document
Question answering system	Get answers to queries directly instead of a set of documents.	A single document or a large collection of documents

With this overview, let us start introducing these topics one by one in a little bit more detail. Our first topic is search and information retrieval.

Search and Information Retrieval

A search engine is an important component of everyone's online activity. We search for information to decide on the best items to purchase, nice places to eat out, and businesses to frequent, just to name a few examples. We also rely heavily on search to sift through our emails, documents, and financial transactions. A lot of these search interactions happen through text (or speech converted to text in voice input). This means that a lot of language processing happens inside a search engine. Thus, we can say that NLP plays an important role in modern search engines.

Let's start with a quick look into what happens when we search. When a user searches using a query, the search engine collects a ranked list of documents that matches the query. For this to happen, an "index" of documents and vocabulary used in them should be constructed first and is then used to search and rank results. One popular form of indexing textual data and ranking search results for search engines is something we studied in Chapter 3: TF-IDF. Recent developments in DL models for NLP can also be used for this purpose. For example, Google recently started ranking search results and showing search snippets using the BERT model. They claim that this has improved the quality and relevance of their search results [1]. This is an important example of NLP's usefulness in a modern-day search engine.

Apart from this major function of storing data and ranking search results, several features in a modern search engine involve NLP. For example, consider the screenshot of a Google search result shown in Figure 7-1, which illustrates some features that use NLP.

Figure 7-1. Screenshot of a Google search query

1. *Spelling correction:* The user entered an incorrect spelling, and the search engine offered a suggestion showing the correct spelling.

2. *Related queries:* The "People also ask" feature shows other related questions people ask about Marie Curie.

3. *Snippet extraction:* All the search results show a text snippet involving the query.

4. *Biographical information extraction:* On the right-hand side, there's a small snippet showing Marie Curie's biographical details along with some specific information extracted from text. There are also some quotes and a list of people related to her in some way.

5. *Search results classification:* On top, there are categories of search results: all, news, images, videos, and so on.

Here, we see a range of concepts we've learned about in this book being put to use. While these are by no means the only places NLP is used in search engines, they are examples of where NLP is useful in the user interface aspect of search. However, there's much more to search than NLP, and building a search engine seems like a massive endeavor requiring a lot of infrastructure. This may make one wonder: when do you need to build a search engine, and how? Do we always build search engines as massive as Google? Let's take a look at two scenarios to answer these questions.

Imagine we work for a company like Broad Reader. Our company wants to develop a search engine that crawls forums and discussion boards from all over the web and lets users query this large collection. Consider another scenario: let's say our client is a law firm where loads of legal documents from clients and other legal sources are uploaded every day. We're asked to develop a custom search engine for the client to search through their database. How are these two scenarios different?

The first scenario requires that we build what we call a generic search engine, where we would have to set up a way to scrape different websites, keep looking for new content and new websites, and constantly build and update our "index." The second scenario is an example of an enterprise search engine, as we don't have to scout for content to index. Thus, these two types of search engines are distinguished as follows:

- Generic search engines, such as Google and Bing, that crawl the web and aim to cover as much as possible by constantly looking for new webpages
- Enterprise search engines, where our search space is restricted to a smaller set of already existing documents within an organization

In our experience, the second form of search is the most common use case you may encounter at your workplace, so we'll only briefly introduce a generic search engine by discussing a few basic components that are also relevant to enterprise search.

Components of a Search Engine

How does a search engine work? What are some of the basic components? We briefly introduce them through Figure 7-2, taken from the now-famous 1998 research paper on the architecture of Google [2].

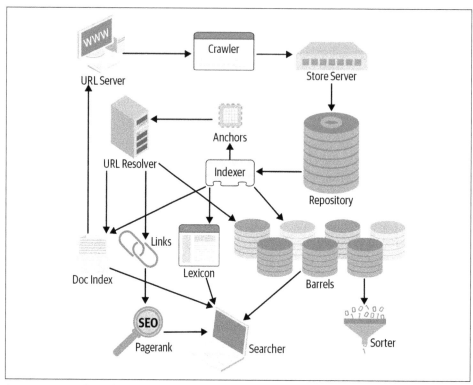

Figure 7-2. Early architecture of the Google search engine [2]

There are several small and large components inside a search engine, as shown in the figure. The three major components that can be considered its building blocks (and a fourth component that is now also common) are:

Crawler

Collects all the content for the search engine. The crawler's job is to traverse the web following a bunch of seed URLs and build its collection of URLs through them in a breadth-first way. It visits each URL, saves a copy of the document, detects the outgoing hyperlinks, then adds them to the list of URLs to be visited next. Typical decisions that need to be made when designing a crawler include identifying what to crawl, when to stop crawling, when to re-crawl, what to re-crawl, and how to make sure we don't crawl duplicate content. From our experience, even when you have to develop some sort of generic search engine (say, a blog search engine), you're unlikely to encounter a scenario where you should design your own crawler. Production-ready crawlers, such as Apache Nutch [3] and Scrapy [4], can be customized and used for your project in such scenarios.

Indexer

Parses and stores the content that the crawler collects and builds an "index" so it can be searched and retrieved efficiently. While it's possible to index videos, audio, images, etc., text indexing is the most common type of indexing in real-world projects. Data structures for a search engine index are developed keeping in mind the need for fast and efficient search of its crawl in response to a user query. An example of a popular indexing algorithm used in web search engines is an "inverted index," which stores the list of documents associated with each word in its vocabulary. As with crawlers, you're unlikely to encounter a situation where you have to develop your own indexer. Software like Apache Solr [5] and Elasticsearch [6] are typically used in the industry to build an index and search over it.

Searcher

Searches the index and ranks the search results for the user query based on the relevance of the results to the query. A typical search query on Google or Bing will likely yield hundreds and thousands of results. As users, we can't go through them manually to decide whether the result is relevant to our query. This is where a ranking of search results becomes important. An intuitive approach to ranking based on what we've seen so far in this book is to obtain a vector representation of the result document and user query and rank the documents based on some measure of similarity. In fact, as we mentioned at the start of the chapter, TF-IDF, which we saw in detail in Chapter 3 and used for text classification in Chapter 4, is one of the popular methods of searching and ranking search results.

Feedback

A fourth component, which is now common in all search engines, that tracks and analyzes user interactions with the search engine, such as click-throughs, time spent on searching and on each clicked result, etc., and uses it for continuous improvement of the search system.

We hope this short discussion gave a quick glance into what a typical search engine is made up of. Information retrieval is a major research area in itself, and search engine development is a massive undertaking involving a lot of computation and infrastructure. All the topics discussed above are not completely solved problems yet. In this section, we only provided an overview of how a search engine works in order to lead into a discussion on where NLP comes into the picture and how to develop custom search engines. Interested readers can refer to [7] for a detailed discussion on the algorithms and data structures behind search engine development.

With this introduction, let's move on to what a typical search engine pipeline looks like in the use cases you may encounter in your workplace and what NLP methods we've learned so far can be put to use in this pipeline.

A Typical Enterprise Search Pipeline

Say we work for a large newspaper and are tasked with developing a search engine for its website. We already mentioned that Solr and ElasticSearch are typically used for addressing such scenarios. How will we use them? Let's do a step-by-step walkthrough and also discuss which NLP tools we'll need in this process.

Crawling/content acquisition
> We don't really need a crawler in this case, as we don't need data from external websites. What we need is a way to read data from the location where all the news articles are stored (e.g., in a local database or in some cloud location).

Text normalization
> Once we collect the content, depending on its format, we start by first extracting the main text and discarding additional information (e.g., newspaper headers). It's also common to do some pre-processing steps, such as tokenizing, lowercasing, stop word removal, stemming, etc., before vectorizing.

Indexing
> For indexing, we have to vectorize the text. TF-IDF is a popular scheme for this, as we discussed earlier. However, like Google, we can also use BERT instead. How do we use BERT for search? We can use BERT to get a vector representation of the query and documents and generate a ranked list of closest documents for a given query in terms of vector distance. [8] shows how we can use such text embeddings to index and search using Elasticsearch.

In addition to indexing the entire content of an article, we can also add additional fields/facets to the index for each document and later search by these facets. For example, for a newspaper, this can be the news category, other tags like the state involved (e.g., California for a news article about something in the USA), and so on. Text classification approaches we saw in Chapter 4 can be used to get such categories and tags, if necessary. At the time of displaying the search results, we can combine this with filters like date to enrich the user experience. We'll see an example of such a faceted search in Chapter 9.

So, let's assume we've built our search engine following the above process. What next? What happens when the user types a query? At this point, the pipeline typically consists of the following steps:

1. *Query processing and execution:* The search query is passed through the text normalization process as above. Once the query is framed, it's executed, and results are retrieved and ranked according to some notion of relevance. Search engine libraries like Elasticsearch even provide custom scoring functions to modify the ranking of documents retrieved for a given query [9].

---

2. *Feedback and ranking:* To evaluate search results and make them more relevant to the user, user behavior is recorded and analyzed, and signals such as click action on result and time spent on a result page are used to improve the ranking algorithm. An example in our newspaper's case could be to learn the reader's preference (e.g., the reader prefers reading local news from Region X) and show them a personalized ranking of suggested articles.

We hope this newspaper use case shows what a typical enterprise search engine development pipeline looks like. Like with many software applications, recent developments in the field of machine learning have also influenced enterprise search. We briefly mentioned how BERT and other such embedding-based text representations can be used with Elasticsearch. Amazon Kendra [10], an enterprise search engine powered by machine learning, is a recent addition to this space.

Setting Up a Search Engine: An Example

Now that we have an idea of the components of a search engine and how they work together in an example scenario, let's take a quick look at building a small search engine using Elasticsearch's Python API. We'll use the CMU Book Summaries dataset [11], which consists of plot summaries of over 16,000 books extracted from Wikipedia pages. We'll illustrate the process using 500 documents, but the notebook associated with this section (*Ch7/ElasticSearch.ipynb*) can be used to build a search engine with the full dataset. We already have our content in place, so we don't need a crawler. Taking a simple use case that doesn't involve additional pre-processing (no stemming, for example), the following code snippet shows how to build an index using Elasticsearch:

```
#Build an index from booksummaries dataset, using only 500 documents.
path = "../booksummaries/booksummaries.txt"
count = 1
for line in open(path):
    fields = line.split("\t")
    doc = {'id' : fields[0],
           'title': fields[2],
           'author': fields[3],
           'summary': fields[6]
          }
      #Index is called myindex
    res = es.index(index="myindex", id=fields[0], body=doc)
    count = count+1
    if count%100 == 0:
        print("indexed 100 documents")
    if count == 501:
        break
res = es.search(index="myindex", body={"query": {"match_all": {}}})
print("Your index has %d entries" % res['hits']['total']['value'])
```

This code builds an index with four fields per document—id, title, author, and sum mary—which are all available in the dataset itself. Once the index is built, it runs a query to check the size of the index. In this case, the output will show as 500 entries. Once the index is built, we have to figure out how to use it to perform search. While we won't go into the user interface design aspects of the search process, the following code snippet illustrates how to search with Elasticsearch:

```
#match query works as a OR query when the query string has multiple words
#match_phrase looks for exact matches. So using that here.
while True:
    query = input("Enter your search query: ")
    if query == "STOP":
        break
    res = es.search(index="myindex", body={"query": {"match_phrase":
                                            {"summary": query}}})
    print("Your search returned %d results:"
                    %res['hits']['total']['value'])
    for hit in res["hits"]["hits"]:
        print(hit["_source"]["title"])
        #to get a snippet 100 characters before and after the match
        loc = hit["_source"]["summary"].lower().index(query)
        print(hit["_source"]["summary"][:100])
        print(hit["_source"]["summary"][loc-100:loc+100])
```

This snippet keeps asking the user to enter a search query until the word STOP is typed and shows the search results, along with a short snippet containing the search phrase. For example, if the user searches for the word "countess," the results look as follows:

```
Enter your search query: countess
Your search returned 7 results:
All's Well That Ends Well
71
 Helena, the orphan daughter of a famous physician, is the ward of the Countess
 of Rousillon, and ho
 ...
 ...
 ...
Enter your search query: STOP
```

Elasticsearch has many features to alter the scoring function, to change the search process in terms of query formulation (e.g., exact match versus fuzzy match), to add pre-processing steps like stemming during the indexing process, and so on. We leave them as further exercises for the reader. Now, let's look at a case study of building an enterprise search engine from scratch and improving it.

A Case Study: Book Store Search

Imagine a scenario where we have a new e-commerce store focused on books and we have to build its search pipeline. We have metadata like author, title, and summary. The search functionality we saw earlier can serve as the baseline at the start. We can set up our own search engine backend or use online services like Elasticsearch [12] or Elastic on Azure [13].

This default search output might have a bunch of issues. For instance, it may show the results with exact query matches in title or summary to be higher than more relevant results that aren't an exact match. Some of the exact matches might be poorly written books with bad reviews, which we're not accounting for in our search ranking. For example, consider these two books on Marie Curie: *Marie Curie Biography* and *The Life of Marie Curie*. The latter is an authoritative biography on Marie Curie, while the former is a new and poorly reviewed book. But while querying for "marie curie biography," the less-relevant book, *Marie Curie Biography*, is ranked higher than the popular *The Life of Marie Curie*.

We can incorporate real-world metrics that account for this into our search engine. For instance, the number of times a book is viewed and sold, the number of reviews, and the book's rating can all be incorporated into the search ranking function. In Elasticsearch, this can be done by using function scoring and giving a manually selected weightage to number of ratings, number of books sold, and average rating. So, we might want to give more weightage to books sold than the number of times it was viewed. These heuristics will provide more relevant results as more books get sold and reviewed. This method of manually defining search relevance weights can be a good starting point when there's no data or the data is limited.

We should start collecting user interactions with the search engine to improve it further. These interactions can include the search query, the kind of user, and their actions on the books. When recording such granular search information, various patterns can be found—for example, when searching for "science books for children," scientists' biographies get purchased at a higher rate even when they're ranked lower. Over time, with increasing amounts of data, we can learn relevance ranking from these logs. We can use a tool like Elasticsearch Learning to Rank [14] to learn this information and improve search relevance. Over time, more advanced techniques like neural embeddings can also be incorporated into search query analysis [15].

As more user information is collected, search results can also be personalized based on the user's past preferences. Generally, such systems are built as a layer over the initial ranking retrieved from the search engine.

Another point to consider in this journey of building an advanced search engine is how important it is to keep complete control of the system and data. If such a search engine is not a core part of your offering and the organization is comfortable with data sharing, many of these features also come as a managed service. These managed search engine services include Algolia [16] and Swiftype [17].

Since the implementation of a search engine involves many other factors beyond NLP and is typically reserved for larger-sized datasets, we're not showing a running example covering all the aspects of a search engine in this book. However, we hope this short introduction gave you an overview of how to get started developing custom search engines involving textual data and of where the NLP techniques you learned so far may play a role. For more details on implementing search engines with Elasticsearch, refer to [18]. Now, let's move on to the second topic of this chapter: topic modeling.

Topic Modeling

Topic modeling is one of the most common applications of NLP in industrial use cases. For analyzing different forms of text from news articles to tweets, from visualizing word clouds (see Chapter 8) to creating graphs of connected topics and documents, topic models are useful for a range of use cases. Topic models are used extensively for document clustering and organizing large collections of text data. They're also useful for text classification.

But what is topic modeling? Say we're given a large collection of documents, and we're asked to "make sense" out of it. What will we do? Clearly, the task is not well defined. Given the large volume of documents, going through each of them manually is not an option. One way to approach it is to bring out some words that best describe the corpus, like the most common words in the corpus. This is called a *word cloud*. The key to a good word cloud is to remove stop words. If we take any English text corpus and list out the most frequent k words, we won't get any meaningful insights, as the most frequent words will be stop words (the, is, are, am, etc.). After doing appropriate preprocessing, the word cloud may yield some meaningful insights depending on the document collection.

Another approach is to break the documents into words and phrases, then group these words and phrases together based on some notion of similarity between them. The resulting groups of words and phrases can then be used to build some understanding of what the corpus is about. Intuitively, if we pick one word from each group, then the set of selected words represents (in a semantic sense) what the corpus is about. Another possibility is to use TF-IDF (See Chapter 3). Consider a corpus of documents wherein some documents are on farming. Then, terms like "farm," "crops," "wheat," and "agriculture" should form the "topics" in the documents on farming. What's the easiest way to find these terms that occur frequently in a document but do not occur much in other documents in the corpus?

Topic modeling operationalizes this intuition. It tries to identify the "key" words (called "topics") present in a text corpus without prior knowledge about it, unlike the rule-based text mining approaches that use regular expressions or dictionary-based keyword searching techniques. Figure 7-3 shows a visualization of a topic model's results for a humanities corpus.

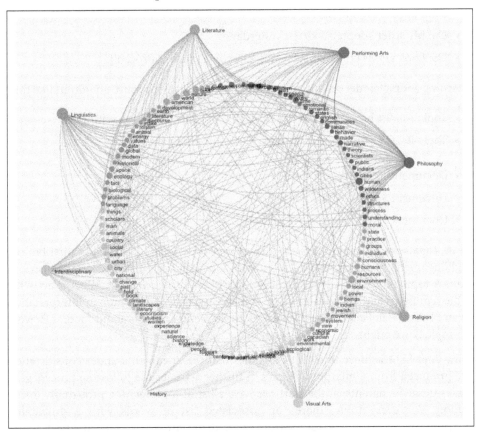

Figure 7-3. Illustration a of topic modeling visualization [19].

In this figure, we see a collection of keywords for individual humanities disciplines—and also how some keywords overlap between disciplines—obtained through a topic model. This is an example of how we can use a topic model to discover what the topics in a large corpus are about. It has to be noted that there's no single topic model. Topic modeling generally refers to a collection of unsupervised statistical learning methods to discover latent topics in a large collection of text documents. Some of the popular topic modeling algorithms are latent Dirichlet allocation (LDA), latent semantic analysis (LSA), and probabilistic latent semantic analysis (PLSA). In practice, the technique that's most commonly used is LDA.

What does LDA do? Let's start with a toy corpus [20]. Say we have a collection of documents, D1 to D5, and each document consists of a single sentence:

- D1: I like to eat broccoli and bananas.
- D2: I ate a banana and salad for breakfast.
- D3: Puppies and kittens are cute.
- D4: My sister adopted a kitten yesterday.
- D5: Look at this cute hamster munching on a piece of broccoli.

Learning a topic model on this collection using LDA may produce an output like this:

- Topic A: 30% broccoli, 15% bananas, 10% breakfast, 10% munching
- Topic B: 20% puppies, 20% kittens, 20% cute, 15% hamster

- Document 1 and 2: 100% Topic A
- Document 3 and 4: 100% Topic B
- Document 5: 60% Topic A, 40% Topic B

Thus, topics are nothing but a mixture of keywords with a probability distribution, and documents are made up of a mixture of topics, again with a probability distribution. A topic model only gives a collection of keywords per topic. What exactly the topic represents and what it should be named is typically left to human interpretation in an LDA model. Here, we might look at Topic A and say, "it is about food." Likewise, for topic B, we might say, "it is about pets."

How does LDA achieve this? LDA assumes that the documents under consideration are produced from a mixture of topics. It further assumes the following process generates these documents: at the start, we have a list of topics with a probability distribution. For every topic, there's an associated list of words with a probability distribution. We sample k topics from topic distribution. For each of the k topics selected, we sample words from the corresponding distribution. This is how each document in the collection is generated.

Now, given a set of documents, LDA tries to backtrack the generation process and figure out what topics would generate these documents in the first place. The topics are called "latent" because they're hidden and must be discovered. How does LDA do this backtracking? It does so by factorizing a document-term matrix (M) that keeps count of words across all documents. It has all the m documents $D_1, D_2, D_3 \ldots D_m$ arranged along the rows and all the n words $W_1, W_2, \ldots, W_n$ in the corpus vocabulary arranged as columns. $M[i,j]$ is the frequency count of word W_j in Document D_i. Figure 7-4 shows one such matrix for a hypothetical corpus consisting of five documents, with a vocabulary of six words.

	W1	W2	W3	W4	W5	W6
D1	0	3	0	0	1	2
D2	1	0	0	1	1	1
D3	2	1	2	2	4	2
D4	1	1	1	4	0	0
D5	0	1	2	1	0	4

Figure 7-4. Document–term matrix (M)

Note that if each word in the vocabulary represents a unique dimension and the total vocabulary is of size n, then the ith row of this matrix is a vector that represents the ith document in this n-dimensional space. LDA factorizes M into two submatrices: M1 and M2. M1 is a document–topics matrix and M2 is a topic–terms matrix, with dimensions (M, K) and (K, N), respectively. With four topics (K1–K4), the submatrices for M may look like the ones shown in Figure 7-5. Here, k is the number of topics we're interested in finding.

	K1	K2	K3	K4
D1	1	0	0	1
D2	1	1	0	0
D3	1	0	0	1
D4	1	0	1	0
D5	0	1	1	1

	W1	W2	W3	W4	W5	W6
K1	1	0	0	1	0	0
K2	0	1	1	0	1	1
K3	1	1	0	1	1	0
K4	1	0	0	0	1	0

Figure 7-5. Factorized matrices

> k, the number of topics, is a hyperparameter. The optimal value for k is found by trial and error.

These submatrices can then be used to understand the topic structure of a document and the keywords a topic is made up of. Now that we have some idea of what happens behind the scenes when we train a topic model, let's look at how to build one.

Training a Topic Model: An Example

We've seen the intuition behind LDA. How do we build one ourselves? Here, we'll use an LDA implementation from the Python library gensim [21] and the CMU Book Summary Dataset [11] we used earlier for demonstrating how to create a search engine. The notebook associated with this section (*Ch5/TopicModeling.ipynb*) contains more details. The following code snippet shows how to train a topic model using LDA:

```
from nltk.tokenize import word_tokenize
from nltk.corpus import stopwords
from gensim.models import LdaModel
from gensim.corpora import Dictionary
from pprint import pprint

#tokenize, remove stopwords, non-alphabetic words, lowercase
def preprocess(textstring):
    stops =  set(stopwords.words('english'))
    tokens = word_tokenize(textstring)
    return [token.lower() for token in tokens if token.isalpha()
            and token not in stops]

data_path = "/PATH/booksummaries/booksummaries.txt"
summaries = []
for line in open(data_path, encoding="utf-8"):
    temp = line.split("\t")
    summaries.append(preprocess(temp[6]))

# Create a dictionary representation of the documents.
dictionary = Dictionary(summaries)
# Filter infrequent or too frequent words.
dictionary.filter_extremes(no_below=10, no_above=0.5)
corpus = [dictionary.doc2bow(summary) for summary in summaries]
# Make a index to word dictionary.
temp = dictionary[0]  # This is only to "load" the dictionary.
id2word = dictionary.id2token
# Train the topic model
model = LdaModel(corpus=corpus, id2word=id2word,iterations=400, num_topics=10)
top_topics = list(model.top_topics(corpus))
pprint(top_topics)
```

If we visually inspect the topics, one of them shows words such as police, case, murdered, killed, death, body, etc. While topics themselves will not get names in a topic model, in looking at the keywords, we may infer that this relates to the topic of crime/thriller novels.

How do you evaluate the results? Given the topic–term matrix for LDA, we sort each topic from highest to lowest term weights and then select the first n terms for each topic. We then measure the *coherence* for terms in each topic, which essentially measures how similar these words are to one another. Additionally, in this example, we made a few choices for the model parameters, such as number of iterations, number of topics, and so on, and did not do any fine-tuning. The notebook associated with this section (*Ch7/TopicModeling.ipynb*) shows how to evaluate the coherence of topic models.

As with any real-world project, we need to experiment with different parameters and topic models before choosing a final model to deploy. Gensim's tutorial on LDA [22] provides more information on how to build, tune, and evaluate a topic model.

 Removing words with low frequency or keeping only those words that are nouns and verbs are some ways of improving a topic model. If the corpus is big, divide it into batches of fixed sizes and run topic modeling for each batch. The best output comes from the intersection of topics from each batch.

What's Next?

Now that we know how to build a topic model, how exactly can we use it? In our experience, some of the use cases for topic models are:

- Summarizing documents, tweets, etc., in the form of keywords based on learned topic distributions
- Detecting social media trends over a period of time
- Designing recommender systems for text

Also, the distribution of topics for a given document can be used as a feature vector for text classification.

Although there is clearly a range of use cases for topic models in industry projects, there are a few challenges associated with their use. The evaluation and interpretation of topic models is still challenging, and there's no consensus on it yet. Parameter tuning for topic models can also take a lot of time. In the above example, we provided the number of topics manually. As mentioned previously, there's no straightforward procedure to know the number of topics; we explore with multiple values based on our estimates about the topics in the dataset. Another thing to keep in mind is that models like LDA typically work only with long documents and perform poorly on short documents, such as a corpus of tweets.

Despite all these challenges, topic models are an important tool in any NLP engineer's toolbox, and they have a wider reach in terms of where they can be used. We hope we gave you enough information to help you identify its suitable use cases at your work-place. An interested reader can start at [23] to delve deeper into this topic. Let's move on to the next topic of this chapter: text summarization.

Text Summarization

Text summarization refers to the task of creating a summary of a longer piece of text. The goal of this task is to create a coherent summary that captures the key ideas in the text. It's useful to do a quick read of large documents, store only relevant information, and facilitate better retrieval of information. NLP research on the problem of auto-matic text summarization was actively pursued by different research groups around the world starting in the early 2000s as a part of the Document Understanding Con-ference [24] series. This series of conferences held competitions to solve several sub-tasks within the larger realm of text summarization. Some of them are listed below:

Extractive versus abstractive summarization
> Extractive summarization refers to selecting important sentences from a piece of text and showing them together as a summary. Abstractive summarization refers to the task of generating an abstract of the text; i.e., instead of picking sentences from within the text, a new summary is generated.

Query-focused versus query-independent summarization
> Query-focused summarization refers to creating the summary of the text depending on the user query, whereas query-independent summarization creates a general summary.

Single-document versus multi-document summarization
> As the names indicate, single-document summarization is the task of creating a summary from a single document, whereas multi-document summarization cre-ates a summary from a collection of documents.

We'll look at some use cases to help you understand how these can be applied to actual tasks.

Summarization Use Cases

In our experience, the most common use case for text summarization is a single-document, query-independent, extractive summarization. This is typically used to create short summaries of longer documents for human readers or a machine (e.g., in a search engine to index summaries instead of full texts). A well-known example of such a summarizer in action in a real-world product is the autotldr bot on Reddit [25], a screenshot of which is shown in Figure 7-6. The autotldr bot summarizes long Reddit posts by selecting and ranking the most important sentences in the post.

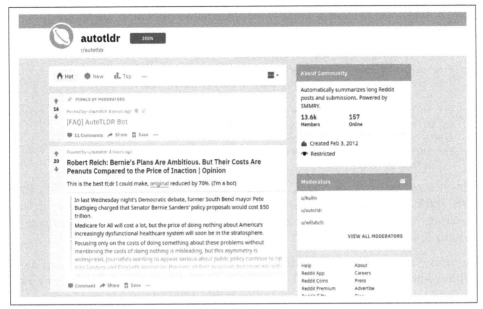

Figure 7-6. Screenshot of Reddit's autotldr bot

Two other use cases one of the authors implemented in their past workplaces are:

- An automatic sentence highlighter for news articles that colors "summary" sentences (i.e., sentences that capture the gist of the text) instead of creating full-length summaries.

- A text summarizer to index only the summaries of documents instead of the full content, with the goal of reducing the size of a search engine's index.

You may encounter similar scenarios for implementing a text summarizer at your workplace. Let's look at an example of how we can leverage existing libraries to implement a single-document, query-independent, extractive summarizer.

Setting Up a Summarizer: An Example

Research in this area has explored rule-based, supervised, and unsupervised approaches and, more recently, DL-based architectures. However, popular extractive summarization algorithms used in real-world scenarios use a graph-based sentence-ranking approach. Each sentence in a document is given a score based on its relation to other sentences in the text, and this is captured differently in different algorithms. The Top N sentences are then returned as a summary. Sumy [26] is a Python library that contains implementations of several popular query-independent, extractive summarization algorithms. The code snippet below shows an example of how to use sumy's implementation of a popular summarization algorithm, TextRank [27], to summarize a Wikipedia page:

```
from sumy.parsers.html import HtmlParser
from sumy.nlp.tokenizers import Tokenizer
from sumy.summarizers.text_rank import TextRankSummarizer

url = "https://en.wikipedia.org/wiki/Automatic_summarization"
parser = HtmlParser.from_url(url, Tokenizer("english"))
summarizer = TextRankSummarizer()
for sentence in summarizer(parser.document, 5):
    print(sentence)
```

This library takes care of HTML parsing and tokenization for the given URL, then uses TextRank to choose the most important sentences as the summary of the text. Running this code shows the five most important sentences in the Wikipedia page on automatic summarization.

Sumy is not the only library with such implementations of summarization algorithms. Another popular library is gensim, which implements an improvised version of TextRank [28]. The following code snippet shows how to use gensim's summarizer to summarize a given text:

```
from gensim.summarization import summarize
text = "some text you want to summarize"
print(summarize(text))
```

Note that, unlike sumy, gensim does not come with an HTML parser, so we'll have to incorporate an HTML parsing step if we want to parse web pages. Gensim's summarizer also allows us to experiment with the length of the summaries. We'll leave the exploration of other summarization algorithms in sumy and further investigation of gensim as exercises for the reader.

So, now we know how to implement a summarizer in our projects. However, there are a few things to keep in mind when using these libraries to deploy a working summarizer. Let's take a look at some of them based on our experiences with building summarizers for various application scenarios.

Practical Advice

If you encounter a scenario where you have to deploy a summarizer as a product feature, there are a few things to keep in mind. It's very likely that you'll use one of the off-the-shelf summarizers like in the example above rather than implementing your own summarizer from scratch. However, if existing algorithms don't suit your project scenario or if they perform poorly, you may have to develop your own summarizer. A more common reason to work on your own summarizer is if you're in an R&D organization, working toward pushing the state of the art in summarization systems. So, assuming you're using off-the-shelf summarizers, how do you compare the multiple summarization algorithms available and choose the one that works best for your use case?

In research, summarization approaches are evaluated using a common dataset of reference summaries created by humans. Recall-Oriented Understudy for Gisting Evaluation (ROUGE) [29] is a common set of metrics based on n-gram overlaps used for evaluating automatic summarization systems. However, such datasets may or may not suit your exact use case. Hence, the best way to compare different approaches is to create your own evaluation set or ask human annotators to rate the summaries produced by different algorithms in terms of coherence, accuracy of the summary, etc.

There are a few practical issues to keep in mind when deploying a summarizer:

- Pre-processing steps like sentence splitting (or HTML parsing in the above example) play a very important role in what comes out as output summary. Most libraries have built-in sentence splitters, but even those can do erroneous sentence splitting for different input data (e.g., what if there's a news article with a letter quoted in the middle?). To our knowledge, there's no one-stop solution for such issues, and you may need to develop custom solutions for the data formats you encounter in your project.

- Most summarization algorithms are sensitive to the size of the text given as input. For example, TextRank runs in polynomial time, so it can easily take up a lot of computing time to generate summaries for larger pieces of text. You need to be aware of this limitation when using a summarizer with very large texts. A workaround could be to run the summarizer on partitions of the large text and stringing the summaries together. Another alternative could be to run the summarizer on the top M% and bottom N% of the text instead of the whole text (assuming that these parts contain the gist of a long document).

Summarizers are sensitive to text length. So, it may make sense to run a summarizer on selected parts of the text.

So far, we've only seen examples of extractive summarization. In comparison, abstractive summarization is more of a research topic than a practical application. Three interesting use cases that come up frequently in abstractive summarization research are: news headline generation, news summary generation, and question answering. Deep learning and reinforcement learning approaches have shown some promising results for abstractive summarization in the recent past [30]. Because this topic has so far been primarily a research bastion and is restricted to academics and organizations with dedicated AI teams, we won't discuss it in further detail in this book. However, we hope this discussion gave you enough of an overview about summarization to get started with an MVP in case you need one. Now, let's take a look at another interesting problem where NLP is useful: offering recommendations for textual data.

Recommender Systems for Textual Data

We're all familiar with seeing related searches, related news articles, related jobs, related products, and other such features on the various websites we browse in our day-to-day lives, and it's not unusual for clients to request them. How do these "related texts" features work?

News articles, job descriptions, product descriptions, and search queries all contain a lot of text. Hence, textual content and the similarities or relatedness between different texts is important to consider when developing recommender systems for textual data. A common approach to building recommendation systems is a method called *collaborative filtering*. It shows recommendations to users based on their past history and on what users with similar profiles preferred in the past. For example, Netflix recommendations use this type of approach at a large scale.

In contrast, there are content-based recommendation systems. An example of one such recommendation is the "related articles" feature on newspaper websites. Look at an example from CBC, a Canadian news website, shown in Figure 7-7.

Below the article text, we see a collection of related stories that are topically similar to the source article, which is titled "How Desmond Cole wrote a bestselling book about being black in Canada." As you can see, the related stories cover black history and racism in Canada and list another article about Desmond Cole. How do we build such a feature based on content similarity among texts? One approach to building such a content-based recommendation system is to use a topic model like we saw earlier in this chapter. Texts similar to the current text in terms of topic distribution can be shown as "related" texts. However, the advent of neural text representations has changed the ways we can show such recommendations. Let's take a look at how we can use a neural text representation to show related text recommendations.

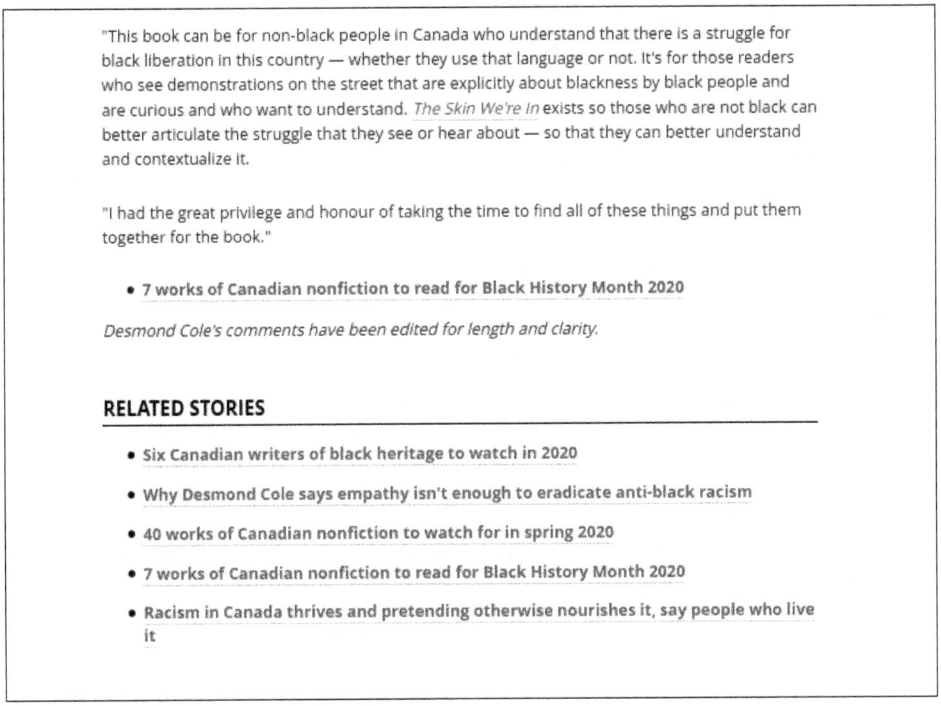

"This book can be for non-black people in Canada who understand that there is a struggle for black liberation in this country — whether they use that language or not. It's for those readers who see demonstrations on the street that are explicitly about blackness by black people and are curious and who want to understand. *The Skin We're In* exists so those who are not black can better articulate the struggle that they see or hear about — so that they can better understand and contextualize it.

"I had the great privilege and honour of taking the time to find all of these things and put them together for the book."

- **7 works of Canadian nonfiction to read for Black History Month 2020**

Desmond Cole's comments have been edited for length and clarity.

RELATED STORIES

- **Six Canadian writers of black heritage to watch in 2020**

- **Why Desmond Cole says empathy isn't enough to eradicate anti-black racism**

- **40 works of Canadian nonfiction to watch for in spring 2020**

- **7 works of Canadian nonfiction to read for Black History Month 2020**

- **Racism in Canada thrives and pretending otherwise nourishes it, say people who live it**

Figure 7-7. Screenshot showing the related stories feature on cbc.ca [31]

Creating a Book Recommender System: An Example

We've seen a few examples of neural network–based text representations (Chapter 3) and how some of them can be useful for text classification (Chapter 4). One of the representations we saw was Doc2vec. The following code snippet shows how to use Doc2vec for serving related book recommendations using the CMU Book Summary Dataset we used earlier in this chapter for topic modeling and the Python libraries NLTK (for tokenization) and gensim (for Doc2vec implementation):

```
from nltk.tokenize import word_tokenize
from gensim.models.doc2vec import Doc2Vec, TaggedDocument

# Read the dataset's README to understand the data format.
data_path = "/DATASET_FOLDER_PATH/booksummaries.txt"
mydata = {} #titles-summaries dictionary object
for line in open(data_path, encoding="utf-8"):
    temp = line.split("\t")
    mydata[temp[2]] = temp[6]

# Prepare the data for doc2vec, build and save a doc2vec model.
d2vtrain = [TaggedDocument((word_tokenize(mydata[t])), tags=[t])
                        for t in mydata.keys()]
model = Doc2Vec(vector_size=50, alpha=0.025, min_count=10, dm =1, epochs=100)
```

```
model.build_vocab(train_doc2vec)
model.train(train_doc2vec, total_examples=model.corpus_count,
  epochs=model.epochs)
model.save("d2v.model")

# Use the model to look for similar texts.
model= Doc2Vec.load("d2v.model")

# This is a sentence from the summary of "Animal Farm" on Wikipedia:
# https://en.wikipedia.org/wiki/Animal_Farm
sample = """
Napoleon enacts changes to the governance structure of the farm, replacing
meetings with a committee of pigs who will run the farm.
"""
new_vector = model.infer_vector(word_tokenize(sample))
sims = model.docvecs.most_similar([new_vector]) #gives 10 most similar titles
print(sims)
```

This prints the output as:

```
[('Animal Farm', 0.6960548758506775), ("Snowball's Chance", 0.6280543208122253),
('Ponni', 0.583295464515686), ('Tros of Samothrace', 0.5764356255531311),
('Payback: Debt and the Shadow Side of Wealth', 0.5714253783226013),
('Settlers in Canada', 0.5685930848121643), ('Stone Tables',
0.5614138245582581), ('For a New Liberty: The Libertarian Manifesto',
0.5510331988334656), ('The God Boy', 0.5497804284095764),
('Snuff', 0.5480046272277832)]
```

Note that we just tokenized the text in this example and did not do any other pre-processing, nor did we do any model tuning. This is just an example of how we can approach the development of a recommendation system, not a detailed analysis. More recent approaches to implementing such systems use BERT or other such models to calculate document similarity. We also briefly mentioned text similarity–based search options in Elasticsearch earlier in this section; that's another option for implementing a recommender system for our use case. We'll leave exploring them further as an exercise for the reader.

Now that we have an idea of how to build a recommendation system for textual data, let's take a look at some practical advice for building such recommendation systems based on our past experiences.

Practical Advice

We just saw a simple example of a textual recommendation system. This kind of approach will work for some use cases, such as recommending related news articles. However, we may have to consider aspects beyond text in many applications where we need to provide more personalized recommendations or where other non-textual aspects of the item need to be considered. An example of such a case is similar listing recommendations in Airbnb, where they combine embedding-based neural text representations with other information, such as location, price, etc., to provide personalized recommendations [32].

How do we know our recommendation system is working? In a real-world project, the impact of recommendations can be measured by performance indicators, such as user click-through rates, conversion into a purchase (if relevant), customer engagement on the website, etc. A/B tests where different groups of users are exposed to different recommendations are used to compare these performance indicators. A third (and perhaps more time consuming) way is to conduct carefully designed user studies where participants are shown specific recommendations and asked to rate them. Finally, if we have a small test set with appropriate recommendations for a given item, we can evaluate a recommendation system by comparing it to this test set. In our experience, a combination of these indicators, along with an analytics platform like Google Analytics, is used in evaluating industry-scale recommendation systems.

Last but not least, our pre-processing decisions play a significant role in the recommendations served by our system. So, we need to know what we want before going ahead with an approach. In the example above, we just did plain tokenization. In the real world, it's not uncommon to see lowercasing, removal of special characters, etc., as parts of the pre-processing pipeline.

This concludes our overview of text recommendation systems. We hope this provides you enough information to identify suitable use cases at your workplace and build recommendation systems for them. Let's move to the next topic of this chapter: machine translation.

Machine Translation

Machine translation (MT)—translating text from one language to another automatically—is one of the original problems of NLP research. Early MT systems employed rule-based approaches that required a lot of linguistic knowledge, including the grammars of source and target languages, to be explicitly coded along with resources like dictionaries between languages. This was followed by several years of research and application development using statistical methods that relied on the existence of lots and lots of parallel data between languages. Such datasets were usually collected from resources where texts were translated into multiple languages, such as European parliamentary proceedings. The past five years have seen explosive growth in DL-based neural MT approaches, which have become the state of the art in both research and production-scale MT systems. Google Translate is a popular example. However, owing to the amount of data and resources required to build them, research and development of such systems has been primarily the bastion of large organizations.

Clearly, MT is a large research area, and building MT systems seems like a large effort. Where is MT useful in the industry? Here are two example scenarios where MT may be required to develop solutions:

- Our client's products are used by people around the world who leave reviews on social media in multiple languages. Our client wants to know the general sentiment of those reviews. For this, instead of looking for sentiment analysis tools in multiple languages, one option is to use an MT system, translate all the reviews into one language, and run sentiment analysis for that language.

- We work with a lot of social media data (e.g., tweets) on a regular basis and notice that it's unlike the kind of text we encounter in typical text documents. For example, consider the sentence, "am gud," which, in formal, well-formed English is, "I am good." (More details on how social media text differs from normal, well-formed text are in Chapter 8.) MT can be used to map these two sentences by treating the conversion from "am gud" to "I am good" as an informal-to-grammatical English translation problem.

While we may or may not develop our own MT systems, there are many scenarios where we may need to implement an MT solution in our NLP projects. [33] discusses some of the industry use cases of MT. So what should we do, then, if we face a similar situation? Let's look at an example of how to set up an MT system in our project.

Using a Machine Translation API: An Example

Building an MT system from scratch is a time- and resource-consuming exercise. A more common way to set up an MT system for a project is to use one of the pay-per-use translation services APIs provided by large research organizations such as Google or Microsoft, which are powered by state-of-the-art neural MT models. The following code snippet shows how to use the Bing Translate API [34] (after obtaining the subscription key and the endpoint URL by registering) to translate from English to German:

```
import os, requests, uuid, json

subscription_key = "XXXXX"
endpoint = "YYYYY"
path = '/translate?api-version=3.0'
params = '&to=de' #From English to German (de)
constructed_url = endpoint + path + params

headers = {
    'Ocp-Apim-Subscription-Key': subscription_key,
    'Content-type': 'application/json',
    'X-ClientTraceId': str(uuid.uuid4())
}
```

```
body = [{'text' : 'How good is Machine Translation?'}]
request = requests.post(constructed_url, headers=headers, json=body)
response = request.json()

print(json.dumps(response, sort_keys=True, indent=4, separators=(',', ': ')))
```

This example requests a translation of the sentence "How good is Machine Translation?" from English to German. The output in JSON format is shown below:

```
[
    {
    "detectedLanguage": {
            "language": "en",
            "score": 1.0
    },
    "translations": [
            {
                "text": "Wie gut ist maschinelle Übersetzung?",
                "to": "de"
            }
    ]
    }
]
```

This shows the translated sentence in German as "Wie gut ist maschinelle Übersetzung?" We can use the service as we need it by calling the Bing Translate API. Similar setups exist for other providers of such services. Before concluding this topic, let's take a look at some practical advice for readers who want to incorporate MT into an NLP project.

Practical Advice

First, as we explained earlier, don't build your own MT system if you don't have to. It's more practical to make use of translation APIs. When using such APIs, it's important to pay close attention to pricing policies. Considering the costs involved, it might be a good idea to store the translations of frequently used text (called a translation memory or a translation cache).

 Maintain a translation memory, which can be used for translations that repeat frequently.

When working with an entirely new language, or, say, a new domain where existing translation APIs do poorly, it makes sense to start with a domain knowledge–based, rule-based translation system addressing the restricted scenario we're dealing with. Another approach to addressing such data-scarce scenarios is to augment our training data by doing "back translation." Let's say we want to translate from English to the Navajo language. English is a popular language for MT, while Navajo is not, but we do have a few examples of English–Navajo translation. In such a case, we can build an MT model between Navajo and English, then use this system to translate a few Navajo sentences into English. At this point, these machine-translated Navajo–English pairs can be added as additional training data to the English–Navajo MT system. This results in a translation system with more examples to train on (even though some of these examples are synthetic). In general, though, if accuracy of translation is paramount, it might make sense to form a hybrid MT system that combines the neural models with rules and some form of post-processing.

 Data augmentation is a useful approach to collect more training data for building an MT system.

MT is a large area of research with dedicated annual conferences, journals, and data-driven competitions where academics and industry groups involved in MT research compete and evaluate their systems. We've only scratched the surface to give you some idea about the topic. A collection of learning materials on MT [35] are available for readers interested in further study. With this overview of MT, let's move on to the next topic of this chapter: question-answering systems.

Question-Answering Systems

When searching online with a search engine such as Google or Bing, for some of the queries, we see "answers" along with a bunch of search results. These answers can be a few words or a listing or definition. In Chapter 5, we saw some examples of one such query to illustrate named entity recognition's role in search. Let's now go a little bit farther than that. Consider the screenshot in Figure 7-8 from Google search for the query "who invented penicillin."

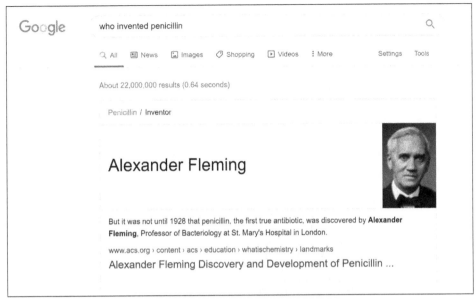

Figure 7-8. Screenshot for the query "who invented penicillin"

Here, the search engine performs an additional task of question answering along with information retrieval. If we follow the search engine pipeline described earlier with the aim of answering such a question, the processing steps look like the ones shown in Figure 7-9.

Clearly, NLP plays an important role in understanding the user query, deciding what kind of question it is and what kind of answer is needed, and identifying where the answers are in a given document after retrieving documents relevant to the query.

While this is an example of a large, generic search engine, we may also encounter scenarios where we have to implement a question-answering system for internal consumption, using a company's data or some other custom setting. Following the pipeline approach mentioned earlier in "Search and Information Retrieval" on page 243 can lead us toward a solution in such cases.

There may be other relatively simpler scenarios of question answering in the workplace, too. A common scenario is an FAQ-answering system. We saw how this works in Chapter 6. Let's briefly discuss one more scenario, based on one of the author's past experiences at their workplace.

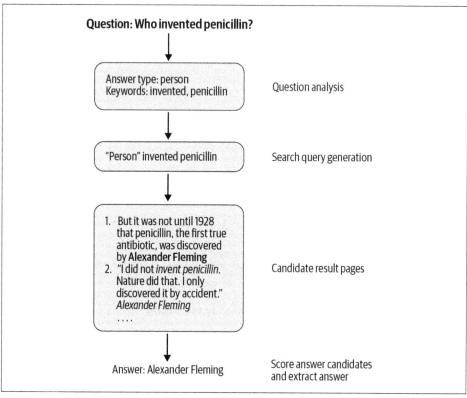

Figure 7-9. Answer extraction

Developing a Custom Question-Answering System

Let's say we're asked to develop a question-answering system that answers all user questions about computers. We've identified a few websites with question-and-answer discussions (e.g., Stack Overflow) and have a crawler in place. At this point, how can we get started with the first version of the question-answering system? One way to build an MVP is to start looking at the markup structure of the websites. Generally, the questions and answers are distinguished using different HTML elements. Collecting this information and using it specifically to build an index of question–answer pairs will get us started on a question-answering system for this task. The next step could be using text embeddings and performing a similarity-based search using Elasticsearch.

Looking for Deeper Answers

In the approaches described above, we would still expect the user question to have a significant amount of exact overlap with the indexed question and answer. However, DL-based text embeddings, which we've seen in different chapters throughout this book so far, are capable of going beyond exact matches and capturing semantic similarities. Such a neural question-answering approach looks for the answer span in a text by comparing the question's embedding with that of the text's subunits (words, sentences, and paragraphs). Question answering using deep neural networks is very much an active area of research and is typically studied as a supervised ML problem using specific datasets designed for this task, such as the SQuAD [36] dataset. DeepQA, which is a part of Allen NLP [37], is a popular library for developing experimental question-answering systems using DL architectures.

Another approach to question answering is knowledge-based question answering, which relies on the presence of a huge knowledge database and a way to map user queries to the database. This is typically used for answering short, factual questions. Real-world question-answering systems like IBM Watson, which beat human participants in the popular quiz show *Jeopardy!*, use a combination of both approaches. Bing Answer Search API [38], which allows subscribed users to query the system for answers, is an example of a research system that follows such a hybrid approach.

Developing any such question-answering system that can model deeper knowledge at web scale requires a substantial amount of data and computing resources coupled with a lot of experimentation. It's not yet a common scenario in a typical software company working on NLP projects, so we won't discuss it further in this book. To get a historical overview of question answering along with the most recent developments in research, we recommend reading Chapter 25 of the upcoming edition of the popular NLP textbook, *Speech and Language Processing* [39]. If you want to implement a DL-based question-answering system for your own dataset (e.g., internal documents in an organization), libraries such as CDQA-Suite [40] provide the backbone to get started.

As can be seen from this discussion, question answering is an area of search that has a wide-ranging array of solutions, ranging from simple and straightforward approaches like extracting markup, to complex, DL-based solutions. We hope this overview provided you with enough examples of the use cases you may encounter in your workplace to develop question-answering systems.

Wrapping Up

In this chapter, we saw how NLP plays a role in a range of problem scenarios, starting from search engines to question answering. We saw how some of the topics we learned earlier in the book can be used to address these problems. While these topics seem disparate at first glance, some of them are also related to one another—for example, search, recommendation systems, and question answering are all some form of information retrieval. Even summarization can be treated as such, as we retrieve relevant sentences from a given text. Additionally, all of them, except machine translation, typically do not require large, annotated datasets. Thus, we can see some similarities among these topics. Note that each of the topics we discussed are still active research questions in NLP, and a lot of new developments happen every day, so the treatment of topics in this chapter is not exhaustive. However, we hope this gave you enough of an overview to get started should you encounter a related use case at work.

With this, we've reached the end of the "Essentials" part of the book. In the next part, we'll take a look at how all these different topics come together in specific domains.

References

[1] Nayak, Pandu. "Understanding Searches Better than Ever Before" (*https://oreil.ly/-syhq*). *The Keyword (blog)*, October 25, 2019.

[2] Brin, Sergey and Lawrence Page. "The Anatomy of a Large-Scale Hypertextual Web Search Engine." *Computer Networks and ISDN Systems* 30.1–7 (1998): 107–117.

[3] Apache Nutch (*https://oreil.ly/P8cnm*). Last accessed June 15, 2020.

[4] Scrapy, a fast and powerful scraping and web crawling framework (*https://scrapy.org*). Last accessed June 15, 2020.

[5] Apache Solr, an open source search engine (*https://oreil.ly/fTcCt*). Last accessed June 15, 2020.

[6] Elasticsearch, an open source search engine (*https://www.elastic.co*). Last accessed June 15, 2020.

[7] Manning, Christopher D., Prabhakar Raghavan, and Hinrich Schütze. *Introduction to Information Retrieval*. Cambridge: Cambridge University Press, 2008. ISBN: 978-0-52186-571-5

[8] Tibshirani, Julie. "Text similarity search with vector fields" (*https://oreil.ly/3K7_F*). *Elastic (blog)*, August 27, 2019.

[9] Elasticsearch. "Function score query" documentation (*https://oreil.ly/4vM6S*). Last accessed June 15, 2020.

[10] Amazon Kendra (*https://oreil.ly/n4DJI*). Last accessed June 15, 2020.

[11] Bamman, David and Noah Smith. "CMU Book Summary Dataset" (*https://oreil.ly/TEpOW*), 2013.

[12] Amazon Elasticsearch Service (*https://oreil.ly/hyQOj*). Last accessed June 15, 2020.

[13] Elastic on Azure (*https://oreil.ly/2eOjQ*). Last accessed June 15, 2020.

[14] Elasticsearch. "Elasticsearch Learning to Rank: the documentation" (*https://oreil.ly/o_P9q*). Last accessed June 15, 2020.

[15] Mitra, Bhaskar and Nick Craswell. "An introduction to neural information retrieval." *Foundations and Trends in Information Retrieval* 13.1 (2018): 1–126.

[16] Search engine services by Algolia (*https://www.algolia.com*). Last accessed June 15, 2020.

[17] Search engine services by Swiftype (*https://swiftype.com*), and Amazon Kendra (*https://oreil.ly/n4DJI*). Last accessed June 15, 2020.

[18] Gormley, Clinton and Zachary Tong. *Elasticsearch: The Definitive Guide* (*https://oreil.ly/cpIGq*). Boston: O'Reilly, 2015. ISBN: 978-1-44935-854-9

[19] "EH Topic Modeling II" (*https://oreil.ly/xxC-O*). Last accessed June 15, 2020.

[20] Keshet, Joseph. "Latent Dirichlet Allocation" (*https://oreil.ly/KE20W*). Lecture from Advanced Techniques in Machine Learning (89654), Bar Ilan University, 2016.

[21] RaRe Consulting. "Genism: topic modelling for humans" (*https://oreil.ly/hDr-a*). Last accessed June 15, 2020.

[22] Gensim's LDA tutorial (*https://oreil.ly/I80VD*). Last accessed June 15, 2020.

[23] Topic modeling is a broad area, with entire books written on the topic, so we won't discuss how they work in this book. Interested readers can refer to the following article as a starting point: Blei, David M. "Probabilistic Topic Models." *Communications of the ACM* 55.4 (2012): 77–84.

[24] NIST. Document Understanding Conference series (*https://duc.nist.gov*). Last accessed June 15, 2020.

[25] Reddit. autotldr bot (*https://oreil.ly/WpFTr*). Last accessed June 15, 2020.

[26] Sumy, an automatic text summarizer (*https://oreil.ly/8OQ1l*). Last accessed June 15, 2020.

[27] Mihalcea, Rada and Paul Tarau. "TextRank: Bringing Order into Text." *Proceedings of the 2004 Conference on Empirical Methods in Natural Language Processing* (2004): 404–411.

[28] Mortensen, Ólavur. "Text Summarization with Gensim" (*https://oreil.ly/wu1xO*). *RARE Technologies (blog)*, August 24, 2015.

[29] Wikipedia. "ROUGE (metric)" (*https://oreil.ly/uBsUq*). Last updated September 3, 2019.

[30] Paulus, Romain, Caiming Xiong, and Richard Socher. "Your TLDR by an ai: a Deep Reinforced Model for Abstractive Summarization" (*https://oreil.ly/SDWDy*). *Salesforce Research (blog)*, 2017.

[31] Patrick, Ryan B. "How Desmond Cole Wrote a Bestselling Book about Being Black in Canada" (*https://oreil.ly/X-txd*). *CBC*, February 27, 2020.

[32] Grbovic, Mihajlo et al. "Listing Embeddings in Search Ranking" (*https://oreil.ly/C0pWw*). *Airbnb Engineering & Data Science (blog)*, March 13, 2018.

[33] Way, Andy. "Traditional and Emerging Use-Cases for Machine Translation." *Proceedings of Translating and the Computer* 35 (2013): 12.

[34] Azure Cognitive Services. Translator Text API v3.0 (*https://oreil.ly/9NV4W*). Last accessed June 15, 2020.

[35] Machine Translation courses (*http://mt-class.org*). Last accessed June 15, 2020.

[36] SQuAD2.0. "The Stanford Question Answering Dataset" (*https://oreil.ly/XHL2-*). Last accessed June 15, 2020.

[37] Allen Institute for AI. AllenNLP (*https://oreil.ly/v1bKA*). Last accessed June 15, 2020.

[38] Microsoft. Project Answer Search API (*https://oreil.ly/J7Nkz*). Last accessed June 15, 2020.

[39] Jurafsky, Dan and James H. Martin. *Speech and Language Processing* (*https://oreil.ly/Ta16f*), Third Edition (Draft). 2018.

[40] CDQA-Suite, a library to help build a QA system for your dataset (*https://oreil.ly/uxXnj*). Last accessed June 15, 2020.

## PART III

Applied

## CHAPTER 8

Social Media

*In today's world, we don't need to speak English
because we have social media.*
—*Vir Das*

Social media platforms (Twitter, Facebook, Instagram, WhatsApp, etc.) have revolutionized the way we communicate with individuals, groups, communities, corporations, government agencies, media houses, etc. This, in turn, has changed established norms and etiquette and the day-to-day practices of how businesses and government agencies carry out things like sales, marketing, public relations, and customer support. Given the huge volume and variety of data generated daily on social media platforms, there's a huge body of work focused on building intelligent systems to understand communication and interaction on these platforms. Since a large part of this communication happens in text, NLP has a fundamental role to play in building such systems. In this chapter, we'll focus on how NLP is useful for analyzing social media data and how to build such systems.

To give an idea of the volume of data that's generated on these platforms [1, 2, 3], consider the following numbers:

Volume: 152 million monthly active users on Twitter; for Facebook, it's 2.5 billion
Velocity: 6,000 tweets/second; 57,000 Facebook posts/second
Variety: Topic, language, style, script

The infographic shown in Figure 8-1 presents how much data is generated per minute across different platforms [4].

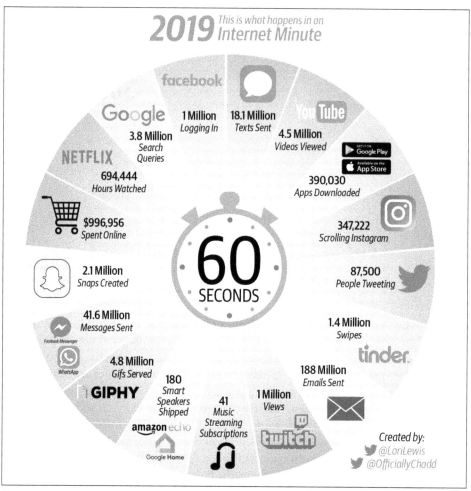

Figure 8-1. Data generated in one minute on various social platforms

Given these numbers, social platforms have to be the largest generators of unstructured natural language data. It's not possible to manually analyze even a fraction of this data. Since a lot of content is text, the only way forward is to design NLP-based intelligent systems that can work with social data and bring out insights. This is the focus of this chapter. We'll look at some important business applications, such as topic detection, sentiment analysis, customer support, and fake news detection, to name a few. A large part of this chapter will be about how the text from social platforms is different from other sources of data and how we can design subsystems to handle these differences. Let's begin by looking at some of the important applications that use NLP to extract insights from social media data.

Applications

There's a wide variety of NLP applications that use data from social platforms, including sentiment detection, customer support, and opinion mining, to name a few. This section will briefly discuss some of the popular ones to give an idea of where we could begin applying these applications for our own needs:

Trending topic detection
> This deals with identifying the topics that are currently getting the most traction on social networks. Trending topics tell us what content people are attracted to and what they think is noteworthy. This information is of immense importance to media houses, retailers, first responders, government entities, and many more. It helps them fine-tune their strategies of engaging with their users. Imagine the insights it could bring when done at the level of specific geolocations.

Opinion mining
> People often use social media to express their opinions about a product, service, or policy. Gathering this information and making sense of it is of great value to brands and organizations. It's impossible to go through thousands of tweets and posts manually to understand the larger opinion of the masses. In such scenarios, being able to summarize thousands of social posts and extract the key insights is highly valuable.

Sentiment detection
> Sentiment analysis of social media data has to be by far the most popular application of NLP on social data. Brands rely extensively on using signals from social media to better understand their users' sentiments about their products and services and that of their competitors. They use it to better understand their customers, from using sentiment to identify the cohorts of customers they should engage with to understanding the shift in the sentiment of its customer base over a long duration of time.

Rumor/fake news detection
> Given their fast and far reach, social networks are also misused to spread false news. In the past few years, there have been instances where social networks were used to sway the opinion of masses using false propaganda. There is a lot of work going on toward understanding and identifying fake news and rumors. This is part of both preventive and corrective measures to control this menace.

Adult content filtering
> Social media also suffers from people using social networks to spread inappropriate content. NLP is used extensively to identify and filter out inappropriate content, such as nudity, profanity, racism, threats, etc.

Customer support

> Owing to the widespread use of social media and its public visibility, customer support on social media has evolved into a must-have for every brand across the globe. Users reach out to brands with their complaints and concerns via social channels. NLP is used extensively to understand, categorize, filter, prioritize, and in some cases even automatically respond to the complaints.

There are many other applications that we haven't dug into, such as geolocation detection, sarcasm detection, event and topic detection, emergency situation awareness, and rumor detection, to name a few. Our aim here is to give you a good idea of the landscape of applications that can be built using social media text data (SMTD).

Now, let's look into why building NLP applications using SMTD is not a straightforward application of the concepts we've learned so far in this book and why SMTD requires special treatment.

Unique Challenges

Until now, we've (implicitly) assumed that the input text (most of the time, if not always) follows the basic tenets of any language, namely:

- Single language
- Single script
- Formal
- Grammatically correct
- Few or no spelling errors
- Mostly text-like (very few non-textual elements, such as emoticons, images, smileys, etc.)

These assumptions essentially stem from the properties and characteristics of the domain(s) from which the input text data comes. Standard NLP systems assume that the language they deal with is highly structured and formal. When it comes to text data coming from social platforms, most of the above assumptions go for a toss. This is because users can be extremely terse when posting on social media; this extreme brevity is a hallmark of social posts. For example, users may write "are" as "r," "we" as "v," "laugh out loud" as "lol," etc. This brevity has given rise to a new recipe for language: one that's very informal and consists of nonstandard spellings, hashtags, emoticons, new words and acronyms, code-mixing, transliteration, etc. These characteristics make the language used on social platforms so unique that it's altogether considered a new language—the "language of social."

Because of this, the NLP tools and techniques designed for standard text data don't work well with SMTD. To illustrate this point better, let's look at some sample tweets, shown in Figures 8-2 and 8-3. Notice how the language used here is very different from the language used in newspapers, blog posts, emails, book chapters, etc.

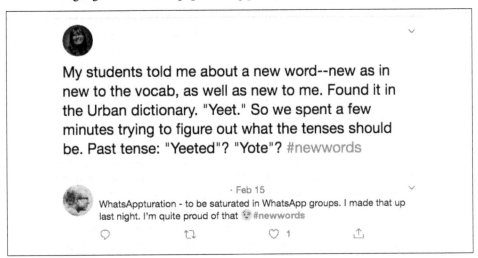

Figure 8-2. Examples of new words being introduced in vocabulary

Figure 8-3. New recipe for language: nonstandard spellings, emoticons, code-mixing, transliteration [5]

These differences pose challenges to standard NLP systems. Let's look at the key differences in detail:

No grammar

Any language is known to strictly follow the rules of grammar. However, conversations on social media don't follow any grammar and are characterized by inconsistent (or absent) punctuation and capitalization, emoticons, incorrect or nonstandard spelling, repetition of the same character multiple times, and rampant abbreviations. This departure from standard languages makes basic preprocessing steps like tokenization, POS tagging, and identification of sentence boundaries difficult. Modules specialized to work with SMTD are required to achieve these tasks.

Nonstandard spelling

Most languages have a single way of writing any word, so writing a word in any other way is a spelling mistake. In SMTD, words can have many spelling variations. As an example, consider the following different ways in which the English word "tomorrow" is written on social [6]—tmw, tomarrow, 2mrw, tommorw, 2moz, tomorro, tommarrow, tomarro, 2m, tomorrw, tmmrw, tomoz, tommorow, tmrrw, tommarow, 2maro, tmrow, tommoro, tomolo, 2mor, 2moro, 2mara, 2mw, tomaro, tomarow, tomoro, 2morr, 2mro, tmoz, tomo, 2morro, 2mar, 2marrow, tmr, tomz, tmorrow, 2mr, tmo, tmro, tommorrow, tmrw, tmrrow, 2mora, tommrow, tmoro, 2ma, 2morrow, tomrw, tomm, tmrww, 2morow, 2mrrw, tomorow. For an NLP system to work well, it needs to understand that all these words refer to the same word.

Multilingual

Take any article from a newspaper or a book, and you'll probably find it's written in a single language. Seldom will you see where large parts of it are written in more than one language. On social media, people often mix languages. Consider the following example from a social media website [7]:

> *Yaar tu to,* GOD *hain.* **tui**
> JU te ki korchis? Hail u man!

It means, "Buddy you are GOD. What are you doing in JU? Hail u man!" The text is a mix of three languages: English (normal font), Hindi (italics), and Bengali (boldface). For Bengali and Hindi, phonetic typing has been used.

Transliteration

Each language is written in its own script, which refers to how the characters are written. However, on social media, people often write the characters of one script using characters of another script. This is called "transliteration." For example, consider the Hindi word "आप" (devanagari script, pronounced as "aap"). In

English, it means "you" (roman script). But people often write it in roman script as "aap." Transliteration is common in SMTD, usually due to the typing interface (keyboard) being in roman script but the language of communication being non-English.

Special characters

SMTD is characterized by the presence of many non-textual entities, such as special characters, emojis, hashtags, emoticons, images and gifs, non-ASCII characters, etc. For example, look at the tweets shown in Figure 8-4. From an NLP standpoint, one needs modules in the pre-processing pipelines to handle such non-textual entities.

Figure 8-4. Special characters in social media data

Ever-evolving vocabulary

Most languages add either no or very few new words to their vocabulary every year. But when it comes to the language of social, the vocabulary increases at a very fast rate. New words pop up every single day. This means that any NLP system processing SMTD sees a lot of new words that were not part of the vocabulary of the training data. This has an adverse impact on the performance of the NLP system and is known as the out of vocabulary (OOV) problem.

In order to get an idea of the severity of this problem, look at the infographic shown in Figure 8-5. We did this experiment [8] a few years ago, where we collected a large corpus of tweets and quantified the amount of "new vocabulary" seen on a month-by-month basis. The figure shows the fraction of new words seen in a month as compared to the previous month's data. As evident from the image, when compared to the vocabulary of the previous month, there are 10–15% new words every month.

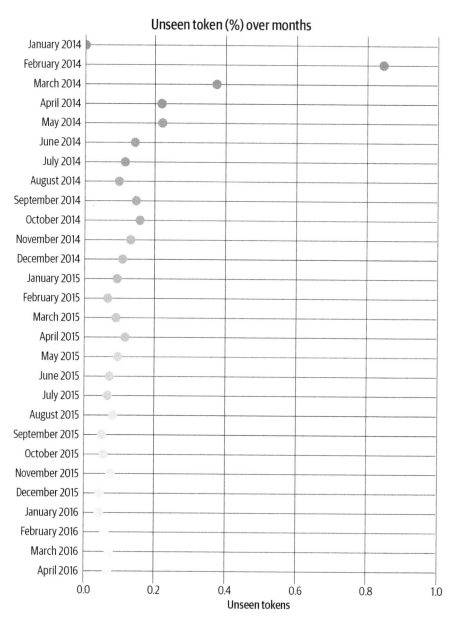

Figure 8-5. Fraction of new vocabulary words seen every month [8]

Length of text

The average length of text on social media platforms is much smaller compared to other channels of communication like blogs, product reviews, emails, etc. The reason is that shorter text can be typed quickly while preserving understandability. This was driven primarily by Twitter's 140-character restriction. For example, "This is an example for texting language" might be written as "dis is n eg 4 txtin lang." Both mean the same, but the former is 39 characters long while the latter has only 24 characters. As Twitter's popularity and adoption grew, being terse on social platforms became the norm. This way of condensed writing has become so popular that now it can be seen in every informal communication, such as messages and chats.

Noisy data

Social media posts are full of spam, ads, promoted content, and all manner of other unsolicited, irrelevant, or distracting content. Thus, we cannot take raw data from social platforms and consume it as is. Filtering out noisy data is a vital step. For example, imagine we're collecting data for an NLP task (say, sarcasm detection) from a Twitter handle or Facebook page, either by scraping or using the Twitter API. It's important to run a check that no spam, ads, or irrelevant content has come into our dataset.

In short, text data from social media is highly informal compared to text data from blogs, books, etc., and this lack of formality can manifest in the various ways described above. All of these can have adverse impacts on the performance of NLP systems that don't have built-in ways to handle them. Figure 8-6 [5] shows the spectrum of formalism in text data and where different sources of text data appear on it.

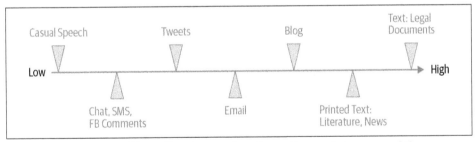

Figure 8-6. Spectrum of formalism in text data depending on data sources [5]

Owing to the characteristics and peculiarities that stem from the informal nature of the language of social, standard NLP tools and techniques face difficulties when applied to SMTD. NLP for SMTD relies on either converting the text from social to standard text (normalization) or building systems that are specifically designed to tackle SMTD. We'll see how to go about doing this while building various applications in the next section.

It's important to identify, understand, and address the language peculiarities found in SMTD. Building submodules that can handle these peculiarities often goes a long way toward improving the performance of models working with SMTD.

Now, let's focus on building business applications using SMTD.

NLP for Social Data

We'll now take a deep dive into applying NLP to SMTD to build some interesting applications that we can apply to a variety of problems. We may need to know how customers are responding to a particular announcement or product we've released, or be able to identify user demographics, for example. We'll start with simple applications like word clouds and ramp up to more complex ones, like understanding sentiment in posts on social media platforms like Twitter.

Word Cloud

A word cloud is a pictorial way of capturing the most significant words in a given document or corpus. It's nothing but an image composed of words (in different sizes) from the text under consideration, where the size of the word is proportional to its importance (frequency) in the text corpus. It's a quick way to understand the *key terms* in a corpus. If we run a word cloud algorithm on this book, we're likely to get a word cloud similar to one shown in Figure 8-7.

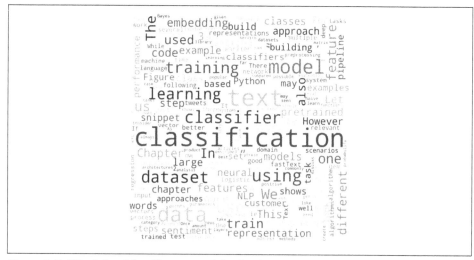

Figure 8-7. Word cloud for Chapter 4 of this book

Words like NLP, natural language processing, and linguistics occur many times compared to other words in the book, so they show up prominently in the corresponding word cloud. So, how do we create word clouds from a collection of tweets? What's the NLP pipeline for this?

Here's a step-by-step process for building a word cloud:

1. Tokenize a given corpus or document

2. Remove stop words

3. Sort the remaining words in descending order of frequency

4. Take the top *k* words and plot them "aesthetically"

The following code snippet illustrates how to implement this pipeline in practice (the complete code can be found in *Ch8/wordcloud.ipynb*). For this, we'll use a library called wordcloud [9] that has a built-in function for generating word clouds:

```
from wordcloud import WordCloud
document_file_path = './twitter_data.txt'
text_from_file = open(document_file_path).read()

stop_words = set(nltk.corpus.stopwords.words('english'))

word_tokens = twokenize(text_from_file)
filtered_sentence = [w for w in word_tokens if not w in stop_words]
wl_space_split = " ".join(filtered_sentence)
my_wordcloud = WordCloud().generate(wl_space_split)

plt.imshow(my_wordcloud)
plt.axis("off")
plt.show()
```

Depending on the styling, we can generate word clouds in various shapes to suit our application [10], as shown in Figure 8-8.

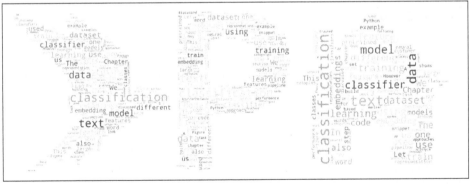

Figure 8-8. The same word cloud in various shapes

Tokenizer for SMTD

One of the key steps in the above process is to correctly tokenize the text data. For this, we used twokenize [11] to get tokens from the text corpus. This is a specialized function for getting tokens from tweets' text data. This function is part of a set of NLP tools specially designed to work with SMTD [12, 13]. Now, we might ask: why do we need a specialized tokenizer, and why not use the standard tokenizer available in NLTK? We discussed this briefly in Chapters 3 and 4, but it's worth spending time on again. The answer lies in the fact that the tokenizer available in NLTK is designed to work with standard English language. Specifically in the English language, two words are separated by space. This might not necessarily be true for English used on Twitter.

This suggests that a tokenizer that uses space as a way to identify word boundaries might not do well on SMTD. Let's understand this with an example. Consider the following tweet: "Hey @NLPer! This is a #NLProc tweet :-D". The ideal way to tokenize this text is as follows: ['Hey', '@NLPer', '!', 'This', 'is', 'a', '#NLProc', 'tweet', ':-D']. Using a tokenizer designed for the English language, like nltk.tokenize.word_tokenize, we'll get the following tokens: ['Hey', '@', 'NLPer', '!', 'This', 'is', 'a', '#', 'NLProc', 'tweet', ':', '-D']. Clearly, the set of tokens given by the tokenizer in NLTK is not correct. It's important to use a tokenizer that gives correct tokens. twokenize is specifically designed to deal with SMTD.

Once we have the correct set of tokens, frequency counting is straightforward. There are a number of specialized tokenizers available to work with SMTD. Some of the popular ones are nltk.tokenize.TweetTokenizer [14], Twikenizer [15], Twokenizer by ARK at CMU [12], and twokenize [11]. For a given input tweet, each of them can give slightly different output. Use the one that gives the best output for your corpus and use case.

Now, we'll move on to the next application, where we'll try to extract topics that are trending.

Trending Topics

Just a couple of years ago, keeping yourself updated with the latest topics was pretty straightforward—pick up the day's newspaper, read through the headlines, and you're done. Social media has changed this. Given the volume of traffic, what is trending can (and often does) change within a few hours. Keeping track of what's trending by the hour may not be so important for an individual, but for a business entity, it can be very important.

How can we keep track of trending topics? In the lingo of social media, any conversation around a topic is often associated with a hashtag. Thus, finding trending topics is all about finding the most popular hashtags in a given time window. In Figure 8-9, we show a snapshot of trending topics in the area of New York.

New York trends · Change

#LittleThingsBuildLove
Similarly, regular investments build
wealth! Happy Valentine's day!
⬜ Promoted by RELIANCE MUTUAL FUND

#TheBachelor 👤
18.5K Tweets

#BlackPantherLive 🐾
17.9K Tweets

Chloe Kim
Chloe Kim sets the bar super high with her first
medal-round run

Bari Weiss
1,808 Tweets

Boston Dynamics
People are terrified of a robot that opens a door
for its robot friend

#LegendsOfTomorrow
12.8K Tweets

#westminsterdogshow

#VisibleWomen
26.1K Tweets

New Music
108K Tweets

Figure 8-9. Snapshot of trending topics on Twitter [16]

So how do we implement a system that can collect trending topics? One of the simplest ways to do this is using a Python API called Tweepy [17]. Tweepy gives a simple function, `trends_available`, to fetch the trending topics. It takes the geolocation (WOEID, or Where On Earth Identifier) as an input and returns the trending topics in that geolocation. The function `trends_available` returns the top-10 trending topics for a given WOEID, on the condition that the trending information for the given WOEID is available. The response of this function call is an array of objects that are "trending." In response, each object encodes the following information: name of the topic that's trending, the corresponding query parameters that can be used to search for the topic using Twitter search, and the URL to Twitter search. Below is a code snippet that demonstrates how we can use Tweepy to fetch trending topics (full code at *Ch8/TrendingTopics.ipynb*):

```
import tweepy, json

CONSUMER_KEY = 'key'
CONSUMER_SECRET = 'secret'
ACCESS_KEY = 'key'
ACCESS_SECRET = 'secret'
auth = tweepy.OAuthHandler(CONSUMER_KEY, CONSUMER_SECRET)
auth.set_access_token(ACCESS_KEY, ACCESS_SECRET)
```

```
api = tweepy.API(auth)

# Where On Earth ID for the entire world is 1.
# See https://dev.twitter.com/docs/api/1.1/get/trends/place and
# http://developer.yahoo.com/geo/geoplanet/

WORLD_WOE_ID = 1
CANADA_WOE_ID = 23424775 # WOEID for Canada

world_trends = api.t
trends_place(_id=WORLD_WOE_ID)
canada_trends = api.trends_place(_id=CANADA_WOE_ID )
world_trends_set = set([trend['name'] for trend in world_trends[0]['trends']])

canada_trends_set = set([trend['name'] for trend incanada_trends[0]['trends']])

# This gives the top trending hashtags for both world and Canada.
common_trends = world_trends_set.intersection(us_trends_set)

trend_queries = [trend['query'] for trend in results[0]['trends']]

for trend_query in trend_queries:
    print(api.search(q=trend_query))

# this will return the tweets for each of the trending topic
```

This small snippet of code will give us the live top trends for a given location. The only problem is that Tweepy is a free API, so it has rate limits. Twitter imposes rate limits on how many requests an application can make to any given API resource within a given time window—you can't make thousands of requests. Twitter's rate limits are well documented. In case you need to make calls beyond the rate limits, look at Gnip [18], a paid data hosepipe from Twitter.

Now, let's see how to implement another popular NLP application: sentiment analysis with social media data.

Understanding Twitter Sentiment

When it comes to NLP and social media, one of the most popular applications has to be sentiment analysis. For businesses and brands across the globe, it's crucial to listen to what people are saying about them and their products and services. It's even more important to know whether people's opinion is positive or negative and if this sentiment polarity is changing over time. In the pre-social era, this was done using customer surveys, including door-to-door visits. In today's world, social media is a great way to understand people's sentiment about a brand. Even more important is how this sentiment changes over time. Figure 8-10 shows how sentiment changes over time for a given organization. Visualizations like these provide great insights to marketing teams and organizations—dissecting their audience's reactions to their campaigns and events helps them plan strategically for future campaigns and content.

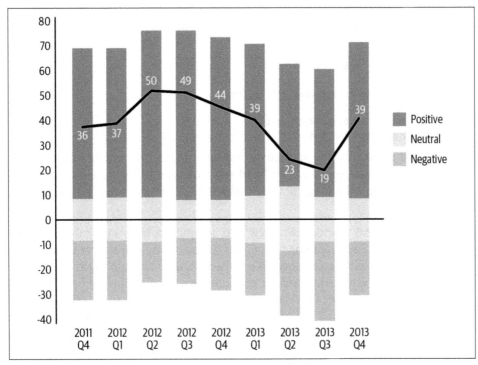

Figure 8-10. Tracking change in sentiment over time [19]

In this section, we'll focus on building sentiment analysis for Twitter data using a dataset from the public domain. There are many datasets available on the internet—for example, the University of Michigan Sentiment Analysis competition on Kaggle [20] and Twitter Sentiment Corpus by Niek Sanders [21].

How is sentiment analysis for Twitter different from the sentiment analysis models we built in Chapter 4? The key difference lies in the dataset. In Chapter 4, we used the IMDB dataset, which consists of sentences that are well formed and have a structure to them. On the other hand, the data in the Twitter sentiment corpus consists of tweets written informally. This leads to the various issues we discussed in "Unique Challenges" on page 280. These issues, in turn, impact the performance of the model. A great experiment is to run the sentiment analysis pipeline from Chapter 4 on our Twitter corpus and take a deep dive into the kind of mistakes the model makes. We leave this as an exercise for the reader.

We'll move forward by building a system for sentiment analysis and setting up a baseline. For this, we'll use TextBlob [22], which is a Python-based NLP toolkit built on top of NLTK and Pattern. It comes with an array of modules for text processing, text mining, and text analysis. All it takes is five lines of code to get a basic sentiment classifier:

```
from textblob import TextBlob

for tweet_text in tweets_text_collection:
    print(tweet_text)
    analysis = TextBlob(tweet_text)
    print(analysis.sentiment)
```

This will give us polarity and subjectivity values of each of the tweets in the corpus. Polarity is a value between [–1.0, 1.0] and tells how positive or negative the text is. Subjectivity is within the range [0.0, 1.0] where 0.0 is very objective and 1.0 is very subjective.

It uses a simple idea: tokenize the tweet and compute polarity and subjectivity for each of the tokens. Then combine the polarity and subjectivity numbers to arrive at a single value for the whole sentence. We leave it to the reader to get into the finer details. This simple sentiment classifier might not work well, primarily because of the tokenizer used by TextBlob. Our data comes from social media, so it will most likely not follow formal English. Thus, after tokenization, many of the tokens may not be standard words found in the English dictionary, so we won't have the polarity and subjectivity for all such tokens.

Say we've been asked to improve our classifier. We can try various techniques and algorithms we learned in Chapter 4. However, we might not see a great improvement in performance because of the noise present in the data (discussed in "Unique Challenges" on page 280). Thus, the key to improving the system lies in better cleaning and pre-processing of the text data. This is crucial for SMTD. Below, we'll discuss some important parts of pre-processing for SMTD. For the rest of the pipeline, we can follow the pipeline discussed in Chapter 4.

 Pre-processing and data cleaning are crucial when working with SMTD. This step is likely to provide the most gains in model performance.

Pre-Processing SMTD

Most NLP systems that work with SMTD have a rich pre-processing pipeline that includes many steps. In this section, we'll cover some of the steps that come up often in dealing with SMTD.

Removing markup elements

It's not surprising to see markup elements (HTML, XML, XHTML, etc.) in SMTD, and it's important to remove them. A great way to achieve this is to use a library called Beautiful Soup [23]:

```
from bs4 import BeautifulSoup

markup = '<a href="http://nlp.com/">\nI love <i>nlp</i>\n</a>'
soup = BeautifulSoup(markup)
soup.get_text()
```

This gives the output `\nI love nlp\n`.

Handling non-text data

SMTD is often full of symbols, special characters, etc., and they're often in encodings such as Latin and Unicode. In order to understand them, it's important to convert the symbols present in the data to simple and easier-to-understand characters. This is often done by converting to a standard encoding format like UTF-8. In the example below, we see how the entire text is converted into a machine-readable form:

```
text = 'I love Pizza 🍕!  Shall we book a cab 🚕 to gizza?'
Text = text.encode("utf-8")
print(Text)

b'I love Pizza \xf0\x9f\x8d\x95!
Shall we book a cab \xf0\x9f\x9a\x95 to get pizza?'
```

Handling apostrophes

Another hallmark of SMTD is the use of the apostrophe; it's quite common to see scenarios like 's, 're, 'r, etc. The way to handle this is to expand apostrophes. This requires a dictionary that can map apostrophes to full forms:

```
Apostrophes_expansion = {
"'s" : " is",
"'re" : " are",
"'r" : " are", ...} ## Given such a dictionary
words = twokenize(tweet_text)

processed_tweet_text = [Apostrophes_expansion[word] if word
                        in Apostrophes_expansion else word for word in words]

processed_tweet_text = " ".join(processed_tweet_text)
```

To the best of our knowledge, such a mapping between apostrophes and their expansion is not available anywhere off the shelf, so it needs to be created manually.

Handling emojis

Emojis are at the very core of communication over social channels. One small image can completely describe one or more human emotions. However, they pose a huge challenge for machines. How can we design subsystems that can understand the meaning of an emoji? A naive thing to do during pre-processing would be to remove all emojis. This could result in significant loss of meaning.

A good way to achieve this is to replace the emoji with corresponding text explaining the emoji. For example, replace "🔥" with "fire". To do so, we need a mapping between emojis and their corresponding elaboration in text. Demoji [24] is a Python package that does exactly this. It has a function, findall(), that gives a list of all emojis in the text along with their corresponding meanings.

```
tweet = "#startspreadingthenews yankees win great start by 🔥 going 5strong
innings with 5k's 🔥  🐂 solo homerun 🌋 🌋 with 2 solo homeruns
and🐂 3run homerun… 🤡  🚣 👨 with rbi's … 🔥 🔥 🇲🇽 and 🇳🇮
to close the game 🔥 🔥 !!!….WHAT A GAME!! "
```

```
demoji.findall(tweet)

{
    "🔥": "fire",
    "🌋": "volcano",
    "👨": "man judge: medium skin tone",
    "🎅": "Santa Claus: medium-dark skin tone",
    "🇲🇽": "flag: Mexico",
    "🐂": "ogre",
    "🤡": "clown face",
    "🇳🇮": "flag: Nicaragua",
    "🚣": "person rowing boat: medium-light skin tone",
    "🐂": "ox",
}
```

We can use the output of findall() to replace all emojis in a text with their corresponding meaning in words.

Split-joined words

Another peculiarity of SMTD is that users sometimes combine multiple words into a single word, where the word disambiguation is done by using capital letters, for example GoodMorning, RainyDay, PlayingInTheCold, etc. This is simple to handle. The following code snippet does the job for us:

```
processed_tweet_text = " ".join(re.findall('[A-Z][^A-Z]*', tweet_text))
```

For GoodMorning, this will return "Good Morning."

Removal of URLs

Another common feature of SMTD is the use of URLs. Depending on the application, we might want to remove the URL all together. The code snippet replaces all URLs with a constant; in this case, `constant_url`. While in simpler cases, we could use a regex, such as `http\S+`, in most cases, we'll have to write a custom regex like the one shown in the following snippet. This code is complex because some social posts contain tiny URLs instead of full URLs:

```python
def process_URLs(tweet_text):
    '''
    replace all URLs in the tweet text
    '''
    UrlStart1 = regex_or('https?://', r'www\.')
    CommonTLDs  = regex_or( 'com','co\\.uk','org','net','info','ca','biz',
                        'info','edu','in','au')
    UrlStart2 = r'[a-z0-9\.-]+?' + r'\.' + CommonTLDs +
                pos_lookahead(r'[/ \W\b]')
    # * not + for case of:  "go to bla.com." -- don't want period
    UrlBody = r'[^ \t\r\n<>]*?'
    UrlExtraCrapBeforeEnd = '%s+?' % regex_or(PunctChars, Entity)
    UrlEnd = regex_or( r'\.\.+', r'[<>]', r'\s', '$')
    Url =       (optional(r'\b') +
            regex_or(UrlStart1, UrlStart2) +
            UrlBody +
        pos_lookahead( optional(UrlExtraCrapBeforeEnd) + UrlEnd))

    Url_RE = re.compile("(%s)" % Url, re.U|re.I)
    tweet_text = re.sub(Url_RE, " constant_url ", tweet_text)

    # fix to handle unicodes in URL
    URL_regex2 = r'\b(htt)[p\:\/]*([\\x\\u][a-z0-9]*)*'
    tweet_text = re.sub(URL_regex2, " constant_url ", tweet_text)
    return tweet_text
```

Nonstandard spellings

On social media, people often write words that are technically spelling mistakes. For example, people often write one or more characters multiple times, as in "yessss" or "ssssh" (instead of "yes" or "ssh"). This repetition of characters is very common in SMTD. Below is a simple way to fix this. We use the fact that, in the English language, there are hardly any words that have the same character three times consecutively. So we trim accordingly:

```python
def prune_multple_consecutive_same_char(tweet_text):
    '''
    yessssssssss  is converted to yes
    sssssssssssh is converted to ssh
    '''
        tweet_text = re.sub(r'(.)\1+', r'\1\1', tweet_text)
        return tweet_text
```

This gives the output `yess ssh`.

Another idea is to use spelling-correction libraries. Most of them use some form of distance metric, such as edit distance or Levenshtein distance. TextBlob itself has some spelling-correction capabilities:

```
from textblob import TextBlob

data = "His sellection is bery antresting"
output = TextBlob(data).correct()
print(output)
```

This gives the output: `His selection is very interesting`.

We hope this gives you a good idea of why, when it comes to SMTD, pre-processing is so important, and of how it can be accomplished. This is by no means an exhaustive list of pre-processing steps. Now, we'll focus on the next step in our NLP pipeline (from back in Figure 2-1): feature engineering.

Text Representation for SMTD

Previously, we saw how to make a simple sentiment classifier for tweets using Text-Blob [22]. Now, let's try to build a more sophisticated classifier. Let's say we've implemented all the pre-processing steps we discussed in the previous section. Now what? Now we need to break the text into tokens and then represent them mathematically. For tokenization, we use twokenize [11], which is a specialized tokenizer designed to work with Twitter data. How do we represent the tokens we get? We can try various techniques we learned in Chapter 3.

In our experience, basic vectorization approaches like BoW and TF-IDF do not work well with SMTD, primarily due to noise and variation in text data (e.g., the variations of "tomorrow" we discussed earlier in this chapter). The noise and variations lead to extremely sparse vectors. This leaves us with the option of using embeddings. As we saw in Chapter 3, training our own embeddings is very expensive. So, we can begin by using pre-trained embeddings. In Chapter 4, we saw how to use Google's pre-trained word embeddings to build a sentiment classifier. Now, if we run the same code on our dataset collected from social media platforms, we may not get impressive numbers like we got there. One of the reasons may be that the vocabulary of our dataset is dramatically different from the vocabulary of the Word2vec model. To verify this, we just tokenize our text corpus and build a set on all tokens, then compare it with the vocabulary of Word2vec. The following code snippet does this:

```
combined = tokenizer(train_test_X)

# This is one way to create vocab set from our dataset.
flat_list = chain(*combined)
dataset_vocab = set(flat_list)
len(dataset_vocab)
```

```
w2v_vocab = set(w2v_model.vocab.keys())

print(dataset_vocab - w2v_vocab)
```

Here, `train_test_X` is the combined set of reviews from training and test chunks of our corpus. Now, you may ask why this wasn't true when we worked with the IMDB movie review dataset. The reason is that Google's Word2vec is trained on Wikipedia and news articles. The language and vocabulary used in these articles is similar to the language and vocabulary used in the IMDB movie review dataset. This is unlikely to be true with our dataset from social media. So, it's highly likely that, for our dataset from social media, the set difference will be pretty high.

So, how do we fix this? There are a few ways:

1. Use pre-trained embeddings from social data, such as the ones from Stanford's NLP group [25]. They trained word embeddings on two billion tweets [26].

2. Use a better tokenizer. We highly recommend the twokenize tokenizer from Allen Ritter's work [11].

3. Train your own embeddings. This option should be the last resort and done only if you have lots and lots of data (at least 1 to 1.5 million tweets). Even after training your own embeddings, you may not get any considerable bump in performance metrics.

 In our experience, if you're going for word-based embeddings, (1) and (2) can give you the best return on investment for your efforts.

Even if you get a considerable boost in the performance metrics, as the time gap between training data and production data keeps increasing, the performance can keep going down. This is because as the time gap increases, the overlap between the vocabulary of the training data and production data keeps reducing. One of the main reasons for this is the fact that the vocabulary of social media is always evolving—new words and acronyms are created and used all the time. You might think that new words get added only once in a while, but, surprisingly, this is far from true. Figure 8-11 shows how fast the vocabulary on social media can evolve [8]. The plot on the left shows the percentage of unseen tokens on a month-by-month basis. This analysis was done using approximately 2 million tweets over a span of 27 months. The plot in the middle shows the same statistics as a bar plot of total versus new tokens on a monthly basis. The plot on the right is a cumulative bar chart. On average, approximately 20% of the vocabulary for any month are new words.

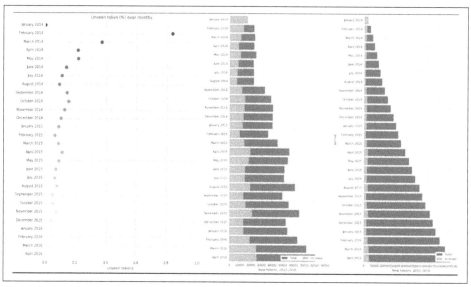

Figure 8-11. Plots depicting how fast the vocabulary of social media can evolve [8]

What does this mean for us? No matter how good our word embeddings are, because of the ever-evolving vocabulary of social media, within a couple of months, our embeddings will become obsolete (i.e., a large portion of our vocabulary won't be present in our word embeddings). This means that when we query the embedding model with a word to fetch its embedding, it will return null since the query word was not present in the training data when the embeddings were trained. This is analogous to saying that all such words were completely ignored. This, in turn, will dramatically reduce the accuracy of our sentiment classifier with time, because with time, more and more words will end up getting ignored.

Word embeddings are not the best way to represent SMTD, especially when you want to use them for more than four to six months.

Researchers working in this area identified this problem pretty early and tried various ways to circumvent it. One of the better ways to deal with this persistent OOV problem with SMTD is to use character n-gram embeddings. We discussed this idea when we covered fastText in Chapters 3 and 4. Each character n-gram in the corpus has an embedding for it. Now, if the word is present in the vocabulary of the embeddings, then we use the word embedding directly. If not—i.e., the word is OOV—we break the word into character n-grams and combine all these embeddings to come up with the embedding for the word. fastText has pre-trained character n-gram embeddings but they're not not Twitter or SMTD specific. Researchers have also tried character embeddings. An interested reader can look into various works along these lines [27, 28, 29, 30].

Customer Support on Social Channels

From its inception to present day, social media has evolved as a channel of communication. It started primarily with the objective of helping people across the globe get connected and express themselves. But the widespread adoption of social media has forced brands and organizations to take another look at their communication strategies. A great example of this is brands providing customer support on social platforms like Twitter and Facebook. Brands never intended to do this to begin with.

Early in this decade, as the adoption of social platforms grew, brands started to create and own properties and assets like Twitter handles and Facebook pages primarily to reach out to their customers and users and run branding and marketing campaigns. However, over time brands saw that users and customers were reaching out to them with complaints and grievances. As the volume of the complaints and issues grew, this prompted brands to create dedicated handles and pages to handle support traffic. Figure 8-12 shows the support pages of Apple and Bank of America. Twitter and Facebook have launched various features to support brands [31], and most customer relationship management (CRM) tools support customer service on social channels. A brand can connect their social channels to the CRM tool and use the tool to respond to inbound messages.

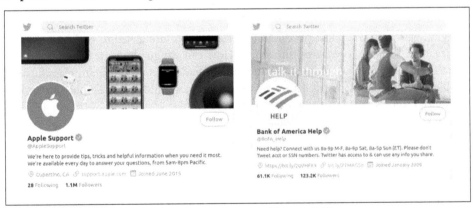

Figure 8-12. Example of brands' support pages on Twitter [32]

Owing to the public nature of conversations, brands are obligated to respond quickly. However, brands' support pages receive a lot of traffic. Some of this is genuine questions, grievances, and requests. These are popularly known as "actionable conversations," as customer support teams should act on them quickly. On the other hand, a large portion of traffic is simply noise: promos, coupons, offers, opinions, troll messages, etc. This is popularly called "noise." Customer support teams cannot respond to noise and want to steer clear of all such messages. Ideally, they want only actionable messages to be converted into tickets in their CRM tools. Figure 8-13 shows examples of both actionable messages and noise.

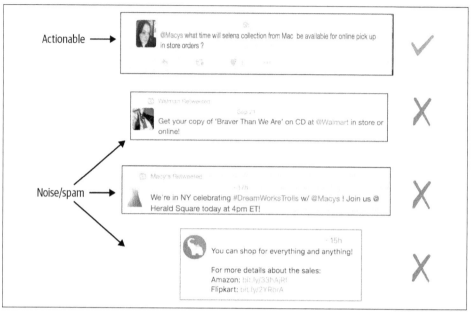

Figure 8-13. Example of actionable versus noisy messages [8]

Imagine we work at a CRM product organization and are asked to build a model to segregate actionable messages from noise. How can we go about it? The problem of identifying noise versus actionable messages is analogous to the spam classification problem or sentiment classification problem. We can build a model that can look at the inbound messages. The pipeline will be very similar:

1. Collect a labeled dataset

2. Clean it

3. Pre-process it

4. Tokenize it

5. Represent it

6. Train a model

7. Test model

8. Put it in production

We've already discussed various aspects of this pipeline in this chapter. Much like sentiment analysis on SMTD, the key here, too, is the pre-processing step. With this, we're now ready to move to the last topic of this chapter: identifying controversial content on social platforms.

Memes and Fake News

Users on social platforms are known to share various kinds of information and thoughts in various ways. These platforms were initially designed to be self-regulating. However, over time, users have evolved to behave beyond community norms; this is known as "trolling." A large portion of posts on social platforms are full of controversial content such as trolls, memes, internet slang, and fake news. Some of it might be advocacy of propaganda, or it could be just for fun. In any case, this content needs to be monitored and filtered out. In this section, we'll discuss how to study the trends of such content and the role NLP has to play in it.

Identifying Memes

Memes are one of the most interesting elements that have been curated by social media users to communicate messages with fun or satire. These memes get reused with minimal changes in form, such as the image of "grumpy cat" (Figure 8-14), which has been used in many scenarios with different text associated with it. This resembles the original concept of "genes" as coined by Richard Dawkins [33]. Lada Adamic from Facebook studied information flow via these memes in the Facebook network [34]; she says, "…memes propagating via a manual copy and paste mechanism can be exact, or they might contain a "mutation," an accidental or intentional modification." Figure 8-14 shows examples of two popular memes that you might have come across.

Figure 8-14. Examples of memes [35]

Before we cover some key methods for understanding the trends in memes, let's discuss why it's important to understand these trends. Misuse of trolling memes in a live feed of a professional network platform like LinkedIn may not be desirable. This is similar to groups on Facebook or Google that intend to spread awareness or information related to official processes or group events (e.g., a Facebook page for a fundraiser event or a Google group for helping students applying to their graduate school). Identifying content that could be a meme that's heckling others or is otherwise offensive or violating other group or platform rules is important. There are two primary ways in which a meme could be identified:

Content-based

> Content-based meme identification uses content to match with other memes of similar patterns that have already been identified. For example, in a community, it has been identified that "This is Bill. Be like Bill" (Figure 8-14) has emerged as a meme. To identify if a new post belongs to the same template, we can extract the text and use a similarity metric like Jaccard distance to identify problematic content. In this way, it's possible to identify memes of this pattern: "This is PersonX. Be like PersonX." In our running example, even a regular expression would be able to identify such templates from a new post.

Behavior-based

> Behavior-based meme identification is done mainly using the activity on the post. Studies have shown that the sharing behavior of a meme changes drastically from its inception to later hours. Usually, viral content can be identified by analyzing the number of shares, comments, likes for a particular post. In general, these numbers often go beyond the average metrics for other non-meme posts. This is more in the realm of anomaly detection. An interested reader can read the survey of such methods studied extensively on the Facebook network [34].

Now that we've discussed the basic definition of memes in the context of social media and briefly touched on how to identify or measure their effects, we'll now move to another important and pressing issue in social media: fake news.

Fake News

In the last few years, fake news on social platforms has become a huge issue. The number of incidents related to fake news has risen significantly along with the rise in users on social platforms. This consists of users both creating fake content and constantly sharing it on social networks to make it viral. In this section, we'll take a look at how we can detect fake news using the NLP techniques we've learned so far.

Let's look at an example of such fake news: "Lottery Winner Arrested for Dumping $200,000 of Manure on Ex-Boss' Lawn." [36] This got over 2.3 million Facebook shares in 2018 [37].

Various media houses and content moderators are actively working on detecting and weeding out such fake news. There are some principled approaches that can be used to tackle this menace:

1. *Fact verification using external data sources*: Fact verification deals with validating various facts in a news article. It can be treated as a language understanding task where, given a sentence and a set of facts, a system needs to find out if the set of facts supports the claim or not.

   Consider we have access to external data sources, such as Wikipedia, where we assume the facts have been entered correctly. Now, given a piece of news text, such as, "Einstein was born in 2000," we should be able to verify it using data sources consisting of facts. Note that, at the beginning, we don't know which piece of information could be wrong, so this cannot be solved trivially just by pattern matching.

   Amazon Research at Cambridge created a curated dataset to deal with such cases of misinformation present in natural text [38]. The dataset consists of examples that look like:

   ```
   {
       "id": 78526,
       "label": "REFUTES",
       "claim": "Lorelai Gilmore's father is named Robert.",
       "attack": "Entity replacement",
       "evidence": [
           [
               [<annotation_id>, <evidence_id>, "Lorelai_Gilmore", 3]
           ]
       ]
   }
   ```

   As you might be able to see, we can develop a model that takes the {claim, evidence} as an input and produces the label REFUTES. This is more of a classification task with three labels: AGREES, REFUTES, and NONE. The evidence set contains the Wikipedia URL of the related entities of the sentence, and 3 denotes the sentence that has the correct fact in the corresponding Wikipedia article.

   A similar dataset could be built by individual media houses to extract knowledge from existing articles related to their domains. For example, a sports news company might build a set primarily containing facts related to sports.

   We can use BoW-based methods to represent both the claim and the evidence and pass them as a pair through a logistic regression to obtain a classification label. More advanced techniques include using DL methods such as LSTM or pre-trained BERT to obtain encodings of these inputs. We can then concatenate these embeddings and pass it to a neural network to classify the claim. An interested reader can look at [39, 40, 41].

2. *Classifying fake versus real*: A simple setup for this problem would be to build a parallel data corpus with instances of fake and real news excerpts and classify them as real or fake. While the setup is simple, it could be very hard for a machine to solve this task reasonably well due to the fact that people may use various linguistic nuances to confuse the machine in flagging fake content.

Researchers from Harvard recently developed a system [42] to identify which text is written by humans and which text is generated by machines (and therefore could be fake). This system uses statistical methods to understand the facts and uses the fact that, when generating text, machines tend to use generic and common words. This is different from humans, who tend to use words that are more specific and adhere to an individual's writing style. Their methods show that there could often be a clear distinction in the statistical properties of word usage that can be used to distinguish fake text from real text. We encourage readers to look into the work of Sebastian Gehrmann et al. [42, 43] for a complete understanding of the method.

A similar technique was used by the AllenNLP team to develop a tool called Grover [44], which uses an ML model to generate text that looks human-written. They exploit the nuances present in the text generated to understand the quirks and attributes, which can then be used to build a system that helps in detecting potentially fake, machine-generated articles. We encourage you to play with the demo [44] that's been open sourced by the team to understand its mechanism.

We discussed two critical issues in social media—memes and fake news—and provided a quick survey of how to detect them. We also discussed how we can pose these problems as a simple natural language understanding task (such as classification) and what a potential dataset to solve that task might look like. This section should give you a good starting point to build systems that can identify malicious or fake content present in social media.

Wrapping Up

In this chapter, we started with an overview of the various applications of NLP in social media and discussed some of the unique challenges social media text data poses to traditional NLP methods. We then took a detailed look at different NLP applications, such as building word clouds, detecting trending topics on Twitter, understanding tweet sentiment, customer support on social media, and detecting memes and fake news. We also saw a range of text processing issues we might encounter while developing these tools and how to solve them. We hope this gave you a good understanding of how to apply NLP techniques on SMTD and solve an NLP problem dealing with social media text data you may encounter in your workplace. Let's now move on to the next chapter, where we'll address another vertical where NLP has proven to be very useful: e-commerce.

References

[1] Twitter. Quarterly results: 2019 Fourth quarter (*https://oreil.ly/RasvL*). Last accessed June 15, 2020.

[2] Internet Live Stats. "Twitter Usage Statistics" (*https://oreil.ly/Tx2U7*). Last accessed June 15, 2020.

[3] Zephoria Digital Marketing. "The Top 20 Valuable Facebook Statistics–Updated May 2020" (*https://oreil.ly/f3LTg*).

[4] Lewis, Lori. "This Is What Happens In An Internet Minute" (*https://oreil.ly/YVU3C*). March 5, 2019.

[5] Choudhury, Monojit. "CS60017 - Social Computing, Indian Institute of Technology Kharagpur, Lecture 1: NLP for Social Media: What, Why and How?" (*https://oreil.ly/CbIUH*). Last accessed June 15, 2020.

[6] Ritter, Alan, Sam Clark, and Oren Etzioni. "Named Entity Recognition in Tweets: An Experimental Study." *Proceedings of the 2011 Conference on Empirical Methods in Natural Language Processing* (2011): 1524–1534.

[7] Barman, Utsab, Amitava Das, Joachim Wagner, and Jennifer Foster. "Code Mixing: A Challenge for Language Identification in the Language of Social Media." *Proceedings of the First Workshop on Computational Approaches to Code Switching* (2014): 13–23.

[8] Gupta, Anuj, Saurabh Arora, Satyam Saxena, and Navaneethan Santhanam (*https://oreil.ly/P7c_a*). "Continuous Learning Systems: Building ML systems that learn from their mistakes" (*https://oreil.ly/39r6_*). *Open Data Science Conference* (2019).

[9] Mueller, Andreas. word_cloud: A little word cloud generator in Python (*https://oreil.ly/7whtP*), (GitHub repo). Last accessed June 15, 2020.

[10] Mueller, Andreas. "Gallery of Examples" (*https://oreil.ly/SyhSL*). Last accessed June 15, 2020.

[11] Ritter, Allen. "Twokenize" (*https://oreil.ly/z8wWs*). Last accessed June 15, 2020.

[12] Ritter, Allen. "OSU Twitter NLP Tools" (*https://oreil.ly/QdtZq*). Last accessed June 15, 2020.

[13] Noah's ARK lab. "Tweet NLP" (*https://oreil.ly/xlhX-*). Last accessed June 15, 2020.

[14] Natural Language Toolkit. TweetTokenizer (*https://oreil.ly/g3P5x*). Last accessed June 15, 2020.

[15] Routar de Sousa, J. Guilherme. Twikenizer (*https://oreil.ly/TNRdM*). Last accessed June 15, 2020.

[16] Twitter's Trending Topics (*https://oreil.ly/Fxn6S*). Last accessed June 15, 2020.

[17] Tweepy, an easy-to-use Python library for accessing the Twitter API (*http://www.tweepy.org*). Last accessed June 15, 2020.

[18] Twitter. Enterprise Data: Unleash the Power of Twitter Data (*https://oreil.ly/5-ojY*). Last accessed June 15, 2020.

[19] Wexler, Steve. "How to Visualize Sentiment and Inclination" (*https://oreil.ly/gQw6H*). *Tableau (blog)*, January 14, 2016.

[20] Kaggle. UMICH SI650—Sentiment Classification (*https://oreil.ly/7CoBZ*). Last accessed June 15, 2020.

[21] Sanders Twitter sentiment corpus (*https://oreil.ly/ZlnRf*), (GitHub repo). Last accessed June 15, 2020.

[22] Loria, Steven. "TextBlob: Simple, Pythonic, text processing––Sentiment analysis, part-of-speech tagging, noun phrase extraction, translation, and more" (*https://oreil.ly/18zLK*). Last accessed June 15, 2020.

[23] Beautiful Soup (*https://oreil.ly/4DpmK*). Last accessed June 15, 2020.

[24] Solomon, Brad. Demoji (*https://oreil.ly/IJ643*). Last accessed June 15, 2020.

[25] Pennington, Jeffrey, Richard Socher, and Christopher D. Manning. "GloVe: Global Vectors for Word Representation" (*https://oreil.ly/MMche*). Last accessed June 15, 2020.

[26] The Stanford Natural Language Procesisng Group. "Pre-trained GloVe embeddings from Tweets" (*https://oreil.ly/WKYcd*). Last accessed June 15, 2020.

[27] Dhingra, Bhuwan, Zhong Zhou, Dylan Fitzpatrick, Michael Muehl, and William W. Cohen. "Tweet2Vec: Character-Based Distributed Representations for Social Media" (*https://oreil.ly/mQymq*). (2016).

[28] Yang, Zhilin, Bhuwan Dhingra, Ye Yuan, Junjie Hu, William W. Cohen, and Ruslan Salakhutdinov. "Words or Characters? Fine-grained Gating for Reading Comprehension" (*https://oreil.ly/0EQm1*). (2016).

[29] Kuru, Onur, Ozan Arkan Can, and Deniz Yuret. "CharNER: Character-Level Named Entity Recognition." *Proceedings of COLING 2016, the 26th International Conference on Computational Linguistics: Technical Papers* (2016): 911–921.

[30] Godin, Fredric. "Twitter word embeddings" (*https://oreil.ly/QuySb*) and "Twitter-Embeddings" (*https://oreil.ly/9cM4I*). Last accessed June 15, 2020.

[31] Lull, Travis. "Announcing new customer support features for businesses" (*https://oreil.ly/Jsa6v*). *Twitter (blog)*, September 15, 2016; Facebook Help Center. "How does my Facebook Page get the 'Very responsive to messages' badge?" (*https://oreil.ly/*

23UNN); Facebook Help Center. "How are response rate and response time defined for my Page?" (*https://oreil.ly/KRmGH*).

[32] Apple's and Bank of America's support handles on Twitter: *https://twitter.com/AppleSupport* and *https://twitter.com/BofA_Help*. Last accessed June 15, 2020.

[33] Rogers, Kara. "Meme: Cultural Concept" (*https://oreil.ly/4J7g7*). *Encyclopedia Britannica*. Last modified March 5, 2020.

[34] Adamic, Lada A., Thomas M. Lento, Eytan Adar, and Pauline C. Ng. "Information Evolution in Social Networks." *Proceedings of the Ninth ACM International Conference on Web Search and Data Mining* (2016): 473–482.

[35] Popsugar Tech (*https://oreil.ly/zpWRu*). Last accessed June 15, 2020.

[36] "Lottery Winner Arrested for Dumping $200,000 of Manure on Ex-Boss' Lawn" (*https://oreil.ly/mOsAp*). *World News Daily Report*. Last accessed June 15, 2020.

[37] Silverman, Craig. "Publishers Are Switching Domain Names to Try and Stay Ahead of Facebook's Algorithm Changes" (*https://oreil.ly/1SX-j*). *BuzzFeed News*, March 1, 2018.

[38] Thorne, James, Andreas Vlachos, Christos Christodoulopoulos, and Arpit Mittal. "FEVER: a large-scale dataset for Fact Extraction and VERification" (*https://oreil.ly/PCI0H*), (2018).

[39] Hassan, Naeemul, Bill Adair, James T. Hamilton, Chengkai Li, Mark Tremayne, Jun Yang, and Cong Yu. "The Quest to Automate Fact Checking." *Proceedings of the 2015 Computation+ Journalism Symposium* (2015).

[40] Graves, Lucas. "Understanding the Promise and Limits of Automated Fact-Checking." *Reuters Institute*, February 28, 2018.

[41] Karadzhov, Georgi, Preslav Nakov, Lluís Màrquez, Alberto Barrón-Cedeño, and Ivan Koychev. "Fully Automated Fact Checking Using External Sources." *Proceedings of the International Conference Recent Advances in Natural Language Processing* (2017).

[42] Strobelt, Hendrik and Sebastian Gehrmann. "Catching a Unicorn with GLTR: A Tool to Detect Automatically Generated Text" (*http://gltr.io*). Last accessed June 15, 2020.

[43] Gehrmann, Sebastian, Hendrik Strobelt, and Alexander M. Rush. "GLTR: Statistical Detection and Visualization of Generated Text" (*https://oreil.ly/vb1z7*), (2019).

[44] Allen Institute for AI. "Grover: A State-of-the-Art Defense against Neural Fake News" (*https://oreil.ly/0Ssr-*). Last accessed June 15, 2020.

## CHAPTER 9

E-Commerce and Retail

Today's new marketplaces must nurture
and manage perfect competition to thrive.
—*Jeff Jordan, Andreessen Horowitz*

In today's world, e-commerce has become synonymous with shopping. An enriched customer experience compared to what a physical retail store offers has fueled this growth of e-commerce. Worldwide retail e-commerce sales in 2019 were $3.5 trillion and are projected to reach $6.5 trillion by 2022 [1]. Recent advancements in ML and NLP have played a major role in this rapid growth.

Visit the home page of any e-retailer, and you'll find a lot of information in the form of text and images. A significant portion of this information consists of text in the form of product descriptions, reviews, etc. Retailers strive to utilize this information intelligently to deliver customer delight and build competitive advantage. An e-commerce portal faces a range of text-related problems that can be solved by NLP techniques. We saw different kinds of NLP problems and solutions in the previous section (Chapters 4 through 7). In this chapter, we'll give an overview of how NLP problems in the e-commerce domain can be addressed using what we've learned in this book so far. We'll discuss some of the key NLP tasks in this domain, including search, building a product catalog, collecting reviews, and providing recommendations.

Figure 9-1 shows some of these e-commerce tasks. Let's start with an overview of them.

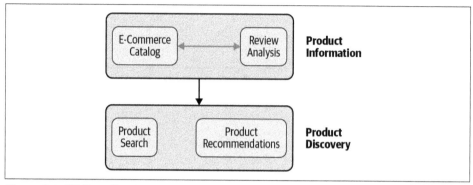

Figure 9-1. NLP applications in e-commerce

E-Commerce Catalog

Any large e-commerce enterprise needs an easy-to-access product catalog. A product catalog is a database of the products that the enterprise deals or a user can purchase. This contains product description attributes as well as images for each product. Better product descriptions with relevant information help the customer choose the right product through the catalog. Such information can also help in product search and recommendations. Imagine a recommendation engine that automatically knows that you like the color blue! That's certainly not possible unless and until the engine notices that most of your recent purchases or searches were on apparel of the color blue. The first thing needed to achieve this is identifying that "blue" is associated with the products as a color attribute. Extracting such information automatically is called *attribute extraction*. Attribute extraction from product descriptions can guarantee that all the relevant product information is properly indexed and displayed for each product, improving product discoverability.

Review Analysis

The most notable part of an e-commerce platform is the user reviews section for every product. Reviews provide a different perspective of the product that cannot be obtained from the product attributes alone, such as quality, usability, comparisons with other products, and delivery feedback. All reviews may not be useful, or they might not come from trusted users. Further, it's hard to process multiple reviews for a given product manually. NLP techniques provide an overall perspective for all reviews by performing tasks such as sentiment analysis, review summarization, identifying review helpfulness, and so on. We saw one example of NLP for review analysis in Chapter 5 when we discussed keyphrase extraction. We'll see other use cases later in this chapter.

Product Search

Search systems in e-commerce are different compared to general search engines like Google, Bing, and Yahoo. An e-commerce search engine is closely tied to the products available and the different kinds of information associated with them. For instance, in a regular search engine, we're dealing largely with free-form text data (like news articles or blogs) as opposed to structured sales and review data for e-commerce. We might search for "red checkered shirt for a wedding," and the e-commerce search engine should be able to fetch it. Similar forms of focused search can also be seen on travel websites for flight and hotel bookings, such as Airbnb and TripAdvisor. The specific nature of the information associated with each type of e-commerce business calls for a customized pipeline of information processing, extraction, and search.

Product Recommendations

Without a recommendation engine, any e-commerce platform would be incomplete. A customer likes when the platform intelligently understands their choices and suggests products to buy next. It actually helps the customer organize their thoughts about shopping and helps to achieve better utility. Recommendations of discounted items, same-brand products, or products with favorite attributes can really engage the customer on the website and make them spend more time. This directly increases the possibility of the customers buying those products. In addition to transaction-based recommendation facilities, there is a rich set of algorithms that are developed based on product content information and reviews that are textual in nature. NLP is used to build such recommendation systems.

With this overview, we're all set to explore the role of NLP in e-commerce in more detail. Let's start with how it's used in building search for e-commerce.

Search in E-Commerce

Customers visit an e-commerce website to find and purchase their desired products quickly. Ideally, a search feature should enable the customer to reach the right product with the least number of clicks. The search needs to be fast and precise and fetch results that closely match customers' needs. A good search mechanism positively impacts the conversion rate, which directly impacts the revenue of the e-retailer. Globally, on average, only 4.3% of user search attempts convert to a purchase. By some estimates, 34% of results in search on the top 50 portals do not produce useful results [2], and there's often a large scope for improvement.

In Chapter 7, we discussed how general search engines work and where NLP is useful. However, for e-commerce, the search engine needs to be more fine-tuned to the business needs. Search in e-commerce is closed domain—i.e., the search engine typically fetches items from within the product information, rather than from a generic set of documents or content on the open web (like Google or Bing). The underlying product information is built on the product catalog, attributes, and reviews. Search works on different facets of this information, like color, style, or category. This kind of search in e-commerce is generally called "faceted search," which is the focus of this section.

Faceted search is a specialized variant of search that allows the customer to navigate in a streamlined way with filters. For example, if we're planning to buy a TV, then we might look for filters like brand, price, TV size, etc. In e-commerce websites, users are presented with a set of search filters depending on the product. Figures 9-2 and 9-3 illustrate search in e-commerce through Amazon and Walmart.

The left-most section of both images depicts a set of filters (alternatively, "facets") that allows the customer to guide their search in a way that matches their buying needs. In Figure 9-2, we see a search for television models, so the filters show aspects such as resolution and display size. Along with such custom filters, there are also some general features that are valid for many such product searches, such as brand, price range, and mode of shipping, as shown in Figure 9-3. These filters are explicit dimensions to perceive the product. And this guided search enables the user to arrange the search results on their own to get more control over shopping, rather than having to sift through a lot of results to get what they're looking for.

Figure 9-2. Faceted search on Amazon.com

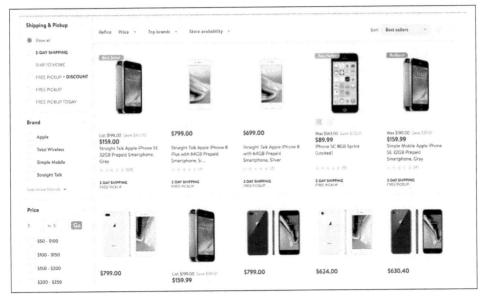

Figure 9-3. Faceted search on Walmart.com

These filters are the key that defines the faceted search. However, they may not always be readily available for all products. Some reasons for that are:

- The seller didn't upload all the required information while listing the product on the e-commerce website. This is typically the case when a new e-commerce business ramps up and aggressively promotes quick onboarding of various sellers. To achieve this, they often allow the sellers to list without having quality checks in place for the product metadata.

- Some of the filters are difficult to obtain, or the seller may not have the complete information to provide—for example, the caloric value of a food product, which is typically derived from the nutrient information provided on the product case. E-retailers don't expect this information to be provided by the seller, but it's crucial because it may capture important customer signals that are directly related to the conversation of that product sale.

Faceted search can be built with most popular search engine backends like Solr and Elasticsearch. Besides regular text search, different facet attributes are also added to the search query. Elasticsearch's DSL also comes with a built-in faceted search interface [3].

In an e-commerce setting, we also need to account for business needs other than relevance in terms of facets and text. For instance, products that are part of a promotion or sale may be bumped up in results. This can be built by utilizing features like Elasticsearch boosting.

Apart from search algorithms, there are many nuances associated with faceted search, and we'll focus on these for the rest of this chapter. The issues mentioned above relate to the problem we'll discuss in the next section: building an e-commerce catalog.

Building an E-Commerce Catalog

As we saw earlier in this chapter, building an informative catalog is one of the primary problems in e-commerce. It can be split into several subproblems:

- Attribute extraction
- Product categorization and taxonomy creation
- Product enrichment
- Product deduplication and matching

Let's take a look at each of these in this section.

Attribute Extraction

Attributes are properties that define a product. For example, in Figure 9-2, we saw brand, resolution, TV size, etc., as relevant attributes. An accurate display of these attributes will provide a complete overview of the product on the e-commerce website so that the customer can make an informed choice. A rich set of attributes relates directly to the improvement of clicks and click-through rates, which influence the product's sale. Figure 9-4 shows an example of a product description obtained by a set of filters or attributes.

As you can see, attributes like {clothing, color, size} are basically what defines this product to a customer. Each of these attributes can have multiple values, as shown in the figure. In this example, color takes seven values. However, directly obtaining attributes from the sellers for all products is difficult. Moreover, the quality of the attributes should be consistent enough to allow a customer to have the correct and relevant information about a product.

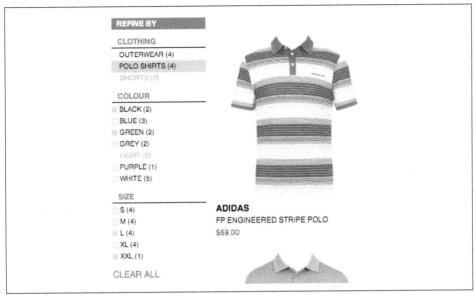

Figure 9-4. Product obtained by a set of filters or attributes

Traditionally, e-commerce websites employed manual labeling or crowdsourcing techniques to obtain the attributes. This is typically done by third-party companies or crowdsourcing platforms (e.g., Mechanical Turk), where specific questions about each product are asked and the crowd workers are expected to answer them. Sometimes, the questions are framed in a multiple-choice way to restrict the answer into a set of values. But generally, it's expensive and not scalable with the increase in the volume of products. That's where techniques from machine learning step in. This is a challenging task because it requires an understanding of the context of the information present in the product. For example, look at the two product descriptions shown in Figure 9-5.

Pink is a popular brand with younger women. Similarly, pink is a very common color of apparel. Hence, in the first case, Pink is a brand name attribute, whereas in the other case, pink is just a color. In Figure 9-5, we see that the backpack is from the brand "Pink" with a color of neon red, whereas the sweatshirt is of the color pink. Cases like these and many more are prevalent and pose a challenging task for a computer to solve.

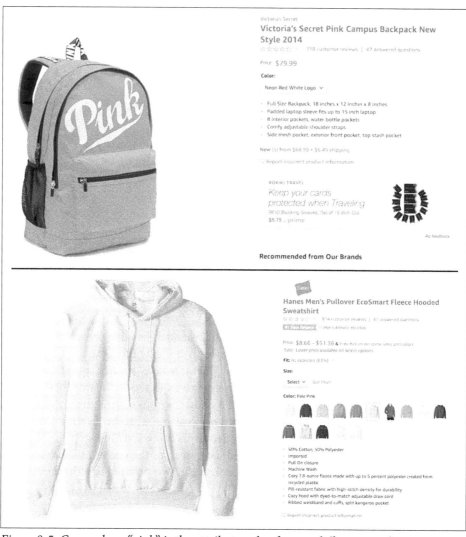

Figure 9-5. Cases where "pink" is the attribute value for two different attributes

If we can obtain a set of attributes in some structured data format, then the search mechanism can accurately utilize them to retrieve results according to customer needs. The algorithms that extract the attribute information from various product descriptions are generally called *attribute extraction algorithms*. These algorithms take a collection of textual data as input and produce the attribute-value pairs as output. There are two types of attribute extraction algorithms: *direct* and *derived*.

Direct attribute extraction algorithms assume the presence of the attribute value in the input text. For example, "Sony XBR49X900E 49-Inch 4K Ultra HD Smart LED TV (2017 Model)" contains the brand "Sony." A brand is typically an attribute that's expected to be present in the product title in most cases. On the other hand, *derived attribute extraction algorithms* do not assume that the attribute of interest is present in the input text. They derive that information from the context. Gender is one such attribute that is usually not present in the product title, but from the input text, the algorithm can identify if the product is specifically for men or women. Consider the product description: "YunJey Short Sleeve Round Neck Triple Color Block Stripe T-Shirt Casual Blouse." The product is for women, but the gender "female" is not explicitly mentioned in the product description or title. In this case, the gender has to be inferred from the text (for instance, from the product description).

Direct attribute extraction

Typically, the direct attribute extraction is modeled as a sequence-to-sequence labeling problem. A sequence labeling model takes a sequence (e.g., of words) as input and outputs another sequence of the same length. In Chapter 5, we briefly touched on this kind of problem in the notebook on training a named entity recognizer. Following a similar approach, let's take a look at how direct attribute extraction algorithms work.

Our training data will be of the form shown in Figure 9-6, for an example product titled, "The Green Pet Shop Self Cooling Dog Pad."

The	Green	Pet	Shop	Self	Cooling	Dog	Pad
B-attribute	I-attribute	I-attribute	I-attribute	O	O	O	O

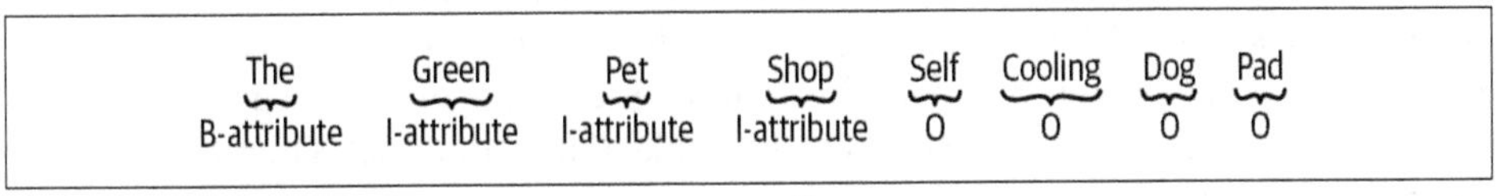

Figure 9-6. Training data format for direct attribute extraction

Here, what we have to extract is "The Green Pet Shop," which is indicated by the -attribute tags, whereas the rest of it is indicated by an O (Other) tag. Getting labeled data in BIO is crucial for any direct attribute extraction process. We should also have data that represents various categories (e.g., B-Attribute1, B-Attribute2, etc.).

There are two broad ways to collect this data. A simpler one would be to use regular expressions on existing text descriptions with brands and attributes and use that dataset. This is akin to weak supervision. We can also get a subset of the data labeled by human annotators. With such labeled data, a rich set of features needs to be extracted to train an ML model. Ideally, the input features should capture the attribute characteristics and locational and contextual information. Here's a list of some of the features that can capture all three of these aspects. We can develop more complex features along similar lines and perform analysis to understand if they're significant in improving performance. Some common features for this task are:

Characteristic features
> These are typically token-based features, such as the letter case of the token, length of the token, and its character composition.

Locational features

These features capture the positional aspect of the token in the input sequence, such as the number of tokens before the given token or the ratio of the token position and the total length of the sequence.

Contextual features

These features mostly encode information about the neighboring tokens, such as the identity of the preceding/succeeding token, POS tag of the token, whether the preceding token is a conjunction, etc.

Once the features are generated and output tags are encoded properly, we get the sequence pairs for training the model. At this point, the training process is similar to that of an NER system. Even though the pipeline looks simple and similar to NER systems, there are challenges with these feature-generation schemes and modeling techniques because of domain-specific knowledge. Further, it's a challenge to obtain large enough datasets that cover a range of attributes.

To deal with such data sparsity and other feature incompleteness issues, some approaches suggest the use of a sequence of word embeddings in the input. The input sequence will be passed to the model as is, and it's supposed to predict the output sequence. Recent efforts include deep recurrent structures like RNN or LSTM-CRF to perform the seq2seq labeling task [4]. We saw how word embeddings and RNNs are useful in NLP in Chapters 3 and 4. This is another example of where such representations can be useful. Figure 9-7 shows an example of how one such DL model [5] performs better than the typical ML models.

Product Title	Previous Best	Current Deep Model
Woodland Imports Decorative Bottle	Woodland	**Woodland Imports**
Home Essentials White Essentials Sugar & Creamer	unbranded	**Home Essentials**
Plum Island Silver Sterling Silver Fairy Piece Ear Cuf	Plum Island	**Plum Island Silver**

Figure 9-7. Characteristic performance improvement in the LSTM framework for attribute extraction [5]

Indirect attribute extraction

Indirect attributes are attributes that are not directly mentioned in the description. These attributes, however, can be inferred from other direct attributes or the overall description. For instance, gender- or age-specific words can be inferred from the text. A phrase like "Suit for your baby aged 1–5 years" implies that the product is for toddlers. Due to the absence of explicit mentions, a sequence labeling approach won't work.

For indirect attribute classification, we use text classification, since instead of extracting information, we can infer high-level classes (i.e., indirect attributes) from the overall input. Recall the example of "YunJae Short Sleeve Round Neck Triple Color Block Stripe T-Shirt Casual Blouse." For this case, we represent the whole input string using any of the sentence representation methods from Chapter 3. We can also create features, such as the presence of class-specific words, character n-grams, and word n-grams. Then, we can train a model to classify the input to an indirect attribute label. In this example here, for the "gender" attribute, we should use men, women, unisex, and child as different class labels.

 For the models that use deep recurrent structures, the amount of data needed is typically much more than what's needed when less-complex ML models such as CRF and HMM are used. The more data there is, the better the deep models learn. This is common to all DL models, as we saw in earlier chapters, but for e-commerce, getting a large set of well-sampled, annotated data is very expensive. Hence, it needs to be taken care of before we to build any sophisticated models.

So far, we've discussed attribute extraction from textual data and the various recent approaches that extend this to multimodal attribute extraction, incorporating various modalities such as title, description, image, reviews, etc., about the product [6].

In the next sections, we'll talk about expanding techniques similar to the ones we applied to product attributes to other facets of e-commerce and retail.

Product Categorization and Taxonomy

Product categorization is a process of dividing products into groups. These groups can be defined based on similarity—e.g., products of the same brand or products of the same type can be grouped together. Generally, e-commerce has pre-defined broad categories of products, such as electronics, personal care products, and foods. When a new product arrives, it should be categorized into the taxonomy before it's put in the catalog. Figure 9-8 shows a taxonomy for the electronics category with a hierarchy of granular subcategories.

We can further define successively smaller groups with stricter definitions of products, such as laptops and tablets inside the computer category. For a more contextual example, this book will have a level category of technical books, while it's subcategories will be related to AI or natural language processing. This task is a lot like the text classification we covered in Chapter 4.

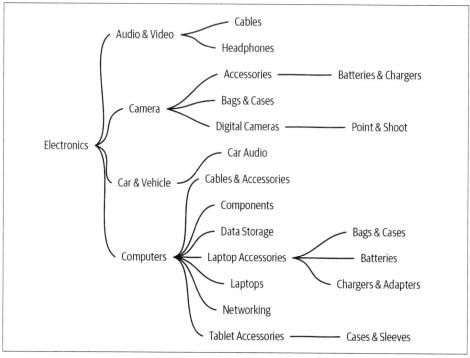

Figure 9-8. A typical category hierarchy—taxonomy of a product

A good taxonomy and properly linked products can be critical because it allows an e-commerce site to:

- Show products similar to the product searched
- Provide better recommendations
- Select appropriate bundles of products for better deals for the customer
- Replace old products with new ones
- Show price comparisons of different products in the same category

This categorization process is typically manual to start at small scale, but as the variety of products increases, it gets harder and harder to process them manually. At scale, this categorization is typically posed as a classification task where the algorithm takes information from a variety of sources and applies the classification technique to solve it [7, 8].

Specifically, there are cases where algorithms take input as the title or description and classify the product into a suitable category when all the categories are known. This again falls into the typical case of text classification. In this way, the categorization process can be automated. Once the category is determined, it's extended directly to the relevant attribute extraction process that we discussed earlier. It's logical that a product will be passed to the attribute extraction process only when its category is discovered.

The accuracy of the algorithm can be improved when both images and text can be used to solve the problem. Images can be passed to a convolutional neural network for generating image embedding, and the text sequence can be encoded via LSTM, both of which, in turn, can be concatenated and passed to any classifier for the final output [6].

Building a taxonomy tree is an extensive process. Placing the products at the right level in the taxonomy can be done via a hierarchical text classification. A hierarchical text classification in context is nothing more than applying classification models in hierarchy according to levels in a taxonomy.

Generally simple rule-based classification methods are used mainly for the high-level categories. They can use a dictionary-based matching as a start. Subcategories that are complex and require deeper context to determine the right taxonomic level are dealt with by ML classification techniques such as SVM or decision tree [9]. Figure 9-9 shows various taxonomy levels for a specific product example.

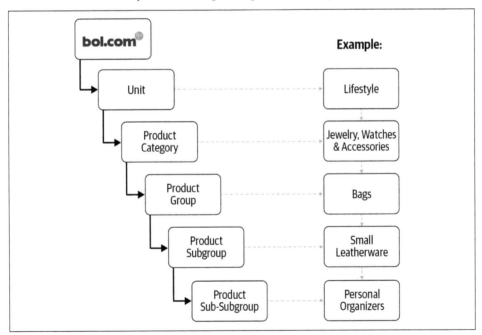

Figure 9-9. Taxonomy tree with different levels [9]

For a new e-commerce platform, creating a product taxonomy via product categorization can be an insurmountable task. Building rich content requires a huge amount of relevant data, manual interventions, and category experts' domain knowledge. All these can be expensive for a nascent e-commerce platform. However, there are some APIs offered by Semantics3, eBay, and Lucidworks that can help with the process.

These APIs typically build on large catalog content of various big retailers and provide the intelligence inside to categorize a product by scanning its unique product code. Small-scale e-commerce can use the power of such cloud APIs for bootstrapping taxonomy creation and categorization. Figure 9-10 shows a snapshot of one such API from Semantics3 [10]. Their API helps categorize a product from its name.

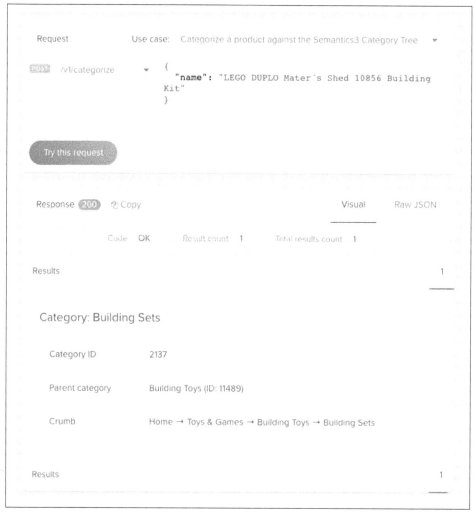

Figure 9-10. Semantics3 terminal snapshot

Once a significant amount of product information has been gathered, it's advisable to use custom rule-based systems. Some of these APIs also support user-defined rules, as well as product enrichment and deduplication, which we'll cover in the next sections.

Product Enrichment

For better search and recommendations, it's important to gather richer product information. Some potential sources of this information are short and long titles, product images, and product descriptions. But this information is often either incorrect or incomplete. For example, a misleading title can hamper the faceted search in an e-commerce platform. Improving a product title will not only improve the click-through rate in search, but also the conversion rate in terms of product purchase.

In the example shown in Figure 9-11, the product title is too long and contains words like iPad, iPhone, and Samsung, which can easily mislead the search. The full title is "Stylus Pen LIBERRWAY 10 Pack of Pink Purple Black Green Silver Stylus Universal Touch Screen Capacitive Stylus for Kindle Touch ipad iphone 6/6s 6Plus 6s Plus Samsung S5 S6 S7 Edge S8 Plus Note." This text is too complicated even for a human to parse and make sense of, let alone a machine. Such cases are ideal for product enrichment.

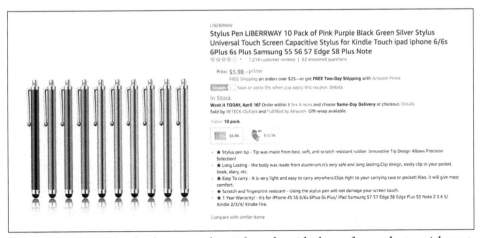

Figure 9-11. Example of a clumsy product title and an ideal case for product enrichment

First, we'll go through the problem scenario shown in Figure 9-11. When different taxonomic and enrichment levels are filled, at least to an acceptable threshold (typically defined by the retail platform itself), then we can attempt to make the product title more expressive and accurate.

The process can start with direct string matching. It's also necessary to filter out tokens that are not part of the product's attribute values. In the example, the product is a stylus, and iPad and iPhone are not part of its attribute values. These tokens are misleading and can affect the quality of faceted search. Hence, such tokens should be removed from the product title, unless they're important to indicate domain-specific context for the product.

Ideally, a pre-defined template for the product titles helps maintain consistency across products. A good approach is to build a template composed of attributes from the taxonomy tree. The product category or type could be the first token in the product title—e.g., "iPad" or "Macbook." That will follow lower-level or granular attributes from the taxonomy tree, such as brand, size, color, etc. So, the combined title would be: "iPad 64GB - Space Grey." Attributes from the leaf of the taxonomy can be omitted to keep the product title simple.

Product enrichment is typically seen as a larger and more continuous process than just improving product titles in any online retail setup. Apart from taxonomic levels, there are other ways to define the enrichment levels. Most of them are based on the importance of the attribute information. [9] has defined these taxonomies, shown in Figure 9-12. Mandatory attributes are part of every product, while nice-to-have attributes provide a high level of detail that can be missing.

Enrichment Level	Importance	Description
0	Mandatory	If attributes with this enrichment level are missing, the product is not added to the product database.
1	Crucial	If attributes with this enrichment level are missing, the product is not added to the webshop.
2	Essential	These attributes generally describe product characteristics and there are no consequences if these attributes are missing.
3	Nice-to-have	These attributes describe product characteristics to a high level of detail and are considered nice-to-have.

Figure 9-12. Table showing the categorization of various enrichment levels [9]

Next, we'll turn our attention to product duplication and matching.

Product Deduplication and Matching

Products are often added to the platform by third-party sellers, and different sellers can refer to the same product by different names. They seldom follow the same terminology, which can result in the same product getting listed with multiple titles and product images. For example, "Garmin nuvi 2699LMTHD GPS Device" and "nuvi 2699LMTHD Automobile Portable GPS Navigator" refer to the same product.

In addition to product categorization and attribute extraction, product deduplication is also an important aspect of e-commerce. Identifying duplicate products is also a challenging task, and we'll discuss ways to handle this problem via attribute match, title match, and image match.

Attribute match

If two products are the same, then the values of various attributes must be the same. Hence, once the attributes are extracted, we compare values for attributes for both of the products in question. Ideally, maximum overlap of the attributes will indicate strong product matching. In order to match the attribute values, we can use string matching [11]. Two strings can be matched via exact character match or using string similarity metrics. String similarity metrics are typically built to take care of slight spelling mistakes, abbreviations, etc.

Abbreviations are a big problem in product-related data. The same word can be represented in multiple accepted abbreviations. They should be mapped to a consistent form (discussed in "Product Enrichment" on page 323) or form agnostic rules formulated to tackle the problem. An intuitive rule to tackle abbreviations while matching two words could be matching the first and last characters and checking whether those characters belong to the shorter or longer word.

Title match

One product can often have multiple title variants. Below are some title variants for the same GPS navigator, sold by different sellers:

- Garmin nuvi 2699LMTHD GPS Device
- nuvi 2699LMTHD Automobile Portable GPS Navigator
- Garmin nuvi 2699LMTHD — GPS navigator — automotive 6.1 in
- Garmin Nuvi 2699lmthd Gps Device
- Garmin nuvi 2699LMT HD 6" GPS with Lifetime Maps and HD Traffic (010–01188–00)

To retrieve all such instances, a matching mechanism is needed to identify them as the same. A simple method could be to compare bigrams and trigrams among these titles. It's also possible to generate title-level features (such as counts of common bigrams and trigrams) and then calculate the Euclidean distance between them. We could use sentence-level embedding and a pair of textual phrases simultaneously to learn a distance metric that improves matching accuracy [12]. This can also be done with a neural network architecture called the Siamese network [13]. The Siamese network takes two sequences simultaneously and learns to generate the embeddings in such a way that, if the sequences are similar, they appear closer to each other in the embedding space, else farther.

Image match

Finally, there could still be irregularities (e.g., abbreviations or domain-specific word usage) in attributes and titles, which are difficult to align with one another. In those cases, product images can serve as rich source information for product matching and deduplication. For image matching, pixel-to-pixel match, feature map matching, or even advanced image-matching techniques like Siamese networks are popular [14], and when applied in this setting can reduce the amount of product duplication. Most of the algorithms are based on the principles of computer vision approaches and depend on image quality and other size-related particulars.

 A/B testing is a good method of measuring the results and effectiveness of different algorithms in the e-commerce world. For procedures like attribute extraction, product enrichment and A/B testing different models will lead to an impact on business metrics. These metrics can be direct or indirect sales, click-through rates, time spent on one web page, etc., and an improvement in relevant metrics shows that a model works better.

In a practical setting, all these algorithms are used in conjunction, and their results are combined to deduplicate the products. In the next few sections, we'll discuss NLP for analyzing product reviews, which are a fundamental part of any online shopping experience.

Review Analysis

Reviews are an integral part of any e-commerce portal. They capture direct feedback from customers about products. It's important to leverage this abundant information and create important signals to send feedback to the e-commerce system so that it can use them to further improve the customer experience. Moreover, reviews can be viewed by all customers, and they directly affect the sales of the products. In this section, we'll delve deeper into the different facets of review sentiment analysis.

Sentiment Analysis

We covered generic sentiment analysis as a classification task in Chapter 4. But there are various nuances when it comes to sentiment analysis for e-commerce reviews. Figure 9-13 shows a screenshot of customer reviews of iPhone X on Amazon. Most of us are familiar with seeing such aspect-level reviews on e-commerce websites—this is where you can slice and dice reviews based on aspects and attributes.

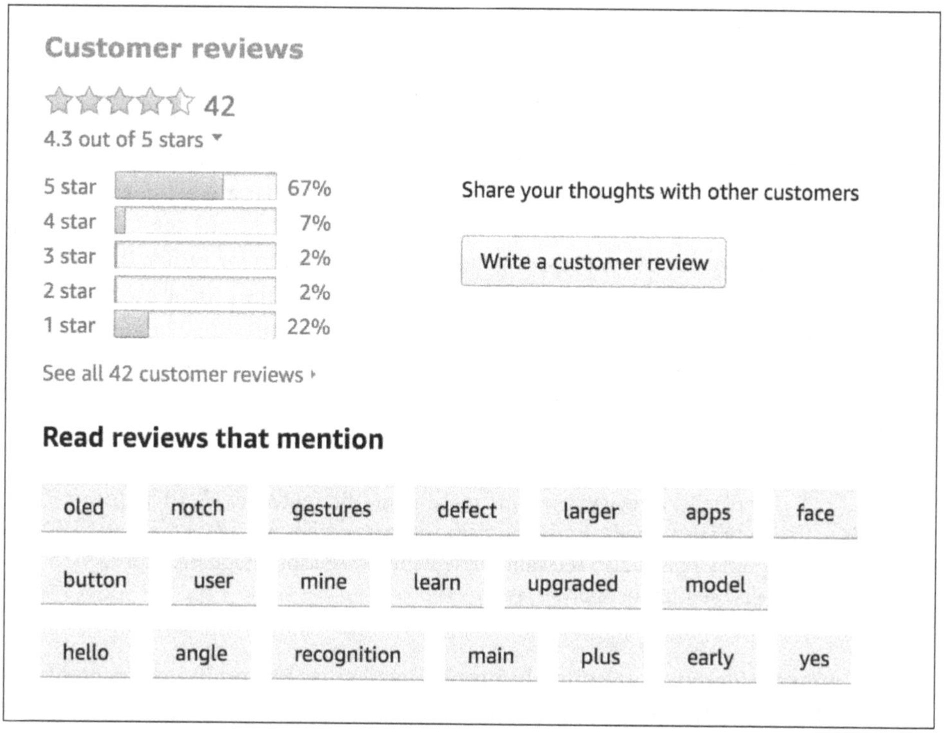

Customer reviews

☆☆☆☆☆ 42
4.3 out of 5 stars ▾

5 star		67%
4 star		7%
3 star		2%
2 star		2%
1 star		22%

See all 42 customer reviews ›

Share your thoughts with other customers

Write a customer review

Read reviews that mention

oled   notch   gestures   defect   larger   apps   face

button   user   mine   learn   upgraded   model

hello   angle   recognition   main   plus   early   yes

Figure 9-13. Analysis of customer reviews: ratings, keywords, and sentiments

As you can see, 67% of the reviews have a rating of five stars (i.e., the highest), and 22% of the reviews have the lowest rating of one star. It's important for an e-commerce company to know what leads customers to give bad ratings. To illustrate this point, Figure 9-14 shows two examples of extreme reviews of the same product.

Figure 9-14. A positive and a negative review

Certainly, both of these reviews contain some information about the product, which gives the retailer cues about what customers are thinking. Specifically, negative reviews are more important to understand. In Figure 9-14, look at the first review where the customer states that there are issues with phones that are being shipped. It's mostly related to the defective screen, which the retailer should take care of. In contrast, the positive review expresses generic positive sentiment rather than explicitly pointing out what aspects the user really liked. Hence, it's crucial to have a full understanding of the reviews. By nature, they're in the text and mostly in an unstructured format, full of unforced errors such as spelling mistakes, incorrect sentence constructions, incomplete words, and abbreviations. This makes review analysis even more challenging.

> Typically, a review contains more than one sentence. It's advisable to break a review into sentences and pass each sentence as one data point. This is also relevant for sentence-wise aspect tagging, aspect-wise sentiment analysis, etc.

Ratings are considered to be directly proportional to the overall sentiment of the reviews. There are cases where the user mistakenly rates the product poorly but gives a positive review. Understanding emotions directly from the text will help retailers rectify these anomalies during analysis. But in most cases, a review doesn't talk about just one aspect of the product but tries to cover most aspects of it, ultimately reflecting everything in the review rating.

Take another look at the iPhone X review screenshot in Figure 9-13. Look at the section where it reads: "Read reviews that mention." These are nothing but the important keywords Amazon has found may help customers navigate better when skimming through the reviews. This clearly indicates that there are certain aspects customers are talking about. It could be user experience, manufacturing aspects, price, or something else. How can we know what the customer's emotions or feedback are? So far, we've provided only a high-level index of emotion for the entire review, but that won't allow us to dig down deeper to understand it better. This necessitates an aspect-level understanding of the reviews. These aspects could be pre-defined or extracted from the review data itself. Based on that, the approaches will be supervised or unsupervised accordingly.

Aspect-Level Sentiment Analysis

Before we start the discussion of various techniques for aspect-level sentiment analysis, we need to understand what an aspect is. An *aspect* is a semantically rich, concept-centric collection of words that indicates certain properties or characteristics of the product. For example, in Figure 9-15, we'll see the kind of aspects a travel website might have: location, value, and cleanliness.

This isn't constrained only to the inherent attributes of the product, but also to anything and everything related to the supply, presentation, delivery, return, quality, etc., around the product. Typically, a clear distinguishing of these aspects is difficult unless already assumed.

If the retailer has a clear understanding of the product's aspects, then finding aspects falls under the supervised category of algorithms. There's a common technique for using seed words or seed lexicons, which essentially hints at the crucial tokens that could be present under a particular aspect. For example, regarding user experience as an aspect for iPhone X, seed words could be screen resolution, touch, response time, etc. Again, it's up to the retailer at what level of granularity they'd like to operate. For example, screen quality alone could be a more granular aspect. In the next sections, we'll look at supervised and unsupervised techniques of aspect-level sentiment analysis.

Supervised approach

A supervised approach depends mainly on seed words. It tries to identify the presence of these seed words in a sentence. If it identifies a particular seed word in a sentence, it tags the sentence with the corresponding aspect. Once all the sentences are tagged to any of the aspects, the sentiment analysis has to be done at a sentence level. Now, since we already have an additional tag for each sentence, sentences having one tag can be filtered, and sentiments for them can be aggregated to understand the customer's feedback for that aspect. For example, all review sentences related to screen quality, touch, and response time can be grouped together.

For a change, let's look at an example from a travel website in Figure 9-15, where the aspect-level sentiment analysis is apparent. As you see, there are specific ratings for location, check-in, value, and cleanliness, which are semantic concepts rightfully extracted from the data to present a more detailed view of the reviews.

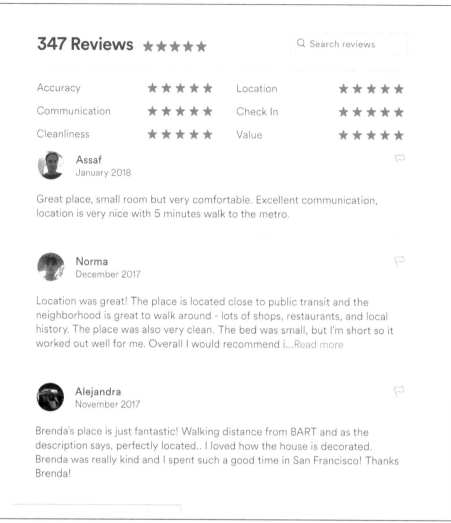

Figure 9-15. Aspect-level ratings on reviews given on a travel website

Unsupervised approach

As it's understood, arranging a good-quality seed lexicon is difficult, so there are unsupervised ways of detecting aspects. Topic modeling is a useful technique in identifying latent topics present in a document. We can think of these topics as aspects in our case. Imagine if we can group sentences that are talking about the same aspect. That's exactly what a topic modeling algorithm does. One of the most popular topic modeling approaches is the latent Dirichlet algorithm (LDA). We covered LDA in more detail in Chapter 7.

In a similar fashion, we can pre-define the number of aspects we expect out of the set of sentences. The topic modeling algorithm also outputs the probability of each word to be in all the topics (here, aspects). Hence, it's also possible to group words that have a high chance of belonging to a certain aspect and call them characteristic words for that particular aspect. This will ultimately help annotate the unannotated aspects.

Further, a more unsupervised approach can be performed by creating sentence representation and then performing clustering as opposed to LDA. In our experience, the latter sometimes gives better results when there are fewer review sentences. In the next section, we'll see how we can predict ratings for all of these aspects and provide a more granular view of user preferences.

Connecting Overall Ratings to Aspects

We've already seen how we can detect the sentiment for each aspect. Typically, users also give an overall rating. The idea here is to connect that rating to individual aspect-level sentiment. For this, we use a technique called latent rating regression analysis (LARA) [15]. Details of LARA implementation are outside the scope of this book, but here's an example of the system generating aspect-level ratings for a hotel review. The table shown in Figure 9-16 from [15] gives some details on these aspect-based ratings.

Aspect	Summary	Rating
Value	Truly unique character and a great location at a reasonable price, Hotel Max was an excellent choice for our recent three-night stay in Seattle.	3.1
	Overall not a negative experience, however considering that the hotel industry is very much in the impressing business there was a lot of room for improvement.	1.7
Room	We chose this hotel because there was a Travelzoo deal where the Queen of Art room was $139.00/night.	3.7
	Heating system is a window AC unit that has to be shut off at night or guests will roast.	1.2
Location	The location, a short walk to downtown and Pike Place market, made the hotel a good choice.	3.5
	When you visit a big metropolitan city, be prepared to hear a little traffic outside!	2.1
Business Service	You can pay for wireless by the day or use the complimentary Internet in the business center behind the lobby though.	2.7
	My only complaint is the daily charge for Internet access when you can pretty much connect to wireless on the streets anymore.	0.9

Figure 9-16. Aspect-wise sentiment prediction using LARA

We can assume that the final rating is nothing but a weighted combination of individual aspect-level sentiments. The objective will be estimating the weights and the aspect-level sentiment together. It's also possible to perform these two operations sequentially—i.e., first determining the aspect-level sentiment and then the weights.

These weights on top of various sentiments present for each aspect will ultimately indicate how much importance a reviewer places on that specific topic. It's possible that a customer is extremely unhappy with some aspect, but maybe that aspect isn't their priority. This information is crucial for e-retailers to have before they take any action. More details of this implementation are covered in [15].

User information is also key in handling reviews. Imagine a scenario where a popular user, as opposed to a less-popular user, writes a good review. The user matters! While performing the review analysis, a "user weight" can be defined for all users based on their ratings (generally given by other peers) and can be used in all calculations to discount the reviewer bias.

We'll now go deeper into an example algorithm to understand aspects.

Understanding Aspects

It's a business objective for retailers to analyze a particular aspect of a product and how various sentiments and opinions have been reflected in reviews. Similarly, a user might be interested in a specific aspect of a product and may want to scan through all the reviews on it. Hence, once we derive all the aspects and tag each sentence with them, it's possible to group the sentences by aspects. But given the huge volume of reviews an e-commerce website encounters, there will still be a lot of sentences under an aspect. Here, a summarization algorithm may save the day. Think about a situation where we need to take an action regarding an aspect but we don't have the capacity to go through all the sentences regarding that particular aspect. We'd need an automatic algorithm that can pick and choose the best representative sentences for that aspect.

LexRank [16] is an algorithm, similar to PageRank, that assumes each sentence is a node and connects via sentence similarity. Once done, it picks the most central sentences out of it and presents an extractive summary of the sentences under an aspect. An example pipeline for review analysis, covering overall and aspect-level sentiments, is shown in Figure 9-17.

In this pipeline, we start with a set of reviews. After applying review-level aspect detection, we can run sentiment analysis for every aspect as well as aggregate them based on aspects. After aggregation, summarization algorithms such as LexRank can be used to summarize them. In the end, we can take away the overall sentiment for an aspect of a product as well as get a summary of opinions explaining the sentiment.

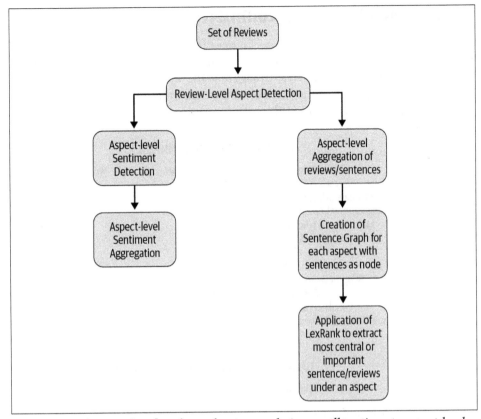

Figure 9-17. The complete flowchart of review analysis: overall sentiments, aspect-level sentiments, and aspect-wise significant reviews

A complete understanding of a product can only be achieved by both user reviews and editorial reviews. Editorial reviews are generally provided by expert users or domain experts. These reviews are more reliable and can be shown at the top of the review section. But on the other hand, general user reviews reveal the true picture of the product experience from all users' perspectives. Hence, melding editorial reviews with general user reviews is important. That may be achieved by mixing both kinds of reviews in the top section and ranking them accordingly.

We've seen how review analysis can be done from the perspective of aspects, sentiment, and ratings. In the next sections, we'll briefly cover the nuances of personalization for e-commerce.

Recommendations for E-Commerce

In Chapter 7, we discussed various techniques for recommendations using textual data. Along with product search and review analysis, product recommendation is another main pillar in e-commerce. In Figure 9-18, we show a comprehensive study on the different algorithms used as well as the data utilization required for recommendations in various scenarios [17].

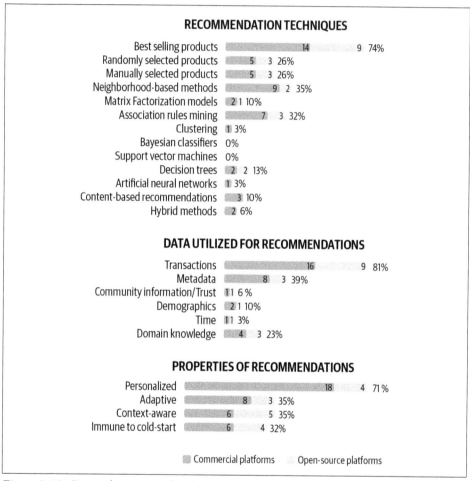

Figure 9-18. *Comprehensive study of techniques for various e-commerce recommendation scenarios*

In e-commerce, products are recommended based on a user's purchase profile: fashionista, book lover, enjoyer of popular products, etc. These purchase profiles can be inferred from the user's behavior on the platform. Imagine a user has interacted with a set of products in the platform via viewing or clicking or purchasing them. These interactions contain information that can help decide the set of products the user will be interested in next. This can be achieved by neighborhood-based methods where we look for similar products (in terms of attributes, purchase history, customers who purchased them, etc.) and provide them in the form of recommendations.

Clicks, purchase history, etc., are mainly numerical data, whereas e-commerce also has a huge amount of textual data that can be utilized in product recommendations. Along with numerical sources, the recommendation algorithm can include product descriptions in text to induce better understanding about those products and provide more similar products that match with even more granular attributes. For example, the clothing material (e.g., 52% cotton, 48% polyester) mentioned in a product description could be important textual information to consider while looking for similar apparel.

Recommendation engines deal with information from various sources. Proper matching of various data tables and consistency of the information across various data sources is important to maintain. For example, while collating the information about product attributes and product transaction history, the consistency of the information should be checked carefully. Complementary and substitute data can give indications about data quality. One should check for anomalous behavior while working with multifarious data sources, as in the case of e-commerce recommendation.

Reviews contain a lot of nuanced information and user opinions about products, which can guide product recommendations. Imagine a user providing feedback regarding the screen size of a mobile device (e.g., "I would have preferred a smaller screen"). The specific feedback from the user for a specific attribute of the product can provide a strong signal to filter the set of related products to make the recommendation more useful to the user. We'll look at a detailed case study relating to this and see how we can potentially build a recommendation system for e-commerce leveraging product reviews. Reviews are not only useful for finding better products for recommendation but can also reveal the interrelationships between various products via nuanced feedback from customers.

A Case Study: Substitutes and Complements

Recommender systems are built on the idea of "similar" products. This similarity can be defined as content based or user profile based. There's another way of identifying item interrelationships specifically in an e-commerce setting.

Complements are products that are typically bought together. On the other hand, there are pairs that are bought in lieu of the other, and they're known as substitute pairs. Even though the economic definition is much more rigorous, these lines of thought typically capture the behavioral aspect of product purchase. Sometimes, due to huge disparities in individual user behavior, it's difficult to infer the interrelationships between products from them. But in aggregation, these user interactions can reveal interesting properties about substitution and complementarity between products. There are several ways [18] we can identify substitutes and complements using user interaction data, but here, we'll focus on an approach that relies primarily on the reviews as a form of textual information present in the products.

Julian McAuley has presented [19] a comprehensive way of understanding product interrelationships in a framework where the query product is given and the framework returns the ranked products, both substitutes and complements, (see Figure 9-19). We'll discuss this application as a case study in the context of e-commerce.

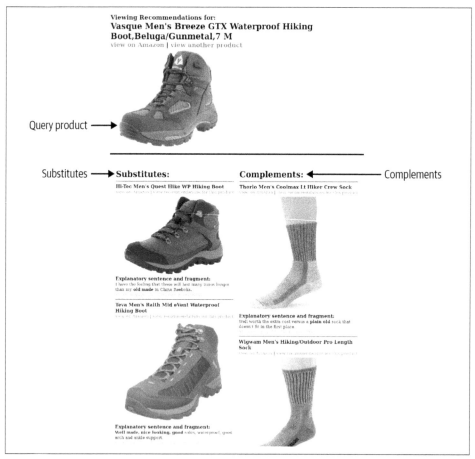

Figure 9-19. Substitutes and complements based on product reviews [19]

Latent attribute extraction from reviews

Typically, as we've discussed, reviews contain specific information about product attributes. Explicit extraction of attributes from reviews may have limitations in representation, as we need to define an explicit ontology, so instead, we learn them via a latent vector representation. The details of latent factor models are outside the scope of this book, but an interested reader can find the relevant material at [20].

Each product is associated with a review. One review can discuss or mention various opinions regarding aspects related to the product. While these topics are latent and can't be identified distinctly, we can obtain a distribution of the share of discussion on various attributes as they're discussed in the review. This distribution can be modeled on all the reviews related to that product using popular topic models like LDA [21]. This provides a vectorial representation, or "topic vector," which tells us how a particular product has been discussed in reviews. This representation can be thought of as a feature representation (from the usual ML terminology) of the product itself.

Product linking

The next task is to understand how the two products are linked. We already obtained topic vectors, which capture the intrinsic properties of the product in a latent attribute space. Now, given a pair of products, we want to create a combined feature vector out of the respective topic vectors for the products and then predict if there's any relationship between them. This can be viewed as a binary classification problem where the features have to be obtained from the respective topic vectors for the product pair. We call this process "link prediction," similar to [22].

To ensure that the topic vector is expressive enough to predict a link or relationship between a product pair, the objectives of obtaining topic vectors and link prediction can be solved jointly rather than one after the other—i.e., we learn topic vectors for each product as well as the function to combine them for a product pair.

Figure 9-20 depicts the interpretation of a topic vector after it's learned, which is covered in detail in [19]. It shows how a topic vector becomes expressive enough to capture the intrinsic attributes of the product. Hierarchical dependence also emerges from such a representation, which in a way depicts the taxonomy that the product belongs to.

This case study shows that reviews contain useful information that reveals various interrelationships between products. Such latent representation, which has more expressivity than exact extraction of attributes from reviews, has shown to be efficient not only for the link prediction task, but also for revealing meaningful notions about the product taxonomy. Such representation can be useful for making better product recommendations via better product linking and obtaining more similar products.

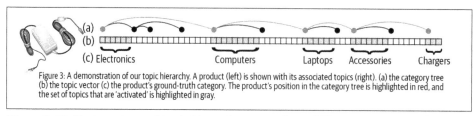

Figure 3: A demonstration of our topic hierarchy. A product (left) is shown with its associated topics (right). (a) the category tree (b) the topic vector (c) the product's ground-truth category. The product's position in the category tree is highlighted in red, and the set of topics that are 'activated' is highlighted in gray.

Figure 9-20. Topic vector and topic hierarchy express how different taxonomic identities and relations are captured in reviews [19]

Wrapping Up

A primary driver behind the e-commerce industry's immense success has been massive data collection and adaptation of data-driven decisions. NLP techniques have played a significant role in improving user experience and driving more revenue in e-commerce and retail industries.

In this chapter, we covered different aspects of NLP in e-commerce. We started with an introduction on faceted search, then delved deep into product attributes. These areas are closely linked to product enrichment and categorization. We then covered review analysis and product recommendations for e-commerce. Most of the examples and the setting in this chapter are product commerce, but the same techniques can be used in other areas as well, such as travel and food. We hope this chapter will be a good starting point for baking NLP and intelligence into your domain.

References

[1] Clement, J. "Global Retail E-commerce Sales 2014–2023" (*https://oreil.ly/RyAAZ*). *Statista*, March 19, 2010.

[2] Fletcher, Iain. "How to Increase E-commerce Conversion with Site Search" (*https://oreil.ly/mfr4s*). *Search and Content Analytics (blog)*. Last accessed June 15, 2020.

[3] Elasticsearch DSL. Faceted Search (*https://oreil.ly/KdKVS*). Last accessed June 15, 2020.

[4] Huang, Zhiheng, Wei Xu, and Kai Yu. "Bidirectional LSTM-CRF Models for Sequence Tagging" (*https://oreil.ly/iE4ag*). 2015.

[5] Majumder, B. P., Aditya Subramanian, Abhinandan Krishnan, Shreyansh Gandhi, and Ajinkya More. "Deep Recurrent Neural Networks for Product Attribute Extraction in eCommerce" (*https://oreil.ly/nvrly*). 2018.

[6] Logan IV, Robert L., Samuel Humeau, and Sameer Singh. "Multimodal Attribute Extraction" (*https://oreil.ly/Jt11M*). 2017.

[7] Popescu, Ana-Maria, and Oren Etzioni. "Extracting Product Features and Opinion from Reviews." *Proceedings of the Conference on Human Language Technology and Empirical Methods in Natural Language Processing* (2005): 339–346.

[8] Wang, Tao, Yi Cai, Ho-fung Leung, Raymond YK Lau, Qing Li, and Huaqing Min. "Product Aspect Extraction Supervised with Online Domain Knowledge." *Knowledge-Based Systems* 71 (2014): 86–100.

[9] Trietsch, R. C. "Product Attribute Value Classification from Unstructured Text in E-Commerce." (master's thesis, Eindhoven University of Technology, 2016).

[10] "Product Classification with AI: How Machine Learning Sped Up Logistics for Aeropost" (*https://oreil.ly/UkKcp*). *Semantics3 (blog)*, June 25, 2018.

[11] Cheatham, Michelle, and Pascal Hitzler. "String Similarity Metrics For Ontology Alignment." *International Semantic Web Conference*. Berlin: Springer, 2013: 294–309

[12] Bilenko, Mikhail and Raymond J. Mooney. "Adaptive Duplicate Detection Using Learnable String Similarity Measures." *Proceedings of the Ninth ACM SIGKDD International Conference on Knowledge Discovery and Data Mining* (2003): 39–48.

[13] Neculoiu, Paul, Maarten Versteegh, and Mihai Rotaru. "Learning Text Similarity with Siamese Recurrent Networks." *Proceedings of the First Workshop on Representation Learning for NLP* (2016): 148–157.

[14] Zagoruyko, Sergey and Nikos Komodakis. "Learning to Compare Image Patches via Convolutional Neural Networks." *Proceedings of the IEEE Conference on Computer Vision and Pattern Recognition* (2015): 4353–4361.

[15] Wang, Hongning, Yue Lu, and Chengxiang Zhai. "Latent Aspect Rating Analysis on Review Text Data: A Rating Regressions Approach." *Proceedings of the 16th ACM SIGKDD International Conference on Knowledge Discovery and Data Mining* (2010): 783–792.

[16] Erkan, Günes and Dragomir R. Radev. "LexRank: Graph-Based Lexical Centrality as Salience in Text Summarization." *Journal of Artificial Intelligence Research* 22 (2004): 457–479.

[17] Sarwar, Badrul, George Karypis, Joseph Konstan, and John Riedl. "Analysis of Recommendation Algorithms for E-Commerce." *Proceedings of the 2nd ACM Conference on Electronic Commerce* (2000): 158–167.

[18] Misra, Subhasish, Arunita Das, Bodhisattwa Majumder, and Amlan Das. "System for calculating competitive interrelationships in item-pairs." US Patent Application 15/834,054, filed April 25, 2019.

[19] McAuley, Julian, Rahul Pandey, and Jure Leskovec. "Inferring Networks of Substitutable and Complementary Products." *Proceedings of the 21th ACM SIGKDD International Conference on Knowledge Discovery and Data Mining* (2015): 785–794.

[20] McAuley, Julian and Jure Leskovec. "Hidden Factor and Hidden Topics: Understanding Rating Dimensions with Review Text." *Proceedings of the 7th ACM Conference on Recommender Systems* (2013): 165–172.

[21] Blei, David M., Andrew Y. Ng, and Michael I. Jordan. "Latent Dirichlet Allocation." *Journal of Machine Learning Research* 3 (2003): 993–1022.

[22] Menon, Aditya Krishna and Charles Elkan. "Link Prediction via Matrix Factorization." *Joint European Conference on Machine Learning and Knowledge Discovery in Databases.* Berlin: Springer, 2011: 437–452

## CHAPTER 10

Healthcare, Finance, and Law

> *Software is eating the world,*
> *but AI is going to eat software.*
> *—Jensen Huang, Nvidia CEO*

NLP is affecting and improving all major industries and sectors. In the last two chapters, we covered how NLP is being utilized in the e-commerce, retail, and social media sectors. In this chapter, we'll cover three major industries where the impact of NLP is rapidly increasing to have a substantial influence on the global economy: healthcare, finance, and law. We've chosen these areas to demonstrate a wide range of problems, solutions, and challenges you might face in your organization.

The term *healthcare* encompasses all goods and services for maintenance and improvement of health and well-being. It's estimated to be worth over 10 trillion dollars as a market globally and accounts for tens of millions of people in the workforce [1]. The financial industry is one of the bedrocks of modern civilization and is estimated to be worth over 26.5 trillion dollars. The legal services industry is estimated to be worth over 850 billion dollars annually and is projected to cross a trillion dollars by 2021.

In this first section, we'll start with an overview of the healthcare industry. Then we'll cover broad applications in the healthcare landscape, along with a detailed discussion of specific use cases.

Healthcare

Healthcare as an industry encompasses both goods (i.e., medicines and equipment) and services (consultation or diagnostic testing) for curative, preventive, palliative, and rehabilitative care.

Curative care is provided to cure a patient suffering from a curable disease, and preventative care is meant to prevent one from falling sick. Rehabilitative care helps patients recuperate from illness and includes activities like physical therapy. Palliative care focuses on improving the quality of life for patients suffering from terminal conditions.

For most advanced economies, healthcare accounts for a substantial part of the gross domestic product, often exceeding 10%. Being such a large segment, there are massive benefits to automating and optimizing these processes and systems, and that's where NLP comes in. Figure 10-1 from Chilmark Research [2] shows a range of applications where NLP helps. Each column shows the broad area, like clinical research or revenue cycle management. The blue cells show the applications that are used currently, the purple cells are applications that are emerging and being tested, and the red cells are more next generation and will be practically applicable in a longer time horizon.

Research	Treat	Capture	Population Health	Revenue Cycle Management	Analytics/ Reporting
Data Mining					
Cohost Discovery	Clinical Decision Support	Speech Recognition	Pharmacosurveillance	Computer Assisted Coding	Registry Reporting
Clinical Trial Matching	Computations Phenotyping	Clinical Documentation Improvement (CDI)	Population Surveillance	Prior Authorization	Descriptive Analytics
Drug Discovery	Biomarker Discovery	Patient Reported Outcomes	Adverse Event Detection	Risk Adjustment	Predictive Analytics
Precision Medicine	Virtual Therapy	Ambient Virtual Scribe	Social Determinants of Health	Payer Provider Convergence	Prescriptive Analytics
	Triage		Readmissions		

Next-Generation   Emerging   Proven

Figure 10-1. NLP in healthcare use cases by Chilmark Research [2]

Healthcare deals with large amounts of unstructured text, and NLP can be used in such places to improve health outcomes. Broad areas where NLP can help include but are not limited to analyzing medical records, billing, and ensuring drug safety. In the next sections we'll briefly cover some of these applications.

Health and Medical Records

A large proportion of health and medical data is often collected and stored in unstructured text formats. This includes medical notes, prescriptions, and audio transcripts, as well as pathology and radiology reports. An example of such a record is shown in Figure 10-2.

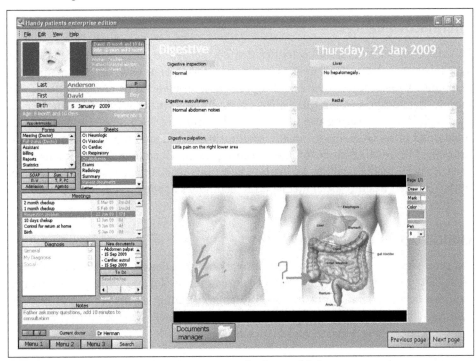

Figure 10-2. An example of an electronic medical record [3]

This makes the data hard to search, organize, study, and understand in its raw form. This is exacerbated by a lack of standardization in how the data is stored. NLP can help doctors search and analyze this data better and even automate some of the workflows, such as by building automated question-answering systems to decrease time to look up relevant patient information. We'll cover some of these in detail later in the chapter.

Patient Prioritization and Billing

NLP techniques can be used on physician notes to understand their state and urgency to prioritize various health procedures and checkups. This can minimize delays and administrative errors and automate processes. Similarly, parsing and extracting information from unstructured notes to identify medical codes can facilitate billing.

Pharmacovigilance

Pharmacovigilance entails all activities that are needed to ensure that a drug is safe. This involves collection and detection and monitoring of adverse drug or medication reactions. A medical procedure or drug can have unintended or noxious effects, and monitoring and preventing these effects is essential to making sure the drug acts as intended. With increasing use of social media, more of such side effects are being mentioned in social media messages; monitoring and identifying these is part of the solution. We covered some of these techniques in Chapter 8, which focused on generic social media analysis. We'll also cover some social media–specific cases later in this chapter. Besides social media, NLP techniques applied to medical records also facilitate pharmacovigilance.

Clinical Decision Support Systems

Decision support systems assist medical workers in making healthcare-related decisions. These include screening, diagnosis, treatments, and monitoring. Various text data can be used as an input to these systems, including electronic health records, column-tabulated laboratory results, and operative notes. NLP is utilized on all of these to improve the decision support systems.

Health Assistants

Health assistants and chatbots can improve the patient and caregiver experiences by using various aspects of expert systems and NLP. For instance, services like Woebot [4] (Figure 10-3) can keep the spirits of patients suffering from mental illness and depression high. Woebot combines NLP with cognitive therapy to do this by asking relevant questions reinforcing positive thoughts.

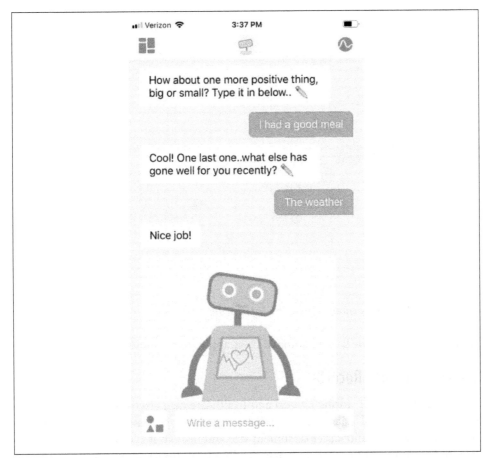

Figure 10-3. A Woebot conversation

Similarly, assistants can assess patients' symptoms to diagnose potential medical issues. Depending on the urgency and critical nature of the diagnoses, chatbots can book appointments with relevant doctors. One example of such a system is Buoy [5]. These systems can also be built based on the user's specific needs by utilizing existing diagnostic frameworks. One example of such a framework is Infermedica [6] (Figure 10-4), where a chat interface can elicit symptoms from the user as well as give a list of possible ailments with their probability.

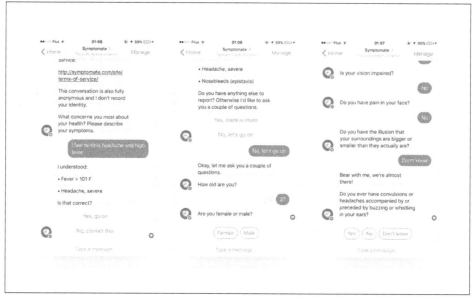

Figure 10-4. Diagnosis chatbot made by Infermedica API

In the next sections, we'll cover some of these applications in more detail.

Electronic Health Records

Increased adoption of storing clinical and healthcare data electronically has led to an explosion of medical data and overwhelmingly large personal records. With this increasing adoption and larger document size and history, it's getting harder for doctors and clinical staff to access this data, leading to an information overload. This, in turn, leads to more errors, omissions, and delays and affects patient safety.

In the next few sections, we'll broadly cover how NLP can help manage this overload and improve patient outcomes. In this section, we'll deal with electronic health records (EHRs).

HARVEST: Longitudinal report understanding

Various tools have been built to overcome the informational overload we mentioned earlier. A notable effort is called HARVEST [7] from Columbia University. The tool has been used extensively across hospitals in New York City. To start with, however, we need to cover how a standard clinical information system works.

Figure 10-5 shows a screenshot of a standard clinical information review system that's used at New York Presbyterian Hospital (iNYP). iNYP delivers text-heavy, dense, time-consuming, and generally unwieldy reports. There's an option for basic text search, but the text-heavy information lends itself to being skimmed over, which is an impediment in the context of a busy, minute-to-minute hospital environment.

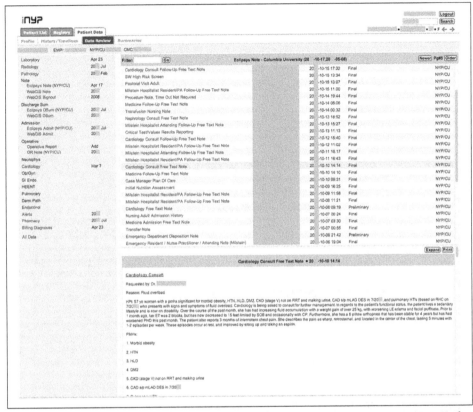

Figure 10-5. Screenshot of the standard clinical information review system at New York Presbyterian Hospital

In contrast, HARVEST parses all of the medical data to make it easy to analyze and can sit on top of any medical system. Figure 10-6 demonstrates how HARVEST is used on the iNYP system, showing the revamped and evolved visual depiction of the formerly text-heavy reporting format.

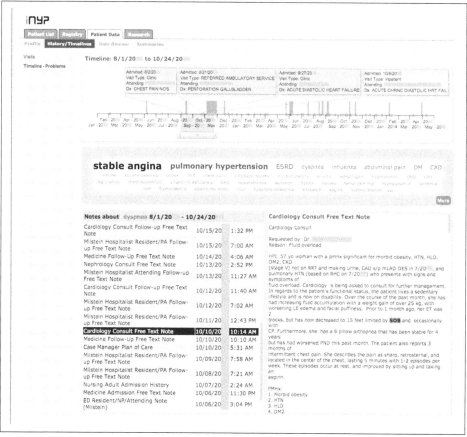

Figure 10-6. HARVEST system [7] for the same patient from Figure 10-5

We can see a timeline of each visit to the clinic or hospital. It's accompanied by a word cloud of important medical conditions for the patient in the given time range. The user can drill down to detailed notes and history if needed as well. All of this is also supported by summaries of each report so a user can get the gist of a patient's medical history quickly. HARVEST is much more than a reformatted novelty—it's extremely useful for giving not just doctors, but also general medical staff and caregivers, a near real-time, informative snapshot of what's going on with a patient.

All historical observations (from doctors, nurses, nutritionists, etc.) related to that patient are run through a named entity recognizer called HealthTermFinder. This finds all healthcare-related terms, which are then mapped to the Unified Medical Language System (UMLS) semantic group. These terms are visualized in the word cloud. Word cloud weights are determined by TF-IDF, which we covered in detail in Chapter 7. Also, the larger to smaller font sizes indicate the degree and frequency of the various issues a patient has been carrying. This visual pattern can also drive the identification and exploration of issues that otherwise might not have been considered.

HARVEST is able to depict a patient's medical history across a period of time, however long that might be, in a much more effective and easy-to-comprehend fashion. What becomes more valuable in such instances is that it helps with the analytical capability of the medical professional to home in on root issues and not get caught up in merely treating symptoms or biased misdiagnoses. A study was conducted where the HARVEST system was tested by medical practitioners at New York Presbyterian Hospital. In this test, more than 75% of participants said they would definitely use HARVEST regularly in the future, despite it being a completely new user interface, while the rest also showed some leaning toward using the system. Figure 10-7 shows a snapshot of some of the feedback provided by these practitioners at the time.

HARVEST delivers understandable summaries and conclusions by collating a patient's history of healthcare issues across their lifetime. Its unique selling point is that it can mine, extract, and visually present content at a macro level—based on detailed micro-level observations—irrespective of where and by whom in the hospital a patient might have been seen. Such systems can be built to visualize and analyze a large amount of information. When the underlying knowledge base is unstructured text, as it is in the case of EHRs, NLP techniques play a key role in such analytics and information visualization tools.

Table 4:

Subject feedback on the overall use of Harvest (A) and applicable usage in the clinical workflow (B)

A.

▶ "It's a great adjunctive tool to visually represent the patient's chart history"

▶ "Good visual representation of the patient's clinic and [ED] visits and admissions, and gives a good overall sense of the patient's medical problems"

▶ "[Allows for] review [of] the medical record to find specific instances when things were diagnosed or managed"

▶ "Useful tool to quickly tell burden of disease"

▶ "Made me more confident that I wasn't missing information that can sometimes be buried in the list of [past medical history]"

▶ "[I]t helped pick up on diagnoses within the chart that I otherwise would've had a lot of difficulty finding"

▶ "The tool was very helpful in quickly getting a sense of how many (and what type of) encounters a patient had"

B.

▶ "[T]he Harvest tool would be most helpful when taking care of new patients and patient not already well-known

▶ "I would use it in pre-scrolling patients prior to seeing them both in the outpatient and inpatient setting"

▶ "[Harvest] would allow me to better become acquainted with other people's patients in the event I was covering for them in clinic"

▶ "[When] admitting a patient to the hospital, I feel like it would allow me to gather information to write a pertinent admission note in less time

▶ "[I]n the emergency department this tool would allow me to get a rapid view of the important terms in the patient's medical record"

ED, emergency department.

Figure 10-7. Clinical feedback on HARVEST at New York Presbyterian Hospital [7]

Question answering for health

In the last section, we looked at how basic NLP techniques like NER can be used to improve the user's experience with handling records and information at scale. But to take the user experience to the next level, we can consider building a question-answering (QA) system on top of these records.

We've covered question-answering systems in Chapter 7, but our focus here is on the nuances of questions that arise specifically in healthcare scenarios. For example, these questions can include:

- What dosage of a particular medicine is a patient required to take?
- For what ailment is a particular medication taken?
- What were the results of a medical test?
- By how much was the result of a medical test out of range for a given test date?
- What lab test confirmed a particular disease?

As we've discussed throughout the book, building the right dataset for a particular task is often the key to solving any NLP problem. For the particular problem of the QA system in the healthcare domain, we'll focus on a dataset known as emrQA, which was created by a joint collaboration between IBM Research Center, MIT, and UIUC [8, 9]. Figure 10-8 shows an example of what such a dataset entails. For instance, for the question, "Has the patient ever had an abnormal BMI?", a correct answer is extracted from past health records.

Record Date: 08/09/98

08/31/96 ascending aortic root replacement with homograft with omentopexy. The patient continued to be hemodynamically stable making good progress. Physical examination: BMI: 33.4 Obese, high risk. Pulse: 60. resp. rate: 18

Question: Has the patient ever had an abnormal BMI?
Answer: BMI: 33.4 Obese, high risk
Question: When did the patient last receive a homograft replacement ?
Answer: 08/31/96 ascending aortic root replacement with homograft with omentopexy.

Figure 10-8. Example of a question-answer pair in emrQA

To create such datasets of questions and answers and build a QA system on them, a general question-answering dataset creation framework consists of:

1. Collecting domain-specific questions and then normalizing them. For instance, a patient's treatment can be asked about in multiple ways, like, "How was the problem managed?" or "What was done to correct the patient's problem?" These all have to be normalized in the same logical form.

2. Question templates are mapped with expert domain knowledge and logical forms are assigned to them. The question template is an abstract question. For example, for a certain type of question, we expect a number or a medication type as a response. More concretely, a question template is "What is the dosage of medication?", which then maps to an exact question, like, "What is the dosage of Nitroglycerin?" This question is of a logical form that expects a dosage as response. We'll see this in more detail in Figure 10-9.

3. Existing annotations and the information collected in (1) and (2) are used to create a range of question-and-answer pairs. Here, already available information like NE tags as well as answer types linked to the logical form are used to bootstrap data. This step is especially relevant, as it reduces the manual effort needed in the creation of the QA dataset.

More specifically for emrQA, this process involved polling physicians at the Veterans Administration to gather prototypical questions, which led to over 2,000 noisy templates that were normalized to around 600. These prototypical questions were then logically mapped to an i2b2 dataset [10]. i2b2 datasets are already expertly annotated with a range of fine-grained information like medication concepts, relations, assertions, coreference resolution, etc. Although they're not made explicitly for QA purposes, by using logical mapping and existing annotations, questions and answers are generated out of them. A high-level overview of this process is shown in Figure 10-9. This process is closely supervised by a set of physicians to ensure the quality of the dataset.

To build a baseline QA system, neural seq-to-seq models and heuristic-based models were used. These models are covered in more detail in the emrQA team's work. To evaluate these models, they divided the dataset into two sets: emrQL-1 and emrQL-2. emrQL-1 had more diversity in vocabulary in test and training data. Heuristic models performed better than neural models for emrQL-1, while neural models did better for emrQL-2.

More broadly, this is an interesting use case on how to build complex datasets using heuristics, mapping, and other simpler annotated datasets. These learnings can be applied to a range of other problems, beyond processing health records, that require generation of a QA-like dataset. Now, we'll cover how health records can be used to predict health outcomes.

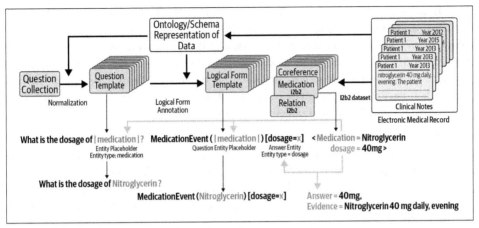

Figure 10-9. QA dataset generation using existing annotations

Outcome prediction and best practices

We've seen how NLP can aid exploration and how doctors can ask questions from patient health records. Here, we'll cover a more cutting-edge application using health records: predicting health outcomes. Health outcomes are a set of attributes that explain the consequences of a disease for a patient. They include how fast and how completely a patient recovers. They're also important in measuring efficacies of different treatments. This work is a joint collaboration between Google AI, Stanford Medicine, and UCSF [11].

Besides predicting health outcomes, another focus of scalable and accurate deep learning with electronic health records is to ensure that we can build models and systems that can be both scalable as well as highly accurate. Scalability is necessary, as healthcare has a diverse set of inputs—data collected from one hospital or department can be different from another. So it should be simple to train the system for a different outcome or different hospital. It's necessary to be accurate in order not to raise too many false alarms; the need for accuracy is obvious in the healthcare industry, where people's lives are on the line.

As simple as EHRs might sound, they are far from it; there are a lot of nuances and complexity attached to them. Even something as simple as body temperature can have a range of diagnoses depending on whether it was taken via tongue, forehead, or other body parts. To handle all these cases, an open Fast Healthcare Interoperability Resources (FHIR) standard was created, which used a standardized format with unique locators for consistency and reliability.

Once the data is in a consistent format, it's fed into a model based on RNNs. All historical data is fed from the start of the record to its end. The output variable is the outcome we're looking to predict.

The model was evaluated on a range of health outcomes. It achieved an AUC score (or area under the curve) of 0.86 on whether the patients would stay longer in the hospital, 0.77 on unexpected readmissions, and 0.95 on predicting patient mortality. An AUC score [12] is a measure used often in such cases because AUC is a summary measure of performance across all potential diagnostic thresholds for positivity, rather than performance at any specific threshold [13]. A score of 1.0 indicates perfect accuracy, while 0.5 is the same as a random chance.

It's important in healthcare that models are interpretable. In other words, they should pinpoint why they suggested a particular outcome. Without interpretability, it's hard for doctors to accommodate the results in their diagnosis. To achieve this, *attention*, a concept in deep learning, is used to understand what data points and incidents are most important for an outcome. An example of this attention map can be seen in Figure 10-10.

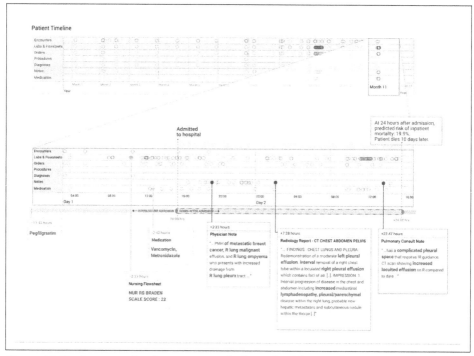

Figure 10-10. An example of attention applied to a health record

This Google AI team also came up with some of the best practices one should keep in mind while building ML models for healthcare, outlining ideas in all parts of the machine learning life cycle, from defining the problem and collecting data to validating the results. These suggestions are relevant to NLP and computer vision as well as structured data problems. The reader can peruse them in detail in [14].

These techniques focus mostly on managing the physical well-being of humans, which is relatively easy to quantify because there is a variety of numerical measures available, but there are no obvious quantifiable measures for a person's mental well-being. Let's look at some techniques for monitoring a person's mental health.

 The following section includes discussions of mental health issues and suicide.

Mental Healthcare Monitoring

Given the fast-moving pace of economic and technological change and the fast pace of life in today's world, it's no surprise that most people, particularly in generations X, Y, and Z, tend to experience some form of mental health issue in their lifetimes. By some estimates, over 790 million people are affected by mental health–related issues globally, which translates to more than 1 in every 10 people [15]. A study by the National Institutes of Health estimated that one in four Americans are likely to be affected by one or more mental health conditions in a given year. Over 47,000 Americans committed suicide in 2017, and this number has been increasing at a rapid pace [16].

With social media usage at an all-time high, it's increasingly possible to use signals from social media to track the emotional state and mental balance of both particular individuals and across groups of individuals. It should also be possible to gain insights into these aspects across various demographic groups, including age and gender. In this section, we'll briefly cover an exploratory analysis [17] on public data from Twitter users and how techniques learned in Chapter 9 can be applied to this problem.

There are innumerable aspects to evaluating an individual's mental well-being. The study by Glen Coppersmith et al. focuses, as an illustrative example, on utilizing social media in identifying individuals who are at risk for suicide. The goal of the study was to develop an early warning system along with identifying the root causes of the issues.

In this study, 554 users were identified and evaluated who stated that they attempted to take their lives. 312 of these users gave an explicit indication of their latest suicide attempt. Profiles that were marked as private were not included in this study. They only examined public data, which does not include any direct messages or deleted posts.

Each user's tweets were analyzed with the following perspectives:

- Is the user's statement of attempting to take their life apparently genuine?
- Is the user is speaking about their own suicide attempt?
- Is the suicide attempt localizable in time?

See Figure 10-11 for a few example tweets.

I'm so glad I survived my suicide attempt to see the wedding today.
I was so foolish when I was young, so many suicide attempts!
I have been out of touch since I was hospitalized after my suicide attempt last week.
It's been half a year since I attempted suicide, and I wish I had succeeded
I'm going to go commit suicide now that the Broncos won... #lame
It is going to be my financial suicide, but I NEEEEEEEEEED those shoes.

Figure 10-11. Nuances of building a social dataset

The first two tweets refer to genuine suicide attempts, while the bottom two are sarcastic or false statements. The middle two are examples where an explicit suicide attempt date is mentioned.

In order to analyze the data, the following steps were followed:

1. *Pre-processing*: Because Twitter data is often noisy, it was normalized and cleaned first. URLs and usernames are represented with homogenous tokens. We covered various aspects of cleaning social media data in detail in Chapter 9.

2. *Character models*: Character n-gram–based models followed by logistic regression were used to classify various tweets. Performance was measured with 10-fold cross validation.

3. *Emotional states*: To estimate emotional content in tweets, a dataset was bootstrapped using hashtags. For instance, all tweets containing #anger but not containing #sarcasm and #jk were put into an emotional label. Tweets with no emotional content were also classified as No Emotion.

These models were then tested on how well they could flag potential suicide risks. They were able to identify 70% of people who were very likely to attempt suicide, with only 10% false alarms. Figure 10-12 shows a confusion matrix detailing misclassification of various emotions that were modeled.

Identifying potential mental health issues can be used to intervene in flagged cases. With accurate monitoring and alerting, NLP bots like Woebot can also be used to elevate the moods of folks at higher risk. In the next section, we'll dig deeper into extracting entities from medical data.

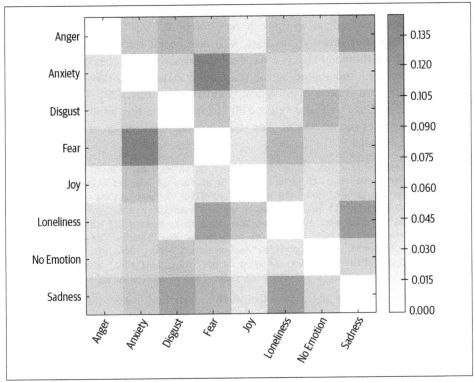

Figure 10-12. Confusion matrix for emotion classification

Medical Information Extraction and Analysis

We've seen a range of applications built on health records and information. If we were to start building applications using health records, one of the first steps would be to extract medical entities and relations from it. Medical information extraction (IE) helps to identify clinical syndromes, medical conditions, medication, dosage, strength, and common biomedical concepts from health records, radiology reports, and discharge summaries, as well as nursing documentation and medical education documents. We can use both cloud APIs and pre-built models for it.

First, we'll start with understanding Amazon Comprehend Medical [18]. It's a part of a larger suite by AWS, Amazon Comprehend, that allows us to do popular NLP tasks like keyphrase extraction, and sentiment and syntax analysis, as well as language and entity recognition in the cloud. Amazon Comprehend Medical helps process medical data, including medical named entity and relationship extraction and medical ontology linking.

We can use Amazon Comprehend Medical as a cloud API on our medical text. We cover the cloud API in detail in this chapter's notebooks, but here, we'll give a short overview of how they function. To start, we'll take health records from FHIR as an input [19]. As a reminder, FHIR is a standard that describes how healthcare information is documented and shared across the United States. We'll take a sample electronic health record from a hypothetical Good Health Clinic [20]. To robustly test Comprehend Medical, we'll also remove all formatting and line breaks from it to see how well the system can do on this. As a starting input, let's consider a small sequence of this medical record:

Good Health Clinic Consultation Note Robert Dolin MD Robert Dolin MD Good Health Clinic Henry Levin the 7th Robert Dolin MD History of Present Illness Henry Levin, the 7th is a 67 year old male referred for further asthma management. Onset of asthma in his twenties teens. He was hospitalized twice last year, and already twice this year. He has not been able to be weaned off steroids for the past several months. Past Medical History Asthma Hypertension (see HTN.cda for details) Osteoarthritis, right knee Medications Theodur 200mg BID Proventil inhaler 2puffs QID PRN Prednisone 20mg qd HCTZ 25mg qd Theodur 200mg BID Proventil inhaler 2puffs QID PRN Prednisone 20mg qd HCTZ 25mg qd

When we provide this as an input to Comprehend Medical, we get the output shown in Figure 10-13.

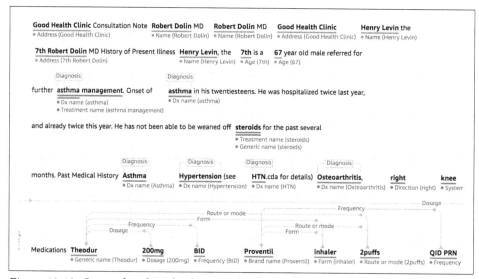

Figure 10-13. Comprehend Medical output for the FHIR record example

As we can see, we were able to extract everything, from clinic and doctor details to diagnosis and medications, as well as their frequency, dosage, and route. If we need to, we can also link extracted information to standard medical ontologies such as ICD-10-CM or RxNorm. Access to all Comprehend Medical features is through an AWS boto library, which we cover in more detail in the notebooks for Chapter 10.

Cloud APIs and libraries can be a good starting point for building medical information extraction, but if we have specific requirements and prefer to build our own system, we recommend BioBERT as a starting point. We've covered BERT, Bidirectional Encoder Representations, throughout the book. However, the default BERT model is trained on regular web text, which is very different from medical text and records. For instance, the different word distributions vary substantially between regular English and medical records. This affects the performance of BERT in medical tasks.

In order to build better models for biomedical data, BERT for Biomedical Text (BioBERT) was created [21]. It adapts BERT to biomedical texts to get better performance. In the domain adaptation phase, we initialize the model weights with a standard BERT model and pre-trained biomedical texts, including texts from PubMed, a search engine for medical results. Figure 10-14 shows the process of pre-training and fine-tuning BioBERT.

This model and weights were open sourced and can be found on GitHub [22, 23]. BioBERT can be fine-tuned on a range of specific medical problems like medical named entity recognition and relation extraction. It has also been applied to question-answering on healthcare texts. BioBERT obtains significantly higher performance than BERT and other state-of-the-art techniques. It can also be adapted depending on the medical task and dataset.

We've discussed a range of healthcare applications where NLP can help. We covered different facets of applications that can be built on health records and learned how social media monitoring can be applied to mental health issues. At the end, we saw how to lay the foundations of our healthcare application. Now, we'll delve into the world of finance and law and see how NLP helps.

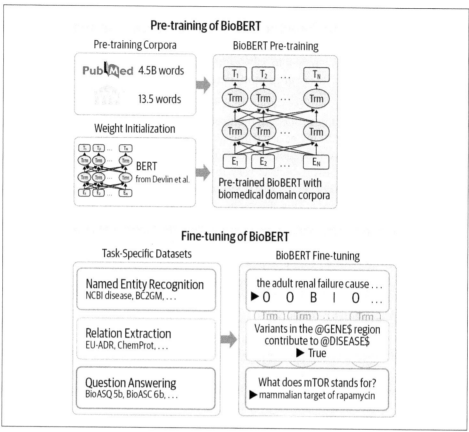

Figure 10-14. BioBERT pre-training and fine-tuning

Finance and Law

Finance is a diverse area that encompasses a wide spectrum, from public company monitoring to investment banking deal flow. Globally, the financial services industry is expected to grow to 26 trillion USD by 2022 [24]. As finance and law are more interrelated, we'll cover them in the same section. In the context of integrating and utilizing NLP in the context of finance frameworks, operations, reporting, and evaluation, we can look at finance from the following three angles:

Organization perspectives
    Different organization types have different requirements and perspectives that need to be taken into account. These perspectives include:

- Private companies
- Public companies

- Non-profit enterprises
- Governmental organizations

Actions

There are different actions that an organization can take, including:

- Allocating and reallocating funds
- Accounting and auditing, which includes identifying anomalies and outliers to investigate for both value and risk
- Prioritization and resource planning
- Compliance with legal and policy norms

Financial context

These actions can have various contexts, including:

- Forecasting and budgeting
- Retail banking
- Investment banking
- Stock market operations
- Cryptocurrency operations

To make real-time, thoughtful, planned decisions around structuring, viewing, managing, and reporting financial flows, there must be a constant focus on the changing nature of the company, and the financial infrastructure must be built and designed accordingly. ML and NLP can help design such a system. Figure 10-15 [25] shows how UK bankers think ML and NLP can improve their operations and in what areas.

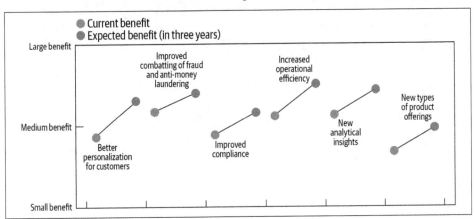

Figure 10-15. Estimated ML benefits survey in the UK [25]

They estimate large improvements in operational efficiency as well as analytics insights. With the application of ML and NLP, anti-fraud and anti–money laundering efforts are also expected to yield better benefits.

NLP Applications in Finance

In this section, we'll cover some specific applications of NLP in finance, including loan risk assessments, auditing and accounting problems, and financial sentiment analysis.

Financial sentiment

Stock market trading relies on a set of information about specific companies. This knowledge helps create a set of actions that determine whether to buy, hold, or sell off stock. This analysis can be based on companies' quarterly financial reports or on what analysts are commenting about the companies in their reports. This can also come from social media.

Social media analysis, which we covered in detail in Chapter 8, helps in monitoring social media posts and pointing out potential opportunities for trading. For instance, if a CEO is resigning, that sentiment is often negative, which can negatively affect the company's stock price. On the other hand, if the CEO is not performing well and markets welcome their resignation, that could lead to an increase in stock price. Examples of companies that provide this information for trading include DataMinr and Bloomberg. Figure 10-16 shows the DataMinr terminal, where alerts and marketing-affecting news related to Dell is surfaced to the user.

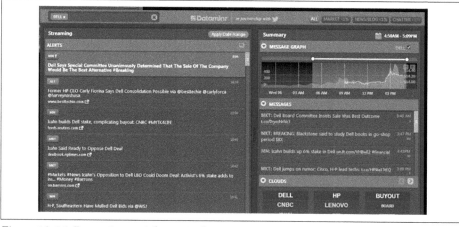

Figure 10-16. Dataminr social terminal

Financial sentiment analysis is different from regular sentiment analysis. It's not just different in domain, but also in purpose. Generally, the purpose is to guess how the markets will react to a piece of news, as opposed to whether the news is inherently positive or not. Just like we saw earlier in BioBERT for healthcare, there have been efforts to adapt BERT to the financial domain. One of these is FinBERT [26].

FinBERT uses a subset of financial news from Reuters. For sentiment classification, it uses Financial PhraseBank, which has over 4,000 sentences labeled by people with backgrounds in business and finance. Unlike regular sentiment analysis, where positive means that something is of positive emotion, in Financial PhraseBank, a positive sentiment indicates that the stock price of the company will increase based on the news in the sentence. FinBERT led to an accuracy of 0.97 and an F1 of 0.95—a substantial improvement over other general state-of-the-art methods. FinBERT is a library that's available on GitHub, along with its data [26]. We can build on this library for custom problems and use the pre-trained models for financial sentiment classification.

Risk assessments

Credit risk is a way to quantify the chances of a successful loan repayment. It's generally calculated by an individual's past spending and loan repayment history. However, this information is limited in many scenarios, especially in underprivileged communities. It's estimated that more than half of the world's population is excluded from financial services [27]. NLP can help alleviate this problem. NLP techniques can add a lot more data points that can be used to assess credit risk. For example, in business loans, entrepreneurial ability and attitude can be measured using NLP. This approach is used by Capital Float and Microbnk. Similarly, incoherencies in data provided by the borrower can also be surfaced for more scrutiny. Other more nuanced aspects, such as lenders' and borrowers' emotions while applying for a loan, can also be incorporated. This is covered in more detail in [27].

Often in personal loan agreements, various information has to be captured from loan documents, which are then fed to credit risk models. The information captured helps in identifying credit risk, and erroneous data extraction from these documents can lead to flawed assessments. Named entity recognition (NER), which we covered in detail in Chapter 5, can improve this. An example of such a loan agreement is shown in Figure 10-17, where we see a loan agreement and different relevant entities extracted from it. This example is taken from a work [28] on domain adaptation of NER for the finance domain. We'll cover such entity extraction in more detail in "NLP and the Legal Landscape" on page 365.

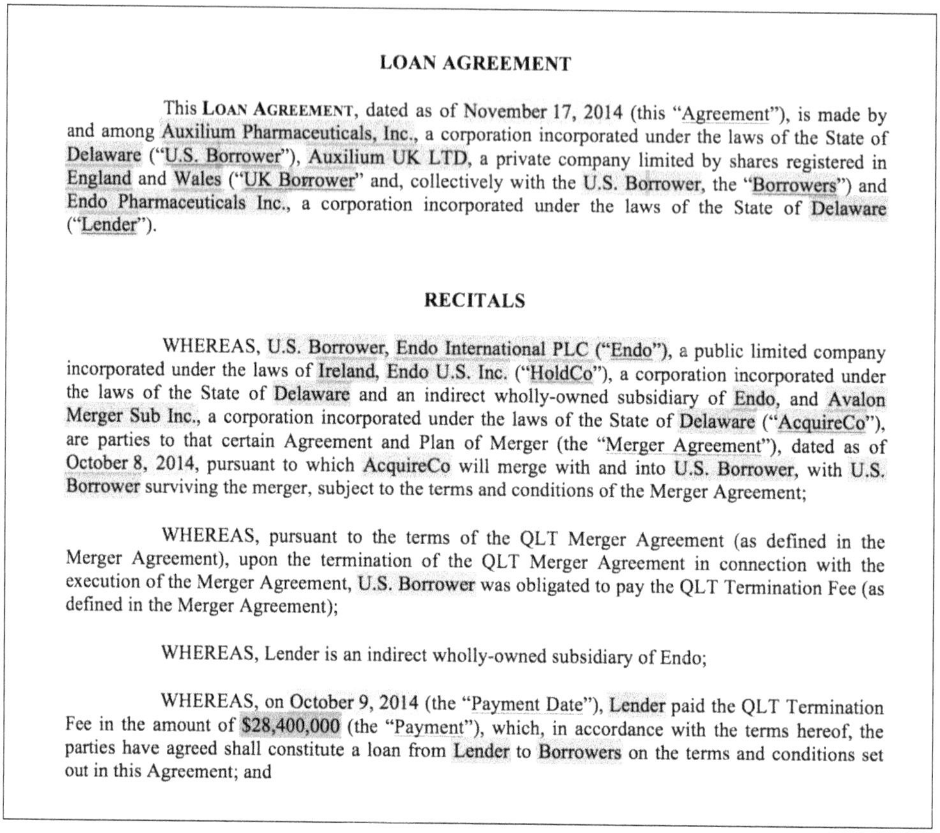

LOAN AGREEMENT

This LOAN AGREEMENT, dated as of November 17, 2014 (this "Agreement"), is made by and among Auxilium Pharmaceuticals, Inc., a corporation incorporated under the laws of the State of Delaware ("U.S. Borrower"), Auxilium UK LTD, a private company limited by shares registered in England and Wales ("UK Borrower" and, collectively with the U.S. Borrower, the "Borrowers") and Endo Pharmaceuticals Inc., a corporation incorporated under the laws of the State of Delaware ("Lender").

RECITALS

WHEREAS, U.S. Borrower, Endo International PLC ("Endo"), a public limited company incorporated under the laws of Ireland, Endo U.S. Inc. ("HoldCo"), a corporation incorporated under the laws of the State of Delaware and an indirect wholly-owned subsidiary of Endo, and Avalon Merger Sub Inc., a corporation incorporated under the laws of the State of Delaware ("AcquireCo"), are parties to that certain Agreement and Plan of Merger (the "Merger Agreement"), dated as of October 8, 2014, pursuant to which AcquireCo will merge with and into U.S. Borrower, with U.S. Borrower surviving the merger, subject to the terms and conditions of the Merger Agreement;

WHEREAS, pursuant to the terms of the QLT Merger Agreement (as defined in the Merger Agreement), upon the termination of the QLT Merger Agreement in connection with the execution of the Merger Agreement, U.S. Borrower was obligated to pay the QLT Termination Fee (as defined in the Merger Agreement);

WHEREAS, Lender is an indirect wholly-owned subsidiary of Endo;

WHEREAS, on October 9, 2014 (the "Payment Date"), Lender paid the QLT Termination Fee in the amount of $28,400,000 (the "Payment"), which, in accordance with the terms hereof, the parties have agreed shall constitute a loan from Lender to Borrowers on the terms and conditions set out in this Agreement; and

Figure 10-17. Loan agreement with annotated entities

Accounting and auditing

The global firms Deloitte, Ernst & Young, and PwC now have a significant focus on delivering more meaningful, actionable, and relevant audit conclusions and observations on a company's annual performance. While applying aspects of NLP and ML to areas like contract document reviews and long-term procurement agreements, Deloitte, for example, has evolved its Audit Command Language into a more efficient NLP application. This is covered in more detail in their report on government data [29].

In addition, after decades of long, drawn-out ticking and tying of reams of endless, typical day-to-day transactions and other pieces of paper like invoices, companies have finally realized that NLP and ML has a significant advantage in the audit process. This advantage manifests in the direct identification, focus, visualization, and trend analysis of outliers in transaction types. Time and effort are spent on the investigation of these outliers and their causes. This results in early identification of potentially significant risks and possible fraudulent activity like money laundering along with potentially value-generating activities that can be emulated and extrapolated across a company and customized for various business processes.

Next, we'll turn our attention to the use of NLP in legal matters.

NLP and the Legal Landscape

The integration and utilization of technological tools in the law profession has been in progress for decades. Given the amount of research, case referencing, brief preparation, document review, contract design, background analysis, and opinion drafting, those in the legal profession, including law offices and court systems, have long looked for a multitude of ways, means, and tools to slash their hours of manual effort. We won't cover legal NLP in as much detail, as research work in the domain is protected by patents instead of open or partially open. So, we'll discuss the ideas in general terms.

Some core tasks where NLP helps legal services include:

Legal research
> This involves finding relevant information for a specific case, including searching both legislatures and case law and regulations. One such service is ROSS Intelligence [30]. It allows matching of facts and relevant cases and also analyzes legal documents. We can see it in action in Figure 10-18.

Figure 10-18. ROSS match for relevant passages

Contract review
> This refers to reviewing a contract and making sure it follows a set of norms and regulations. It involves making comments and suggesting edits for different clauses. One example is SpotDraft [31], which focuses on GPDR-based regulations.

Contract generation
> This refers to generating contracts based on a question-and-answer setup. Simple cases may just require a simple form, whereas for more complex cases, an interactive chatbot system may be more suitable. After taking in all the responses, a slot-filling algorithm generates the contract.

Legal Discovery

This refers to finding anomalies and patterns in electronically stored information that can be used for the case. In some cases, this discovery is completely unsupervised. In other cases, it can involve more active learning (i.e., providing an initial set of tagged documents). One such product is siren.io [32], which aids discovery for intelligence, law enforcement, cyber security, and financial crime domains.

Legal entity extraction with LexNLP

In any kind of contract, there are a bunch of legal terms and entities we need to extract before building any kind of intelligent application. LexNLP [33] helps with that because it has legal word segmentation and tokenization. This is important because of legal abbreviations like LLC or F.3d, which regular parsers can't handle. Similarly, LexNLP helps us segment documents into sections and extract facts like recurring contract dates or regulations. Moreover, it plugs into the ContraxSuite, which has a range of other legal features that we'll cover later.

Now, let's see how this works in action:

```
import lexnlp.extract.en.acts
import lexnlp.extract.en.definitions

print("List of acts in the document")

data_contract = list(lexnlp.extract.en.acts.get_acts(text))
df = pd.DataFrame(data=data_contract,columns=data_contract[0].keys())
df['Act_annotations'] = list(lexnlp.extract.en.acts.get_acts_annotations(text))

df.head(10)

print("Different ACT definitions in the contract")

data_acts = list(lexnlp.extract.en.definitions.get_definitions(text))
df = pd.DataFrame(data=data_acts,columns=["Acts"])
df.head(20)
```

Figure 10-19 shows the list of acts in the document extracted using LexNLP.

As shown in the code, we extracted information from a SAFE (simple agreement for future equity), a common document for investments. We extracted all the acts and their definitions that were present in the document. Similarly, this can be extended to extract companies, citations, constraints, legal durations, regulations, etc. We cover some of these in the notebook for Chapter 10.

```
List of acts in the document
   location_start  location_end            act_name  section  year  ambiguous                          value               Act_annotations
0          6233          6264  Securities Exchange Act            1934      False  Securities Exchange Act of 1934   [act] at (6233..6264), loc: en
1          6346          6377  Securities Exchange Act            1934      False  Securities Exchange Act of 1934   [act] at (6346..6377), loc: en
2          9158          9176          Securities Act                    False              Securities Act.\n\n"   [act] at (9158..9176), loc: en
3         15403         15419          Securities Act                    False              Securities Act,   [act] at (15403..15419), loc: en
4         15691         15707          Securities Act                    False              Securities Act,   [act] at (15691..15707), loc: en
5         15806         15821          Securities Act                    False               Securities Act   [act] at (15806..15821), loc: en

Different ACT definitions in the contract
                        Acts
0             SECURITIES ACT
1            Purchase Amount
2                   Investor
3            Cash-Out Amount
4          Conversion Amount
5              Capital Stock
6           Change of Control
7        Converting Securities
8           Dissolution Event
9            Dividend Amount
10            Equity Financing
11      Initial Public Offering
12             Liquidity Event
13             Liquidity Price
14                    Options
15                   Proceeds
16            Promised Options
17                       Safe
18       SafePreferred Stock
19                 Safe Price
```

Figure 10-19. Output from LexNLP

Besides legal entity extraction, LexNLP also provides legal dictionaries [34] and knowledge sets for multiple countries for accounting, financial information, regulators, and legal and medical areas. It also integrates with ContraxSuite [35], which allows us to deduplicate documents, cluster legal entities according to how they're mentioned (as seen in Figure 10-20), and so on. When building custom applications, we can also inject code to build on the baseline platform.

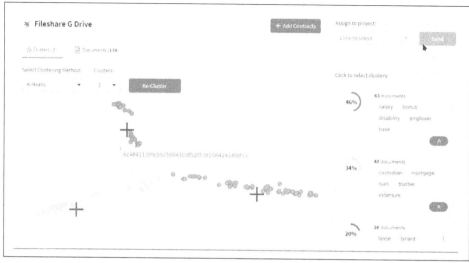

Figure 10-20. Clustering of legal entities from a set of documents

Wrapping Up

In this chapter, we learned about how NLP is utilized in healthcare, finance, and law, covering everything from model building, using online APIs, and dataset creation. These areas offer a diverse set of issues and solutions, so even if the domain you're working in is unrelated to these areas, the techniques learned here may be applicable in solving any unconventional problem. In the next chapter, we'll see how all of this comes together in building a complete NLP solution.

References

[1] Business Wire. "The $11.9 Trillion Global Healthcare Market: Key Opportunities & Strategies (2014–2022)" (*https://oreil.ly/JfILB*). June 25, 2019.

[2] Chilmark Research. "NLP Use Cases for Healthcare Providers" (*https://oreil.ly/3iIJr*). July 17, 2019.

[3] Wikipedia. "Electronic health record" (*https://oreil.ly/FU5DC*). Last modified April 17, 2020.

[4] Woebot (*https://woebot.io*). Last accessed June 15, 2020.

[5] Buoy: a healthcare chatbot (*https://oreil.ly/vrKwD*). Last accessed June 15, 2020.

[6] Infermedica (*https://oreil.ly/mEkxK*). Last accessed June 15, 2020.

[7] Hirsch, Jamie S., Jessica S. Tanenbaum, Sharon Lipsky Gorman, Connie Liu, Eric Schmitz, Dritan Hashorva, Artem Ervits, David Vawdrey, Marc Sturm, and Noémie

Elhadad. "HARVEST, a longitudinal patient record summarizer." *Journal of the American Medical Informatics Association* 22.2 (2015): 263–274.

[8] Raghavan, Preethi and Siddharth Patwardhan. "Question Answering on Electronic Medical Records." *Proceedings of the 2016 Summit on Clinical Research Informatics* (2016).

[9] Raghavan, Preethi, Siddharth Patwardhan, Jennifer J. Liang, and Murthy V. Devarakonda. "Annotating Electronic Medical Records for Question Answering" (*https://oreil.ly/UYbrD*), (2018).

[10] i2b2. "NLP Research Datasets" (*https://oreil.ly/WFPqh*). Last accessed June 15, 2020.

[11] Rajkumar, Alvin and Oren, Eyal. "Deep Learning for Electronic Health Records" (*https://oreil.ly/RM9ic*). *Google AI Blog*, May 8, 2018.

[12] Google Machine Learning Crash Course. "Classification: ROC Curve and AUC" (*https://oreil.ly/TIatR*). Last accessed June 15, 2020.

[13] Hilden, Jørgen. "The Area Under the Roc Curve and Its Competitors." *Medical Decision Making* 11.2 (1991): 95–101.

[14] Liu, Yun and Po-Hsuan Cameron Chen. "Lessons Learned from Developing ML for Healthcare" (*https://oreil.ly/p-Bat*). *Google AI Blog*, December 10, 2019.

[15] Ritchie, Hanna and Max Roser. "Mental Health" (*https://oreil.ly/TdVZv*). *Our World In Data*, April 2018.

[16] National Institute of Mental Health (NIMH). "Suicide" (*https://oreil.ly/YZ1t0*). Last accessed June 15, 2020.

[17] Coppersmith, Glen, Kim Ngo, Ryan Leary, and Anthony Wood. "Exploratory Analysis of Social Media Prior to a Suicide Attempt." *Proceedings of the Third Workshop on Computational Linguistics and Clinical Psychology* (2016): 106–117.

[18] Amazon Comprehend Medical (*https://oreil.ly/hKZft*). Last accessed June 15, 2020.

[19] Fast Healthcare Interoperability Resources (FHIR) specification (*https://oreil.ly/OmShK*). Last accessed June 15, 2020.

[20] FHIR sample healthcare record (*https://oreil.ly/fjDIY*), (download).

[21] Lee, Jinhyuk, Wonjin Yoon, Sungdong Kim, Donghyeon Kim, Sunkyu Kim, Chan Ho So, and Jaewoo Kang. "BioBERT: A Pre-Trained Biomedical Language Representation Model for Biomedical Text Mining." *Bioinformatics* 36.4 (2020): 1234–1240.

[22] DMIS Laboratory - Korea University. BioBERT: a pre-trained biomedical language representation model (*https://oreil.ly/VZhCv*), (GitHub repo). Last accessed June 15, 2020.

[23] NAVER. BioBERT: a pre-trained biomedical language representation model for biomedical text mining (*https://oreil.ly/IYKfX*), (GitHub repo). Last accessed June 15, 2020.

[24] Ross, Sean. "What Percentage of the Global Economy Is the Financial Services Sector?" (*https://oreil.ly/jb2x7*) *Investopedia*, February 6, 2020.

[25] Bank of England. "Machine Learning in UK Financial Services" (*https://oreil.ly/a7q8-*). October 2019.

[26] Araci, Dogu. "FinBERT: Financial Sentiment Analysis with Pre-trained Language Models" (*https://oreil.ly/TqnOX*), (2019).

[27] Crouspeyre, Charles, Eleonore Alesi, and Karine Lespinasse. "From Creditworthiness to Trustworthiness with Alternative NLP/NLU Approaches." *Proceedings of the First Workshop on Financial Technology and Natural Language Processing* (2019): 96–98.

[28] Alvarado, Julio Cesar Salinas, Karin Verspoor, and Timothy Baldwin. "Domain Adaption of Named Entity Recognition to Support Credit Risk Assessment." *Proceedings of the Australasian Language Technology Association Workshop* (2015): 84–90.

[29] Eggers, William D., Neha Malik, and Matt Gracie. "Using AI to Unleash the Power of Unstructured Government Data." *Deloitte Insights* (2019).

[30] Ross Intelligence (*https://oreil.ly/_uvv-*). Last accessed June 15, 2020.

[31] SpotDraft (*https://spotdraft.com*). Last accessed June 15, 2020.

[32] Siren: Investigative Intelligence Platform (*https://siren.io*). Last accessed June 15, 2020.

[33] LexPredict. LexNLP by LexPredict (*https://oreil.ly/3WS6x*), (GitHub repo). Last accessed June 15, 2020.

[34] LexPredict. LexPredict Legal Dictionaries (*https://oreil.ly/NdU6O*), (GitHub repo). Last accessed June 15, 2020.

[35] ContraxSuite (*https://oreil.ly/UdSgi*). Last accessed June 15, 2020.

## PART IV

Bringing It All Together

CHAPTER 11

The End-to-End NLP Process

The process is more important than the goal. The person you become
is infinitely more valuable than whatever the result is.
—Anthony Moore

So far in the book, we've addressed a range of NLP problems, starting from what an NLP pipeline looks like to how NLP is applied in different domains. Efficiently applying what we've learned to build end-to-end software products involving NLP takes more than just stitching together various steps in an NLP pipeline—there are several decision points during the process. While a lot of this knowledge comes only with experience, we've distilled some of our knowledge about the end-to-end NLP process in this chapter to help you hit the ground running faster and better.

In Chapter 2, we already saw what a typical pipeline for an NLP system looks like. How is this chapter then any different from that? In Chapter 2, we focused primarily on the technical aspects of the pipeline—for example, how do we represent text? What pre-processing steps should we do? How do we build a model, and then how do we evaluate it? In the subsequent chapters in Parts I and II of the book, we delved deeper into different algorithms to perform various NLP tasks. We also saw how NLP is used in various industry domains, such as healthcare, e-commerce, and social media. However, in all these chapters, we spent little time on the issues related to deploying and maintaining such systems and on the processes to follow when managing such projects. These are the focus of this chapter. Most of the points discussed here are broadly applicable not just to NLP, but also to other concepts, such as data science (DS), machine learning, artificial intelligence (AI), etc. Throughout this chapter, we use these terms interchangeably; where the focus is specifically on NLP tasks, we mention that explicitly.

We'll start the discussion by revisiting the NLP pipeline we introduced in Chapter 2 and take a look at the last two steps: deployment, followed by monitoring and updating the model, which we didn't cover in earlier chapters. We'll also see what it takes to build and maintain a mature NLP system. This is followed by a discussion on the data science processes followed in various AI teams, especially with respect to building NLP software in particular. We'll conclude the chapter with a lot of recommendations, best practices, and do's and don'ts to successfully deliver NLP projects. Let's start by looking at how to deploy NLP software.

Revisiting the NLP Pipeline: Deploying NLP Software

In Chapter 2, we saw that a typical production pipeline for NLP projects consists of the following stages: data acquisition, text cleaning, text pre-processing, text representation and feature engineering, modeling, evaluation, deployment, monitoring, and model updating. When we encounter a new problem scenario involving NLP in our organization, we have to first start thinking about creating an NLP pipeline covering these stages. Some of the questions we should ask ourselves in this process are:

- What kind of data do we need for training the NLP system? Where do we get this data from? These questions are important at the start and also later as the model matures.

- How much data is available? If it's not enough, what data augmentation techniques can we try?

- How will we label the data, if necessary?

- How will we quantify the performance of our model? What metrics will we use to do that?

- How will we deploy the system? Using API calls over the cloud, or a monolith system, or an embedded module on an edge device?

- How will the predictions be served: streaming or batch process?

- Would we need to update the model? If yes, what will the update frequency be: daily, weekly, monthly?

- Do we need a monitoring and alerting mechanism for model performance? If yes, what kind of mechanism do we need and how will we put it in place?

Once we've thought through these key decision points, a broad design of our pipeline is ready! We can then start to focus on building version 1 of the model with strong baselines, implementing the pipeline, deploying the model, and from there, iteratively improving our solution. In Chapter 2, we saw how different stages of the NLP pipeline before deployment are implemented for various NLP tasks. Let's now take a look at the final stages of the pipeline: deployment, monitoring, and model updating.

What does deployment mean? Any NLP model we build is typically a part of some larger software system. Once our model is working well in isolation, we plug it into a larger system and ensure that everything is working well. The set of all of the tasks related to integrating the model with the rest of the software and making it production-ready is called *deployment*. Typical steps in deployment of a model include:

1. *Model packaging*: If the model is large, it might need to be saved in persistent cloud storage, such as AWS S3, Azure Blob Storage, or Google Cloud Storage, for easy access. It might also be serialized and wrapped up in a library call for easy access. There are also open formats like ONNX [1] that provide interoperability across different frameworks.

2. *Model serving*: The model can be made available as a web service for other services to consume. In cases where a more tightly coupled system and batch process is more applicable, the model could be part of a task flow system like Airflow [2], Oozie [3], or Chef [4], instead of a web service. Microsoft has also released reference pipelines for MLOps [5] and MLOps in Python [6].

3. *Model scaling*: Models that are hosted as web services should be able to scale with respect to request traffic. Models that are running as part of a batch service should also be able to scale with respect to the input batch size. Public cloud platforms as well as on-premise cloud systems have technologies that enable that. Figure 11-1 shows one such pipeline for text classification on AWS. More details on the engineering of this pipeline can be found in the AWS post [7].

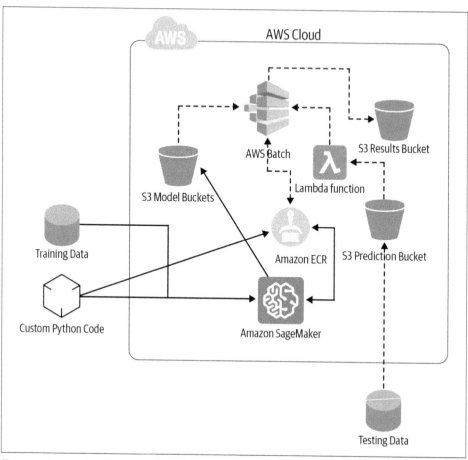

Figure 11-1. AWS Cloud and SageMaker to serve text classification [8]

Let's look at an example to understand the deployment of an NLP model into a larger system.

An Example Scenario

Let's say we work for a social media platform and are asked to build a classifier to identify abusive user comments. The goal of this classifier is to prevent abusive content from appearing on the platform by flagging any content that's potentially abusive and sending it for human moderation. We worked hard on collecting the data relevant to this task, designing a set of features, and testing a range of algorithms, and we built a predictive model that takes a new comment as input and classifies it as abusive or safe. What next?

Our model is just a small part of the larger social media platform. There are several components: content is being rendered dynamically, and there are various modules to interact with users, components responsible for storage and retrieval of data, and so on. It's possible that different subsystems of the platform are written in different programming languages. Our classifier is just a small component of the product, and we need to integrate it into the larger setup. How do we go about doing this? A common way to address this scenario is to create a web service where the model sits behind the web service. The rest of the product interacts with the model via this web service. It queries the service with the new comment(s) and gets back the prediction(s). The call to this web service is integrated into the product wherever necessary. Popular web application frameworks such as Flask [9], Falcon [10], and Django [11] are typically used to create such web services.

Developing various NLP solutions involves relying on a range of pre-existing libraries. Setting up a web service and hosting what we built in the cloud or some server requires us to ensure that there are no compatibility issues. To address this, there is a range of options available. The most common option is to package various libraries into a container like Docker [12] or Kubernetes [13]. Operationalizing a web service for production requires addressing many other issues, such as tech stack, load balancing, latency, throughput, availability, and reliability. Building and making a model production ready includes a whole lot of engineering tasks, which can often be time consuming. Cloud services such as AWS SageMaker [14] and Azure Cognitive Services [15] try to make these engineering tasks easy. Sometimes, the whole process, to the last detail, is automated to such an extent that it's as simple as one-click-get-done to set up the service. The idea is to let the AI teams focus on the most important part: model building.

Another important issue to address is model size. Modern NLP models can be quite large. For example, Google's Word2vec model is 4.8 GB in size and takes over 100 seconds just to load into memory (refer back to *Ch3/Pre_Trained_Word_Embeddings.ipynb*). Likewise, a fastText classification model is typically over 2 GB in size. DL models like BERT are known to be even bulkier. Hosting such large models in the cloud can be both challenging and expensive. There's a lot of work happening in the area of model compression to address such scenarios. Some of them are listed below:

- "Compressing BERT for Faster Prediction," a blog post by a team at Rasa NLP [16]
- "A Survey of Model Compression and Acceleration for Deep Neural Networks," a report by a team at Microsoft Research and Tsinghua University [17]
- "FastText.zip: Compressing text classification models," a report by a team at Facebook AI Research [18]

- "Awesome ML Model Compression," a GitHub repository by Cedric Chee that includes relevant papers, videos, libraries, and tools [19]

This is just a brief overview of various steps that go into deploying our NLP model. There are books and other materials that cover this in complete detail. As a start, interested readers can look at the later chapters of the book *Machine Learning Engineering* [20].

For most industry use cases, model building is seldom a one-time activity. As the deployed system gets used more, the models built need to adapt to new scenarios and new data points. Hence, the models should be updated regularly. Let's discuss the issues to consider while building and maintaining mature NLP software.

Building and Maintaining a Mature System

In most real-world settings, the underlying patterns in data change over a period of time. This means that the models that were trained long before can become stale—i.e., the data used to train the model is very different from the data in the production environment that's being fed to the model for predictions. This is called *covariate shift*, and it results in a performance drop of the model. Model update is a common approach to deal with such scenarios. On a similar note, in most industrial settings, once the first version of a model is consumed, improving the model becomes inevitable. Updating and improving an existing NLP model could just mean retraining with newer or additional training data, or it sometimes involves adding new features. When updating such models, the goal is to ensure that the deployed system performs at least as well as the existing system. Most model updates and improvements lead to more complex models. As the models grow in complexity, we need to ensure that the system doesn't crumble under increasing complexity. We need to manage the complexity of a mature NLP model while making sure it's also maintainable. Some of the issues we need to consider in this process are:

- Finding better features
- Iterating existing models
- Code and model reproducibility
- Troubleshooting and testing
- Minimizing technical debt
- Automating the ML process

In this section, let's take a look at these issues one by one, starting with a discussion about how to find better features.

Finding Better Features

Throughout this book, we've repeatedly stressed the importance of building a simple model first. This version 1 model is seldom an end in itself. We may keep on adding new features and periodically retraining the model beyond V1. Our goal is to find the features that are most expressive to capture the regularities in the data that are useful for making predictions. How can we develop such features? We saw different ways to generate textual feature representations in Chapter 3. We can start with one of those that doesn't require prior knowledge about the problem domain (e.g., basic vectorization, distributed representations, and universal representations) or use our prior knowledge about the problem and domain to develop specific features for our problem (i.e., handcrafted features) or use a combination of both.

Designing specific features for a given problem (or feature engineering) can be both difficult and expensive. This is why problem-agnostic text representations are commonly used as a starting point. However, domain-specific features have their own value. For example, in a task of sentiment classification, more than vector representations of raw text, domain-specific indicators, such as count of negative words, count of positive words, and other word- and phrase-level features, are useful to extract the sentiment in a more robust manner.

Let's say we implemented a bunch of features to build our NLP models. Does the best model need each one of these features? How do we choose the most informative features among the several we implemented? For example, if we use two features where one can be derived from the other, we're not adding any extra information to the model. Feature selection is a great technique to handle such cases and make informed decisions. There are plenty of statistical methods that can be used to fine-tune our feature sets by removing redundant or irrelevant features. This broad area is called *feature selection*.

Two popular techniques for feature selection are wrapper methods and filter methods. Wrapper methods use an ML model to score feature subsets. Each new subset is used to train a model, which is tested on a hold-out set and then used to identify the best features based on the error rate of the model. Wrapper methods are computationally expensive, but they often provide the best set of features. Filter methods use some sort of proxy measure instead of the error rate to rank and score features (e.g., correlation among the features and correlation with the output predictions). Such measures are fast to compute while still capturing the usefulness of the feature set. Filter methods are usually less computationally expensive than wrappers, but they produce a feature set that's not as well optimized to a specific type of predictive model. In DL-based approaches, while feature engineering and feature selection is automated, we have to experiment with various model architectures.

Since feature selection methods are usually task specific (i.e., methods for classification tasks are different from methods for, say, machine translation), interested readers can look into resources such as sparse features, dense features, and feature interactions from Wide and Deep Learning from Google AI [21]. The book *Feature Engineering for Machine Learning* [22] would also be useful. However, we hope this overview convinced you of feature selection's role in building mature, production-quality NLP systems. Assuming we're going through this process of adding new features and evaluating them, how should we incorporate them into our training process and update our NLP models? Let's take a look at this question now.

Iterating Existing Models

As we mentioned earlier, any NLP model is seldom a static entity. We're often required to update our models even in production systems. There are several reasons for this. We may get more (and newer) data that differs from previous training data. If we don't update our model to reflect this change, it will soon become stale and churn out poor predictions. We may get some user feedback on where the model predictions are going wrong. This will then require us to reflect on the model and its features and make amendments accordingly. In both cases, we need to set up a process to periodically retrain and update the existing model and deploy the new model in production.

When we develop a new model, intuitively, it's always good to compare the results with our previous best models to understand the incremental value addition. How do we know this new model is better than the existing one? The analysis of model performance can be based on comparing raw predictions from both models, or it could be from a perspective of a derived performance based on the predictions. Let's explain these two cases by revisiting the abusive comments detection example from earlier in this chapter.

Let's say we have a gold standard test set of abusive versus non-abusive comments. We can always use this to compare an old model with the new one in terms of, say, classification accuracy. We can also follow an external validation approach and look for other aspects, such as how many model decisions were contested by users every day. It would be practical to set up a dashboard to monitor these metrics periodically and display them for each model so that we can choose the one that's the best improvement over the current model among the various models we may build. We can also A/B test a new model with an old model (or any baseline system) and measure business KPIs to see how well the new model performs. When onboarding a new model, it might also be a good practice to first roll it out to a small fraction of users, monitor its performance, and then progressively expand it to the entire user base.

Code and Model Reproducibility

Making sure your NLP models continue working in the same fashion in different environments can be critical for the long-term success of any project. A model or result that's reproducible is generally considered more robust. There is a range of best practices you can use to achieve this while building systems.

Maintaining separation between code, data, and model(s) is always a good strategy. Separating code and data is generally a best practice in software engineering, and it becomes even more critical for AI systems. While there are established version control systems for code, such as Git, versioning of models and datasets can be different. As of recently, there are tools like Data Version Control [23] that address this issue. It's always a good practice to name model and data versions appropriately so that we can revert back easily, if needed. While storing the models, you should try to have all your model parameters, along with other variables, in a separate file. Similarly, try to avoid hardcoded parameter values in your model. If you have to use arbitrary numbers in your training process (e.g., a seed value somewhere), explain it in the code as comments.

Another good practice is creating checkpoints in your code and model often. You should store your learned model in a repository both periodically and at milestones. When training a model, it's also a good idea to use the same seed wherever random initialization is used. This ensures that the model creates similar results (and internal representation) every time the same parameters and data are used.

A keystone for improving reproducibility is to make sure to note all steps explicitly. This is especially necessary in the exploratory phase of data analysis. On the same note, it helps to record as many intermediate steps and data outputs as possible. This helps in transforming your experimental model to an in-production model without any loss of information. To read further, we would suggest a report on AI reproducibility state of the art [24] and an interview of a reproducibility researcher at Facebook, Joelle Pineau [25]. This brings us to the next topic in this section. While making all these iterations and building multiple models, how do we ensure there are no errors and bugs in the training process and that our data isn't noisy? How do we troubleshoot and test our code and models?

Troubleshooting and Interpretability

To maintain the quality of software, testing is a key step in any software development process. However, considering the probabilistic nature of ML models, how to test ML models is not obvious. Figures 11-2 and 11-3 illustrate some of the good practices for testing out AI systems. We already saw how to use Lime (Figure 11-3) in Chapter 4.

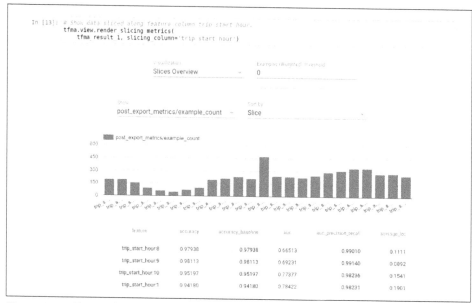

Figure 11-2. TensorFlow Model Analysis (TFMA) [26]

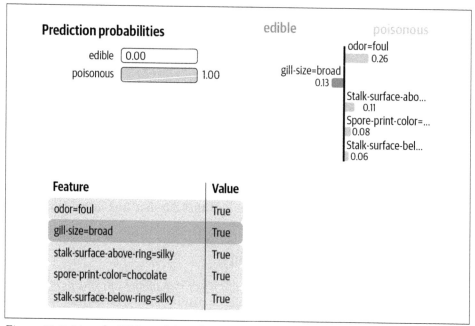

Figure 11-3. Lime for NLP model analysis

As we discussed earlier in the chapter, a model is just a small component of any AI system. When it comes to testing the entire system, barring the model, most techniques for testing of software engineering are applicable and work well. When it comes to testing the model, the following steps are helpful:

- Run the model on train, validation, and test datasets used during the model-building phase. There should not be any major deviation in the results for any of the metrics. K-fold cross validation is often used to verify model performance.

- Test the model for edge cases. For example, for sentiment classification, test with sentences with double or triple negation.

- Analyze the mistakes the model is making. The findings from the analysis should be similar to the findings from the analysis of the mistakes it was making during the development phase. For NLP, packages and techniques like TensorFlow Model Analysis [26], Lime [27], Shap [28], and attention networks [5] can give a deeper understanding of what the model is doing deep down. You can see this in action in Figures 11-2 and 11-3. The insights from these during development and production should not change much.

- Another good practice is to build a subsystem that keeps track of key statistics of the features. Since all features are numerical, we can maintain statistics like mean, median, standard deviation, distribution plots, etc. Any deviation in these statistics is a red flag, and we're likely to see the system churning out wrong predictions. The reason could be as simple as a bug in the pipeline or as complex as a covariate shift in the underlying data. Packages like TensorFlow Model Analysis [26] can track these metrics. Figure 11-4 shows distributions for metrics of various features for a dataset that can be tracked to find covariate shift or bugs.

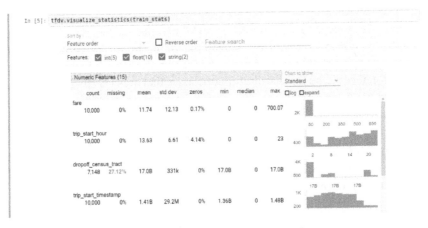

Figure 11-4. Feature statistics in TensorFlow Extended [29]

- Create dashboards for tracking model metrics and create an alerting mechanism on them in case there are any deviations in the metrics. We'll discuss this point in detail in the next section.

- It's always good to know what a model is doing inside. This goes a long way toward understanding why a model is behaving in a certain way. A key question in AI has been how to create intelligent systems where we can explain why the model is doing what it is doing. This is called *interpretability*. It's the degree to which a human can understand the cause of a decision [30]. While many algorithms in machine learning (such as decision trees, random forest, XGboost, etc.) and computer vision have been very interpretable, this is not true for NLP, especially DL algorithms. With recent techniques such as attention networks, Lime, and Shapley, we have greater interpretability in NLP models. Interested readers can look at *Interpretable Machine Learning* by Christoph Molnar [31] for further discussion on this topic.

Monitoring

Once an ML system has been deployed and is in production, we need to make sure the model continues working well. As an example deployment, if the model is being trained automatically every day with new data points, certain bugs can creep in, or the model can malfunction. To ensure that this doesn't happen, we need to monitor the model for a range of things and trigger alerts at the right points:

- Model performance has to be monitored regularly. For a web service–based model, it can be the mean and various percentiles—50th (median), 90th, 95th, and 99th (or deeper)—for response time. If the model is deployed as a batch service, statistics on the batch processing and task times have to be monitored.

- Similarly, it helps to store monitor model parameters, behavior, and KPIs. Model KPIs for the abusive comments example would be the percentage of comments that were reported by users but not flagged by the model. For a text classification service, it could be the distribution of classes that are classified each day.

- For all the metrics we're monitoring, we need to periodically run them through an anomaly detection system that can alert changes in normal behavior. This could be a sudden spike in the response rate of a web service or a sudden drop in retraining times. In the worst case, when the performance drops substantially, we may also want to hit circuit breakers (i.e., move to a more stable model or a default approach).

- If our overall engineering pipeline is using a logging framework, there's a good chance it also has support for monitoring anomalies over time for any metric. For instance, ELK stack by Elastic offers built-in anomaly detection [7].

Sumo Logic also flags outliers that can be queried as needed [32]. Microsoft also offers anomaly detection as a service [33].

Monitoring our ML models and their deployments can save substantial time as the project scales. As the system matures and the model stabilizes, proper monitoring allows MLOps teams to largely manage it, so data scientists can solve other harder problems. Although, as systems mature, we also start accumulating more technical debt, which we'll cover in the next section.

Minimizing Technical Debt

Throughout this book, and especially in this chapter, we've seen various aspects of training NLP models, deploying them as a part of a larger system, and iteratively improving from there on. As we start iterating from the first version of the system, the system and various components, including the model, can easily become complex. This brings the challenges of maintaining the system. We may have scenarios where we don't know if the incremental improvements justify the complexity. Such scenarios can create a technical debt. Let's take a brief look at addressing technical debt in building AI software.

It's important to plan and build for the future when working with any software system. We have to ensure that our system continues being both performant and easy to maintain after all these continuous iterations and testing. Unused and poorly implemented improvements can create technical debt. If we're not using a feature or any of its combinations with other features, it's important to drop it out of the pipeline. A feature or part of the code that doesn't work just clogs our infrastructure, hinders fast iteration, and brings down clarity.

A good rule of thumb is to look at the coverage a feature provides. If a feature is present in only a few data points, say, 1%, then maybe it's not worth keeping. But even something like this can't be applied blindly. For example, if the same feature covers just 1% of the data but gives 95% classification accuracy just based on that feature, then it's really effective and most certainly worth continuing to use. From our experience, an important tip (that we've also reiterated several times in the book) is: *opt for a simpler model that has performance comparable to a much more complex model if you want to minimize technical debt.* Complex models may become necessary if there's no equivalent simple model though.

Besides these recommendations, we'd also like to share some landmark work on building mature ML systems:

- "A Few Useful Things to Know About Machine Learning" by Pedro Domingoes of the University of Washington [34]
- "Machine Learning: The High-Interest Credit Card of Technical Debt" by a team at Google AI [35]
- "Hidden Technical Debt in Machine Learning Systems" by a team at Google AI [36]
- *Feature Engineering for Machine Learning*, a book written by Alice Zheng and Amanda Casari [22]
- "Ad Click Prediction: A View from the Trenches," a work by a Google Search team on the issues faced by a large online ML system [37]
- "Rules of Machine Learning," an online guide created by Martin Zenkovich of Google [38]
- "The Unreasonable Effectiveness of Data," a report by renowned UC Berkeley researcher Peter Norvig and a Google AI team [39]
- "Revisiting Unreasonable Effectiveness of Data in Deep Learning Era," another modern look at the previous report by a team from Carnegie Mellon University [40]

So far, we've discussed various best practices used in building mature AI systems. From finding better features to version control of datasets, these practices are manual and effort intensive. Driven by the ultimate goal of building intelligent machines and reducing manual effort, an interesting recent work has been to automate some aspects of building AI systems. Let's look at some key efforts in this direction.

Automating Machine Learning

One of the holy grails of machine learning is to automate more and more of the feature engineering process. This has led to the creation of a subarea called AutoML (automated machine learning), which aims to make machine learning more accessible. In most cases, it generates a data analysis pipeline that can include data preprocessing, feature selection, and feature engineering methods. This pipeline essentially selects ML methods and parameter settings that are optimized for a specific problem and data. As all of these steps can be time consuming for the ML expert and may be intractable for a beginner, AutoML can be a much-needed bridge for a gap in the world of machine learning. AutoML is itself essentially "doing machine learning using machine learning," making this powerful and complex technology more widely accessible for those hoping to make use of massive amounts of data.

As an example, one research group at Google has used AutoML techniques [41] for language modeling with the Penn Treebank dataset. Penn Treebank is a benchmark dataset for linguistic structure [42]. The research group at Google found that their AutoML approach can design models that achieve accuracies on par with state-of-the-art models designed by world-class machine learning experts. Figure 11-5 shows an example of a neural network generated by AutoML.

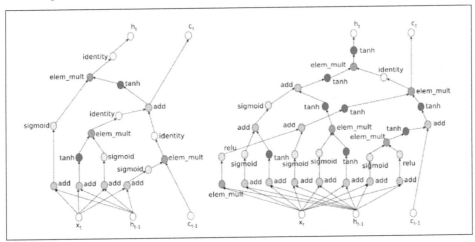

Figure 11-5. AutoML-generated network [41]

On the left side of the figure is a neural network that Google experts created to parse text. On the right side is another network that was created automatically by Google's AutoML. AutoML that explores various neural network architectures automatically performed as well as the handcrafted model. It's fascinating to see that their system did almost as well as humans even for designing ML models.

AutoML is the cutting edge of machine learning. One should only build it from the bottom up when more traditional methods for improving performance are exhausted. It often requires a high amount of computing and GPU resources and a higher level of technical skill when doing it from scratch.

auto-sklearn

As we mentioned previously, it's generally a good idea to work on automating machine learning only after most other options have been exhausted. In cases where the need for AutoML [43] is more clear, one of the best libraries for applying it is auto-sklearn. It uses recent advancements in Bayesian optimization and meta-learning to search in a huge hyperparameter space to figure out a reasonably good ML model on its own. As it's integrated with sklearn, which is one of the more popular ML libraries, using it is quite simple:

```
import autosklearn.classification
import sklearn.model_selection
import sklearn.datasets
import sklearn.metrics
X, y = sklearn.datasets.load_digits(return_X_y=True)
X_train, X_test, y_train, y_test = \
        sklearn.model_selection.train_test_split(X, y, random_state=1)
automl = autosklearn.classification.AutoSklearnClassifier()
automl.fit(X_train, y_train)
y_hat = automl.predict(X_test)
print("Accuracy", sklearn.metrics.accuracy_score(y_test, y_hat))
```

This code builds an autosklearn classifier for the MNIST digits dataset [44]. It splits the dataset into training and test sets. While running for about an hour, this will automatically yield accuracy of over 98%.

When we peek through what's happening internally, we see different stages of AutoML, as shown in the snippet below:

```
[(0.080000, SimpleClassificationPipeline({'balancing:strategy': 'none',
'categorical_encoding:__choice__': 'one_hot_encoding', 'classifier:__choice__':
'lda',
'imputation:strategy': 'mean', 'preprocessor:__choice__': 'polynomial',
'rescaling:__choice__': 'minmax',
'categorical_encoding:one_hot_encoding:use_minimum_fraction': 'True',
'classifier:lda:n_components': 151,
'classifier:lda:shrinkage': 'auto', 'classifier:lda:tol':
0.02939556179271624,
'preprocessor:polynomial:degree': 2, 'preprocessor:polynomial:include_bias':
'True',
'preprocessor:polynomial:interaction_only': 'True',
'categorical_encoding:one_hot_encoding:minimum_fraction': 0.0729529152649298},
dataset_properties={
  'task': 2,
  'sparse': False,
  'multilabel': False,
  'multiclass': True,
  'target_type': 'classification',
  'signed': False})),
...
...
...
...
(0.020000, SimpleClassificationPipeline({'balancing:strategy': 'none',
'categorical_encoding:__choice__':
'one_hot_encoding', 'classifier:__choice__': 'passive_aggressive',
'imputation:strategy': 'mean',
'preprocessor:__choice__': 'polynomial', 'rescaling:__choice__': 'minmax',
'categorical_encoding:one_hot_encoding:use_minimum_fraction': 'True',
'classifier:passive_aggressive:C':
0.03485276894122253, 'classifier:passive_aggressive:average': 'True',
'classifier:passive_aggressive:fit_intercept': 'True',
```

```
  'classifier:passive_aggressive:loss': 'hinge',
  'classifier:passive_aggressive:tol': 4.6384320611389e-05,
  'preprocessor:polynomial:degree': 3,
  'preprocessor:polynomial:include_bias': 'True',
  'preprocessor:polynomial:interaction_only': 'True',
  'categorical_encoding:one_hot_encoding:minimum_fraction': 0.11994577706637469},
  dataset_properties={
    'task': 2,
    'sparse': False,
    'multilabel': False,
    'multiclass': True,
    'target_type': 'classification',
    'signed': False})),
]
auto-sklearn results:
  Dataset name: d74860caaa557f473ce23908ff7ba369
  Metric: accuracy
  Best validation score: 0.991011
  Number of target algorithm runs: 240
  Number of successful target algorithm runs: 226
  Number of crashed target algorithm runs: 1
  Number of target algorithms that exceeded the time limit: 2
  Number of target algorithms that exceeded the memory limit: 11
```

Next, let's take a look at Google Cloud services, as well as a few other approaches to NLP problems.

Google Cloud AutoML and other techniques

Google Cloud Services has also recently released AutoML as a service. This doesn't require any technical knowledge beyond providing training data in the expected format. They've specifically built Cloud AutoML services for different parts of AI, including computer vision and structured tabular data, as well as for NLP.

For NLP, their Cloud AutoML is applied automatically when training custom models for:

- Text classification
- Entity extraction
- Sentiment analysis
- Machine translation

For all these tasks, Google Cloud has defined a specific format that the AutoML models expect the data to be in. More information on these can be found in their documentation [45, 46]. Microsoft also has tooling for AutoML in their Azure Machine Learning [47].

Another interesting approach to tackling an NLP problem in a more automated way is to use the AutoCompete framework created by Abhishek Thakur [48], a top-ranked Kaggle Competitions Grandmaster. Even though his initial approach was to focus on any data science problem specifically targeted to competitions, it has now evolved to a general framework to solve such problems. He has also released a detailed notebook titled "Approaching (Almost) Any NLP Problem on Kaggle" [49] that creates a general modeling framework for NLP problems with a well-defined dataset and goals. While this may not completely solve the specific NLP task you're working at, it's a good start to look at creating baseline models.

So far, we've addressed a range of issues that might come up when trying to build, deploy, and maintain NLP software. However, an equally important component of such an endeavor is to follow standard product development processes. While the field of software development processes and life cycle is well established, there are some important things to consider while working on projects that involve predictive models like the ones we've discussed throughout the book. Let's now take a look at that aspect.

The Data Science Process

Data science is a broad term describing the algorithms and processes used to extract meaningful information and actionable insights from all forms of data. Thus, all NLP work in the industry can be categorized under the data science umbrella. While data science as a term is relatively new, it's been around in some form or another for the past few decades. Over the years, people have formulated and formalized the best processes and practices of working with data. Two popular processes in the industry are the KDD process and the Microsoft Team Data Science Process.

The KDD Process

The ACM SIGKDD Conference on Knowledge Discovery and Data Mining (KDD) is one of the oldest and most reputed data mining conferences in the world. Some of the founders of the conference also created the KDD process in 1996. The KDD process [50], depicted in Figure 11-6, consists of a series of steps that should be applied to a data science or data mining problem to get better results.

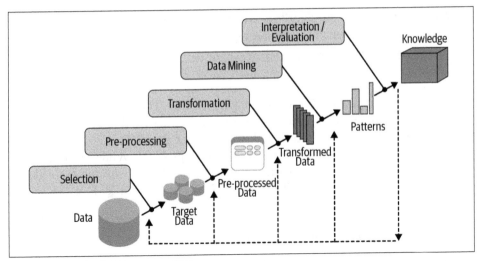

Figure 11-6. The KDD process [50]

These steps are ordered as follows:

1. *Understanding the domain:* This includes learning about the application and understanding the goals of a problem. It also involves getting deeper into the problem domain and extracting relevant domain knowledge.

2. *Target dataset creation:* This includes selecting a subset of data and variables the problem will focus on. We may have a plethora of data sources at our disposal, but we focus on the subset we need to work on.

3. *Data pre-processing:* This encompasses all activities needed so that the data can be treated coherently. This includes filling missing values, noise reduction, and removing outliers.

4. *Data reduction:* If the data has a lot of dimensions, this step can be used to make it easier to work with. This includes steps like dimensionality reduction and projecting the data into another space. This step is optional depending on the data.

5. *Choosing the data mining task:* Various classes of algorithms can be applied to a problem. They may be regression, classification, or clustering. It's important to select the right task based on our understanding from Step 1.

6. *Choosing the data mining algorithm:* Based on the selected data mining task, we need to select the right algorithm. For instance, for classification, we can choose algorithms such as SVM, random forests, CNNs, etc., as we saw in Chapter 4.

7. *Data mining:* This is a core step of applying the selection algorithm from Step 6 to the given dataset and creating predictive models. Tuning with respect to parameters and hyperparameters also happens here.

8. *Interpretation:* Once the algorithm is applied, the user has to interpret the results. This can be done partially by visualizing various components of results.

9. *Consolidation:* This is the final step where we deploy the built model into an existing system, document the approach, and generate reports.

As seen in the figure, the KDD process is highly iterative. There can be any number of loops between various steps. At each step, we can and may need to go back to earlier steps and refine the information there before moving ahead. This process is a good reference when working on a specific data science problem. While not exactly the same, the pipelines we've discussed throughout the book deal with the same idea of bringing structure to building NLP systems. Now, let's take a look at the second process.

Microsoft Team Data Science Process

The KDD process was introduced in the late '90s. As the fields of machine learning and data science grew, bigger teams working exclusively on such data science projects began to emerge. Further, in the fast-moving world of data-driven development, more flexible and iteration-based frameworks were needed, so other data science processes began to emerge. The Microsoft Team Data Science Process (TDSP) addresses this. It was released by the Microsoft Azure team in 2017 and is one of the modern processes for applying machine learning and working in data science [51].

TDSP is an agile, iterative data science process for executing and delivering advanced analytics solutions. It's designed to improve the collaboration and efficiency of data science teams in enterprise organizations. The main features of TDSP are:

- A data science life cycle definition
- A standardized project structure, which includes project documentation and reporting templates
- An infrastructure for project execution
- Tools for data science, like version control, data exploration, and modeling

The TDSP documentation [52] provides detailed insight into all of these aspects, so we'll just take a brief look in this section. The TDSP data science life cycle, showing different phases of a data project, is shown in Figure 11-7.

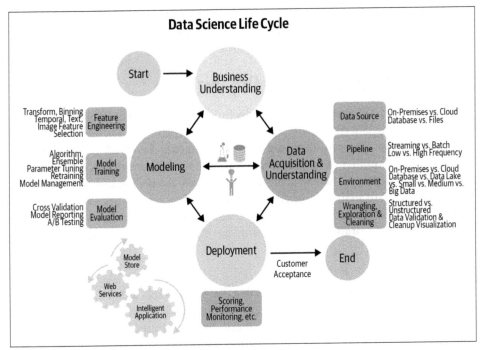

Figure 11-7. *The Microsoft TDSP life cycle [51]*

While TDSP shares some similarities with the KDD process, an interesting aspect of TDSP is that it defines a life cycle of a data science project from a business and team management perspective. This includes the following stages:

- Business understanding
- Data acquisition and understanding
- Modeling
- Deployment
- Customer acceptance

At a high level, the data science life cycle showcases how various components of an effective and agile data science team should operate. The "Charter" and "Exit Report" documents in the TDSP documentation are particularly important to consider. They help define the project at the start of an engagement and provide a final report to the customer or client.

Overall, these processes can be useful for taking the problems and solutions we've discussed so far in this book from prototyping to deployment in a production system. These processes are of course not specific to NLP and are more generic recommendations for any data-driven projects involving ML approaches. While there are other similar project management processes for data science that are emerging as the field grows, we hope this gives you an overview of what to look out for in managing your own NLP projects in a software development setting.

Making AI Succeed at Your Organization

So far, this book has focused on successfully building and deploying solutions for various AI problems. Success of any AI project is dependent not just on the technical superiority of the solution—there are many other factors involved, too. It's a known fact that a large number of AI projects in industry fail because the model doesn't get deployed or, if deployed, fails to achieve its objectives. According to a recent study by Gartner [53], more than 85% of AI projects fail. Here, we discuss some key points and rules of thumb to make AI projects succeed. Many of these points come from our own experience of working in various domains of AI across various organizations.

Team

It's important to have the right team to solve the AI problems at hand. In understanding the problem statement, prioritizing, developing, deploying, and consuming, a lot depends on the skills of the team. While there's no fixed recipe, in our experience, the right blend comes with having (1) scientists who build models, (2) engineers who operationalize and maintain models, and (3) leaders who manage AI teams and strategize. It's good to have (4) scientists who have worked in industry after graduate school, (5) engineers who understand scale and data pipelines, and 6) leaders who have also been individual contributor scientists in the past. While (5) is pretty self-explanatory, (4) and (6) warrant some explanation.

Let's look at (4) first. It's important that scientists understand the fundamentals of machine learning and are able to think of novel solutions. Graduate school (especially a PhD) prepares you well for that. But, in industry, solving an AI problem is not just applying novel algorithms. It's also about collecting and cleaning the data, making the data consumption-ready, and applying known techniques. This is very different from academia, where most work happens on known public datasets that are both readily available and clean. Most researchers in academia work on devising novel approaches to beat the state-of-the-art results. In many cases, scientists fresh from academia end up applying sophisticated approaches that prove counterproductive. One is building AI for products—AI is just a means, and not the end. That's why it's important that senior scientists on the team have built and deployed models in industrial settings.

Moving on to (6): AI leadership is very different from software engineering leadership. Even though what runs in production in any AI system is code, AI is fundamentally different from software engineering. Many leaders and organizations are not aware of this nuance. They believe that, because it's code, all the principles of software engineering apply to it. From defining the problem statement to planning project timelines, developing an AI system is different from developing a traditional IT system. This is why it's recommended that AI leaders in your organization have the experience of having been individual contributors (ICs) in the AI field.

Right Problem and Right Expectations

In many cases, either the problem at hand is ill defined or AI teams set the wrong expectations. Let's understand this better with some examples. Consider a scenario where we're given a dump of what customers say about a particular product or brand, and we're asked to bring out "interesting" insights. This is a very common scenario in industry; we discussed similar scenarios in "Topic Modeling" on page 252. Now, can we apply topic modeling to this particular scenario? It depends on what "interesting" means in this context. It could be what the majority of customers are saying, or it could be what a small subset of customers belonging to a particular region are saying, or it could be what customers are saying about a specific product feature. The possibilities are many. It's important to work with the stakeholders first to clearly define the task. A great way to do this is to take a set of diverse example inputs that include edge cases and ask the stakeholders to write down the desired output. An important thing to keep in mind is that the ready availability of a lot of data does not make something an AI problem by default; many problems can be solved using engineering and rule-based and human-in-the-loop approaches.

Another common problem is stakeholders having wrong expectations of AI technology. This often happens because of articles in popular media that tend to compare AI to the human brain. While that's correct as a motivation behind the area of AI, it's far from the truth. For example, consider a scenario where we built a sentiment analysis system and, for a given input sentence, our system predicts a wrong output. It gives a very high accuracy, but not 100%. Most stakeholders coming from the world of software engineering treat this as a bug and are not willing to accept anything that's not 100% correct. They are not aware of the fact that any AI system (as of today) will give wrong output for a subset of inputs. Another expectation of AI is that it will replace human effort completely, thus saving money. This is seldom the case. It's better to treat AI as augmented intelligence to *support* human efforts rather than artificial intelligence to *replace* human efforts. Also, beyond a point, model performance stagnates and doesn't continue rising with time. We see this in Figure 11-8, where reality behaves more like an S curve while the expectation continues rising.

Even a very mature and advanced AI system requires human supervision. In many cases, we can reduce human efforts, but that happens over a long period of time. In the same vein, stakeholders coming from software engineering may not understand the importance of building responsible AI. Responsible AI ensures trustworthy solutions that are fair, transparent, and accountable. Google [54] and Microsoft [55] have published best practices for building responsible AI systems.

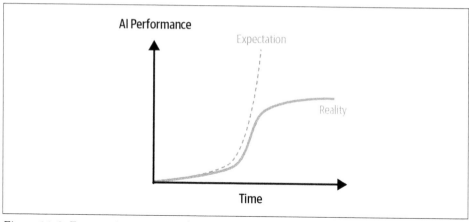

Figure 11-8. Expectation versus reality in AI performance

Data and Timing

Data is at the heart of any AI system. We've discussed various aspects of data in detail in previous chapters. Let's look at one more: in many cases, just because an organization has gigabytes or even petabytes of data, it doesn't mean they're ready for AI and can quickly reap its benefits. There's a difference between having data and having the right data. Let's understand this:

Quality of data

    To perform well, any AI system needs a high quality of data for both training and prediction. What does high quality mean? Data that is structured, homogenous, cleaned, and free of noise and outliers. Going from a dump of noisy data to high-quality data is often a long process. The best way to think of it is the following analogy: raw data is crude oil and AI models are fighter jets. Fighter jets need aviation fuel to fly; they cannot fly on crude oil. So, to enable fighter jets, someone must set up the petroleum refinery to systematically extract the aviation fuel from the crude oil. And setting up this refinery is a long and expensive process.

    Another important point is to have the right representative data: data that allows us to solve the problem at hand. For example, there's no way we can improve our search feature if we don't already have the metadata about what we want to search. So, if we don't have "Adidas Shoes Size 10 Tennis Shoes" but only have "Adidas Shoes Size 10," there's no way we can easily make our search help find tennis shoes.

Quantity of data

    Most AI models are a compressed representation of the dataset used to train them. Not having enough data that's a true representation of the data the model will see in production is a big reason for models not performing well. How much data is enough? This is a hard question to answer, but there are some rules of thumb. For instance, for sentence classification using baseline algorithms such as Naive Bayes or random forest, we've observed that having at least two to three thousand data points per class is a must to be able to build an acceptable classifier.

Data labeling

As of today, most success stories of AI in industry have come from supervised AI. As we discussed in initial chapters, it's the subarea where, for each data point, we have the ground truth. For many problems, the ground truth comes from human annotators. This is often a time-consuming and expensive process. In many industrial settings, stakeholders aren't aware of the importance of this step.

Data labeling is often a continuous process. While we do get data labeled in bulk as a one-time effort to build the first versions of our model, once the model is put in production and stabilizes, getting the production data annotated is a continuous process from there on. Further, we need to define processes for labeling and enforce quality checks to improve the accuracy and consistency of human annotators. This is done using metrics like kappa to measure inter-annotator agreement [56].

Currently, AI talent comes at a high cost. Without the right data, it will be futile to hire AI talent; having the right data is a prerequisite for AI teams to deliver well and fast. By this, we don't mean that we must have all of the prerequisites in place before bringing in AI talent. What we mean is that we must be fully aware of other prerequisites, such as the right data, and have realistic expectations in the absence of it.

A Good Process

Another important factor that often leads to the failure of AI projects is not following the right process. In this chapter, we've already discussed both the KDD and Microsoft processes. Both of them are great starting points. Here are some other important points to consider when getting started:

Set up the right metrics

Most AI projects in industry aim to solve a business problem. In many cases, teams set up AI metrics like precision, recall, etc., as success metrics. But we must also set up the right business metrics along with AI metrics. For example, let's say we're building a text classifier to automatically assign customer complaints to the right customer care teams. The right metric for this is the number of times a complaint is reassigned to another team. A classifier that has a 95% F1 score but leads to many complaints being reassigned multiple times is of no use. Another example of this is a chatbot system that correctly detects intent but has high user drop-off rates. User interaction and drop-off rates provide a complete picture that's missed by using only AI-specific metrics.

Start simple, establish strong baselines

AI scientists are often influenced by the latest techniques and recent state-of-the-art (SOTA) models and apply those in their work straight away. Most SOTA techniques are both compute- and data-intensive, which leads to cost and time overruns. The best way is to start with simple approaches and build strong baselines. Many times, a SOTA technique might only give us marginal improvement over a rule-based system! Try multiple simple approaches first before pondering over complex approaches.

Make it work, make it better

Building a model is often only 5–10% of most AI projects; the remaining 90% is made up of various steps, ranging from data collection to deployment, testing, maintenance, monitoring, integration, pilot testing, etc. It's always good to build an acceptable model quickly and complete one full project cycle instead of spending a huge amount of time building an amazing model. This helps all stakeholders realize the value proposition of the project.

Keep shorter turnaround cycles

Even when solving a standard problem with well-known approaches, we must still apply them to our dataset to see if they work or not. For example, if we're building a sentiment analysis system, it's a well-known fact that Naive Bayes gives very strong baselines. Yet it's very much possible that for our dataset, Naive Bayes might not give good numbers. Building AI systems involves a lot of experiments to figure what works and what doesn't. Hence, it's important to build models quickly and present the results to stakeholders frequently. This helps raise any red flags early and get early feedback.

There are a few other important things to consider, which we'll cover next.

Other Aspects

In addition to the various points we've discussed so far, there are some more key points to consider, including compute costs and return on investment. Let's discuss those now:

Cost of compute

Many AI models (especially DL-based models) are compute-intensive. Over time, GPUs on the cloud or physical hardware prove to be considerably expensive. Many organizations are known to spend huge amounts on GPU and other cloud services—so much that they have to create parallel projects to reduce these costs.

Blindly following SOTA

Practitioners are often keen to apply SOTA models in their work. This often proves to be disastrous. For example, Meena [57], a SOTA chatbot system from

Google that gave amazing results, took over 2,048 TPU for 30 days for training. That compute time is worth $1.4M. While Meena has shown some very impressive results, imagine using Meena techniques to build a chatbot for automating customer support that saves $1,000 a day. We would need to run the chatbot for over four years just to break even on the training cost.

ROI

AI projects are expensive; various stages, such as data collection, labeling, hiring AI talent, and compute all involve costs. For this reason, it's important to estimate the gains at the start of the project itself. We must establish the process and clear metrics to measure the returns early on in the project.

Full automation is hard

We can never achieve complete automation, at least for any moderately complex AI project—it will continue to require some manual effort. Figure 11-9 represents this in the same S curve we discussed earlier. Levels for complete automation and acceptable performance might change depending on the project, but the broad point will hold true.

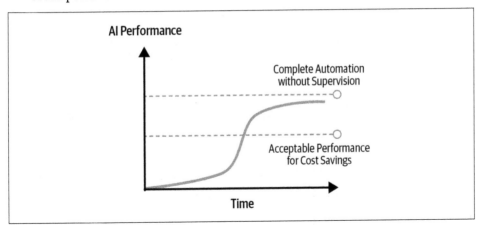

Figure 11-9. Complete automation can be hard

We've covered some key points in this section, but making AI succeed in business is a vast topic. We suggest a few articles for further reading. While some of them bring out the distinctions between software engineering and AI, others discuss rules of thumb for building AI systems:

- "Why Is Machine Learning 'Hard'?," a blog post by S. Zayd Enam, a Stanford researcher [58]
- "Software 2.0," a blog post on AI as a different way of writing software by Andrej Karpathy, a well-known researcher, educator, and scientist at Tesla [59]

- "NLP's Clever Hans Moment Has Arrived," an article by Benjamin Heinzerling that argues the validity of SOTA results obtained on certain popular datasets [60]
- "Closing the AI Accountability Gap," a report by a team at Google AI and the nonprofit Partnership on AI [61]
- "The Twelve Truths of Machine Learning for the Real World," a blog post by Delip Rao, researcher and O'Reilly author [62]
- "What I've Learned Working with 12 Machine Learning Startups," an article by Daniel Shenfeld, a startup veteran and ML consultant [63]

These will give you a more holistic picture. Figure 11-10 demonstrates what we've covered in this section and the chapter.

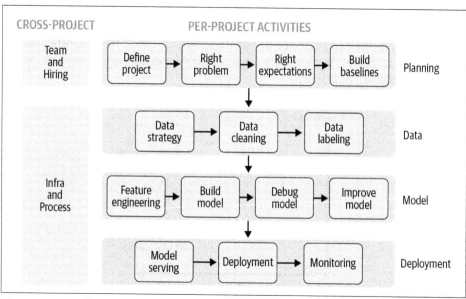

Figure 11-10. Life cycle of an AI project

Many of these suggestions are not hard rules set in stone; their application will depend on the context of your project, problem, data, and organization. We hope the discussion in this section will help in making your AI endeavors succeed.

Peeking over the Horizon

We'd like to end this chapter and the book with various perspectives of how machine learning is evolving. ML will continue improving on the cutting edge, and its applications will be more relevant to business in the coming years. One way to look at this is the influential lecture by renowned scientist C.P. Snow in 1959, titled *The Two Cultures and the Scientific Revolution* [64]. In this lecture, Snow states that the intellectual world can be seen from two distinct perspectives, which seem to be getting more divided over time. One perspective is of science and technology and the other is concerned with arts and humanities. He argues why it's important for these two perspectives to have a common core for better advancements of the entire area. This is true for AI as well.

Analogously, in the world of AI, we see a similar set of two distinct perspectives emerging. On one hand, we have the advances made by researchers and scientists working on the forefront. On the other hand, we have businesses trying to leverage AI. This includes everyone from Fortune 500 companies to early stage startups. The world increasingly believes that the successful adoption of AI in industry will stem from an intersection of both.

From the perspective of researchers and scientists, we see two macro trends: building *truly intelligent machines* and applying *AI for social good*. For instance, François Chollet of Google has stressed the importance of building better metrics to measure intelligence in "On the Measure of Intelligence" [65]. Most evaluation of AI models at present is inherently narrow in nature and measures specific skills as opposed to broad abilities and general intelligence. Chollet proposes certain measures inspired by testing of human intelligence, including efficiencies in new skill acquisition. They introduce a dataset called Abstraction and Reasoning Corpus (ARC) that's inspired by a classic IQ test: the Raven's Progressive Matrices [66]. One such example is presented in Figure 11-11, where the task is for the computer to infer the missing area by looking at the overall input matrix pattern. Work on improving measures of AI is necessary for developing better and more robust AI in the future.

AI and technology in general can be a force for social good. And there are now various initiatives that are working on AI for social good. Wadhwani AI is working on improving maternal and early childhood health with AI [67]. Google AI for Social Good has a range of initiatives, including applying AI to predict and better manage floods [68]. Similarly, Microsoft is using AI to solve global climate issues, improve accessibility, and preserve cultural heritage [69]. Allen AI has been improving common-sense reasoning in NLP through the WinoGrande dataset [70]. Such work by foundations and research labs is helping to incorporate the forefront of ML and NLP to improve human well-being.

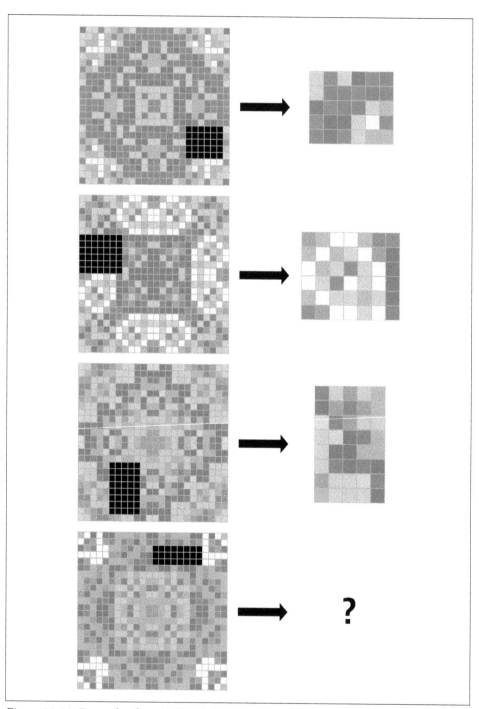

Figure 11-11. Example of an ARC task for general intelligence from [66]

A completely different perspective comes from the world of business. This is more practical and is concerned with business impact and business models. For instance, several consulting firms have conducted surveys across organizations on use cases and effectiveness of AI across industry verticals. McKinsey & Company's Global AI survey is one such example [71]. They discuss how AI has helped different verticals save money by reducing inefficiencies and make more money by expanding the market. They also assess the impact of AI on the workforce and on which parts of organizations it's most impactful. Another such study is a report by MIT Sloan and BCG [72]. This is immensely useful for business leaders to learn how to onboard and grow AI inside their organizations.

Venture capital (VC) firms have been investing heavily in startups building AI-powered businesses. Based on their understanding of how new AI businesses are formed and how they can succeed, they're compiling reports and debriefs. Andressen Horowitz, a major VC firm, has published a report, "The New Business of AI," based on their learnings in many AI investments [73]. The report addresses business issues that AI startups are facing despite the hype, like lower gross margins and product-scaling challenges. They've provided practical advice on building AI businesses that can scale better and be more competitive.

This range of perspectives will be applicable depending on where your organization is in their AI journey. First, when starting a new AI business, lessons from VCs will help you decide what to build. Second, to formulate an AI strategy in a large organization, surveys and reports from industry will align you better. Last but not least, as your organization matures, incorporating SOTA techniques can lead to a step change in your products.

Final Words

And here we come to the end of *Practical Natural Language Processing*! We hope you've learned a few things about NLP tasks and pipelines and their applications in various domains and that these will help you in your day-to-day work. The advances in NLP are just starting to bear big fruits. Some of the most fundamental questions in NLP, like context and common sense, have probably yet to even be asked properly.

True mastery of any skill requires a lifetime of learning, and we hope that our references, research papers, and industry reports will help you continue the journey.

References

[1] ONNX (*https://onnx.ai*): An open format built to represent machine learning models. Last accessed June 15, 2020.

[2] Apache Airflow (*https://oreil.ly/pJRzj*). Last accessed June 15, 2020.

[3] Apache Oozie (*https://oreil.ly/TW8xV*). Last accessed June 15, 2020.

[4] Chef (*https://www.chef.io*). Last accessed June 15, 2020.

[5] Microsoft. "MLOps examples" (*https://oreil.ly/z8SZa*). Last accessed June 15, 2020.

[6] Microsoft. MLOps using Azure ML Services and Azure DevOps (*https://oreil.ly/mS8vB*), (GitHub repo). Last accessed June 15, 2020.

[7] Elastic. "Anomaly Detection" (*https://oreil.ly/35PbS*).

[8] Krzus, Matt and and Jason Berkowitz. "Text Classification with Gluon on Amazon SageMaker and AWS Batch" (*https://oreil.ly/oN0jO*). *AWS Machine Learning Blog*, March 20, 2018.

[9] The Pallets Projects. "Flask" (*https://oreil.ly/K6AW-*). Last accessed June 15, 2020.

[10] The Falcon Web Framework (*https://oreil.ly/ipNIv*). Last accessed June 15, 2020.

[11] Django (*https://oreil.ly/jsEyA*): The web framework for perfectionists with deadlines. Last accessed June 15, 2020.

[12] Docker (*https://www.docker.com*). Last accessed June 15, 2020.

[13] Kubernetes (*https://kubernetes.io*): Production-Grade Container Orchestration. Last accessed June 15, 2020.

[14] Amazon. AWS SageMaker (*https://oreil.ly/MCkm-*). Last accessed June 15, 2020.

[15] Microsoft. Azure Cognitive Services (*https://oreil.ly/30cWw*). Last accessed June 15, 2020.

[16] Sucik, Sam. "Compressing BERT for Faster Prediction" (*https://oreil.ly/_Osgi*). *Rasa (blog)*, August 8, 2019.

[17] Cheng, Yu, Duo Wang, Pan Zhou, and Tao Zhang (*https://oreil.ly/nOSC7*). "A Survey of Model Compression and Acceleration for Deep Neural Networks." (*https://oreil.ly/bbjBw*) 2017.

[18] Joulin, Armand, Edouard Grave, Piotr Bojanowski, Matthijs Douze, Hérve Jégou, and Tomas Mikolov. "FastText.zip: Compressing Text Classification Models" (*https://oreil.ly/LEf1y*), 2016.

[19] Chee, Cedric. Awesome machine learning model compression research papers, tools, and learning material (*https://oreil.ly/aRYn_*), (GitHub repo). Last accessed June 15, 2020.

[20] Burkov, Andriy. *Machine Learning Engineering* (Draft) (*https://oreil.ly/1xTP6*). 2019.

[21] Cheng, Heng-Tze. "Wide & Deep Learning: Better Together with TensorFlow (*https://oreil.ly/FBfSY*)." *Google AI Blog*, June 29, 2016.

[22] Zheng, Alice and Amanda Casari. *Feature Engineering for Machine Learning.* Boston: O'Reilly, 2018. ISBN: 978-9-35213-711-4

[23] DVC (*https://dvc.org*): Open source version control system for machine learning projects. Last accessed June 15, 2020.

[24] Gundersen, Odd Erik and Sigbjørn Kjensmo. "State of the Art: Reproducibility in Artificial Intelligence." *The Thirty-Second AAAI Conference on Artificial Intelligence* (2018).

[25] Gibney, E. "This AI Researcher Is Trying to Ward Off a Reproducibility Crisis." *Nature* 577.7788 (2020): 14.

[26] TensorFlow. "Getting Started with TensorFlow Model Analysis" (*https://oreil.ly/dQWKv*). Last accessed June 15, 2020.

[27] Marco Tulio Correia Ribeiro. Lime: Explaining the predictions of any machine learning classifier (*https://oreil.ly/FynST*), (GitHub repo). Last accessed June 15, 2020.

[28] Lundberg, Scott. Shap: A game theoretic approach to explain the output of any machine learning model (*https://oreil.ly/8saPS*), (GitHub repo). Last accessed June 15, 2020.

[29] TensorFlow. "Get started with TensorFlow Data Validation" (*https://oreil.ly/DHec0*). Last accessed June 15, 2020.

[30] Miller, Tim. "Explanation in Artificial Intelligence: Insights from the Social Sciences" (*https://oreil.ly/drgXS*), (2017).

[31] Molnar, Christoph. *Interpretable Machine Learning: A Guide for Making Black Box Models Explainable* (*https://oreil.ly/EXsY8*). 2019.

[32] Sumo Logic. "Outlier" (*https://oreil.ly/Izt9N*). Last accessed June 15, 2020.

[33] Microsoft. "Anomaly Detector API Documentation" (*https://oreil.ly/L9ksb*). Last accessed June 15, 2020.

[34] Domingos, Pedro. "A Few Useful Things to Know about Machine Learning." *Communications of the ACM* 55.10(2012): 78–87.

[35] Sculley, D., Gary Holt, Daniel Golovin, Eugene Davydov, Todd Phillips, Dietmar Ebner, Vinay Chaudhary, and Michael Young. "Machine Learning: The High Interest Credit Card of Technical Debt." *SE4ML: Software Engineering for Machine Learning* (NIPS 2014 Workshop).

[36] D. Sculley, Gary Holt, Daniel Golovin, Eugene Davydov, Todd Phillips, Dietmar Ebner, VinayChaudhary, Michael Young, Jean-Francois Crespo, and Dan Dennison. "Hidden Technical Debt in Machine Learning Systems." *Proceedings of the 28th International Conference on Neural Information Processing Systems* 2 (2015): 2503–2511.

[37] McMahan, H. Brendan, Gary Holt, David Sculley, Michael Young, Dietmar Ebner, Julian Grady, Lan Nie et al. "Ad Click Prediction: A View from the Trenches." *Proceedings of the 19th ACM SIGKDD International Conference on Knowledge Discovery and Data Mining* (2013): 1222–1230.

[38] Zinkevich, Martin. "Rules of Machine Learning: Best Practices for ML Engineering" (*https://oreil.ly/-azsB*). *Google Machine Learning*. Last accessed June 15, 2020.

[39] Halevy, Alon, Peter Norvig, and Fernando Pereira. "The Unreasonable Effectiveness of Data." *IEEE Intelligent Systems* 24.2 (2009): 8–12.

[40] Sun, Chen, Abhinav Shrivastava, Saurabh Singh, and Abhinav Gupta. "Revisiting Unreasonable Effectiveness of Data in Deep Learning Era." *Proceedings of the IEEE International Conference on Computer Vision* (2017): 843–852.

[41] Petrov, Slav. "Announcing SyntaxNet: The World's Most Accurate Parser Goes Open Source" (*https://oreil.ly/tuwnp*). *Google AI Blog*, May 12, 2016.

[42] Marcus, Mitchell, Beatrice Santorini, and Mary Ann Marcinkiewicz. "Building a Large Annotated Corpus of English: The Penn Treebank" (*https://oreil.ly/yk7V4*). *Computational Linguistics* 19, Number 2, Special Issue on Using Large Corpora: II (June 1993).

[43] Feurer, Matthias, Aaron Klein, Katharina Eggensperger, Jost Springenberg, Manuel Blum, and Frank Hutter. "Efficient and Robust Automated Machine Learning." *Advances in Neural Information Processing Systems* 28 (2015): 2962–2970.

[44] Le Cun, Yann, Corinna Cortes and Christopher J.C. Burges. "The MNIST database of handwritten digits" (*https://oreil.ly/d0fDb*). Last accessed June 15, 2020.

[45] Google Cloud. "Features and capabilities of AutoML Natural Language" (*https://oreil.ly/3Ljr4*). Last accessed June 15, 2020.

[46] Google Cloud. "AutoML Translation" (*https://oreil.ly/fq5DQ*). Last accessed June 15, 2020.

[47] Microsoft Azure. "What is automated machine learning (AutoML)?" (*https://oreil.ly/yahkz*), February 28, 2020.

[48] Thakur, Abhishek and Artus Krohn-Grimberghe. "AutoCompete: A Framework for Machine Learning Competition" (*https://oreil.ly/8iFSU*), (2015).

[49] Thakur, Abhishek. "Approaching (Almost) Any NLP Problem on Kaggle" (*https://oreil.ly/ksGdV*). Last accessed June 15, 2020.

[50] Fayyad, Usama, Gregory Piatetsky-Shapiro, and Padhraic Smyth. "The KDD Process for Extracting Useful Knowledge from Volumes of Data." *Communications of the ACM* 39.11 (1996): 27–34.

[51] Microsoft Azure. "What is the Team Data Science Process?" (*https://oreil.ly/N6hzM*), January 10, 2020.

[52] Microsoft. "Team Data Science Process Documentation" (*https://oreil.ly/R8c7d*). Last accessed June 15, 2020.

[53] Kidd, Chrissy. "Why Does Gartner Predict up to 85% of AI Projects Will 'Not Deliver' for CIOs?" (*https://oreil.ly/28IOn*), *BMC Machine Learning & Big Data Blog*, December 18, 2018.

[54] Google AI. "Responsible AI Practices" (*https://oreil.ly/aAicm*). Last accessed June 15, 2020.

[55] Microsoft. "Microsoft AI principles" (*https://oreil.ly/rL2Oh*). Last accessed June 15, 2020.

[56] Artstein, Ron and Massimo Poesio. "Inter-Coder Agreement for Computational Linguistics." *Computational Linguistics* 34.4 (2008): 555–596.

[57] Adiwardana, Daniel and Thang Luong. "Towards a Conversational Agent that Can Chat About...Anything" (*https://oreil.ly/k7Cac*). *Google AI Blog*, January 28, 2020.

[58] Enam, S. Zayd. "Why is Machine Learning 'Hard'?" (*https://oreil.ly/ZcJ6c*), *Zayd's Blog*, November 10, 2016.

[59] Karpathy, Andrej. "Software 2.0" (*https://oreil.ly/XgkWP*). *Medium Programming*, November 11, 2017.

[60] Heinzerling, Benjamin. "NLP's Clever Hans Moment has Arrived" (*https://oreil.ly/oPIA2*). *The Gradient*, August 26, 2019.

[61] Raji, Inioluwa Deborah, Andrew Smart, Rebecca N. White, Margaret Mitchell, Timnit Gebru, Ben Hutchinson, Jamila Smith-Loud, Daniel Theron, and Parker Barnes. "Closing the AI Accountability Gap: Defining an End-to-End Framework for Internal Algorithmic Auditing" (*https://oreil.ly/x7SJR*), (2020).

[62] Rao, Delip. "The Twelve Truths of Machine Learning for the Real World" (*https://oreil.ly/3oDtV*). *Delip Rao (blog)*, December 25, 2019.

[63] Shenfeld, David. "What I've Learned Working with 12 Machine Learning Start-ups" (*https://oreil.ly/dRjPD*). *Towards Data Science (blog)*, May 6, 2019.

[64] Snow, Charles Percy. *The Two Cultures and the Scientific Revolution*. Connecticut: Martino Fine Books, 2013.

[65] Chollet, François. "On The Measure of Intelligence" (*https://oreil.ly/XvV8v*), (2019).

[66] John, Raven J. "Raven Progressive Matrices," in *Handbook of Nonverbal Assessment*, Boston: Springer, 2003.

[67] Wadhwani AI. "Maternal, Newborn, and Child Health" (*https://oreil.ly/zL2BL*). Last accessed June 15, 2020.

[68] Matias, Yossi. "Keeping People Safe with AI-Enabled Flood Forecasting" (*https://oreil.ly/qTp5L*). *Google The Keyword (blog)*, September 24, 2018.

[69] Microsoft. "AI for Good" (*https://oreil.ly/XtOAD*). Last accessed June 15, 2020.

[70] Sakaguchi, Keisuke, Ronan Le Bras, Chandra Bhagavatula, and Yejin Choi. "WinoGrande: An Adversarial Winograd Schema Challenge at Scale" (*https://oreil.ly/0_VLH*), (2019).

[71] Cam, Arif, Michael Chui, and Bryce Hall. "Global AI Survey: AI Proves Its Worth, but Few Scale Impact" (*https://oreil.ly/U61yX*). *McKinsey & Company Featured Insights*, November 2019.

[72] Ransbotham, Sam, Philipp Gerbert, Martin Reeves, David Kiron, and Michael Spira. "Artificial Intelligence in Business Gets Real." *MIT Sloan Management Review* (September 2018).

[73] Casado, Martin and Matt Bornstein. "The New Business of AI (and How It's Different From Traditional Software)" (*https://oreil.ly/MMHTt*). *Andreesen Horowitz*, February 16, 2020.

Index

A

A/B testing, 265, 326, 380
Abstraction and Reasoning Corpus (ARC)
 dataset, 401, 402
abstractive summarization, 258, 261
accounting and auditing, 364
accuracy, 69
ACM SIGKDD Conference on Knowledge Dis-
 covery and Data Mining (KDD), 390
active learning, 42
 NER using, 176-177
 with Prodigy, 153
 text classification, 150-152, 153
Adamic, Lada, 301
adapting to new domains, 149-152
adult content filtering, 279
advanced processing, 49, 57-60
AI (see artificial intelligence)
Airbnb, 264, 311
Airflow (Apache), 375
Algolia, 252
Allen AI, 401
AllenNLP, 175, 184
 DeepQA library, 271
 Grover, 304
Amazon, 5, 122, 242
 faceted search on, 312
 "Reviews that mention" filter, 166
 sentiment analysis APIs, 126
Amazon Alexa, 3, 5, 7, 31, 199
Amazon Comprehend, 65, 190
Amazon Comprehend Medical, 358-359
Amazon Mechanical Turk, 150
Amazon Research, 303

Amazon Translate, 5
Amazon Web Services (AWS), 72
 AWS Cloud, 376
 AWS S3, 375
 SageMaker, 376, 377
ambiguity , 12-13
anomaly detection, 384
answer extraction, 270
answering questions (see question answering)
Apache Airflow, 375
Apache Nutch, 246
Apache Oozie, 375
Apache Solr software, 247
APIs
 integration of, 231
 modeling with, 65
 MT, 266-267
 product categorization and taxonomy, 322,
  323
 text classification with, 126, 153
Apple, 299
Apple Siri, 3, 5, 7, 31
Arabic, 74
ARC (see Abstraction and Reasoning Corpus)
Arria, 5
artificial intelligence (AI), 14, 199, 373
 expectations vs reality, 395
 further reading, 399-400
 key points and rules of thumb, 394-400
 perspectives on, 401
 for social good, 401
aspect-based sentiment analysis, 122-123,
 329-331
aspects, 329

POS (part-of-speech) tagging, 21, 57, 60
post-modeling phases, 72-73
pragmatics, 12
pre-processing, 49-60, 65, 356, 391
    advanced processing, 60
    common steps, 55
    frequent steps, 52-55
    other steps, 55-57
    SMTD, 292-296
pre-trained language models, large, 145-147
pre-training, 26, 108
precision, 69
predicting health outcomes, 353-355
pregex, 18
preliminaries, 50-52
probabilistic latent semantic analysis (PLSA),
    253
Prodigy, 151, 153, 176
product catalogs (see catalogs)
product categorization and taxonomy, 319-323
product deduplication and matching, 325-326
product enrichment, 323-324
product intervention, 40
product linking, 337
product recommendations, 311, 334
    (see also recommendations)
product search, 311
propaganda, false, 279
public datasets, 40, 153, 291
PubMed, 359
punctuation: removing, 53
PwC, 364
PyPDF, 47
Python, 48

Q

quality of data, 396
quantity of data, 396
query-focused summarization, 258
question answering (QA), 7, 242
    with deep neural networks, 271
    knowledge-based, 271
question-answering (QA) systems, 268-271
    dataset creation framework , 352
    dataset generation with existing annota-
        tions, 353
    developing, 270
    DL-based, 271
    for health, 351-352

R

random forest, 397
ranking, 70, 247, 249
Rao, Delip, 400
Rasa, 175, 230-232, 235
Rasa NLP, 377
Rasa NLU, 229-232
recall, 69
Recall at rank K, 70
Recall-Oriented Understudy for Gisting Evalu-
    ation (ROUGE), 70, 261
receipts: data extraction from, 163
recommendation engines, 335
    (see also recommender systems)
recommendations, 242
    case study, 335-337
    for e-commerce, 334-337
    product, 311
    techniques for, 334
recommender systems, 262-265, 335
    creating, 263-264
    e-commerce, 311, 335
    examples, 263-264
    practical advice, 264-265
recurrent neural networks (RNNs), 23, 107,
    140, 318
Reddit autotldr bot, 258
Redis database, 108
RegexNER (Stanford NLP), 171, 176
regression techniques, 19
regression, logistic, 131
regular expressions (regex), 17
reinforcement learning, 15
    deep, 227-228
    for dialogue generation, 227-228
related queries, 244
relation extraction (see relationship extraction)
relationship extraction (RE), 58, 164, 181-185
    approaches to, 182-184
    example, 182
    unsupervised, 183
    with Watson API, 184-185
replacing entities, 41
representative data, 396
reproducibility, 381
research, legal, 365
response generation, 220
    automatic, 221
    case study, 33

About the Authors

Sowmya Vajjala has a PhD in computational linguistics from the University of Tubingen, Germany. She currently works as a research officer at the National Research Council, Canada's largest federal research and development organization. Her past work experience spans both academia, as faculty at Iowa State University, USA, and industry at Microsoft Research and The Globe and Mail.

Bodhisattwa Majumder is a doctoral candidate in NLP and ML at UC San Diego. Earlier he studied at IIT Kharagpur where he graduated *summa cum laude*. Previously, he conducted ML research and built large-scale NLP systems, at Google AI Research and Microsoft Research that went into products serving millions of users. Currently, he is leading his university team in the Amazon Alexa Prize for 2019–2020.

Anuj Gupta has built NLP and ML systems as a senior leader at Fortune 100 companies as well as startups. He has incubated and led multiple ML teams in his career. He studied computer science at IIT Delhi and IIIT Hyderabad. He is currently the head of machine learning and data science at Vahan Inc. Above all, he is a father and a husband.

Harshit Surana is the CTO at DeepFlux Inc. He has built and scaled ML systems and engineering pipelines at several Silicon Valley startups as a founder and an advisor. He studied computer science at Carnegie Mellon University where he worked with the MIT Media Lab on common sense AI. His research in NLP has received over 200 citations.

Colophon

The animal on the cover of *Practical Natural Language Processing* is an eclectus parrot (*Eclectus roratus*). Native to the lowland rainforests of Oceania, they can be found anywhere from northeastern Australia to the islands that make up the Moluccas. For centuries they have been domesticated in Indonesia and New Guinea, where their feathers are used in elaborate headdresses used to communicate one's standing or kinship to the birds.

The male's plumage is bright green with touches of red and blue under the wings, while the female has a red crown and a purplish-blue chest. These birds are the most sexually dimorphic species in the parrot family, which led early biologists to classify them as separate species. Another aspect that distinguishes the eclectus from other parrot species is their polygynandry. This allows the females to safely nest for up to 11 months without often leaving, as they can depend on more than one male to forage for them.

O'REILLY®

There's much more where this came from.

Experience books, videos, live online training courses, and more from O'Reilly and our 200+ partners—all in one place.

Learn more at oreilly.com/online-learning

Milton Keynes UK
Ingram Content Group UK Ltd.
UKHW051614220924
448644UK00002B/9

9 781492 054054